Henry James's New York Edition

The Construction of Authorship

HENRY JAMES'S
New York Edition

The Construction of Authorship

ᆼᄉ

EDITED BY

David McWhirter

STANFORD UNIVERSITY PRESS
STANFORD, CALIFORNIA 1995

Stanford University Press
Stanford, California
© 1995 by the Board of Trustees
of the Leland Stanford Junior University
Printed in the United States of America

CIP data appear at the end of the book

Stanford University Press publications are distributed exclusively by Stanford
University Press within the United States, Canada, Mexico, and Central America;
they are distributed exclusively by Cambridge University Press throughout
the rest of the world.

*This book is dedicated
by its contributors and editor to the memory of
Dorothea Krook.*

Acknowledgments

When I first began thinking about the New York Edition, a colleague asked me why I was planning a collection of essays rather than a monograph. The question, posed, no doubt, with my best interests in mind, nonetheless crystallized my previously vague intuition that the New York Edition, and the many Henry Jameses who authored it, would best be served by a book written in many hands. The rightness of that intuition is, I believe, amply confirmed by the richness, originality, and diversity of the essays in this volume. I am deeply grateful to its contributors for the luxuriant growth—so various and surprising!—that they have succeeded in cultivating from the modest seed provided by its editor. Henry James, I am confident, would have understood and valued this practical demonstration of "the truth of the vanity of the *a priori* test of what an *idée-mère* may have to give" (*9*: viii; *AN*, 101). I would like especially to thank Michael Anesko, Paul B. Armstrong, Martha Banta, Stuart Culver, Carol Holly, Julie Rivkin, and John Carlos Rowe, who have supported my work on this book with generous offerings of practical assistance, critical acuity, and friendly encouragement.

I am indebted as well to members of the community of James scholars whose work is not represented in this volume but who have nonetheless helped to shape it: my thanks to Richard Hocks, Gardner Mein, John Pearson, Vivian Pollak, William Veeder, and Philip Weinstein, and especially to Daniel Mark Fogel, the indefatigable impresario of contemporary James studies. I also wish to acknowledge a number of colleagues, students, and friends at the University of Pennsylvania, Texas A&M University, and elsewhere whose substantive suggestions, thoughtful criticisms, and timely gestures of support have facilitated my work at various stages: Susan Albertine, Daniel Bivona, Peter Conn, Jeffrey Cox, Margreta deGrazia, David DeLaura, Nancy Easterlin, Maura Ives, David Lawrence, Robert Lucid, Howard Marchitello, Jeffrey Masten, Ellen McWhirter, Cecile Mazzucco-Than, Katherine O'Keeffe, Kenneth Price, Larry Reynolds, Terry Spitler, and Peter Stallybrass have all helped in some significant way.

Research awards from the Department of English and the Interdisciplinary Group for Historical Literary Study at Texas A&M University furthered my work by affording me the time to bring it to completion. I am grateful to my department head, J. Lawrence Mitchell, for his support, and to the directors and fellows of the Interdisciplinary Group: my thinking has consistently benefited from the challenging intellectual forum they provide. Funding to secure the illustrations in this book was generously provided by the Department of English at Texas A&M. I wish to thank Helen Tartar, humanities editor at Stanford University Press, for her energetic and informed commitment to this project, and for recognizing its importance when others saw only an odd and narrow focus; I also wish to acknowledge the contributions of copyeditor Nancy Young and indexer Pat Deminna.

A few others deserve special mention. This book might never have gotten off the ground without the help of Alan Filreis, whose practical assistance and sympathetic yet critical responsiveness in the early stages of its conception were invaluable. It could never have been completed without the help of Mary Ann O'Farrell; her generosity, wit, and intelligence, and above all the gift of her companionship, cannot be adequately acknowledged here.

Finally, I am grateful to my sons, Gabriel and Joshua, for their help, patience, and understanding. Their love makes my work possible by keeping it in perspective.

Several of the essays in this volume have previously appeared elsewhere: J. Hillis Miller's "The 'Grafted Image': James on Illustration" is reprinted by permission of the publishers from *Illustration*, by J. Hillis Miller, Cambridge, Mass.: Harvard University Press, Copyright 1992 by J. Hillis Miller. Jerome McGann, "Revision, Rewriting, Rereading; or, 'An Error [Not] in *The Ambassadors*'" originally appeared in *American Literature*, 64: 1. Copyright Duke University Press, 1992. Reprinted by permission. A shorter version of my Introduction—"'The Whole Chain of Relation and Responsibility': Henry James and the New York Edition"—appeared in *Henry James Review* 12 (1991). Sections of Eve Kosofsky Sedgwick's "Shame and Performativity: Henry James's New York Edition Prefaces" have appeared previously in *GLQ*, 1, no. 1 (1993), and in *Negotiating Gay and Lesbian Subjects*, ed. Monica Dorenkamp and Richard Henke (New York: Routledge, 1994).

D.M.
College Station, Texas

Contents

Illustrations

    The Awkward Age

14. A. L. Coburn's "Some of the Spoils," frontispiece to
    The Spoils of Poynton

15. A. L. Coburn's "The Cage," frontispiece to *In the Cage*

16. A. L. Coburn's "Juliana's Court," frontispiece to
    The Aspern Papers

17. A. L. Coburn's "The Court of the Hotel," frontispiece to
    The Reverberator

18. A. L. Coburn's "'On Sundays, now, you might be at
    Home?,'" frontispiece to "Lady Barbarina"

19. A. L. Coburn's "Saltram's Seat," frontispiece to
    "The Coxon Fund"

20. A. L. Coburn's "The New England Street," frontispiece
    to "Europe"

21. A. L. Coburn's "The Halls of Julia," frontispiece to
    "Julia Bride"

22. A. L. Coburn's "By St. Peter's," frontispiece to
    Daisy Miller

23. A. L. Coburn's "The Doctor's Door," frontispiece to
    The Wings of the Dove

24. A. L. Coburn's "The Venetian Palace," frontispiece to
    The Wings of the Dove

25. A. L. Coburn's "By Notre Dame," frontispiece to
    The Ambassadors

26. A. L. Coburn's "The Luxembourg Gardens," frontispiece
    to *The Ambassadors*

27. A. L. Coburn's "The Curiosity Shop," frontispiece to
    The Golden Bowl

28. A. L. Coburn's "Portland Place," frontispiece to
    The Golden Bowl

29. Example of James's revisions for *The American* in the
    New York Edition   148

Note on Citations

Parenthetical references to James's prefaces are keyed to two sources: *The Novels and Tales of Henry James*, New York Edition, 24 [26] vols. (New York: Charles Scribner's Sons, 1907–9 [1917]; reprint, New York: Augustus M. Kelley Publishers, 1971), cited by volume number in italics and page number in Roman type, and *The Art of the Novel: Critical Prefaces by Henry James*, ed. Richard P. Blackmur (New York: Charles Scribner's Sons, 1934; reprint, Boston: Northeastern University Press, 1984), abbreviated as *AN* and cited by page number.

Citations for James's fiction are from the New York Edition except where indicated otherwise. James's practice of leaving a space in contractions (e.g., "does n't") has been modernized in quotations from the New York Edition prefaces.

Contributors

MICHAEL ANESKO teaches at The Pennsylvania State University, where he is Associate Professor of English. His book, *'Friction with the Market': Henry James and the Profession of Authorship*, explores James's relations with the literary marketplace. Anesko has published articles and reviews on various topics in American literature, culture, and history in *American Literary History*, *American Literature*, and elsewhere.

PAUL B. ARMSTRONG is Professor of English and Associate Dean of the College of Arts and Sciences at the University of Oregon. He is the author of *The Challenge of Bewilderment: Understanding and Representation in James, Conrad, and Ford* and *The Phenomenology of Henry James*, and has published numerous articles on modern fiction and literary theory. His most recent book is *Conflicting Readings: Variety and Validity in Interpretation*.

MARTHA BANTA, Professor of English at the University of California, Los Angeles, is the author of *Henry James and the Occult*; *Failure and Success in America: A Literary Debate*; and *Imaging American Women: Idea and Ideals in Cultural History*. Her most recent book is *Taylored Lives: Narrative Productions in the Age of Taylor, Veblen, and Ford*. She has also published many articles on American culture and literature, edited *New Essays on "The American,"* and served as associate editor for *The Columbia Literary History of the United States*. She was president of the American Studies Association from 1990 through 1991.

SARA BLAIR is Assistant Professor of English and Director of the Modern Studies program at the University of Virginia. Her work on James has recently appeared in *American Literary History, American Liter-*

ature, and *ELH*. Her forthcoming book from Cambridge University Press is entitled *Mixed Performances. Race, Nation and Culture in Henry James*.

STUART CULVER is Assistant Professor of English and Comparative Literature at the University of California, Irvine. His articles on American literature have appeared in *ELH*, *Representations*, and *American Literary History*. His Ph.D. dissertation (Berkeley, 1984) is a study of the New York Edition, and he is currently working on a book on Henry and William James.

ALFRED HABEGGER, Professor of English at the University of Kansas, is the author of *Gender, Fantasy, and Realism in American Literature* and *Henry James and the "Woman Business."* He has published in *PMLA*, *American Literature*, *Nineteenth-Century Literature*, *New England Quarterly*, *Women's Studies*, *Novel*, and elsewhere. He recently contributed the Henry James section for *Reconstructing American Literature*. His biography, *The Father: A Life of Henry James, Sr.*, was published in 1994 by Farrar, Straus & Giroux. He is working on a life of Emily Dickinson.

CAROL HOLLY is Professor of English at St. Olaf College. She has published extensively on Henry James and the James family in *American Literature*, *The Henry James Review*, and other journals. A recipient of the NEH Fellowship for College Teachers, she has recently completed *Intensely Family: The Inheritance of Shame and the Autobiographies of Henry James* (University of Wisconsin Press).

JEROME MCGANN is the John Stewart Bryan Professor of English, University of Virginia. His most recent book of criticism is *Black Riders: The Visible Language of Modernism*. He is currently developing *The Complete Writings and Pictures of Dante Gabriel Rossetti: A Hypermedia Research Archive*.

DAVID MCWHIRTER is Associate Professor of English at Texas A&M University, where he teaches modern British and American literature. He is the author of *Desire and Love in Henry James: A Study of the Late Novels*, and of articles on James, Yeats, Meredith, and Woolf. He is currently working on a book project entitled "Abstraction and Empathy: Tragicomic Modes in Literary Modernism."

J. HILLIS MILLER is Distinguished Professor of English and Comparative Literature at the University of California, Irvine. His many publications include *Thomas Hardy: Distance and Desire*; *Fiction and Repetition*; *The Linguistic Moment*; *Versions of Pygmalion*; *Ariadne's Thread*; *The Ethics of Reading: Kant, de Man, Eliot, Trollope, James, and Benjamin*; and *Illustration*. His most recent book, *Topographies*, was published by Stanford University Press in 1995. He was president of the Modern Language Association in 1986.

IRA B. NADEL is Professor of English at the University of British Columbia. He has published numerous articles on Victorian and modern British literature, and has edited essay collections on topics ranging from Victorian biography to Gertrude Stein and George Orwell. He is also the author of *Biography: Fiction, Fact, and Form* and *Joyce and the Jews: Culture and Texts*. He is currently writing a study of the relationship between illustrations and the novel in the Victorian and early modern periods.

ROSS POSNOCK is Professor of English at the University of Washington, where he teaches courses in American literature, American studies, and modern social and cultural thought. He is the author of *Henry James and the Problem of Robert Browning* and *The Trial of Curiosity: Henry James, William James, and the Challenge of Modernity*. His articles on James and other topics have appeared in *Boundary 2*, *Raritan*, and *American Literary History*.

JULIE RIVKIN, Associate Professor of English at Connecticut College, has published articles and reviews on James and other topics in *PMLA*, *Contemporary Literature*, and *The Henry James Review*. Her book, *False Positions: The Representational Logics of Henry James's Fiction*, is forthcoming from Stanford University Press.

JOHN CARLOS ROWE teaches the literatures and cultures of the United States and critical theory at the University of California, Irvine, where he also directs the Critical Theory Institute. He is the author of *The Theoretical Dimensions of Henry James*, *Through the Custom-House: Nineteenth-Century American Fiction and Modern Theory*, and *Henry Adams and Henry James: The Emergence of a Modern Consciousness*; he co-edited, with Rick Berg, *The Vietnam War and American Culture*.

EVE KOSOFSKY SEDGWICK is the Newman Ivey White Professor of English at Duke University. She is the author of *Between Men: English Literature and Male Homosocial Desire* and *Epistemology of the Closet*. Her most recent book, *Tendencies*, was published by Duke University Press in 1993.

Foreword

John Carlos Rowe

In June of 1993, I participated in the Henry James Sesquicentennial Conferences in New York. Along with many others, I was impressed with the vitality and diversity of new scholarly approaches to James's life and works. Although some people in New York spoke of the "revival" of interest in Henry James, I think this exciting new work marks yet another of the several transformations Henry James has undergone in this century. As a novelist, he has been held up as the master of realism, of modernism, and of postmodernism in quick succession. As a theorist, he has been claimed by New Critics, phenomenological and reader-response critics, structuralists, and deconstructive critics. Cultural critics have identified his limitations, but often in ways that have testified to his generally progressive ideals and the subtlety of his understanding of how social power works.

We have not needed, then, to "revive" Henry James for the 1990's, because we continue to construct him according to our changing intellectual methods and literary concerns. Such a statement is likely to lend support to those who have argued recently for a return to so-called "classic" works and authors, and I do not object to paying respect to important works and authors as long as such regard includes our contemporary scene. If James is valued because his hopes and worries still speak to us, then let us celebrate his masterful adaptability, even changeable qualities, rather than his testament to some dubious universal truth. By beginning with his own anxieties concerning sexuality, conventional gender roles, and authorship at the turn of the last century, the most exciting new work on James has done just this. The case is decidedly not that nothing has changed, but that the changes we have passed through are readable historically from James and his contemporaries to us.

Positive change begins with our recognition of certain impasses—repetitions and thus repressions—in our previously settled ways of thinking; this has certainly characterized our transformation of the pompous figure of James as Master of the Novel—captured perfectly in John Singer Sargent's famous 1912 portrait of James at 70—into the vulnerable, sexually anxious, and lonely writer struggling with the new modern art and the new age he had helped make possible. The latter James, decidedly more human and accessible, as Fred Kaplan has rendered him in *Henry James: The Imagination of Genius* (1992), is aptly portrayed in Alvin Langdon Coburn's photographs of him at Rye in June 1906, taken just as James was deciding that Coburn would be "the solution to the problem of illustrations" for the New York Edition. Coburn's studies of James at Rye clearly express vulnerability, self-doubt, worry, even as they offer us the dominance of head and eye, of intellect and vision, which virtually holds James up.

How liberating it is to discover how much James needed other people and how desperately lonely he could be when visitors failed to appear, canceled, or left early! Lifting the repression concerning James's life, especially his passionate friendships with Hendrik C. Anderson and Howard Sturgis, changes not just our own attitudes toward his sexuality but also our attitudes toward his work. In one sense, these changes mean that we are now more able to reread James's later works as rich with homoerotic suggestiveness, more able to overcome critical categories that once refused the wit and fun, as well as the literary disguises, of the diverse sexual performances in *In the Cage*, "The Middle Years," "The Death of the Lion," "The Beast in the Jungle," "The Jolly Corner," and a host of others currently being rediscovered by scholars and critics.

Somewhat less obviously, this new understanding of what I can only term James's *sociability*—a quality essential to his writings all along, of course—affects how we understand the vaunted "craft" of his fiction. The ambitious Henry James vigorously committed to his successful literary career now must be understood in conjunction with the other James, who challenged ideas of literary authority and mastery in ways that would help our teachers announce the "death of the Author," grant new respect to readers, and reduce the myth of literary authority to the rhetorical features of an "author-function." Nowhere is this division in James and his critical reputation better expressed than in the New York Edition, long cited as the proof of James's canonization—how much better when the emperor seizes the crown and places it on his own head!—and yet virtually unread as James's work of literary canonization.

James's prefaces to the New York Edition have, of course, been "bor rowed" to make the case for various kinds of bloodless formalisms from Percy Lubbock's *The Craft of Fiction* (1921) and R. P. Blackmur's *The Art of the Novel* (1934) to the present. For all their insistence upon the integrity of the text, the heresy of paraphrase, and the necessity of "close reading," various formalists (and not just New Critics) used the prefaces as carelessly as the harried tourist thumbs the pages of a guidebook. Rarely did they look up at the actual landscape of the New York Edition, with the different perspectives its several authors afforded it—the young Coburn, the older James, his literary influences, and, of course, his previous writing selves, of which he takes such interested note throughout the prefaces. The "house of fiction" is nowhere more needful of deconstruction than in the form it has assumed for previous critics, the "art of the novel" that took the place of "the New York Edition."

Such critical reconsideration of the supposedly formidable "architecture" of literary mastery in the New York Edition is just what is taken up in the first section of this collection, under the appropriate heading, "Rethinking Mastery." Some may consider the James they knew to be destabilized here, but I find him thrown back among the company he liked to keep. Putting James back into his social and cultural contexts is the work of the next two sections, "Cultural and Publishing Contexts" and "Lines of Revision." It is extraordinary how much in these different essays strikes the specialist in James and the period as significantly "new," in part because the New York Edition is, as if for the first time, being considered as a complex work produced in specific historical contexts.

Such recontextualizations are necessary preludes to the final task of representing Henry James differently than we have usually seen him—once again, in the 1912 portrait by Sargent that James himself had judged "awesome." The Jameses we discover in his place are anxious, conflicted, marginal, even ashamed of themselves, utterly at odds it would seem with the royal "we" that James assumed in his deathbed dictations. These new Henry Jameses are instead full of life and interest, not only in their times but for our time, which as we begin to understand it continues to wind its way back to its early modern origins as it unfurls into our own new century. We recognize belatedly that this is the path of the Jamesian sentence, whose serpentine coils still grip us and yet more than ever offer the possibility of a grateful embrace.

Newport Beach, California

Henry James's New York Edition

The Construction of Authorship

"The Whole Chain of Relation and Responsibility": Henry James and the New York Edition

David McWhirter

Henry James's disappointment at the failure of the New York Edition of his Novels and Tales (1907–9) to sell or garner any significant critical attention is well known. Shortly before his death in 1916, the novelist described the Edition as "really a monument (like Ozymandias) which has never had the least intelligent critical justice done it."[1] And while the vast and proliferating body of criticism devoted to James has often addressed the most salient features of the New York Edition, especially its celebrated critical prefaces and the substantial revisions of his early novels which it occasioned, surprisingly little attention has been paid to the Edition itself *as a text*, and to the extraordinary, deeply ambiguous act of self-presentation that it embodies. Recent James criticism—a virtual encyclopedia of the pluralistic universe of contemporary literary theory—has found in the novelist's work a ready vehicle for current debates about canonicity, intentionality, authority, intertextuality, and literary value. Indeed, as John Carlos Rowe has observed, "Henry James . . . is an especially appropriate figure for the study of the impact of contemporary theory on our ideas of the author."[2] The myth of the master initiated by James and reinforced by generations of his commentators has increasingly been challenged by critics who have sought, in various ways, to restore James's art to what he once called "the conditions of life" (*23*: xxiv; *AN*, 347)—the social, political, historical, and personal contexts in which it was produced. But the New York Edition, arguably the central performance in the construction of that myth, has until very recently gone largely untouched.[3]

The essays gathered in this volume constitute a collective attempt to apprehend the full complexity of Henry James's self-performance—his often

ambivalent construction of self, authorship, and authority—in the New
York Edition. Taken together, they suggest how the Edition might serve as
a locus for considering not only the question of Henry James but also the
problematics and permutations of modern literary authority. For all their
methodological and theoretical diversity, however, the project's contributors would, I believe, agree that any attempt to rethink the New York Edition must begin by questioning its longtime function as a cornerstone in the
cultural and ideological construction of "Henry James"—the "Henry
James" who has come to represent the quintessential high-modernist priest
of art, the creator of an art of fiction committed to pure form, a figure
whose "destiny," as Rowe puts it, "always seems to end in the intricacies of
the late style and its retreat from life into the palace of art."[4] James, of
course, was in many ways the originator of this mythicized "Henry James."
Significantly, the one contemporary response to the Edition that James singled out for approval—it was, James averred, "the most appreciative and
fine tribute I have ever received"[5]—was Percy Lubbock's review in the
Times Literary Supplement, which celebrated the publication of the Edition, and especially its prefaces, as "an event, indeed the first event," in the
history of the novel. Lubbock sets the tone for later New Critical valoriza-
tions (and consequent simplifications) of the Edition by insisting on its
seamless structural coherence and by identifying the essential figure in the
Edition's carpet as James's "gradual solution of the problem" of form.[6] By
1934, when R. P. Blackmur collected the prefaces in *The Art of the Novel*,
the canonization initiated by Lubbock and encouraged, in many ways, by
James himself was well on the way to being a *fait accompli*.[7] Leon Edel's
influential essay "The Architecture of Henry James's 'New York Edition'"
(1951)—with its emphasis on the completeness and "architectural form of
[James's] monument" and its assertion that this was "the *comédie humaine*
of Henry James"—effectively completed the task. The assumption that the
Edition constitutes a "literary monument"[8] or "epitaph," a reliable key to
"the substance and principle of [James's] career"[9] and by extension a systematic modern *Poetics* of fiction, has rarely been seriously questioned.
    Yet as Ross Posnock points out in the essay that opens this volume, the
"cramped aura of sanctity [that] has grown around . . . James's cultural
presence" since the 1930's tends to obscure a "far more provocative figure":
the "pre-canonical James" who actually produced the New York Edition.
Part of the problem with traditional readings of the Edition, moreover, is
that they enshrine not only Henry James but a conception of authorship—

the author as autonomous, unitary, originating, and decidedly masculine genius—that seems increasingly untenable in the wake of poststructuralism, and more than a little suspect in the context of recent historicist, cultural, and gender criticism. We need, it seems clear, to ask not only who but what the author of the New York Edition might be; and many of the contributors to this project would agree with Michel Foucault that "we must entirely reverse the traditional notion of the author" as "the genial creator of a work in which he deposits, with infinite wealth and generosity, an inexhaustible world of significations." "The Master" is, in Foucault's words, an "ideological construction," the "figure which . . . marks the manner in which we fear the proliferation of meaning."[10] James's authority is thus both constructed and compromised by the surrounding social, political, and cultural discourses that in some undeniable sense "wrote" both the New York Edition and its author. Yet this demystification of Jamesian mastery from without need not signal the demise of the author or the reduction of Henry James to an ideological function. For as the essays in this volume show, the authority of the New York Edition is also problematized—destabilized—from within by an author who, I want to insist, is still very much an active, responsible agent in his text, though perhaps no longer the purveyor of the "lessons" habitually attributed to this master.

An initial impetus towards desanctifying the New York Edition has come from critics concerned with the ways in which James's complex relationship with the literary marketplace informed both his decision to undertake the project and its ultimate shape. James was, as Anne Margolis remarks, "genuinely perplexed and dismayed by his relative unpopularity in an age of best sellers and stubbornly obsessed with the idea of achieving commercial success."[11] In his introduction to *The Art of the Novel* Blackmur quotes a letter in which James famously described the New York Edition prefaces as "a plea for Criticism, for Discrimination, for Appreciation on other than infantile lines—as against the almost universal Anglo-Saxon absence of these things; which tends so, in our general trade, it seems to me, to break the heart." What Blackmur neglects to mention is that James immediately follows these remarks with an admission that he hoped the prefaces would help sell "two or three copies more!" "They will have represented much labor to this latter end," James continues—"though in that they will have differed indeed from none of their fellow-manifestations (in general) whatever; and the resemblance will even be increased if the two or three copies *don't*, in the form of an extra figure or two, mingle with my

withered laurels."[12] If the commercial failure of the New York Edition
ironically helped, as Margulis notes, "to cap the extremely seductive legend of the master"[13]—its failure to sell somehow serving to prove the purity of its creator's motives—James himself was willing to hope privately
that "it *may* make a little money for me—the consummation sordidly
aimed at."[14]

The myth that James was serenely unconcerned with popular opinion
and sales of his work has, I think, been decisively laid to rest.[15] And as
James's reference to the prefaces' "fellow-manifestations" suggests, the
New York Edition was in fact an example of a specific kind of publishing
commodity—the deluxe collected edition, complete with fine bindings,
frontispieces, and suitable prefatory remarks by the author—that enjoyed
a considerable vogue in the late nineteenth and early twentieth centuries.[16]
For James, the Edition represented in part a second chance to sell his books
in a repackaged form, a chance that seemed, given the popularity of the
deluxe edition, to offer a reasonable hope for commercial success. James's
correspondence with his publisher and with his agent, James B. Pinker,
consistently demonstrates his keen understanding of the conventions, marketing assumptions, and sales potential of the collected edition format: he
insists, for example, on "a Handsome Book, distinctly, not less so" than the
recent editions of Robert Louis Stevenson and George Meredith,[17] and
welcomes "the prospect of a size greater than the Kipling."[18]

As Michael Anesko and Stuart Culver show in their analyses of the factors—including questions of copyright and literary property, as well as the
sheer fiscal constraints imposed by James's publishers—that helped shape
the ostensibly "pure" architecture of the New York Edition, playing the literary market in the particular manner defined by the deluxe format meant
accepting a whole series of compromises on grounds that were anything but
aesthetically pure.[19] Ira Nadel thus argues that James's decision to break
with his long-standing opposition to textual illustration by commissioning
Alvin Langdon Coburn to provide photographic frontispieces for each of
the Edition's 24 volumes was in part a calculated effort to make it more
attractive to potential buyers who had grown wary (and weary) of the abstractions of the master's later prose style. The organic "unity of being" habitually attributed to the prefaces since Blackmur's 1934 *Art of the Novel*
also demands scrutiny in light of the actual conditions—James was revising
and writing the prefaces for the Edition's later volumes even as the first

were reaching the hands of its subscribers—in which they were produced. The professional and economic realities that helped define the final appearance of the Edition, especially with regard to the number, selection, and ordering of texts, are perhaps summarized most clearly in a remark made by one of the numerous publishers involved in the complex copyright negotiations it necessitated: "You will realise that the difficulty here is that so many different people have the copyright for so many different books by this author."[20] The absence of at least one major novel, *The Bostonians*, from an edition advertised by its publisher as including all of the works James wished to perpetuate is in fact partly attributable to the prohibitive difficulties involved in regaining the copyright from its original publisher.[21] James's consistently hard-nosed attitude about his professional life (he had always been willing to abandon even a trusted publisher when a better bargain beckoned) helped create this situation. But the result was that many people and institutions besides Henry James had a hand in the making of his monument. This is, as Jerome McGann would say, a thoroughly "socialized text"—an assertion borne out by McGann's own recounting of the odd history of "an error [not] in *The Ambassadors*," a text unwittingly revised and reconstructed by an earlier generation of critics in an ironic refusal of the Edition's authority.

This portrait of a professional author persistently, and often astutely, engaged with the business of the literary marketplace provides an important antidote to the iconography of the master and the attendant canonization of the New York Edition as pure aesthetic artifact. But even if, as Culver has remarked, the publishing history of the Edition shows how "the text's fate as a commodity re-wrote [James's] own role as its author,"[22] we are still left with the task of evaluating the nature of the authority claimed by the Edition itself, in the form—undoubtedly achieved through many choices and compromises, "sordid" and otherwise—in which it confronts us as readers. We don't, after all, really need Anesko's systematic debunking of Edel's "proof" that the New York Edition was deliberately modeled on Balzac's *Comédie Humaine*[23] to recognize that the two texts in question— Balzac's massively inclusive, totalizing epic structure (conceived in advance of most of the texts it contains) and James's more controlled, "selective as well as collective" unity (retroactively imposed on an existing body of work)[24]—have very little in common. And however mixed James's motives were in undertaking this representation of himself and his *oeuvre*, it

is to the text of the Edition that we must turn in evaluating the novelist's
claim that "the artistic problem involved in my scheme was a deep & ex
quisite one, & moreover was, as I hold, very effectively solved."[25]

In many respects the New York Edition, named by James after his city
of origin,[26] announces itself as precisely the kind of "literary monument"
for which it has long been taken, and as a unified, authoritative act of self-
definition. James's astonishing attention over a period of several years to the
details of this performance—his revisions and prefaces, his selection, ordering, and arrangement of the texts, his active collaboration with Coburn
on the frontispieces, even his insistent efforts to control the physical appearance of the volumes—seems to signal his conviction that the Edition
could provide a valid image or synecdoche for his large and diverse *oeuvre*,
and by implication for himself and his life as an artist. The Edition thus
authoritatively defines and categorizes a canon by its inclusions and—as
Martha Banta's speculative focus on the seven novels denied "its sanctioning imprint" demonstrates—its omissions, and through its hierarchic ordering and grouping of texts and its critical self-judgments. The prefaces
include self-authorizing narratives that trace the original circumstances of
the novels' and tales' conception and production; the revisions replace
"flawed" versions of early texts with "authorized" versions which, Edel argues, "bring [them] up to the level of [James's] maturity."[27] In many respects a magisterial gesture of authority, the Edition has been crucial to the
construction and maintenance of what Posnock calls "the aura of Henry
James": it shapes the novelist's career into a coherent plot, in part by locating its inevitable and defining destination in the "major phase"; provides
(or invents) a coherent mapping of the Jamesian aesthetic and of its underlying thematic and formal structures; offers, in James's words, "a sort of
comprehensive manual or *vademecum*" for future writers;[28] and secures its
author a prominent place in literary history by constructing a narrative of
the novelistic tradition that has remained extremely influential.

"*Heureux homme*," James wrote to Paul Bourget on the occasion of the
latter's collecting of his own works, "to be building and gilding, carving
and colouring, yourself, already, your marble, your mosaic sarcophagus."[29]
And there can be little doubt that James, whatever hopes for commercial
success he harbored, intended the New York Edition, at least in part, *as* a
monument, as "an image," in R. W. B. Lewis's words, "of a completed
oeuvre, of a lifelong commitment, a career" (*AN*, ix), an edifice equivalent
in dignity if not in kind to Balzac's *Comédie*. But James knew that "the

thing done and dismissed has ever, at the best . . . . a trick of looking dead, if not buried" (*9*: v–vi; *AN*, 99). And perhaps the most intriguing thing about the Edition is the way its structure often serves to undermine the "sarcophagic" authority it appears to claim and to problematize the whole question of authorship in ways that anticipate the discourse of poststructuralist theory. For if the Edition can be seen as an attempt at monolithic self-definition, it also should be apprehended as a conscious experiment in intertextuality which deliberately brings a variety of different "voices"—the original texts, the revisions, the prefaces, the frontispieces, even, as Banta suggests, the eloquent silence of the excluded novels and tales—into relation, without insisting that they converge on any architectural or monumental completeness, or that they reveal some monological intention or underlying "unity of being" (Blackmur, *AN*, xvii).

In his Preface to *The Golden Bowl*, for example, James portrays his practice of revision not as an act of rewriting but as a process of "seeing it again" (*23*: xvi; *AN*, 339), of rereading, as an engagement of the difference between his "original tracks" and his "present mode of motion" (*23*: xiii–xiv; *AN*, 336) which does not necessarily imply a hierarchy of validity or value, and which opens "a myriad more adequate channels" for interpretation (*23*: xvii; *AN*, 340). Most commentators on James's revisions for the New York Edition have followed F. O. Matthiessen (perhaps the most influential of the master's New Critical disciples) in assuming that James was basically attempting to fulfill more completely his original intentions for the texts in question. Yet as Hershel Parker has noted, there is much evidence, especially in the prefaces, to support an opposing conclusion: that James understood his revisions not as "casual elaborations or improvements on the original plan" but as "essential corrections or even transformations."[30] Indeed, the most heavily revised of the texts included in the Edition—notably *The American*, *The Portrait of a Lady*, and *Daisy Miller*—seem in many respects to embody fundamental shifts in James's intentions, especially in his attitudes towards key characters.[31] As Julie Rivkin observes, James's theory and practice thus make revision "the signature both of possession and of dispossession"; the writer, she concludes, "will never know all that will get written in the ever expanding margins of his own revised text"—an assertion echoed by Paul Armstrong when he describes James's prefaces as "disciplining the reader's attention . . . while encouraging its free, unpredictable exercise."

Like the revisions, Coburn's frontispieces serve to multiply the Edition's interpretive possibilities and to problematize James's authority. James argues that the photographs fulfill their function not by imitating the texts they illustrate in any direct sense but by becoming "separate and independent subject[s] of publication," each one "carrying its text in its spirit" and existing outside "the frame" of the original work (*23*: x; *AN*, 332). The photographs, typically of houses, streets, or landscapes, unpeopled scenes or images that indirectly evoke settings from James's narratives, are striking in their radical break with long-prevalent practices in illustrating fiction, which dictated the representation of specific dramatic scenes from a narrative in drawings, and the use of accompanying captions quoted directly from the illustrated text.[32] In the Preface to *The Golden Bowl*, explored here by J. Hillis Miller, James emphatically denounces any method that would thus "graft or 'grow' . . . a picture by another hand on my own picture" (*23*: ix; *AN*, 332). Rather, he sought images that possessed their own strength and integrity as works of art and that could, as Miller puts it, be "kept at a distance": in effect James, however warily, invites another artist, an "independent" reader of his work, into his self-constructed "house of fiction" (*3*: x; *AN*, 46).

Miller's brief but crucial reading of James's "not wholly consistent attempt to adjudicate the relation between picture and dramatic word" in the Preface to *The Golden Bowl*, like Rivkin's examination of the multiple, contradictory theories of revision articulated in the same text, points to a larger, "undecidable question" about the nature of representation: "whether," in Miller's words, "the type or idea preexists its representation in picture or word, or is present in something the representation copies, or is generated by the representation." Such doubts about just what representation re-presents are woven deeply into the fabric of the New York Edition, itself a massive act of re-presentation. What emerges here, repeatedly, is James's reluctance to grant priority to either the original texts or the revised ones, or to subject the frontispieces to the authority of the novels and tales they illustrate. And this reluctance adumbrates James's broader ambivalence, evident in his later fictions generally and, I think, in the New York Edition particularly, about the "myths of filiation" which for Roland Barthes distinguish the classic work's authority from the modern text's openness and indeterminacy.[33] Thus while the prefaces have often been treated as "authorized" interpretations, they are in fact, as Armstrong points out, extremely problematic—and sometimes plainly inaccurate—as guides to the texts they discuss. For all their apparent emphasis on origins and intentions, the prefaces frequently focus on the ways in which James's fictions escaped and continue to escape their creator's original binding intentions. Typically, James seems less concerned with closing in on a formal, definitive analysis of a completed text than with opening up new readings through the discovery of unanticipated sites for further interpretive play. And if the prefaces purport to provide a unified, systematic guide to the Jamesian aesthetic, they also enact a whole array of continuing dialogues, between author and critic or between writer and reader, for example, or even, as Max Beerbohm recognized in his celebrated cartoon (Figure 1), between the young and old Henry James, but also between the opposing impulses and demands of the novelist's art: plot and character, representation and form, the "expansive . . . principle" and "foreshortening" (*18*: xv; *AN*, 278), scene and picture, and so on.

Among the most striking and resonant of these dialogues is the one played out in the prefaces between masculine and feminine genderings of James's fictional and critical discourse. On the one hand, James figures his art through images drawn from such conventionally masculine spheres as war, business, architecture, and law. The novelist is thus the "chief accountant" of his text, or again a "builder," who "places, after an earnest survey, the piers of his bridge," and who works to insure that his characters provide "sufficiently solid *blocks* of wrought material . . . as to have weight and mass and carrying power" (*19*: xii–xiii; *AN*, 296–97). Yet alongside these masculine metaphors, James consistently offers images associated with femininity—in particular, figures of weaving, needlepoint, and embroidery—in his attempt to define or describe his own artistic activity. In addition, James frequently assigns himself the domestic tasks of the housewife or the maternal functions of "the nurse's part": the task of revision is thus figured as "a descent of awkward infants from the nursery into the drawing-room," an occasion requiring "a tidying-up of the uncanny brood," with all "the common decencies of such a case—the responsible glance of some power above from one nursling to another, the rapid flash of an anxious needle, the not imperceptible effect of a certain audible splash of soap and water" (*23*: xiv–xv; *AN*, 337–38). If the novelist is a father, the possessor of the "majesty of authorship" (*23*: vi; *AN*, 328), and the originator of the "exquisite laws" (*23*: xxv; *AN*, 348) that govern his works, he is also a nurturing mother, who protects and encourages the free development of each of his fictional "germs." As Sara Blair shows in her study of the Preface to *The Portrait of a Lady*, James's construction of au-

Figure 1. "How badly you wrote!/write!" A cartoon by Max Beerbohm, and his note in a copy of *Art and the Actor* (1915), containing James's revised essay on Coquelin. The essay originally appeared in *Century Magazine* (1887), and was, according to Beerbohm's note on the facing page, "very obviously—or, rather, deviously and circuitously—revised in the great dark rich fulness of time, for republication in 1915." Reproduced by permission of the Houghton Library, Harvard University.

thorship and authority is both legitimated and undermined by the gendered social discourses in which it self-consciously participates.

The language of priority, paternity, origins, hierarchy, and will—the language of authority—is thus countered everywhere in the New York Edition by James's conception and practice of a kind of writing characterized by relationships of adjacency, openness, difference, and free play. James asserts a centered, coherent narrative of the self only to revise that self again and again in the open-ended intertext of difference and dialogue. And his quest for an authoritative, completed image of his *oeuvre* inevitably leaves him with "a sense for ever so many more of the shining silver fish afloat in the deep sea of one's endeavour than the net of widest casting could pretend to gather in" (23: xxii; *AN*, 345). If Foucault is right in seeing the author—or, as he calls it, "the author function"—as "the principle of thrift in the proliferation of meaning,"[34] then James's New York Edition is the act of an author profoundly suspicious of any such economy. In a famous passage from the Preface to *Roderick Hudson*, James argues that "really, universally, relations stop nowhere," and that "the exquisite problem of the artist is eternally but to draw, by a geometry of his own, the circle within which they shall happily *appear* to do so" (1: 7; *AN*, 5). An awareness of the tension so carefully framed in this ambiguous statement—is the circle drawn where relations "appear" to stop? or where the appearance that "relations stop nowhere" is successfully rendered?—seems an essential premise of any attempt at a full apprehension of the New York Edition.

In his Preface to *The Golden Bowl*, James characterizes his *oeuvre*, and by implication the Edition itself, as very much "a *living* affair" (23: xix; *AN*, 342). And the challenge offered by this project to the quasi-divine authority traditionally attributed to the Edition should be seen not as an attempt simply to dismember the god and scatter his bones but rather as an effort to transform our image of this text and its author, to replace its supposed monological unity—the unity, if you will, of a fixed corpus—and the model of a unitary self that it implies, with the more open and flexible continuities of a living body. This transformation is, I think, part of what James had in mind when he summed up his career as an expression of "the religion of doing," a "religion" guided by his conviction that "if [the writer] is always doing he can scarce, by his own measure, ever have done," and practiced in the New York Edition's "reconstitut[ion]" of "the whole chain of *relation* and *responsibility*" (23: xxiv–xxv; *AN*, 347–48; my emphasis) discoverable in his life and work. For all his talk of monuments and sarcophagi, James understood that the self and the career embodied in the Edition's multi-voiced dialogue of relation and response are always recreatable, revisable, rereadable. And the intertextuality of the New York Edition—its deliberately and admittedly compromised authority—finds its surest confirmation in James's recognition that its reader inevitably enters the text's dialogical continuity through his response, "in his own other medium, by his own other art," to "the images [the writer] has evoked" (23: x; *AN*, 332). Indeed, James concludes his final preface by paraphras-

ing Flaubert's remark "that any imaged prose that fails to be richly rewarding in return for a competent utterance ranks itself as wrong through not
being 'in the conditions of life.'" The New York Edition, like any text, thus
owes the fullest "flower of its effect to the act and process of apprehension
that so beautifully asks most from it. It then infallibly, and not less beautifully, most responds" (*23*: xxiv; *AN*, 347).

James's overt invitation to his readers to participate in the construction
of "Henry James" is perhaps the clearest indicator that the "author" of the
New York Edition is a fractured, radically compromised figure. But it
should also remind us that the Edition still embodies a powerful, if revisionary, fiction of mastery—that it projects a specifically modern conception of authority designed to appeal to the highly specialized, sophisticated
group of readers, most of them, presumably, already familiar with much
of the *oeuvre* the Edition re-presents, who constituted the potential audience at which this particular literary commodity was aimed. The Edition,
like all of James's later work, eschews any claim to the kind of cultural and
moral authority manifested in his nineteenth-century predecessors, who assumed, more or less comfortably, the mantle of the Victorian sage. Nor
does James attempt the comparatively naive totalization, or the blatant assertion of power, implicit in Balzac's description of *his* monument—the
Comédie Humaine—as an effort to "portray all aspects of society, so that not
a single situation of life, not a face, not the character of any man or woman,
not a way of life, not a profession, not a social group, will be missing."
Balzac is unquestionably the master builder, whose fictions are "stories" in
a structure of truly epic proportions:

> Not an aspect of childhood, maturity, old age, politics, justice, war, will be left
> out. On this foundation I shall examine every thread of the human heart, every
> social factor and it will be real. On the second storey I shall place the philosophical
> stories, for after portraying effects, I shall deal with what has caused them. . . .
> Finally I shall turn to an analysis of principles. . . . [The *Comédie* is] the play, the
> causes go behind the scenes, and the principle—he's the novelist himself. . . . The
> whole will be an *Arabian Nights* of the West.[35]

The New York Edition, although wrought, James would like us to believe,
with the artist's "master-hammer" (*9*: xvi; *AN*, 109), generally avoids such
palpable aggressions, relying instead on the perhaps more insidious
aggressions of modernism's veiled power—the power embedded in reti-
cence and ambiguity, in what Martha Banta describes as an "aesthetics of
refusal," or what James himself once called "the felicity of suppression and

omission."[36] Indeed, the Edition's modernity may lie precisely in its more subtle organization of power, its hegemonic construction of an authority capable of containing and managing apparently irreconcilable motives, desires, and selves, and of captivating a "distracted" modern reader who, as James acknowledges in the Preface to *The Turn of the Screw*, is "not easily caught." Like the master's celebrated ghost story, the Edition might be read as "a piece of cold artistic calculation" masquerading as "an excursion into chaos" (*12*: xvi–xviii; *AN*, 171–72), and thus as modernity's disguised reinscription of the traditional author function. Coburn's frontispiece for volume 9 (*The Awkward Age*), a picture of Lamb House, James's home in Rye, England, taken at James's direction but identified in the caption only as "Mr. Longdon's" (fig. 13), is suggestive in this regard: the scene of writing, the site where the author exercises his "exquisite management" (*9*: xvi; *AN*, 110), is inserted in the Edition, but only through a gesture that effectively conceals its presence.

It may be, then, as Shoshana Felman argues, that "James's very mastery consists in the denial and in the deconstruction of his own mastery."[37] I would like, however, to keep open the possibility that the New York Edition enacts a more genuinely subversive conceptualization of literary authority, as well as a related, potentially liberating re-vision of the self. John Carlos Rowe has written that "all of us have our different but particular needs for the Author."[38] And I readily confess my own need, in approaching this vexed question, to keep alive the idea of human agency, the possibility that real human beings, spoken by and speaking from within the dominant ideological discourse, can still alter and rewrite the terms of that discourse, and so effect real changes in the culture that ideology shapes. My purpose then is not to deny the presence of James's authority in the New York Edition but to recognize that that authority is inscribed within a system—what Seán Burke calls "a textual *mise en scène*"[39]—which it no longer dominates, but which it is still capable of shaping in meaningful and necessary ways. "The 'subject' of writing," as Jacques Derrida puts it, "does not exist if we mean by that some sovereign solitude of the author." But the sovereign author need not be construed as authorship per se. "The subject of writing," Derrida continues, "is a *system* of relations between strata: the Mystic Pad, the psyche, society, the world."[40] With the death of the author, "the category of [authorial] intention will not disappear; it will have its place, but from that place it will no longer be able to govern the entire scene and system of utterance."[41]

Instead of refusing any truck with the author, we need to focus, as Nancy K. Miller has suggested, on "changing the subject,"[42] an endeavor that James's own rewriting of authorship in the New York Edition can help us to imagine. Recent "death of the author criticism" has all too often conflated literary authority with a historically specific construction of subjectivity as autonomous and transcendental, a model of the self that James consistently contests in the Edition. That the self is less a structure of autonomous, self-same identity than an ever changing network of differences and relations; that authorship is less a matter of monological, originating intentions than a process of infinite adaptability and responsibility: these, it seems to me, are the most important lessons of the Edition's ambiguously staged, if flamboyantly performed, authority. In confusing literary authority with subjectivity itself, moreover, we risk losing sight of the very possibility the death of the author was meant to promote: the exploration, as Foucault himself asserts, of "new forms of subjectivity through the refusal of the kind of individuality which has been imposed on us for several centuries."[43] At the same time, to the extent that we banish the author from our critical and theoretical discourses—a trend promoted, intentionally or not, by Foucault's own work—we risk excluding the necessary figure of "the poet," whom Plato, as Phillipe Lacoue-Labarthe reminds us, insisted on excluding from his Republic. The reduction of the author to a linguistic or ideological function in recent theory, Lacoue-Labarthe argues, reflects our desire, disturbingly parallel to Plato's, "to be done with the producer, the dangerous poet." And what makes the author as poet so "dangerous" is precisely the possibility that he is "not truly a subject, [but] a subject that is a non-subject or subjectless, and also an infinitely multiplied, plural subject." The *"poetic gift"*—*"the gift of mimesis"*—embodies as well a *"gift of impropriety,"* for "in order to (re)present or (re)produce everything . . . one must oneself be nothing, have nothing *proper* to oneself except an 'equal aptitude' for all sorts of things, roles, characters, functions, and so on." The "mimeticians" are "unassignable, unidentifiable, impossible to place in a determined class or to fix in a function that would be proper to them."[44] Their improper, "subjectless subjectivity" is as threatening to us as it was to Plato, for it destabilizes the very structures that produce, position, and constrain subjects in our complex, bureaucratically administered society.

Michael Millgate has characterized the New York Edition as a massive "testamentary act," the production of an author obsessively and at times ruthlessly engaged in constructing "the image of himself that would be handed down to posterity." In Millgate's view, James attempts to reshape and fix his career in a unified master-narrative of identity and his own mastery: the prefaces and revisions constitute a proleptic effort to determine, once and for all, what Henry James was, an effort that depends on willful, perhaps even unethical distortions of the past to achieve its goals.[45] But in denouncing James's imperial consciousness, Millgate frames the questions about authorship and identity posed by the Edition in terms that, as I have been suggesting, have outlived their usefulness. Millgate paradoxically affirms the author's supreme sovereignty even as he seeks to overthrow it, in part because he fails to distinguish, in Ross Posnock's formulation, "between James's technique of *central* consciousness and the ideology of individualism's belief in *centered* consciousness." Indeed, to see James as engaged in so single-minded an effort to define himself and his career is to misapprehend the main thrust of his revisionary energy. The question James asks in the New York Edition is, I think, less "What was it?" than "Who am I?" And any attempt to answer this latter question depends for James not on *a* totalizing narrative of mastery but on a capacity for establishing multiple, often contradictory lines of connection, relation, and responsiveness to the many Henry Jameses who inhabit this extraordinary text. Through what Posnock describes as a protean dialectic of memory and consciousness, James explores a model of selfhood that celebrates continuity even as it abandons "the logic of identity."[46]

In his recent consideration of "the question of selfhood," suggestively entitled *Oneself as Another*, Paul Ricoeur stages a confrontation between two conceptions of personal identity: "on one side, identity as *sameness* (Latin *idem*) . . . ; on the other, identity as *selfhood* (Latin *ipse*)." "Selfhood," Ricoeur insists, "is not sameness," for it "implies no assertion concerning some unchanging core of personality"[47]—nothing like the "unity of being" that Blackmur approvingly ascribes to the New York Edition, and that Millgate condemns in it. While both conceptions of identity depend on a sense of "permanence in time," and hence on a sense of continuity with the past, *idem* or sameness identity attributes that permanence to a schema rooted in "the category of substance"—to the persistence of an essential, selfsame *whatness* that Ricoeur construes in narratological terms as "character": sameness identity conceives of "change as happening to something which does not change."[48] But there is, Ricoeur asserts, "another model of permanence in time besides that of character. In narrative terms, it is that of keeping one's word in faithfulness to the word that has been given." Ricoeur sees in "this keeping [one's word]" that is the hallmark of selfhood or *Ipse*-identity the emblematic figure of an identity that is the polar oppo site of that depicted by the emblematic figure of character. "Keeping one's word expresses a *self-constancy* which cannot be inscribed, as character was, within the dimension of something in general [i.e., as a substance] but solely within the dimension of 'who?'"[49]

Ricoeur argues that identity in narrative oscillates "between two limits: a lower limit, where permanence in time expresses the confusion of [sameness and selfhood]; and an upper limit, where [selfhood] poses the question of its identity without the aid and support of [sameness] or the *idem*." And it is at this upper limit—where the continuity of "keeping one's word" unfolds without the support, and without the disabling immobilizations, of sameness—that James is exploring his own selfhood in the New York Edition. "The perseverance of faithfulness to a word that has been given"[50] as a model for permanence in time informs James's characters' struggles to construct new modalities of ethical selfhood throughout his career. Isabel Archer, for example, might be seen as moving from the conception of identity as sameness which she articulates in her famous conversation with Madame Merle to a new sense of self embodied in her decision to keep her promise to Pansy. The centrality of "keeping one's word" is manifested in Strether's adherence to his logic "not, out of the whole affair, to have got anything for [him]self" (22: 325); in the strange but moving ways in which Merton Densher's sense of himself is increasingly determined by his need to keep the promises he has made unwillingly, perhaps even unwittingly, to Milly Theale; and in Maggie Verver's successful effort to save her marriage, not by clinging to what it was, even less so to what *she* was, but through a fidelity to her vow that requires a massive revision of her relationship with her husband and a remarkable reconfiguration of her self.

In the New York Edition, what we see is James exploring his *own* cultural, authorial, and personal identity under the sign of this revisionary model of selfhood—a process that increasingly affiliates him with what Posnock calls a "politics of nonidentity."[51] It is in this light, I think, that we can best understand the frontispieces, revisions, and prefaces for the New York Edition: neither as an attempt to adhere to "original intentions" nor as an effort to force the differences of the past to conform to James's present imperial will, but as a new *relation* to his earlier texts, a fully *responsible* keeping of the promise of the words he gave so long ago. James's *ipse*—his

"Here I am" as opposed to any "This is *what* I am" (or was)—finds the contexts for its articulation precisely in his multiplicitous, protean, always proliferating senses of himself, and in his never final, always provisional quest for new circuits of connection and continuity with the past and with the others—Coburn; his readers; the authors of *Roderick Hudson* and *Daisy Miller* and *The Tragic Muse*—who inhabit that past and constitute the self which apprehends it. As Eve Kosofsky Sedgwick remarks in her reading of the "intensely charged," eroticized "relationship between the author of the prefaces and the often much younger man who wrote the novels and tales to which the prefaces are appended," the very act of figuring "one's relation to one's own past as a relation*ship*" opens out "a rich landscape of relational positionalities."

James's understanding of the self as a responsible keeping of one's word—his "faithfulness to the word that has been given"—is nowhere more urgently articulated than in his Preface to *The Golden Bowl*. Locating the "incomparable luxury of the artist" in his "essentially traceable" relation to his past "literary deeds," James remarks that he "can make almost anything [he] like[s]" of the "tie that binds" him to them (*23*: xxiv–xxv; *AN*, 347–48)—a freedom, I would argue, that is made possible precisely by his understanding of that tie as ethical, as a chosen self-constancy, not an ontological persistence of the same. Thus in seeking to "reconstitute" the "whole chain of relation and responsibility," James reminds us that to relate is to speak, but also to listen, to be in relation to others and to the others one has been, and that to be responsible is to acknowledge one's agency, one's responsibility for one's deeds and words, but also to understand that those deeds and words are always formulated in response to other voices and in anticipation of still other responses. The author who emerges in this volume will undoubtedly strike many readers as a disturbingly posthumanist figure. But James's "reconstitution" of the ethics of authorship in the New York Edition may also be understood as a necessary transformation, rather than simply a rejection, of the moral humanism he embodied for previous generations of critics. The humanist Henry James was nowhere more subtly and passionately presented than in Dorothea Krook's *The Ordeal of Consciousness in Henry James*.[52] Although Krook, who was to have been a contributor to this book, and to whose memory it is dedicated, wrote to me shortly before her death of her "unfashionable" intention to defend the intrinsic "authoritativeness" and even "sacredness" of "James's Choice" for the New York Edition, she would, I hope, have approved of this addition

to the chain of critical relation and responsibility in which her work remains a crucial link.

With characteristic ambiguity, James both evoked and questioned traditional concepts of authority in shaping the New York Edition. James was
undoubtedly intent on erecting a monument, if only because, as Alfred
Habegger argues in his essay for this volume, that monument was designed to entomb the personal and familial "losses, defeats, disasters, collapses, and failures" concealed in the "New York" of his Edition's title.
Like Habegger, Carol Holly reads James's claim to possess the "master-
hammer" as an "attempt to compensate for the 'wounds and mutilations' of
a lifetime"; the emotional collapse precipitated by the failure of that attempt suggests that the master's sense of his own authority may have been
very fragile indeed. But as James admits in his Preface to *The Wings of the
Dove*, "one's plan, alas, is one thing and one's result another" (*19*: xiii; *AN*,
296). And for all its monumental aspirations, James's Edition also unfolds
a multi-voiced, dialogic tapestry rich in potentially liberating reconfigu-
rations of authorship, authority, and identity. Whatever his intention for
his neglected monument may have been, its effect is to challenge the most
crucial of Barthes's "myths of filiation"—the author's supreme authority
over the meaning(s) of his text. Indeed, the New York Edition *is*, in the
fullest sense of Barthes's term, a "text," a literary/discursive space where the
author is present "as a 'guest,'" and where his "signature"—the signature
so prominently overlaid on the title page of the Edition's first volume (Figure 2)—"is no longer privileged and paternal, the locus of genuine truth,
but rather, ludic."[53]

Moreover, James's decision to name the Edition after his native city
may signal his own recognition that his quest for an authoritative, monumental permanence had resulted instead in a "wondrous adventure" (*1*: vi;
AN, 4) of ever unfolding difference. In *The American Scene*, a text he completed just before he embarked on the New York Edition, James speaks
with considerable ambivalence of New York's skyscrapers—those "most
piercing notes in that concert of the expensively provisional into which
your supreme sense of New York resolves itself": "they never begin to
speak to you, in the manner of the builded majesties of the world as we have
heretofore known such—towers or temples or fortresses or palaces—with
the authority of things of permanence. . . . One story is good only till another is told, and skyscrapers are the last word of economic ingenuity only
till another word be written."[54] The "New York" in the name of James's

Figure 2. Title page for volume 1 of the New York Edition, with facing frontispiece and facsimile signature overleaf. Reproduced by permission of the Harry Ransom Humanities Research Center, University of Texas at Austin.

Edition suggests that he ultimately saw his *oeuvre*, and his identity as an author, as similarly "provisional," as achievements best memorialized by an openness to many stories, rather than an exclusive commitment to one. The New York Edition resists any "last word," and so defines its singular value as a locus for considering the construction of modern literary authority.

PART I

Rethinking Mastery

Breaking the Aura of Henry James

Ross Posnock

Near the close of *The Ambassadors*, Maria Gostrey and Lambert Strether recall an earlier "curiosity felt by both of them as to where he would 'come out'" if his delicate mission to return Chad to America came "to smash." In the wake of Strether's botched mission, his Parisian pleasures, and his uncertain American future, they realize that "he was out, in truth, as far as it was possible to be" (*22*: 321). Near the end of *The Golden Bowl*, James's last complete novel, Maggie Verver is close to reclaiming her straying husband and renewing their marriage on a new basis of sexual intensity. She compares her husband, an Italian prince "fixed in his place," with her own evolving status. Whereas Amerigo's place "was like something made for him beforehand," Maggie's "own had come to show simply as that improvised 'post' . . . of the kind spoken of as advanced" and serving "a settler or trader in a new country. . . . The only geography marking it would be doubtless that of the fundamental passions" (*24*: 323–24). What these passages disclose are characters' movements beyond the conventional codes that impose intelligibility upon selves. James's late work is concerned not simply to celebrate these figures of illegibility, as might a Whitman or an Emerson, but to socialize them. He does so by redirecting their energy back to a social order whose demands for legibility might then be challenged and modified. So relaxed, democratic psyches and social structures might be shaped by less coercive mappings.

When *The Golden Bowl* ends—not long after the quotation above—it concludes the so-called "major phase" of James's fiction. And there too, in 1904, the canonical James ends. But James did not. What he went on to create, as recent critics increasingly realize, was a second major phase

(1907–14), one of autobiography, cultural criticism, and aesthetics: *A Small Boy and Others, Notes of a Son and Brother, The American Scene,* and the New York Edition prefaces. The motto of this cluster of texts might be James's declaration in the Preface to *The American Scene*: "I would stand on my gathered impressions. . . . I would in fact go to the stake for them." This sounds the most characteristic note—intimate, vulnerable, defiant— of his self-representation throughout the late nonfiction. As if inspired by the extremity of exposure risked by his two greatest fictional creations, James too comes out as far as possible, I will argue, and represents his self not as fixed beforehand by what he calls the "oppressive *a priori*," but as improvisational, "led . . . on and on" by the force of "fundamental passions."[1] With this mobile stance he greets American modernity, disembarking at Hoboken, New Jersey, on August 30, 1904, for a strenuous ten-month tour.

Arguably, my rhetoric above seems rather inflated; after all, one might point out, I am describing the final works of an aging, genteel, bachelor celibate whose last books seem more absorbed in the consolations of memory than in anything else. But these oft-repeated facts of canonical wisdom are redolent of what James calls "fatal futility," for they inform only by simplifying, by smoothing out the incongruities that mark the texture of James's genius. These incongruities, implicit in the quotations that began this essay, are heightened when James likens Maggie, his fabulously wealthy princess, to "some Indian squaw with a papoose on her back and barbarous bead-work to sell" (*24*: 323). What does James intend by having the primitive jostle against the genteel, a tension echoed in his willingness to go to the stake and in likening himself (in his memoirs) to a "subtle savage"? Simply to pose this question suggests the reason for his inflation of diction and metaphor—it is the means of making the question visible. His mock-heroic hyperbole functions less as satire than as the vehicle for expressing the return of inner and outer nature—that which is repressed by the violent strain of holding the bourgeois self together.

If bourgeois respectability in the late-nineteenth-century capitalist world, as Jean-Paul Sartre says, embodies "anti-nature," or the suppression of desire, in both of his major phases James in effect stages a revolt of nature. Yet anti-nature—the condition of culture—"bears without cracking the strongest pressure" James throws on it (*19*: xxi; *AN*, 304).[2] Culture holds fast—Maggie's marriage is remade; Strether will go back to Woollett—but not before its dictatorship over nature has been toppled. The result is that nature and culture in his fiction, like the alien and the assimilated in *The American Scene*, exist in a relation of reciprocal incitation, each "eat[ing] round the edges" of the other's position, "baffling insidiously" the other's "ideal," as James describes the interplay of drama and picture in his aesthetics (*19*: iv; *AN, 298*). This volatile tension characterizes a dynamic democratic social order that since the nineteenth century has been, in the words of political theorist Claude Lefort, "the theatre of an uncontrollable adventure." In turn, this "ungraspable society" engenders the bourgeois values and institutions designed to contain it. And the clash between indeterminacy and the cult of order produces a "certain vertigo" that has been identified since Marx and Baudelaire as modernity's hallmark.[3] James defines the "very *donnée*" of twentieth-century America as the "great adventure of a society" where "fluctuations and variations, the shifting quantity of success and failure," render experience bewilderingly inconclusive.[4]

I

A self-described "restored absentee" risking "exposure" and a "certain recklessness," James in 1904 resolves "to stand naked and unashamed" for the sake of his impressions. Like some voluntary Hester at the Scaffold or some Whitman tramping a perpetual journey, this Henry James stages his own spectacle of public vulnerability. He relishes walking the teeming streets of New York, riding the "densely-packed street-cars," feeling "the whole quality and *allure* . . . of the pushing male crowd," mingling with the "polyglot" visitors to Central Park and the "great swarming" life of the "New Jerusalem" on the Lower East Side (James's emphasis).[5]

Receding from view is the impeccably Olympian formalist and aesthetic idealist who, like his characters, turns his back on an impossibly vulgar modern world to cultivate what critics were once fond of calling redemptive consciousness. This is the James that R. P. Blackmur installed into the modernist pantheon as "the novelist of the free spirit, the liberated intelligence" and "ideal vision." Blackmur's description is from his influential 1934 essay on the prefaces that appeared in the special James issue he edited for *Hound and Horn*. This occasion can conveniently mark James's official canonization.[6]

The canonized Henry James has been and remains one of the most prestigious, indeed sacred, cultural icons on the altar of American high culture. And there is an undeniable and significant measure of truth in the official portrait. The problem is that it purports to be a definitive, fixed image of an author always skeptical of the static, whose restless mind's most characteristic movement is an immanent one that conceives the way out as the way through. A cramped aura of sanctity has grown around what might be called James's cultural presence. "Aura" is meant here in Walter Benjamin's sense of a fetishized cultural artifact that, says one commentator, "exerts an irrational, and thus incontrovertible power . . . within a culture which lends it a sacrosanct inviolability."[7] The Jamesian aura diminishes the novelist by repressing some of the deepest impulses of his art and life. In short, Henry James the cultural icon lacks even a suggestion of the Henry James of *The American Scene*, the work that played a pivotal role in creating what James called his "general renovation" of 1904. That year sparked his late recrudescence of revisionary energy that produced the prefaces and autobiography.[8]

Whether in the mode of cultural analysis, aesthetics, or family chronicle, this cluster of works constitutes the textual site or arena wherein James performs a prolonged act of divestiture that dissolves, as if in slow motion, his persona of master and reconstructs it by initiating an inquiry into "the mystery of human subjectivity in general," to borrow a phrase from Melville's *The Confidence-Man*.[9] James's inquiry focuses upon the nature of mastery and authority in late nineteenth and early twentieth century America and proceeds on at least three entwined levels broadly designated aesthetic, cultural, and psychological.

As the quotation from Melville suggests, Henry James's project partakes of the antinomian, interrogative energies of the American Renaissance, which, in turn, inspired the pragmatism of William James and John Dewey, both loyal admirers of Emerson. Emerson's words from "Circles" express the common ground the two movements traverse: "Nothing is secure but life, transition, the energizing spirit. . . . No truth is so sublime but it may be trivial tomorrow in the light of new thoughts. People wish to be settled; only as far as they are unsettled is there any help for them." By stripping himself of the props of the familiar, Henry James does not hope to recover Emerson's "original relation to the universe" but rather to reenact his "abandonment" of "propriety."[10]

My claim ill-consorts with the canonical Henry James constructed in the 1930's as "the great *genteel* classic, embodying better than any other single man the principles of Anglo-Saxon 'idealism,' " as Wyndham Lewis put it in a representative statement.[11] The pre-canonical James is a far more provocative figure, one who by 1904 was a disquieting curiosity to the reading public. His American visit occasions several extensive evaluations of his career, and the two most important—by H. G. Dwight (1907) and W. C. Brownell (1905)—recognize James as a troubling presence. "While readers expressed . . . the most varied degrees of bewilderment, exaspera-tion, or ridicule, the most frequent point of agreement was that of uncer-tainty as to what, after all, to make of Henry James."[12] This is Dwight's summary of what he calls "the flood of remark" called forth by James's re-turn. Unlike many later critics, James's contemporaries frankly confess their unease rather than defensively displacing it into an attack on his al-leged gentility. Indeed, both Dwight and Brownell conclude that a cause of James's unpopularity among his contemporaries is his ungenteel excess of curiosity.

The value of Dwight's essay is that he links the public's uncertainty about James both to familiar sources—the "strangeness" of his style "for eyes accustomed to the telegraphic brevity of the newspaper"—and to less obvious cultural anxieties that James arouses. Not only does the novelist address an American "public without leisure and a people . . . the least sen-sitive to the movements of the inner life." There is also, says Dwight, "an unmannerly levity about him, as of him who should go into great company whistling, with his hands in his pockets. We relish the grand air better, and a proper sense of one's responsibilities. . . . He does not obviously give you, as Mr. Brownell puts it, a 'synthetic view of life seen from a certain centralizing point of view.'"[13] Instead of the grand air of a central synthe-sis, James gives us an "endless chain of suggested improprieties . . . a tissue of hideous, nameless complications," in the words of a scandalized reviewer of the then recently published *The Golden Bowl*.[14]

According to Brownell, curiosity diverts James from a morally respon-sible synthesis: his work is "an unfolding, a laying bare, but not a putting together. The imagination to which it is due is too tinctured with curiosity to be truly constructive. . . . His curiosity is not merely impartial, but ex-cessive." Comparing the novelist to the great French anatomist Cuvier "lecturing on a single bone and reconstructing the entire skeleton from it," Brownell finds James "a Cuvier absorbed in the fascinations of the single bone itself" and thus perversely indifferent to the responsibility of recon-structing the whole.[15] The causes of James's uncertain cultural status begin to suggest themselves. "He will not fit into any of our comfortable old pi-

geon holes" (Dwight) because he seems to combine disparate, even antithetical, identities: a "scientific aspect" and curiosity (Brownell) that simultaneously mocks and unravels its authority by adopting a certain "levity"
that refuses both a "grand air" and, more important, the major responsibility of cultural authority—to conclude, to reconstruct, to synthesize. The
reactions of his contemporaries adumbrate an irresponsible James. This response powerfully intuits the unsettling energy of his late cultural thought,
which challenges the ideology and ontology of monadic individualism with
its grounding in static, binary logic and its promotion of a selfhood devoted to inner and outer control.

The logic governing his project can begin to be uncovered by applying
to James himself a crucial passage from the prefaces where he describes the
writer of genius. "The interest of his genius is greatest," he says, "when he
commits himself in both directions; not quite at the same time or to the
same effect . . . but by some need of performing his whole possible revolution, by the law of some rich passion in him for extremes." In writers of
"largest responding imagination before the human scene," the "current" of
their genius is "extraordinarily rich and mixed" as it washes us with both
"the near and familiar and the tonic shock . . . of the far and strange" (2:
xv; *AN*, 31). James's immediate concerns here are realism and romance,
but the words reverberate beyond this context to suggest his equation of
genius with passion, agonism, contradiction, and mobility, with the radical
heterogeneity of mutually conflicting impulses that at once incite and doom
efforts at resolution. Implicit too in this urge to move "in both directions"
is the androgynous texture of genius, its refusal of polarities. In sum, genius possesses a dialectical imagination that James, in another Preface, images as a "perpetually simmering cauldron": "we can surely account for
nothing in the novelist's work that hasn't passed through the crucible of his
imagination" (*15*: xvii; *AN*, 230).

Igniting this fiery process is the pressure of dialectical reversal
whereby the crucible of the imagination "destroys" "prime identity" to produce "a new and richer saturation." This famous image of artistic process,
a kind of Jamesian version of what Hegel calls negating the negation (the
overcoming of opposites), leaves ambiguous the final term of the process.
All he says about what passes through the "crucible" is that it achieves a
"final savour. . . . Thus it has become a different and . . . better thing" (*15*:
xviii; *AN*, 230). By omitting from his simmering process a synthetic, har-
monizing moment producing an absolute (as in Hegel), James emphasizes

instead the production of difference generated by the dissolving of identity. Difference is what makes for a "richer saturation" of an ongoing process that avoids closure. This elaborate metaphor of the crucible is hardly exhausted by its immediate purpose of defending the artist's right to alter the identities of "real persons." More generally, James's crucible directs attention to his suspicion (shared by Hegel) of the very concept of individual identity as impoverished unless it is nourished by dialectical mediation.

In emphasizing the dynamism of difference and the propensity of genius to move in "both directions," James manifests a commitment to the power and value of the irreconcilable and the uncontrollable in human experience. Henry shares this allegiance to what defies classification with his brother William's pragmatism, which conceives experience as "unfinished and growing," resisting synthesis and absolutes. This affinity is only the most familiar branch of an intriguing philosophical genealogy that will be sketched below in order to contextualize Henry James's second major phase and reveal its unsuspected intellectual affiliations.

II

The prefatory passages discussed above reveal Henry James practicing his own critique of the "logic of identity," to borrow the phrase that William James used in 1909 to describe Hegel's sacrifice of contingency and particularity to the abstract laws of an absolutist system.[16] Analogously, in identity thinking, our normal mode of thought, ambiguity is tacitly excluded as the flux of reality is converted into the fixity of concepts. This repressive impulse to classify will also concern William James's pragmatist successor, John Dewey, who finds it at the heart of traditional philosophy's fear of the spontaneous or contingent. Because these qualities, found in "struggle, conflict, and error," are barred "by definition from full reality," Dewey seeks to reinstate the "left over"—the contingent, hazardous, and changing.[17] This is one reason why Theodor Adorno would praise him as a "truly emancipated thinker."[18] For Adorno's "negative dialectics" (negative in the sense of rejecting Hegel's reconciling absolute moment) share the pragmatist insistence on honoring what William and Henry both call the "residuum" and what Adorno will dub "nonidentity"—the element of difference that eludes the grasp of identity thinking and homogenizing systems.

Henry sponsors the nonidentical in the course of his 1904 American journey, which is made, he tells us, under the "ensign" of the "*il*legible word." The ensign is apt, for James admires the illegible, the "unconverted residuum" embodied in the aliens he sees as he walks the streets of New York.[19] Another flaneur, Adorno's friend Walter Benjamin, found in the meandering peregrinations of the urban stroller the model for his release of philosophy from the tyranny of system and concept. "Systematic completeness" fails to encompass what digression opens up: the "irreducible multiplicity" of urban life, where meaning resides in the peripheral and the aleatory. From this mingled texture Benjamin derives his critical form called "constellation"—the representation of "fragments of thought" by "immersion in the most minute details of subject matter."[20]

This American and German genealogy of antisubjectivist, historicist cultural inquiry embraces a spirit of skepticism toward conventional notions of mastery, such as the pretensions of philosophic systems, be they Comtean positivism or Hegelian idealism, to totalize and unify all reality. "Totality, order, unity, rationality," says Dewey, are mere "eulogistic predicates" that when "used to describe the foundations and proper conclusions of a philosophic system," can artificially simplify existence.[21]

When Henry James confronted the novelistic equivalent of such overarching ambition—Balzac's *Comédie Humaine*—he reacted with pragmatist suspicion. In 1875 he described Balzac's immense fictional edifice as a

complete social system . . . on the imaginative line very much what Comte's "Positive Philosophy" is on the scientific. These great enterprises are equally characteristic of the French passion for completeness, for symmetry, for making a system as neat as an epigram—of its intolerance of the indefinite, the unformulated. The French mind likes better to squeeze things into a formula that mutilates them, if need be, than to leave them in the frigid vague.[22]

To the positivistic spirit of the French, James opposes "us of English speech" who find "the civilization of the nineteenth century . . . so multitudinous, so complex, so far-spreading . . . it has such misty edges and far reverberations—that the imagination, oppressed and overwhelmed, shrinks from any attempt to grasp it as a whole."[23]

According to the canonical image of James, not only did he eventually overcome his awe before this French challenge but he became a kind of Anglo-American version of the Comtean spirit, preoccupied with symmetry, organic wholeness and building an ultimate monument that was to be his own bid for Balzacian grandeur. This edifice was the New York Edition, replete with a synthesis of the aesthetic wisdom of a lifetime—the prefaces. But, once again, James's "rich passion for extremes" demands a more complicated explanation than the canonical wisdom affords. James's ambition is indeed Balzacian, and he does solicit the aura of cultural sanctity that the monumental New York Edition embodies. Yet he builds his monument on shaky ground: "the tracks of my original passage," notes James in his final Preface, are of such "shifting and uneven character" (23: xix; AN, 341). This statement reminds us not to confuse ambition and achievement. For James is also a parody of grand authority: the Balzacian march of his "original passage" soon digresses from its goal and the New York Edition becomes anything but neatly systematic. The deliberate clash of intention and execution shatters James's auratic pretensions and generates a contradictory, unstable authorial identity that the magisterial honorific "Master" represses. The master's most ironic lesson is of the unavoidably compromised nature of mastery. Thus his memoirs flaunt his abjectness as he describes himself, variously, as envious, embarrassed, inept, and, above all, vague. But he finds a "positive saving virtue" in "vagueness" and decides to work that "force as an ideal" in his effort at redefining mastery as dispersed curiosity open to the contingencies and shocks of experience.[24]

Correlative with Henry James's critique of mastery and its embodiment in "prime identity" is his skepticism of the idealist goal of an autonomous self standing beyond culture. In his book on Hawthorne (1879), James had deftly exposed how romantic individualism functioned sociologically and ideologically: "The doctrine of the supremacy of the individual to himself, of his originality, and, as regards his own character, *unique* quality, must have had a great charm for people living in a society in which introspection, thanks to the want of other entertainment, played almost the part of a social resource."[25] Paradoxically, the revered father of the modern novel of "liberated" consciousness, one of the glorious achievements of bourgeois aesthetics, never mystified the "supremacy of the individual" into a natural birthright. But the paradox dissolves once we invoke the seldom-made distinction between James's technique of *central* consciousness and individualism's ideology of *centered* consciousness ("prime identity"). James did indeed employ the technique, but less to legitimate and authorize centered subjectivity than to reveal its fetishized status and obliviousness to its own solipsism. By neglecting this distinction, Fredric Jameson is able to relegate the "Jamesian point of view" to a bourgeois "containment strategy" that functions as a "powerful ideological instrument in the perpetuation of an increasingly subjectivized and psychologized world."[26] The distinction between central and centered is the source of an ineradicable gap in James's work between form and subject, intention and achievement. He finds this disjunction fertile for his fiction and also, as we shall see, returns to it often in the prefaces. In cultivating formal dissonance, James anticipates what Adorno would later teach: that form, not subject matter, is art's vehicle of critique. "What makes works of art socially significant is content that articulates itself in formal structures." The "unresolved antagonisms of reality reappear in art in the guise of immanent problems of artistic form," says Adorno, and "the aesthetic tensions manifesting themselves in works of art" express social actuality, which, for James as well, is an "antagonistic totality . . . a whole which is made up of contradictions."[27] *The American Scene* is James's most direct confrontation with the fractured totality of modern civilization; by foregrounding at the opening of that book the difficulty of fashioning a "decent form" for his impressions, he finds one way of representing the bewildering impact of modern America. A consequence of James's emphasis on formal mediation is that his cultural critique is most often *embodied* rather than discursively articulated.

His novels also register social and cultural contradictions by articulating these antagonisms technically, through the mediation of artistic form that is structured by the aporia between centered and central consciousness. For instance, Isabel Archer assumes fully the role of central reflector only after the seed of her husband's deceit begins to flower in her famous "vigil" scene in chapter 42. Thus her structural centrality coincides (negatively) with her dawning sense that her centered consciousness is actually decentered, that she has been a mere tool of her husband and his lover. Just as James's form pushes her center stage, Isabel's proud belief in her pristine autonomy and mastery starts crumbling, as she feels "haunted with terrors" and "assailed by visions."[28] This aesthetic tension, which expresses James's understanding of the contradictions of Emersonian individualism—its manufacture of an autonomy at once illusory and powerful—has been all but obliterated in the traditional image of James the aesthetic organicist and idealist. This cultural icon is, predictably, regarded as a loyal advocate of the Emersonian tradition of inviolable individualism. Yet, actually, Emerson's imperative of "abandonment" is most germane to James's late effort to represent what experience is like unburdened of the cultural imperative of "prime identity."

When the compulsion to identity is relaxed (if not removed), nonidentity thinking becomes a way to loosen emotional and sensuous constrictions and abandon oneself to the shocks of experience. In a key moment in his final Preface, as he compares the experience of revising his late and early work, James provides a vivid instance of what nonidentity thinking involves. Rereading his most recent fiction proceeds "without an effort or a struggle," for his "present attentions" and "original expression" sufficiently coincide (23: xiii; AN, 335). But this comfortable harmony, which James characterizes as breeding docility and passivity, "throws into relief . . . the very different dance," the "quite other kind of consciousness," experienced when he comes to revise his earlier work. What proceeds from "*that* return" is a "frequent lapse of harmony between" his "present mode of motion" and his "original tracks." Given James's commitment to incalculability, to pursuing "inevitable deviation . . . the exquisite treachery even of the straightest execution," this "lapse of harmony" is something he cherishes rather than laments (21: xxii, 23: xiv; AN, 325, 336). For it turns the question of revision from the "prepared" and predictable to the improvisational, as James feels pleasure in "shaking off all shackles of theory." Unharnessed, he "unlearns the old pace" of identity and sufficiency and falls into another rhythm, one attuned to the "high spontaneity" of "deviations and differences" produced by the disparity between past and present. So compelling are these "deviations and differences" that they become, says James, "my very terms of cognition." This "very different dance" of nonidentity exhilarates by making rewriting "an infinitely interesting and amusing *act*" alive with all the perils and contingencies missing in "finished and dismissed work" (23: xiv; AN, 335–37).[29]

The dance of difference that James performs upon his "return" to his early fiction is also the "mode of motion" that propels his other late "return"—to America. James re-sees his native land with a "quite other kind of consciousness" that takes disparities to be not merely the objects but the "very terms of cognition." More than a theme with a fixed reference in the immigrant, nonidentity in late James becomes a mode of thinking and acting that conceives individualism, identity, and consciousness as historical categories open to change, to revision in a nonpossessive direction. This emphasis on provisionality extends to James's hope that twentieth-century America can devise social arrangements and institutions that maximize heterogeneity and flexibility.

While it is true that James prizes a "deep-breathing economy and an organic form," organicism is not the essence of James's cultural or aesthetic

vision, as Percy Lubbock (and the generations of James readers he influ-
enced) took it to be.[30] Organic economy emerges as an aesthetic ideal or
potential perennially deferred and complicated by the conditions of artistic
creation. Because they enact James's pragmatist historicism, the prefaces
are far from a tranquil record of difficulties avoided and problems
solved.[31] They do not offer a serene retrospect of James's organic artistry
but instead confess acceptance of makeshift compromises rather than any
fully achieved formal harmony. In short, Lubbock ignored James's admission that it is the "Angel, not to say . . . the Demon of Compromise" who
presides over the prefaces and who is also the source of their chief theme:
the unbridgeable gap between original intentions and actual accomplishment (*19*: xv; *AN*, 298). This fissure engenders the energies of art while
leaving art permanently open to the possibility of failure. This chronic in-
security demands the tentative stance that C. S. Peirce called fallibilism—
the belief that every conceptual organization of experience is subject to revision. Not only have "perfect works of art," says Adorno, "rarely ever existed," but "the fact that no artist knows for sure if his work will amount to
something" testifies to art's "exposed quality."[32]

The hazards of exposure pervade the prefaces. From first to last, artistic making is figured as "crisis" and "torment," arousing "terror" and
"fear," as the writer must perpetually improvise the imperfect "substitute"
to replace his "original design" (*1*: v–vii, *19*: xiii; *AN*, 3–6, 297). The
prefaces narrate what James calls "the thrilling ups and downs, the intricate
ins and outs of the compositional problem" (*21*: xv; *AN*, 319). James describes at least four of his greatest novels as "efforts so redolent of good
intentions baffled by a treacherous vehicle, an expertness too retarded" (*23*:
xxi; *AN*, 344). Since "inevitable deviation" abides in it, the aesthetic is a
force at odds with the totalizing impulses of mastery, harmony, and unity
(*21*: xxii; *AN*, 325). Neither central to James nor irrelevant, these impulses are incessantly being challenged and remade in the "simmering
cauldron" of artistic imagination.

James's aesthetic validates Adorno's claim that "dissonance is the truth
about harmony." Noting the "antiharmonistic postures" of Michelangelo,
Rembrandt, and Beethoven, Adorno finds their original allegiance to harmony replaced by a recognition of its insufficiency: "Harmony is unattain-
able, given the strict criteria of what harmony is supposed to be. These criteria are met only when the aspect of unattainability is incorporated into the
essence of art," as occurs in the mature style of the most eminent artists.[33]

James's discovery of "treachery" in the straightest, most mature intentions incorporates this negative affirmation of harmony. Michelangelo is the "greatest of artists," says James, especially "considering how his imagination embarrassed and charmed and bewildered him." "Moses," the sculptor's supreme achievement, is "so far from perfection, so finite, so full of errors, so broadly a target for criticism as it sits there." Yet James finds its very imperfections a source of "vigor": Michelangelo's "willingness to let it stand" testifies to its "life, health, and movement."[34] Far from being an apostle of organic form and formal unity, James is closer to disavowing the ideal of perfection that, says Adorno, all works of art seek.

James would concur with Adorno that "crisis" (a word they both use) "is as old as the concept of art itself. The possibility and the greatness of art depend on how art handles this antinomy. Art cannot live up to its concept."[35] Judged on Adorno's terms, James's handling of art's antinomic character, what the novelist calls its "cruel crisis," is exemplary. For instead of repressing or resolving the crisis of art's inherent nonidentity, James comes to regard it as an "eternal torment of interest" that generates the "variable process" of "doing" (*1*: x; *AN*, 8–9). For instance, James locates the "power" of the novel "as a literary form" in its ability "to appear more true to its character in proportion as it strains, or tends to burst, with a latent extravagance, its mould" (*3*: vii; *AN*, 46). The responsible artist must not evade this refractory dynamism and the tense and tentative process of representation it demands. To take refuge in "conveniences" and "simplifications" cripples representation, arrests "art's law of motion" (Adorno). Yet rather than regretting this condition of crisis, James finds it a source of fun. "It all comes back to that, to my and your 'fun'—if we but allow the term its full extension," he says near the end of his last Preface (*23*: xxii; *AN*, 345). The full extension of fun involves acquiring the "confidence" to accept being caught in the "beautifully tangled" web of the artistic process. The prefaces, like James's other major late works, are spectacles of exposure and curiosity that find pleasure ("fun") in abandonment that releases impulses and forsakes the comforts of control.

III

Throughout his prefaces and most dramatically in *The American Scene*, James counsels acceptance of the limited, precarious powers of a cultural analyst or novelist to order experience. Relaxing the will to dominate and

surrendering to the accidents of digression constitute the mode of being
and representation that allows the "latent vividness" of urban experience to
flower. What produces dynamism is James's commitment to his "religion
of doing," which demands a mode of being that has "never . . . seen or said
all or . . . ceased to press forward" (*23*: xxiv, xx; *AN*, 347, 343). Loss of
control inheres in James's worship of the "religion of doing," for he who is
"always doing . . . can scarce, by his own measure, ever have done."
James's point is how easily "the religion of doing" gives way to the infinity
of doing. The impossibility of ending doing forces upon us the fact that
"our noted behaviour . . . perpetually escapes our control" (*23*: xxv; *AN*,
348). But the ineradicable indeterminacy of experience and behavior,
which makes substitution unavoidable, is also ameliorative. Thus James's
"accepted vision" of America's "too-defiant scale of numerosity" is a fact he
"can rest in at last, as an absolute luxury, converting it . . . into *the* constant
substitute, for many luxuries that are absent."[36]

   If the "very essence of the novelist's process," notes James, involves
one's being "unduly tempted and led on by 'developments'" (*1*: vi; *AN*, 4),
the same temptation rules his cultural inquiry and artistic representation.
"*The will to grow* was everywhere written large" in America, a motto that
can also serve Jamesian mimesis because both are recalcitrant; hence one's
artistic ordering is always belated and flawed: "yet even here I fall short,"
he notes repeatedly about his effort in *The American Scene* to represent
"much too numerous" impressions. This chronic belatedness partly explains why James describes himself as a "restless analyst," his epithet of self-
description throughout *The American Scene*.

   In this oxymoronic identity, James dissolves the conventional dualism
of action and contemplation, for "restless analyst" is itself a phrase that
challenges the conventional oppositions of activity and passivity, the hazardous and assured, and promotes interaction rather than hierarchy. Because his selfhood lacks impermeability and fixity, qualities central to the
ideology of atomized individualism, James is saturated by incessant waves
of "tonic shock" as soon as he arrives back in America. Rather than dis-
tanced in static contemplation, shock is actively solicited and corporeally
felt as the imprint of the material pressure of historical change and the recovery of "extremest youth."[37] Indeed, on the first page of *The American
Scene*, James is assaulted by "instant vibrations" of curiosity prompted "at
every turn, in sights, sounds, smells, even in the chaos of confusion and
change." This noncognitive, nonconceptual strata of experience charged

with the primal, infant avidity of insatiable curiosity ("I want to see everything," he wrote in anticipation of his trip) is where James will most intensely live throughout his journey.[38]

That his trip will tap deep references is evident in a remark of 1903.
James notes that the "bristling . . . U.S.A. have the merit and the precious
property that they meet and fit into my (creative) preoccupations."[39] This
statement is as suggestive as it is cryptic, but may possibly be illuminated
by a late remark in *The American Scene*: "You are not final. . . . You are
perpetually provisional," says James to his "bristling" native land at the
end of his journey, a judgment that crystallizes his late discovery of revision as the matrix of writing, identity, and nationhood.[40] James's recognition of American provisionality also counts as a seminal moment of self-
recognition. Whereas Emerson believed that American experience comprises two parties—one of hope and one of memory—James's parties
might be labeled the revisionists and the "actual non-revisionists." The latter he describes as having "their lot serene and their peace, above all,
equally protected and undisturbed" (*23*: xx; *AN*, 343). James's re-vision of
his native country, his life history and lifework, enlists him, of course, in
the revisionist camp—those unserene, unprotected, and disturbed figures
committed to the "active sense of life" (*23*: xvii; *AN*, 340).

This willed vulnerability is, for James, a quintessentially urban stance,
one he enacts most vividly on the streets of 1904 New York and in the pages
of *The American Scene*. This work's stylistic triumph is James's discovery of
a form of urban cultural analysis that mimes the dissonant rhythms of his
radical curiosity, which, in turn, feeds on the shocks and transitory attractions of minutiae, including shoe polish, candy, and dental work. Hence,
James strikingly prefigures Benjamin's own peripatetic analyses that also
rescue concrete particulars by fashioning constellations out of what slips
through the "conventional conceptual net." The constellation preserves the
"residuum" deemed by the dominant ideology too marginal to be worthy
of attention, a process of reclamation that Benjamin describes as "mortification," which proceeds "eccentrically and by leaps . . . to rip out of context
and quote that which remained inconsequential and buried."[41] He urges
that philosophy's model should be the treatise, which dispenses with the
"coercive proof of mathematics" for the method of representation:

Method is a digression. Representation as digression—such is the methodological
nature of the treatise. The absence of an uninterrupted purposeful structure is its
primary characteristic. Tirelessly the process of thinking makes new beginnings,

returning in a roundabout way to its original object. This continual pausing for breath is the mode most proper to the process of contemplation.[42]

The "irregular," dissonant rhythms of the urban flaneur are not hard to detect here, nor is the parallel with Henry James, whose image of representation in the opening of his first Preface depicts it as a "widening circle" that demands experience "pause from time to time . . . to measure . . . as many steps taken and obstacles mastered" as possible (*1*: v; *AN*, 3).

In illuminating the specific side of the object, the side, as Adorno notes, "which to a classifying procedure is either a matter of indifference or a burden,"[43] the constellation releases what Henry James had also sought—objects' "mystic meaning proper to themselves to give out."[44] In explaining the logic that breeds a heightened sense of objects, James sounds remarkably like Benjamin: "To be at all critically, or . . . analytically minded . . . is to be subject to the superstition that objects and places . . . must have a sense of their own, a mystic meaning proper to themselves to give out: to give out, that is, to the participant at once so interested and so detached."[45] Like Benjamin and his beloved Proust, James here submits to the mystic spell or aura of objects and places. These are imbued with a "wealth of meaning" elicited only by the participant able to remain precariously poised between desire and distance.[46]

In submitting the aura of Henry James the cultural icon to corrosive critique, I have followed not only Benjamin, with his desire to have texts undergo "mortification," but James as well. For surely one meaning of his American journey, that ordeal propelled by hunger for movement and shock, is his own effort to destroy the aura of Henry James.[47] Thus the immediate fruits of that journey—*The American Scene*, the New York Edition, and the Edition's prefaces—at once memorialize and explode his mastery. The audacity of James's self-interrogating act of authority is one reason his second major phase manages to remain compelling in a postmodern cultural moment generally embarrassed (when not overtly hostile) before anything smacking of the magisterial.

Ozymandias and the
Mastery of Ruins:
The Design of the New York Edition

Stuart Culver

Shortly before his death, Henry James looked back on the labor that had
gone into his New York Edition, recalling the time and effort he had spent
rereading and revising his fiction, clearing the rights to his widely scattered publications, writing the critical prefaces, and even helping Alvin
Langdon Coburn find the right subjects for his photographic frontispieces.
The collected edition now seemed to the novelist "a sort of miniature Ozymandias of Egypt," an ambitious project virtually unpurchased and unap-
preciated. Leon Edel has read this remark as a straightforward confession
of failure: the grand array of volumes that had been intended both to memorialize James's contribution to the literary tradition and to provide a re-
tirement fund of sorts lay in ruins, another example of the reading public's
failure to recognize the genius of the "Master."[1]

Yet, as a reader attentive to irony and interested in the way artistic processes get represented in literature, James may well have seen something
more in Shelley's sonnet than a pathetic tale of ambition frustrated. The
poem in fact describes a conflict between two orders of intention, between
the emperor's desire to broadcast and immortalize his political power and
the sculptor's effort to capture the tyrant's character in stone. Shelley's
"traveller from an antique land" distinguishes "the heart that fed" the
dream of eternal empire from "the hand that mocked" that passion and car-
icatured Ozymandias as it advertised his authority.[2] To Shelley's romantic
sensibility, the triumph of the artist is all the more complete now that the
statue lies in ruins: the sculptor's ironic rendering of his master has been
perfected and not destroyed by the passage of time.

Of course, in sculpting the New York Edition, James was both em-

peror and artist. Nevertheless, the Edition's prefaces seem to echo Shelley's
sonnet when they assert that the author's success "fairly depends on his fallibility": according to James, the author "must be the dupe . . . of his prime
object" in order to become "at all measurably . . . the master of his actual
substitute" (*19*: xiii; *AN*, 297). Taking Shelley's logic one step further,
James suggests that the artist may well benefit from the ruin of his own
grandiose ambitions. This notion of a literary mastery grounded in failure
complicates the project of publishing a collected edition: on the one hand,
the collection is bound to expose the limits of the master's authority; on the
other, such an ambitious venture provides a capital opportunity for the
mocking hand of the servant who would expose the fallibility of his master.

When he set to work on the New York Edition in 1907, James was not
inventing a new literary medium. Indeed, "de luxe" collected editions had
become by then standard publishing commodities that sought to commemorate the careers of cultural heroes by presenting their complete works in
expensive and supposedly definitive formats. The very features that had
cost James so much effort, the ones he felt gave his collection its unique
artistic value, actually undermined the value of the New York Edition on
this market by challenging the assumptions about authorship and textuality
underlying these collections: the Edition's illustrations don't depict familiar scenes or characters from the fiction; its prefaces offer little in the way
of personal anecdote; several of the novelist's most popular works are omitted; the early fiction that is included has been extensively revised; and the
volumes seem to follow in no apparent order. In short, the novelist's artistic
representation of his corpus, like the art of Shelley's sculptor, did more to
call his authority, popularity, and influence into question than it did to confirm or celebrate his place in the American cultural pantheon.

In the pages that follow I want to describe the New York Edition as a
specific deviation from the standard format of the deluxe edition and to
propose that it is designed to challenge the conceptions of text and author
underlying such collections even as it tries to capitalize on the public's appetite for them. In other words, I will be arguing that James allowed
Charles Scribner's Sons to market his fiction in this format not simply because he thought it would be profitable but also because he saw in this project an opportunity to mock the vulgar pretensions behind such efforts to
objectify literary authority and influence and a chance to advance, however
tentatively, another portrait of the artist behind and beneath the official version. More specifically, I want to show how James fails to become a literary
object of a certain sort in order to keep his authority itself alive.

I

During the 1890's James produced a series of parables on the literary life, all of which address the close connection of failure and success in the work of writing. In each of these tales the paradox of success in failure is bound up with the conflict between aesthetic and economic value in the modern literary marketplace. "The Next Time" presents the conflict most sharply as it recounts the career of a literary genius, Ralph Limbert, who positively wants to compromise his sense of aesthetic value in order to produce a best-seller. Despite his conscious conspiracy against his genius, Limbert's novels are inevitably "exquisite failures"; by an inexorable and unconscious law, they prove to be artistic successes but commercial disasters. Wanting to treat his fictions as if they were mere commodities "like potatoes or beer," Limbert can't keep himself from producing texts that are too fine or too complex for the popular taste (*15*: 158, 188).

Even though he is ready "not to do his own work but to do what somebody else would take for it," Limbert ends up transgressing and transcending the popular modes and genres he wants to exploit, producing silk purses where sow's ears are expected. The obvious moral is that his desire for commercial success has no real effect on the quality of his work, that the author's intentions about how others should take his texts have no consequences for a literary practice that is deeper and less conscious than such calculations. But a further lesson awaits Limbert when he leaves London and gives up the pursuit of commercial success for a quiet life in the pastoral countryside. Here he hopes to write one uncompromised masterpiece, but he never completes this final novel, *Derogation*. Written "only for himself" and produced in the closest earthly approximation to "the country of the blue," *Derogation* is supposed to be the unconditioned work of literary genius; yet it is precisely the freedom from conditions that proves the most debilitating condition of all for Limbert. Apparently, the constraints and contradictions of the London publishing industry were precisely what his perverse genius required in order to operate most perfectly. When he tries to write for himself, Limbert can produce only a "splendid fragment" while his potboilers are always masterpieces (*15*: 186, 216).

"The Next Time" was one of three stories about contemporary writers James published in the early numbers of *The Yellow Book*. This trilogy, which also includes "The Death of the Lion" and "The Coxon Fund," represents an odd contribution to the self-consciously avant-garde journal, since all three stories complicate the aesthete's distinction between popular taste and artistic quality. It is a familiar tale that these stories, appearing as they do in the mid-1890's at the moment when the novelist had given up novel writing to try his luck on the London stage, document James's doubts about his pursuit of success and mediate his return to longer fiction with *The Spoils of Poynton* in 1897. But perhaps just as significantly they testify to his willingness in these years to experiment with different publishing media. The short stories he wrote and the longer fictions he subsequently published began to appear in a wide variety of places from the avant-garde *Yellow Book* and *The Chap-Book*, its American counterpart, to the genteel *North American Review*, the venerable *Punch*, and popular magazines like *Collier's Weekly* and *The Illustrated London News*. His book-length works went out to a number of different houses in England and America in a calculated effort to spread his fiction out across a number of markets.

The new strategy was not to look for a single "hit" but to cultivate copyright privileges over serialization, revision, and translation in order to exploit every potential market. This marketing strategy led James to employ the pioneer literary agent James B. Pinker to serve as his delegate in coordinating his arrangements with and commitments to a growing number of publishers and editors. James was now able to distance himself from any particular publishing house and was concerned to enforce the legal difference between his texts as such and each of their various published forms by refusing to sell any of his copyrights outright. He and Pinker doled out piecemeal the privilege to reproduce each text in a single specified form. It is noteworthy that James turned to a literary agent at the same moment he began to organize his texts more systematically around what he would describe as the author's surrogate or delegate, and a complete account of the novelist's later manner would explore the analogies between the author's business practices and his compositional strategies.[3] I want for now, however, simply to suggest that the New York Edition is really just another example of this marketing strategy.

Although it could be considered the crowning achievement of the James-Pinker partnership, the collected Edition deviates from their common practice by consolidating a large selection of the fiction in the hands of a single publisher and in a format that passes itself off as "definitive." Yet the Edition's publishers, Charles Scribner's Sons, were given the right to market this fiction only in sets and to sell it by subscription alone. James insisted all along that he was not simply letting the Scribners repackage his fiction for him wholesale; rather, he believed that he was engaged in a significantly creative and original artistic labor. But in order to perform this difficult work of revision and collection, he had to appear in a commercial format he had come to regard with a great deal of suspicion.

To appreciate the ambivalence with which James approached the deluxe format, we need only to recognize how popular and pervasive these book commodities had become in America after 1891. One year after James finished his last triple-decker novel, *The Tragic Muse* (1890), the United States Congress passed the nation's first international copyright statute. The American book trade had grown up without protecting the rights of foreign authors and had consequently thrived on cheap pirated reprints of British authors. The logic of minimizing copyright protection in order to prevent monopolies in intellectual property had appealed to democratic impulses in the nation's early years, and so American publishing houses developed as mass producers of cheap books, emphasizing the public's right to know over the author's property rights in his work.[4] By the 1880's, however, an alliance of the nation's established publishing houses and its recognized authors—organized by James Russell Lowell into the American Copyright League—initiated a campaign against this system. The publishers argued pointedly that the ruinous cycle of overproduction and underselling undermined the book trade, while the authors expressed concern that their protected works were less viable in a market that thrived on pirated books in cheap, unauthorized editions.

In the course of this debate, publishers began to recast their role in the book trade by portraying themselves as professionals rather than entrepreneurs. At issue, they claimed, was a recognition of the peculiar character of the book as a commodity: "The moment it is treated as a mere commodity it takes severe revenge on its author and its publishers." Since books couldn't be treated like Limbert's potatoes and beer, the publishers began to prescribe for their "clients" and to push new kinds of literary wares that presented themselves as objects of enduring value: "What you want in your own library for your own book-money are good books, made at least as well as the furniture in the room; and you want new books of permanent value."[5] The nature of reading is ultimately at issue here: while the cheap paperback can be quickly consumed in one reading, the well-made book promises never to be used up. From the perspective of these professional publishers, the desire to own the text in a lasting form is an essential part of the process of right reading.

James, in his sole contribution to the debate, envisioned a continuity between the commercial exchange that makes the book available and the act of reading itself: "Our power to pay is certainly as great as our power to understand. . . . It is precisely because we *are* a universally reading public that it is of the greatest importance there should be no impediment to our freedom. . . . The real impediment is that this irresponsibility of ours is tainted with a vice which passes into our intelligence itself."[6] Reversing the logic of the argument against copyright, which saw cheap books as guarantors of the public's access to information, James argues here that the real impediment to free information is the refusal to pay for what you read. Because the exchange that makes the text available helps determine the reading relation, the practice of piracy degrades reading into an "irresponsible," furtive act of theft. For James, the new demand for well-made and expensive books and for expanded copyright protection ought to reflect a new appreciation of the reader's intimacy with the text.

Of course, the cult of the well-made book was in many ways a parody of what James envisioned: books were often too "good" or too well-made actually to be read. Still, the production of expensive books, including deluxe sets, together with the appearance in the last decade of the century of both journals for book collectors and literary supplements in metropolitan newspapers, encouraged and reflected a growing desire among American readers to occupy a different and more privileged relationship to the text and its author. The difference was immediately visible on the shelves of American book-buyers. When Collier's published its Unabridged Dickens in 1879, the house tried to fit all the novelist's major fiction into six cumbersome volumes with crabbed, double-columned pages. The first volume alone contained *Oliver Twist*, *David Copperfield*, and *Our Mutual Friend*. The attraction was simply the economy of getting more for less. By 1897, the Scribners could appeal to quite another order of values with their Gadshill Dickens: this expensive set was edited and introduced by Andrew Lang; its pages had wide margins and large print; the novels were spread out over two volumes; and included among the set's 34 volumes were two devoted to Dickens's essays and travel writings. What counted as "unabridged" had changed along with the quality of the book itself. Purchasers were now supposed to want everything written by the man, and the space the author's volumes occupied on the shelves of their well-appointed libraries was supposed to represent materially both the writer's contribution to culture and the buyers' own status as collectors rather than consumers of literature.

The change was not limited to the works of formerly pirated British authors; the material form in which Americans confronted their own cultural heroes also altered. Houghton Mifflin, anxious to establish its role at the center of the New England tradition, quickly brought out Standard Library Editions of those authors whose titles it had inherited from Ticknor and Fields. The Riverside Press issued in the early 1890's uniform sets of Lowell, Emerson, Longfellow, Whittier, Thoreau, and Stowe. Typically these sets were accompanied by smaller and more expensive limited or deluxe editions. Among these were the Elmwood Lowell (1904), Riverside Stowe (1896), Riverside Thoreau (1892), Walden Thoreau (1900), Manuscript Thoreau (1906), and Old Manse Hawthorne (1902). The Old Manse Hawthorne was presented as a "definitive edition" which would "long remain standard," but the three Thoreau editions suggest that these editions never quite managed to provide the stability and fixity they advertised. The Riverside de Luxe Thoreau was limited to 150 copies and claimed to provide the definitive presentation of the author's work because it included selections from his journals. The Walden supplanted this "complete" Thoreau by offering letters as well as journal entries; its editors acknowledged a "natural division" between the published works and private writings but nonetheless believed that there was no "inherent difference" between the two except that private papers offered a closer access to the man himself. This appeal to the impulse to be in touch with the man behind the text and to be present at the scene of production was all the more apparent in the Manuscript Edition: here the limiting factor was not an arbitrarily chosen round number; rather, each set included a page of the journal manuscript itself. These purchasers were literally buying a piece of Thoreau's text, purchasing not the reproduction but the thing itself.[7]

Ten years before they published the New York Edition, the Scribners introduced an important innovation in the deluxe market when they brought out collections of still-active authors, among them Robert Louis Stevenson and Rudyard Kipling, two of James's closest literary friends. This practice seems to have been the brainchild of then-editor Frank Doubleday, who recognized in such open-ended editions a way to ensure an author's loyalty to the house.[8] The Edinburgh Stevenson appeared in 1895, and Kipling's Outward Bound Edition in the following year. These two sets provided the most immediate models for the New York Edition; and James, as he was furnishing Lamb House, remarked to Kipling on the beauty of his new volumes: "They're more than literature: they're Furniture."[9]

But if James saw his friends and rivals enshrined and enriched by the new format, he was also aware that the deluxe market was characterized by a certain vulgarity. Several specialty houses arose in these years, marketing nothing but arbitrarily produced limited editions of canonical figures. Typical of these was Estes and Lauriat, whose well-made but not particularly distinctive sets were in many ways parodies of collectors' items: each deluxe edition was limited—each set individually numbered—in an effort to disguise the fact that these books were just mass-produced articles. There were more than enough Americans willing to pay extravagantly for these sets, so many that *The Nation* ran a campaign against them by following the lawsuit of a New York woman who had paid $6,000 for a complete edition of Theodore Roosevelt and had subsequently been offered, at $10,000 each, similar sets of Thackeray and Shakespeare only to discover that the salesman had simply purchased "well known and easily procurable copies, removed the bindings, changed the title pages and interleaved certain illustrations of a showy character, but intrinsically of little value." *The Nation* rebuked "rich and silly" book-buyers who thought that "such phrases as 'limited edition,' 'large paper,' 'crushed levant,' 'hand-tooling,' and 'extra-illustrated' are a sure index of value."[10]

By the time James began to work on his idiosyncratic version of the deluxe edition, the commodity had entered a crisis: while the boom was starting to subside, the commodity format had itself become a critical problem as it hardened into a set of standard features, each of which reflected assumptions about what a good book really was and how it was properly possessed. The deluxe edition had emerged as an important technology for establishing what an author was and how he functioned as what Michel Foucault has called "the principle of thrift in the proliferation of meaning."[11] By limiting the circulation of texts and instituting certain authenticating features, these sets cast the reader in a new role as a collector of literature who regards each book she purchases as both an object of value in its own right and a relic testifying to her privileged access to the person behind the texts. The deluxe edition's purchaser sets out to buy the text itself and not its cheap reproduction, and she values her set insofar as it remains both rare and definitive, both continuous with the man behind the text and completely alienated from him in its purchased form.

When Joseph Conrad wrote a critical appreciation of James in 1905, he suggested that the novelist had refused to appear in such a form precisely because he distrusted the notions of author and text that deluxe editions traded on: "There is no collected edition to date, such as some of our 'masters' have been provided with; no neat row of volumes in buckram or half-calf putting forth a hasty claim to completeness."[12] For Conrad this lack is the very proof of James's modernity. The novelist's heroic refusal to countenance closure and completion put him at odds with the deluxe format. "One is never set at rest" by Jamesian fictions, Conrad claimed: "His books end as an episode in life ends." Nevertheless he found the typical Jamesian tale "eminently satisfying" because it was never "final."[13] A compromise with the popular demand for closure on easy terms would, he believed, subvert the master's lesson.

At the very moment Conrad was celebrating his resistance to this particular commodification, James was negotiating for such an edition with the Scribners. In 1900, when the Kipling and Stevenson editions were under way, the publishers had proposed a similar project to James, but, perhaps anticipating Conrad's case against deluxe editions, the novelist turned them down, offering instead the book rights to *The Sacred Fount*.[14] There are any number of reasons for James's rather quick change of heart: he saw the success of his friends' sets; his return to America was inspired by and further encouraged an interest in his place in the nation's cultural tradition; he wanted to renew lapsed copyrights and revive old titles; he may have recognized that his career had taken a certain circular shape as he returned to and revised the international themes of his early novels in his most recent productions; and the very hardening of the deluxe format may well have made him feel that such editions had become sites where one could contest the meaning of literary authority. In any event the Scribners themselves were now reluctant to embark on such an expensive project, not only because the deluxe boom was over but also because they hadn't profited much from the three novels—*The Sacred Fount*, *The Wings of the Dove*, and *The Golden Bowl*—they had published over the last five years.[15]

James managed to persuade both his publishers and himself that such a project was feasible by insisting on the active role he would play in its production. Where authors conventionally were silent partners in these enterprises, passively standing aside as their works, both old and new, appeared in this higher form, he would aggressively revise, select, and arrange his fiction. He explained that only such an active role could justify his use of this ready-made format: "I shouldn't have planned the edition at all unless I had felt close revision . . . to be an indispensable part of it. . . . Its *raison d'être* (the Edition's) is in its being selective as well as collective, and by the mere fact of leaving out certain things . . . I exercise a control, a discrimination, I treat certain portions of my work as unhappy accidents."[16] While the typical deluxe edition was advertised as "collected" and "complete," the New York Edition would be "collective" and "selective." By emphasizing the process of gathering and arranging his fiction, James opens up a gap between the entire set of texts attributable to him and the smaller set properly authored by him, distinguishing his life with all its accidental productions from his career with its steady progression from apprenticeship to mastery.

He returns to this distinction in his Preface to the Edition's tenth volume: "Life being all inclusion and confusion . . . [it] has no direct sense whatever for the subject and is capable, luckily for us, of nothing but splendid waste. Hence the opportunity for the sublime economy of art, which rescues, which saves, and hoards and 'banks,' investing and reinvesting these fruits of toil in wondrous useful 'works'" (*10*: vi; *AN*, 120). Art is described here as an operation performed on life, an editorial process of cutting back and managing the flow of experience, turning pure production into "works" by its "sublime economy." By editing his own literary productions, James in effect treats his earlier works of art as if they too were just so much "life" and required hoarding and reinvesting in order to become once again works of art. When James claims that the Edition was possible for him only if he could exercise "control" over his corpus, he is simply announcing that the process of collecting and compiling his works had to be for him an authorial act.

The early reviewers of the Edition were quick to point out that James's aggressive editorial presence marked a real departure from the deluxe model, and they criticized it precisely for violating notions of textual integrity and cultural authority they expected such editions to uphold. *The Literary Digest* was particularly vehement: "Readers have asked with some heat whether an author's published work does not belong to the public. 'Who am I that I should tamper with a classic?' asked a young writer when requested to revise a bit of his own work. Let Mr. James respect the classics, even from his own pen."[17] Without irony, the reviewer presents the young writer's complacency as virtuous humility and denigrates James's revisions as an act of pride and a trespass against the public domain. In his view, the text once published is no longer the author's but is instead a "classic" just because it passes itself off as complete and finished. To revise is not only to insist presumptuously on a continued right over the text but also to imply that the previous edition was somehow incomplete and imperfect. James is, this reviewer suggests, not letting his reader purchase as definitive a body of fiction as the deluxe format promised; indeed, James seems to demand that his reader occupy an altogether different relation to the text than the privileged situation offered by sets like the Manuscript Thoreau. For this reviewer all such meddling in the published work compromises the public's access to the texts and to the author behind them.

The contemporary legal and legislative effort to extend and clarify copyright protection gave James a vehicle for both conceptualizing and enforcing this alternative notion of literary property. If copyright was now defined as a conditional monopoly over the rights to reproduce, reissue, and revise texts, being an author no longer meant appearing in a set of purchasable classic works but rather entailed the right to control what sort of access the public would have to one's work. In compiling the Edition, James exercised his reserve of rights and, in so doing, made his purchaser feel the difference between the printed object in her hand and the text that

As the moral of "The Next Time" indicates, James understood artistic success as somehow bound up with the struggle against the easy consumption and digestion of fiction. By treating his early fictions as "life" and not as classics, he refuses to let any of them be purchased as definitive. In his hands, the deluxe commodity becomes more explicitly a temporary and partial assemblage and an author's desperate strategy for escaping the fate of being fully possessed by his public.[18] Indeed, he devotes the final paragraph of his last Preface to an argument against the "mere gaping contrition" championed by *The Literary Digest*. Unlike our behavior in general, our literary deeds, James tells his reader, never lose "their attachment and reference" to us just because they are "really 'done' things." The "luxury of the artist" is precisely his ability to retrace his relation to these deeds, and therefore he should recognize that he is obligated not to let himself be "disconnected" from these past works (*23*: xxv; *AN*, 348). The novelist's logic inverts that of the reviewer: the "form" of a literary work is precisely what makes it impossible to alienate or disentangle it from its author.

never—not even in deluxe editions—appears in itself, not because it is some ideal entity that transcends any verbal form but simply because it has not yet appeared in its final form. The novelist preserves his authority by refusing to let the book, even in its most elegant form, embody his text definitively.

II

When William James tried in his *Principles of Psychology* to explain the identity between the thinking subject and his or her past selves, he appealed to the notion of property in ideas. Posing the question of identity as radically as he could, William wondered how an individual as he awakens knows which thoughts are properly his own: "Peter awakening in the same bed with Paul, and recalling what both had in mind before they went to sleep, reidentifies and appropriates the 'warm' ideas as his, and is never tempted to confuse them with those cold and pale-appearing ones which he ascribes to Paul."[19] In William's account, there is no intrinsic feature that marks a given thought as Peter's except his sense of its warmth; it feels like it ought to be his. The bizarre example raises the specter of radical discontinuity only to dismiss it by relocating the self's claim to its own past. In William's psychology, the self appears as "an agent of appropriating and disowning" that is less the producer of its ideas and associations than their "legal representative," the inheritor or proprietor who renews his claim in them as he centers the stream of consciousness.[20]

According to William, the self can lay claim to the sensations of more than one body as long as they feel warm enough, and, conversely, a single body may well harbor more than one self. There remains, however, an implicit argument in *The Principles of Psychology* for the former self, the one ready to stake a claim to every possible idea and thus continually expand its range: "All narrow people entrench in their me," William remarks, hinting at a moral failure in their refusal to lay claim to the "mine" outside their immediate self-presence.[21] One could see in Henry's effort to center his stream of fiction a project somewhat at odds with this ethic of expansion; after all, the novelist justifies his Edition by citing his urge precisely to entrench and disown, his anxiety to show that not every product of his hand is in fact the work of his authorial self. If in his Edition the novelist, like Peter, wakes up to the confusing flood of his past literary deeds, his primary concern is to omit and disavow, to establish control by turning the flood into a manageable stream.[22] The second step is to reinvest and center that stream by discovering a design or continuity among the works he is willing to call his own. Indeed, the novelist always contended that the "value and interest" of his collection depended "on the proper association and collocation" of its member texts.[23]

The Edition actually begins conventionally enough. Its first nine volumes present seven of James's novels in chronological order. The texts of some of these are extensively revised, and certain novels are omitted, most notably *The Bostonians* and his first novel, *Watch and Ward*. With the tenth volume, however, the collection takes a crucial turn; this volume, which includes *The Spoils of Poynton*, *A London Life*, and "The Chaperon," introduces a nine-volume sequence of shorter fictions arranged in no immediately apparent order. Although deluxe editions typically placed the author's shorter works or his experiments in alternative genres at the end of the chronological sequence of his major works, the New York Edition places the tales in the midst of the stream of novels, letting the short fiction appear as an interruption or detour from both the major form and chronology as a principle of order.

W. C. Brownell, who edited the Edition for the Scribners, distrusted James's effort to introduce criteria other than the strictly chronological, unsuccessfully advising him to dispense with "any artificial arrangement based on length."[24] The editor was able to accept this nine-volume detour as a strategy for representing in the sequence the novelist's decade-long vacation from novel writing. But the detour is somewhat oddly placed: the tenth volume follows *The Awkward Age*, which was in fact the first of James's post-theater novels, published only a few months before *The Ambassadors* began to appear and nearly a decade after *The Tragic Muse*, the novel that immediately precedes it in the Edition. *The Awkward Age* is James's most rigorously experimental work, and it introduces the set of short fictions as something like a flashback in the middle of the temporal progression from early to late novels. As a fold or complication in this forward movement from apprentice pieces to masterworks, the set within the set introduces competing principles for organizing the corpus that go far beyond the merely artificial questions of length Brownell feared.

In the plan James first submitted to the Scribners, *The Awkward Age* was in fact placed with the other three late novels in a sequence that seems at first glance more straightforwardly chronological than that of the final version: four early novels (*The American, Roderick Hudson, The Portrait of*

a Lady, and *The Princess Casamassima*) are followed by four volumes of
early short stories, *The Tragic Muse*, an unspecified number of volumes de
voted to "shorter productions," and then the four final novels (*The Awkward Age*, *The Wings of the Dove*, *The Ambassadors*, and *The Golden
Bowl*).[25]

There are, however, two crucial inversions here: *The American* precedes *Roderick Hudson* while *The Ambassadors* and *The Wings of the Dove*
appear in order of publication rather than composition—as they do in the
Edition's final form. The slight departure from strict chronology creates a
subtly symmetrical order as the opening novel, with its story of an American intent on plundering the treasures of Europe, anticipates the themes of
the final text. By the same token, the penultimate *Ambassadors* seems to revise the plot of the second novel, *Roderick Hudson*, while *The Wings of the
Dove* is implicitly paired with *The Portrait of a Lady* as another effort at
telling the story of Minny Temple. This logic of revision gives way in the
Edition's published form to another, equally implicit arrangement that iso-
lates the final trilogy from the sequence of novels and stages the "major
phase" as James's triumphant return to the novel form after an interval of
wandering through a maze of minor works. The multiple and contradictory logics that hold together the volumes of shorter works become ways of
complicating the genealogy of the final novels.

The Edition, therefore, seems to foreground the short works if only
because the principles linking the volumes to one another and binding each
story to the others around it are never spelled out clearly yet are made to
seem crucial to any understanding of how James's artistry grows into its
final form. Though James continually asserts that these volumes are "coherent," he is never willing to articulate any law of genre behind his various "collocations" and "juxtapositions"; instead, he is deliberately vague,
commenting, for instance, that the "shorter things will gain in significance and importance, very considerably, by a fresh grouping or classification, a placing together, from series to series, of those that will help each
other, those that will conduce to something of a common effect."[26] In fact
the criteria seem to shift as one progresses through the nine volumes. At
first, the clustered tales appear to share common compositional strategies;
later, they seem merely to be concerned with similar subjects. In any event,
the supplement at the center of the Edition inserts spatial logics in the midst
of the chronology that links the novels and so complicates the expected tale
of growth into mastery. The tales provide what amounts to a counterstory

about James's practice that insists on his conscious experimentation in form and technique and calls attention to the repetitions and revisions that punctuate his career.

The first of these volumes, *The Spoils of Poynton*, belies the subversive role played by the detour, for it presents three fictions that are all roughly contemporary with each other and address similar themes as they focus on the place of young, unmarried women in British society. Yet the Preface to the volume suggests that what really holds the three together is a shared narrative technique: all of the volume's stories—*A London Life* and "The Chaperon" as well as *Spoils*—are presented through the reflective medium of a young woman's consciousness, a center that is in each case in a false position, seeing more than she is willing to be responsible for knowing. The following volume, which includes *What Maisie Knew*, *In the Cage*, and "The Pupil," takes this false position one step further by finding its centers in consciousnesses that are thoroughly bewildered and fundamentally unable to see their respective stories whole. The next volume, the twelfth, contains four first-person narratives—among them *The Aspern Papers* and *The Turn of the Screw*—all of which cast the reader herself into the false position of having to assume knowledge the text won't give her straightforwardly.

This passage through various points of view comes to an abrupt halt in the thirteenth volume, which includes *The Reverberator* and several early international tales. James suggests that this cluster of fictions reveals the second of his "inveterate habits": if the Edition discovers his penchant for seeing his stories through the eyes of another, it also shows us how automatically he turns to the adventures of Americans in Europe as he tries to organize his various plots. Yet the subsequent volumes can't be said to display any one of the novelist's habits or techniques; they are grouped explicitly according to subject matter. There are more international stories in the fourteenth volume, tales of literary life in the next two, and ghost stories in volume 17 before the detour concludes with the catchall eighteenth volume. The shift from formal criteria to questions of the subject divides the volumes of shorter fictions into two groups and, more crucially, intimates that any work could be placed elsewhere in the sequence.

In his influential account of the Edition's "architecture," Leon Edel proposes that James modeled his collection after Balzac's *Comédie Humaine* and so devoted each volume or group of volumes to a distinct region of his world. Edel names several such regions, among them "American pilgrimages abroad," "scenes in the life of some women," "tales of old 'Europe,'" "early international tales," and "the chase for a husband."[27] While Edel is certainly right to note that James was increasingly concerned with the example of Balzac as his own career evolved, he is wrong to suggest that the American novelist ever came to reconsider his original criticism of Balzac's lifelong project. In a 1902 essay James calls his precursor "the sturdiest-seated mass" in the field of fiction but goes on to refer to the *Comédie* itself as a "tragic waste of effort" just because it condemned Balzac to a "monstrous duality": he had to play both historian and novelist, trying to see his subject clearly and still fit it into his schematic presentation of French society. It is "Balzac's catastrophe" that interests James, who insists that "we are never so curious about successes as about interesting failures."[28]

James was apparently unwilling to repeat Balzac's particular mistake, and, as a quick glance at Edel's proposed categories discerns, the American novelist's work simply doesn't cover a number of distinct regions; rather, it returns compulsively to old topics and approaches, revising rather than expanding its scope. In making the case for the Edition's architecture, Edel ignores the fact that the bulk of the volumes are placed chronologically and that the collection can best be described as structured around a tension between temporal and spatial models for organizing a literary corpus. Perhaps more significantly, by comparing James to the other "master" of fiction, Edel dismisses the more immediate models for the Edition, particularly the one the novelist himself mentions in his first letter to the Scribners: "Messrs. Scribners' complete edition of Rudyard Kipling offers to my mind the right type of form and appearance . . . for our undertaking. I could desire nothing better than this, and should be quite content to have it taken for a model. (But I think, also, . . . that I should like a cover of another colour—to differentiate—than the Kipling.)"[29]

Michael Anesko has done a great deal to redress the imbalances of Edel's account by describing the Edition as at base the novelist's effort to make old titles pay again. There is, Anesko urges, really no design to the Edition at all, since James all too readily accepted the arbitrary constraints of bookmaking as he tried to fit as many works as he could into a set small enough to be marketable. If Edel imagines the project's ending tragically when the Edition exceeded Balzac's 23-volume format, the tales of literary life spilling over into a second volume while the ghost stories failed to fill their own, Anesko presents the failure as a purely commercial one, an effort to exploit the market that took more labor than it was worth. Curiously, in a book devoted to showing how deeply engaged James was with questions of making and marketing his fiction, Anesko still endorses the familiar distinction between pure literary production and the sordid practices of packaging fiction when he argues that James retreated finally to the country of the blue and "the creative life of the mind [which] could always ease the frictions of the market."[30] Again, the lesson of Ralph Limbert is that we can't simply dismiss the frictions of the market as secondary and supplementary to the pure workings of the imagination.

I want to conclude by briefly sketching out the design that I believe governs the Edition, a design that portrays the author as neither a transcendent architect nor a mere fiction of the marketplace. For a self-conscious Limbert, as James was by 1907, the mechanical constraints of the publishing system serve as incitements to discover unities and harmonies that can conceal or redeem the arbitrary violence of the book's space and form. The Edition's genres aren't prescribed by the author's original intentions but are found, if not actually produced, in the editorial process of shuffling and arranging texts. James, I would argue, aggressively solicits the crisis of having too many stories for a given volume because, in such desperate moments, he hopes to discover relations latent among his works and because, just as importantly, he wants to force his purchaser to take up the Edition as something more than a passive, commemorative presentation of classic works.

The eighteenth volume, which closes the sequence of short fictions, is a triumph of this authority lost only to be regained. The volume was supposed to have juxtaposed *Daisy Miller* with "Julia Bride," the latter a more recent effort to "do" the self-made American girl, and thus to have ended the detour with an early and late treatment of the same subject. But "Julia" has been thrown back into the incomplete volume of ghost stories; the tales are still next to each other but are separated by the covers of their respective volumes. Inside the eighteenth volume, one group of stories clusters around *Daisy*, all portraying the American girl, while another, largely drawn from *The Better Sort*, focuses on questions of what counts as a work of art and how society goes about recognizing and rewarding artistic labor. One of these stories, "The Real Thing," actually refers to the deluxe edition as just such a means of recognition. The narrator of that tale is hired to illustrate an edition deluxe of a novelist "long neglected by the multitudinous vulgar and dearly prized by the attentive." The edition is described as both "an act of high reparation" and a way of casting "the full light of a higher criticism" on the great writer's work (*18*: 318). But the narrator never applies the notorious lesson he learns about models and representation to the process of making such editions. If the illustrator is forced to acknowledge that professional models visually represent aristocracy better than aristocrats themselves do, he never quite concludes that the edition he is helping to produce may itself be a representation of the novelist's corpus and not the perfect presentation of the corpus in itself.

III

The opening pages of the Edition characterize the work of assembling the Edition as an editorial labor, of choosing and shuffling; similarly, the Preface to *Roderick Hudson* describes the work of composition itself as primarily an editorial labor, that of cutting back. The apprentice novelist worries not about how to produce "relations" but, rather, about how he can make them "happily *appear*" to find a natural stopping point by "a geometry of his own" (*1*: vii; *AN*, *5*; James's emphasis). Much has been made of James's inability in the prefaces to distinguish rewriting from rereading, a distinction made particularly problematic by the very unconsciousness of the "inveterate habits" that produce James's texts. But this opening passage should forewarn the reader that if the act of writing seems to disappear in the prefaces, it is only so that composition can be described as identical to the editorial process of putting the Edition itself together.

As the collection draws to its close, James returns to the question of closure and enclosure when, in his final Preface, he confesses his fear of illustrators like the narrator of "The Real Thing." His concern is that, whenever the space of the volume exceeds that of the text, publishers are tempted to employ their new reproductive technologies to fill the volume with competing and parasitic representations. When writing fails to naturalize its conditions, it leaves room for the usurping illustrator. James's immediate solution is to play a role in his own illustration by providing his volumes with frontispieces that are prescribed by and still continuous with his authorial vision. Yet he goes on to suggest that the object of every novelist is in fact to incite his readers to illustrate his texts elsewhere and in their own media: "One welcomes illustration, in other words, with pride and joy," but only "as a separate and independent subject of publication, carrying its text in its spirit, just as that text correspondingly carries the plastic possibility" (*23*: x; *AN*, 332–33).

Representation as James describes it here is not Balzac's exhaustive documentation but rather a provisional presentation of the subject, one that is simultaneously complete and not quite definitive. The successful text compels its reader to revise and redo its subject. The task confronting the writer is, then, to give his work the semblance of closure while yet instilling in his reader "a sense for ever so many more of the shining silver fish afloat in the deep sea of [his] endeavour than the net of widest casting could pretend to gather in." And the best strategy for "making that sense contagious," James believes, is to weave "so beautifully tangled a web" that the reader is forced both to acknowledge the proper boundaries of his authority and to feel the degree to which his subjects are still not fully treated (*23*: xxii; *AN*, 345). As just such a tangled web, the New York Edition is not intended to be taken up as a metatext enclosing and explaining the Jamesian corpus but as yet another performance of the artist in his later manner, one that exploits the limits of the ready-made format of the deluxe edition in its effort to make the sea of Jamesian fiction itself emerge, and to redefine its author as a presence that always exceeds efforts to enclose or commemorate its achievements.

In the House of Fiction:
Henry James and the
Engendering of Literary Mastery

Sara Blair

In the canons of Anglo-American literature, Henry James holds sway as
our most philosophical novelist, the literary master whose self-consciousness about the limits and the freedoms of the literary act continues to shape
critical understandings of the author, the reader, and the text.[1] His prefaces
to the New York Edition provoke a reexamination of that mastery in the
complexity of the self-representations they perform. On the one hand, as
Ross Posnock argues, the prefaces openly represent the author's desire for
monolithic authority over language and its circulation as a compromised
will to power; they heuristically surrender the authority they help to con-
solidate, and thereby make ironic James's relationship to the project of
monumentalizing his own literary *corpus*. On the other hand, these very
gestures of what Martha Banta calls "self-authorizing refusal" themselves
become a kind of commodity on which James trades, to recover something
very much like the totalized authority he purports to undermine.[2] In
Jamesian terms, to choose between these ways of reading is to compromise
the vaunted ambiguity and undecidability that make his imagination of
narrative agency so receptive to contemporary theorizing.

I propose to displace the prefaces, to read them against their formida-
bly literary contexts, as documents of engenderment in both senses of the
term—and thereby perhaps to reconsider their production of such critical
counterreadings. In the context of difference, as both a topos of and a legitimating resource for the Edition, James's gestures of refusal constitute
neither a comprehensive ethics of destabilizing their own claims to authority nor an essentially literary act. Rather, they are a strategic form of
self-representation through which the cultural work of representation is le-

gitimized. James's identifications with women in the belated complexity of his prefaces reveal the dynamics of a second-order mastery at work. By rejecting public and male forms of authority, by rehearsing ideologies of gender and difference as a resource for his version of the work of authorship, he ultimately claims a higher kind of meaning for his art. In order to uphold a selectively idealized representation of the literary act, James entertains some of the versions of authority he repudiates. As his figures for female identity and his own heroines suggest, his strategic identification with women and domestic space necessarily risks the work of regulation, conducted so as to promote a self-regulating form of art. In the prefaces' designs of and on femininity, James reveals himself engendering a mastery that "recognizes," "revises," and thereby transcends, its own narrative and political limitations, even as it exposes the social costs of this mode of self-production.

I

Within the New York Edition no document more effectively manages the motives and desires of mastery than the Preface to *The Portrait of a Lady*. Combining with virtually unique seamlessness the intimacy of personal reminiscence and the high seriousness of literary doctrine, the *Portrait* Preface exemplifies the project of the Edition as a whole: it represents literary authority in formalist and socialized terms, making the work of authorship inseparable from the author's capacity for moral attention and his vigilant guardianship of cultural and literary forms. At the literal and conceptual center of the Preface stands James's most powerful figure—in effect, his master trope—for the value and limits of the novel as a social form, the figure of the house of fiction. In impassioned, densely metaphoric prose, James celebrates the "boundless freedom" exercised, and the "'moral' reference" secured, through the artist's ultimately social activity. Within the house of fiction, he is the "figure with a pair of eyes, or at least with a field-glass," who occupies a particular "window" opened onto his subject, "the spreading field" of human practices, by "the need of the individual vision and the pressure of the individual will." From this chosen vantage point, the author-surveyor employs his "unique instrument" for observation, producing an "impression distinct from every other" of the "human scene" he surveys. The literary "subject" in question and the chosen vehicle for representing it are, "singly or together, as nothing without

the posted presence of the watcher—without, in other words, the consciousness of the artist" (3: x–xi; *AN*, 46).

For readers of James with widely varying agendas, this passage has
been taken to stand definitively for James's self-consciousness about the
contingency of literary authority and of the values and practices it defends.[3]
In the context of the Edition for which it was produced, the passage is plau-
sibly read as implicating James's own ambiguous performance of literary
"architecture" in the attempt to craft a "beautifully proportioned," totalizing literary monument.[4] At the same time, however, this figured version of
authorship gestures toward a recovery of the kind of mastery that its rela-
tivism and phenomenological canons apparently undo. Even as James exposes the provisionality of the author's vantage point, its dependence on the
enabling subject positions and sites of intervention provided by literary institutions, his insistence on authorial "will" and "freedom" might be said to
activate tropes of the watcher as a romantic "seer," whose privileged capacity for "consciousness" secures unmediated access to higher categories of
experience. Like the Edition it helps to construct, James's figure imagines
the work of authorship in a simultaneous erasure and exposure of its own
metaphysical desires.

Rather than take James's use of this controlling metaphor at face
value—that is, rather than read it as "purely" metaphoric, secure in its reference to a purely literary act—we might consider how this master trope
participates in a textual politics of engenderment. We might, in other
words, ask what difference it makes that James chooses to imagine his literary authority in a figure of domestic architecture, whose terms as such
have gone virtually unchallenged by his readers.[5] The question is compelling, given the extraordinary power of James's representations of women
and the long-standing ambivalence of feminist readers of his master texts.[6]
His fictions engage acutely and intensely with women's experiences,
oppressions, and values—formalized, for example, in the frequent distance of the prefaces from the security of conventionally masculine forms
of ownership and regulation. Yet his master texts can also be said to reify
problematic terms of difference in the service of James's own literary values, in gestures of self-representation that constitute what has been called a
"covert act of force against women."[7]

As the passage in question suggests, this doubleness persists in part because difference serves as a crucial resource in James's performance of a
particular kind of literary authority. By figuring the work of authorship as

a kind of domestic activity, James strategically revises a powerful romance of origins that resonates throughout modern Anglo-American literary doctrine. Redirecting available metaphors for the locus of self-consciousness—the palace of art, the museum, the narrow chamber of the individual mind, the Emersonian place of experience   he mobilizes sentimental ideologies of femininity, purity, and awakened consciousness and makes them intrinsic to his version of the literary act.[8] He thereby naturalizes, in the performance of a self-consciously ironic mastery, fictions of gender that novels like the *Portrait* so resonantly challenge.

In the context of the Edition as a whole, and of its complex performances of authorship as a social act, the textual life of James's trope begins to evoke a continuity between his project of moral custodianship—in fictions that endeavor to make their readers "finely aware and richly responsible"—and the kind of protective domestic discourses with which the novel in Anglo-America remained knottily entangled. James's self-representations throughout the prefaces consistently engage these discourses, which were designed to provide a bulwark against the rising tides of consumerism and middle-class power, and which were already at hand as a powerful subtext in the ongoing narrative of America's emergent modern identity.[9] Appropriating the sanctified separateness of woman's sphere, the formalist literary doctrine of the prefaces opens out onto the genteel metaphysics James ultimately seeks to undermine. James, in other words, trades on the social capital of difference, locating the work of authorship in the space of a privacy in which forms and values untouched by the marketplace and its strident ethos of male power are protected and preserved. The Edition's governing trope thus performs a dual function: it adumbrates the deeply artificial nature of James's literary authority yet simultaneously exploits the capital of a separate sphere to imagine a mastery that supersedes the public, commercial institutionality it surrenders.

To read domesticity as the authorizing ground of James's performance is to begin to understand his habit, throughout the prefaces, of revisiting domestic architecture to account for the origins of his own texts and thus to legitimate his power to offer right readings for them. In numerous reconstructions of the "germs" of his fictions, James imagines himself occupying the neutral architecture—the "mere hole," "disconnected" from the hard facts of commercial enterprise—of a figurally distinct "domestic" space. Chronicling the provenance of *Roderick Hudson* in his first Preface to the Edition, James both foregrounds and erases the "private" character of the "*accessory* facts" he recounts (*1*: v–vi; *AN*, 4; James's emphasis). He retrospectively instances the work of authorship as a domestic occupation; to "nurse" his characters along through the last installments of the novel "was really to sit again in the high, charming, shabby old room which had originally overarched them," to look out "through the slits of cooling shutters"—like those "pierced," "slit-like" apertures in the house of fiction—at "the rather dusty but ever-romantic glare of Piazza Santa Maria Novella" (*1*: ix; *AN*, 7). In the guise of master surveying the "spreading field" of his own career, James replicates his original surveillance of the Florentine square below his window, with its cabstand, the "clatter" of "horse-pails," and the "discussions" of the "garrulous" *cocchieri*, whose humble conveyances for hire attest to the more serious transport effected by his ardent fidelity to metaphor.

He similarly associates the production of *The American* with the domestic space he occupied during its composition, rooms with a set of windows affording a view of the Rue de Luxembourg and of the "martial clatter" of cuirassiers; their barracks, located directly opposite, sounded "recurrent notes in the organic vastness of the city" (*2*: v; *AN*, 26–27). Characteristically, however, James measures a carefully intentioned distance between the scene of writing and that of muscular discipline, mapped onto the distance of "sharp and quiet" reflection from the "too immediate impression," from the "view" that offers "more than . . . one has use for" (*3*: vi; *AN*, 41). Here as throughout the prefaces, his own images of origin betray a certain psychic distance from those distinctively *foreign* activities, military and commercial, of the public sphere he surveys.

These architectural reminiscences gesture toward a more acute awareness throughout the prefaces and other master texts of the gap between public culture in America, which makes no pretense of concealing its continuity with the activities of the marketplace, and the realm of privacy and purer feeling. In the Preface to volume 18 of the Edition, which includes *Daisy Miller*, James considers at length the difficulty created by this gap for his own production of authentic fictions and authentic claims to representativeness. He carefully conflates past perfect and present tenses, insisting on his own powerlessness, both at the moment of composition of such internationalist tales as "Pandora" and at the moment of his return as master to his "native city," vis-à-vis the masculine world of commerce and sharp practice. Openly advertising the fact of his "insuperably restricted experience," his "various missing American clues," James characterizes himself, in the act of creating the Edition, as an "unfortunate practically banished from the true pasture" of "down-town," in which the "real" American stories, of business and capital, vigorously flourish. In orbit on the periphery of that distinctive arena, James "moon [s] about superficially, circumferentially, taking in, through the pores of whatever wistfulness, no good material at all." Thus banished, he effects a telling distinction between the margins he occupies at the edges of downtown and the Dantesque world of Wall Street; barred from the act of *katabasis*, of "'going' down," James "hover [s]" at "the narrow gates" leading toward the "violently over-scored" landscape of "Capital," "the monstrous labyrinth that stretches from Canal Street to the Battery" (*18*: ix–xi; *AN*, 272–73).[10]

No failed Orpheus, James achieves this strong reading of American culture precisely because he occupies such an extrinsic vantage point. His self-representation as master depends on his exclusion from a cultural space whose values would compromise the distinct project of guardianship, the troubled attempt to redirect the circulation of larger cultural fictions. In the Preface to *Daisy Miller*, James thus remains decidedly and strategically alone—"alone, I mean, with the music-masters and French pastry-cooks, the ladies and children—immensely present and immensely numerous these, but testifying with a collective voice to the extraordinary absence (save as pieced together through a thousand gaps and indirectnesses) of a serious male interest" (*18*: x; *AN*, 273). Self-excluded from that magic circle, the male world of the marketplace, James ponders the "interrogated mystery of what American town-life had left to entertain the observer withal when nineteen twentieths of it, or in other words the huge organised mystery of the consummately, the supremely applied money-passion, were inexorably closed to him." Distancing himself from the organs of enterprise, those "down-town penetralia," James endorses his own literary and moral economy, in which "the true intelligent attention," "piously persisted in," will enable a nearer vision of "'American life'" (*18*: x–xii; *AN*, 274–75). Despite his protests to the contrary, James finally *can* "afford—artistically, sentimentally," and ethically—to advertise his own exclusion from the "Capital characteristics" of the culture he surveys for a living, precisely because that exclusion signifies the legitimacy, the neutrality, the more productive friction, of his own acts of moral attention.

In the guise of literary formalist, discussing the proper limits of the *nouvelle* genre, James can openly connect the domestic sphere he inhabits with the textual metaphysics he apparently seeks to undermine. To "ride the *nouvelle* down-town," to "prance and curvet and caracole with it there," would have been, James ruefully admits of *Daisy Miller* and similar performances, "the true ecstasy" of the master. But "a single 'spill'—such as I so easily might have had in Wall Street or wherever—would have forbidden me, for very shame, in the eyes of the expert and the knowing, ever to mount again" (*18*: xii; *AN*, 274). Such self-revealing figures are offered as gestures of refusal, performances of the master's ironic project of destabilizing the very form of authority to which the prefaces would seem to aspire. In the context of James's careful distinction between public and private spaces, however, his vision of the literary enterprise gone wild seems also to imagine domesticity as a self-transcending economy, one that effects authorial transport to a meaning "beyond" the "Capital characteristics" of commercial New York. If such passages dramatize James's rejection of the consumerist ethos in which public and male forms of power are founded, they also advertise these dramatizations, in part, so as to recover such power. Inhabiting domesticity, James secures the legitimacy of his own particular vantage point, for observation and for cultural critique, as a locus both ideologically and socially "distinct" from the "unredeemed commercialism of down-town."

James's language in the *Daisy Miller* Preface itself plays on the spuriousness of this distinction. In its imagery of pastry cooks, music masters, and other attendants of upward mobility, it reveals the leisure and order of domesticity themselves to be commodities dependent on the enabling activities of the market. These foundations, however, are strategically obscured, both in the cultural ideology of home and in James's narratives of textual origin. As literary master, James oddly resembles that emerging modern persona, the lady of the house; both exploit the value of home as a site of self-production in which all traces of productive labor are erased, and whose finished products—beauty, leisure, or in James's case, literary mastery—market themselves as higher social and ethical goods that supersede the consumer context in which they have been created.[11] The apparent distance of the ideologically pure space of home from the aggressive instrumentality of the public sphere will secure James's very authority therein, to promote and regulate the circulation of his literary products. Thus the paradoxical flourish of the *Daisy Miller* Preface: it offers James's last words on a moral drama centrally concerned with the problem of reading the "'self-made,' or at least self-making girl," the "child of nature and freedom" who abandons the safety of domestic propriety to display herself in public (*18*:

viii; *AN*, 271), yet it secures the legitimacy of its own reading by insisting
on an essentialized difference between private and public, between female
and male, between uptown and downtown, to underwrite James's self-
consciousness about the limitations of his art. In the words of a "charming
hostess's prompt protest" (an ironically appropriate source), James's self-
representation in response to his sensational tale consists in a "'pretty perversion,'" an "'unprincipled mystification'" of his domestic resources, reconstructed as a founding site for the reproduction of cultural power (*18*:
vii; *AN*, 269).

II

In tracing the imprint of sentimental ideology in the prefaces, I mean to
call attention to the ways in which James's self-representation throughout
the Edition can be read as refashioning narratives of gender so as to legitimate a form of authorship that, playfully or dutifully, exposes its own
foundations and thereby challenges the kind of authority it claims. James's
imagination of mastery—particularly in prefaces that centrally concern the
freedom of his troubled heroines—weds the essentializing architecture of
home as a sanctified site of private exchange to a version of representation
that depends on a regulated distinction between higher and lower orders. A
logic of paradox thus underlies James's sympathetic engagement with
women's experience: he identifies, and identifies with, the making of
women in the domestic sphere, but he also exploits this understanding to
secure his own access to male and public forms of power. Insofar as the female stakes out a culturally distinct realm that effectually conceals its complicity with the commodification of identity and feeling, it figures an authorial self-consciousness that consistently—in the words of the Preface to
The Golden Bowl—"recognizes," "revises," "re-represents," its own limitations.

   If the domestic maps a space of origins and critique ostensibly liberated
from the realities of Capital, James must logically exert great effort to
maintain a rigid distinction between woman's sphere and the world of commerce, as between the already figural "up-town" and "down-town" of New
York. In other writings of the master phase concerned with James's management of narrative and national origins, he literalizes such gestures of
regulation in uncharacteristically conventional form—as in his lectures to
the women of Bryn Mawr on "Speech and Manners of American Women,"

and even in the often cited discussion in *The American Scene* of the American girl [12] Throughout the prefaces, James more self-consciously maintains the "architectural" boundaries between woman's sphere, or femininity, and the ultimately public and masculine forms of authority he purportedly undoes. Yet even as he feminizes himself in the image of the domestic, overseeing the "tidying-up" of his "brood" as the "awkward infants" descend "from the nursery to the drawing room" and into the "searching" light of publicity (*23*: xiv–xv; *AN*, 337–38), he performs this role with a certain anxiety. His identifications with woman ultimately turn out to be both canny and, as John Carlos Rowe has repeatedly characterized them, "uncanny," literally *unheimlich*: they register the risks and costs of the unstably gendered identity in which James is never altogether at home. Too, they record his discomfort with the potential failure, and the potential success, of mastery as a cultural gesture. [13]

Nowhere does this uncanniness govern the dialogue between text and pretext more richly than in the *Portrait* Preface. Alfred Habegger has argued that the *Portrait*'s deep structure encodes James's attempt to appropriate, while concealing his dependence on, the plots of Anglo-American women's writing, and in particular the canons of sentimental fiction. [14] This double gesture of identification and distancing records itself in the unusual intensity of the Preface's regulatory impulses, and of its claims for James's power to codify as literary doctrine the dynamic of the novel. Detailing his numerous techniques for "positively organising an ado about Isabel Archer," James replicates the design of the *Portrait* itself, which might be said to sacrifice the ideal of freedom for its heroine to the exercise of a higher authorial consciousness of failed and incomplete forms of mastery.

Like James's discussions of *Roderick Hudson*, *The American*, and numerous other fictions, the *Portrait* Preface expends high energy reconstructing the origins of the novel in question. In the case of the *Portrait*, however, the idiom of genesis is highly overdetermined. James rehearses its "origins" by way of recounting its publication history, the geographical and aesthetic conditions of its production, and the gathering life of the "germ" of the story, the character of Isabel Archer. This extended discussion occupies nearly a third of the text, and it anchors James's creation of a literary genealogy as well his most powerful defenses of formalism. Throughout, he offers a series of figures for his heroine that exemplify his proprietary interest in femininity and the female power of reproduction. Ultimately, the imaginative origin of the novel becomes an oddly parthenogenetic moment: his "first dim move toward" the *Portrait* was "exactly" his "grasp of a single character," the "acquisition" of the heroine, sprung full-blown from the author's imagination ("after a fashion," James announces, "not here to be retraced"). The *Portrait* thus ensues with James in "complete possession" of his heroine: "I had my vivid individual—vivid, so strangely, in spite of being still *at large*, not confined by the conditions, not engaged in the tangle, to which we look for much of the impress that constitutes an identity" (*3*: x; *AN*, 47, emphasis added).

In James's rereading of the text, the task of finding "the right relations," the most compelling "complications" of Isabel's existence, amounts to putting the heroine in her properly feminized place. His authority as revisionary reader of his own art is directed, like the force of the *Portrait* itself, specifically against the danger of a heroine "at large," not "confined" (by pregnancy or otherwise) or even "engaged" (and thus safely "impressed" in the service of proper cultural reproduction). To make Isabel Archer bear the evidence of his power to manage the subtleties of literary architecture, James must suppress the dangerous potential of "the stray figure" to suggest her own imaginative history and thereby to subvert the social function of his authorial design. "Take[n] over straight from life" as "a constituted, animated figure," Isabel becomes virtually foundational to James's regulatory economy of signification:

The figure has to that extent, as you see, *been* placed—placed in the imagination that detains it, preserves, protects, enjoys it, conscious of its presence in the dusky, crowded, heterogeneous back-shop of the mind very much as a wary dealer in precious odds and ends, competent to make an "advance" on rare objects confided to him, is conscious of the rare little "piece" left in deposit by the reduced, mysterious lady of title or the speculative amateur, and which is already there to disclose its merit afresh as soon as a key shall have clicked in a cupboard drawer. (*3*: xii; *AN*, 47–48; James's emphasis)

Even for James, this figure of "the figure" of Isabel is unusually oblique. The hyperbole of his metaphor asks us to read his gesture of authorship against the regulatory terms it invokes. Yet in the case of the *Portrait*, those terms aptly represent the mixed motives of James's tale of the tale. Isabel, imagined as a rare and richly symbolic "treasure" that its owner will return to redeem, must be "detained," "preserved," "protected," but she is also "enjoyed." In the darkness of a figural back room, she is the rare "piece" yielded up by the destitute and desperate "lady" to the "advances" of the owner, who exploits the value of the female body as commer-

cial capital. James's description of his own act of authorship *ironically*
equates him, the beneficent author of Isabel's infinite woe, with the owner
(the shopkeeper to whom Charlotte Stant and the prince apply, that "master" of the psychology of desire, seduction, and deceit), and with his most
notorious collector, Gilbert Osmond, whose vigilant "protection" of his
living bibelots constitutes an ongoing act of sexual regulation. As guardian
of his own *oeuvre*, James is more like these problematic masters than his
indulgence in metaphor would imply; he keeps a wary eye on the goods in
question, consigning Isabel to an enclosure (the locked drawer, the literary after-text) whose key he himself regulates, in the free play of a self-
conscious, ironic literary design.

In a characteristic conflation of moral and sexual economies, James describes such acts of regulation as rituals of "refinement": "I quite remind
myself thus," he comments, "of the dealer resigned not to 'realise,' resigned
to keeping the precious object locked up indefinitely rather than commit it,
at no matter what price, to vulgar hands" (*3*: xii; *AN*, 48). Here, James
encourages the deeper analogy of his mastery with the malevolent authorship of Osmond, who "prefer[s] women like books—good and not too
long," and whose aestheticism consists in acts of self-inscription on the "fair
and smooth" pages, the "pure white surface[s]," of his *tabulae rasae* (*3*:
401; *4*: 26). Adverting to his "pious desire to place my treasure right,"
James advertises the construction of the *Portrait*, his "square and spacious
house" of fiction, as an edifice for incarcerating its heroine. Designed to
showcase "a certain young woman affronting her destiny," it "had to be put
up round my young woman while she stood there in perfect isolation"
(*3*: xii; *AN*, 48). Why, we might ask, does James insist so forcefully on
his power of design? One answer might be that, in the *Portrait* Preface,
he is primarily committed "not to 'realise'"—that is, not to trade on the felt
reality of this enormously compelling fiction, not to allow its felt life to
compromise the distinctly literary ontology and status of his art. By under-
scoring his denial of Isabel Archer as a human "Subject," James represents
his mastery as the "architectural" competence, the self-contained "deep
difficulty," it must, in order to sustain its distinctive function of culture-
building, be.

Yet James's openly regulatory figures ultimately reincorporate a metaphysics and a cultural practice they seek to undermine. His formalist ingenuity, which conduces to "the erect[ion]" on "such a [scant] plot of
ground" as the heroine herself "the neat and careful and proportioned pile

of bricks that arches over it," transfigures the heroine as the grounds for his claims to a higher form of mastery (3: xvi; *AN*, 52). Treated as a purely literary object, Isabel Archer becomes the space in which James carries out his "plot" and the arch constructing his "literary monument"—the bridge that, like the figure of metaphor, bears the weight of passage from mere sign to the "latent extravagance," the "too much," of its higher "reference," its richer signified (3: xi; *AN*, 46). In relation to his heroine, James's self-consciously literary authority amounts to the act of authorial "enjoyment" it intermittently foils; his mastery is built, "brick by brick," on the plot of the femininity he surveys in order to interrogate such acts of surveillance.

Throughout the *Portrait* Preface, a strategic formalism distances James from his own authorial will to power by representing the stakes of his narrative as purely literary ones. In so doing, it elides the broadly social import of James's uses of the feminine; further, it allows him to misread the role of femininity in the history of the novel as a social genre. Here we might remember James's elaborate discussion of the masterful technical design whereby Isabel Archer's "thin" problem of self-fulfillment is transformed into a text of thick moral description. "By what process of logical accretion," asks the master after the fact, "was this slight 'personality,' the mere slim shade of an intelligent but presumptuous girl, to find itself endowed with the high attributes of a Subject?" (3: xii–xiii; *AN*, 48). James's aggressive attenuation of the heroine as a narrative pretext—a "mere slim shade" and a "slight" " 'personality,' " one of the "slimnesses" of novelistic tradition—creates the space for his own moral vigilance; Isabel's disembodiment highlights her author's successful formal manipulation of "the value recognised in the mere young thing" (3: xiv; *AN*, 50).

If we take such catachreses to insist on the distinctively literary status and limits of James's project, we need nonetheless to account for the kinds of *mis*representation they perform. In effect, James doesn't figure Isabel, and other heroines of the Great Tradition, so much as he disfigures them: he links her, somewhat incongruously and unconvincingly, with Shakespeare's Juliet and Portia and Eliot's Maggie Tulliver, as members of a class "difficult" to "make a centre of interest." According to James, these heroines—literary constructs first and foremost—are mere vehicles for the movement of their texts, or of textuality itself; they pant and run ever forward, "with that much of firm ground, that much of bracing air, at the disposal all the while of their feet and their lungs" (3: xiii; *AN*, 49). To such a genealogy of heroines the feminist reader may want to object: in this

Preface, as in the *Portrait* itself, Isabel Archer becomes a victim of metaphor. Initially a careless reader of Osmond's self representation, James's heroine commits the disastrous error of "mistak[ing] a part for the whole" (*4*: 191); in James's critical treatment, she is herself misrepresented in the force of the master's synecdoche. By figuring Isabel and other female centers of consciousness as fragments and absences, James reserves the power of plenitude—that totality of moral insight that, like the novel as a literary form, "tends to burst, with a latent extravagance, its mould"—for his own act of revision (*3*: x; *AN*, 46).

The same logic of reconstruction underwrites James's ardent defense of Isabel's centrality to the novel's moral life—a defense that surely protests too much, given the rich history of the female *bildungsroman* in the novel tradition.[15] In a neatly ironic gesture, James allows a female novelist whose influence he often suppresses to name the logic of his design: "George Eliot has admirably noted it—'In these frail vessels is borne onward through the ages the treasure of human affection'" (*3*: xiii; *AN*, 49). Earlier in the Preface, Turgenev has spoken *in propria persona*, and at a length that strains the reader's tolerance for prosopopoeia; Eliot, by contrast, is a merely textual source. Yet her formulation—which James significantly misquotes, substituting "frail" for the original "delicate"[16]—lies at the center of his rehearsal of the meaning of his fiction: it tacitly insinuates the status of the female body as the cultural space in which the work of James's mastery is undertaken. Not only are women central to the "craft" of fiction as James so conspicuously formalizes it here; they are, in a very literal way, his craft itself, his mode for "transporting" literary conventions and forms into a closer correspondence with redemptive truths. James's great "insight," as he names and recounts it in the *Portrait* Preface, is to make the female "frail vessel" the space that he and his text authoritatively and ironically inhabit; femininity effects the reflective author's transportation from literal to figural meaning, from innocence to knowledge, from felt experience to more deeply felt fine awareness. Just as Isabel becomes James's rare "piece" and the arch supporting his literary monument, she is also his craft, to be inhabited in the service of a higher mastery that "recognises" its own contending motives and desires.

To inflect James's deeply metaphoric language in this way is to ask how his second-order mastery, in the specific terms of the project of engenderment, differs from the baneful authorial will to power that James so compellingly "dramatises" and refuses. At certain moments in the *Portrait* Preface, this form of difference appears to collapse; James's formalism refuses to recognize the uses it makes of gender in the service of literary comprehension and totality. Nowhere does James revise his own text more ruthlessly or inaccurately than in his distinction between legitimate subjects (invested with "the germinal property" of authorship) and mere *ficelles*, those characters-cum-functional devices who ostensibly serve merely to create a web of complex "relations," the warp and woof of the protagonist's inner life. James's mode of representing the function of the *ficelle* reveals how steeped is his self-abnegating authority in the forms of identity and difference that his fictions so powerfully undermine. His command of denotation is more apt than he may let on:[17] in the role of master arraying his own texts, James is the consummate *ficellier*, an "invisible" agent who directs their movements and works to render figural the engenderment of his art.

Not surprisingly, James's named *ficelles* are exclusively female (he discusses none of the "relational" male characters, like "little" Bilham or Waymarsh, who serve in this capacity), precisely because his acts of moral attention depend on suppressing challenges to the structures of difference that underwrite his performances of the literary. His language displays a rigorous need to deny the power of the *ficelle* as an autonomous voice guiding the movement of his craft: "Each of these persons is but wheels to the coach; neither belongs to the body of that vehicle, or is for a moment accommodated with a seat inside." Henrietta Stackpole and Maria Gostrey, in particular,

are cases, each, of the light *ficelle*, not of the true agent; they may cling to it till they are out of breath (as poor Miss Stackpole all so vividly does), but neither, all the while, so much as gets her foot on the step, neither ceases for a moment to tread the dusty road. Put it even that they are fishwives who helped to bring back to Paris from Versailles, on that most ominous day of the first half of the French Revolution, the carriage of the royal family. (*3*: xix; *AN*, 54–55)

In the Preface to *The Ambassadors*, James reiterates the limits of the female authorship practiced by the *ficelle*: if Maria Gostrey is "the reader's friend," an "enrolled" aid to "lucidity," she is finally an inferior domestic servant, "pre-engaged at a high salary," waiting "in the draughty wing with her shawl and smelling-salts" (*21*: xix–xx; *AN*, 322–23). Unlike Maggie Verver, who retains her interest as a moral agent even as she becomes a "compositional resource" (*23*: vii; *AN*, 329), the *ficelle* stands in a "false connexion" to the text's central dramas of power and language, a connection that is strategically disguised by the master himself, "under a due polish, as a real one" (*21*: xxi; *AN*, 324).

In both prefaces, James engages in what he himself disingenuously names an "artfu[l] dissimulat[ion]" (*21*: xxi; *AN*, 323) of his dependence on his *ficelles*. He insists on the exclusion of these telling women from his craft; they run breathless beside the coach, refused admission to the conveyance of the text. Instead, they serve as the instruments of transport— wheels to the coach, feet in the dusty road—whose bodies are expended in the service of the literary mission. Protecting the value of difference as a legitimating resource, James must vigorously suppress the creative power of the *ficelle*; like his heroine in the *Portrait*, he too is "not altogether at ease" with the *ficelle*'s "reproductive instincts" (*3*: 115). In the guise of master, James belies the narrative and moral power of his own surrogate—not an inhabited central consciousness but a figure beyond the scope of narrative penetration, whose presence shapes the "true" agent's acquisition of the highest Jamesian good, self-consciousness. Ironically, the *Portrait* itself foregrounds these female authors and their role in the work of moral attention, celebrating by making literal the power of the *ficelle*'s function: she is the tie that binds subjective agents to a network of desire and knowledge, making possible and morally meaningful the coextension of inner life and institutions that James's fiction so powerfully asserts.[18] No wonder James himself is at a loss to explain how the "breathless" and "dusty" (and utterly compelling) Henrietta Stackpole clings so tenaciously to his coach, how she "has been allowed so officiously, so strangely, so almost inexplicably, to pervade" (*3*: xix; *AN*, 55).

The *Portrait* Preface expends this effort to tie up the loose end of the *ficelle* for the reason suggested in James's own figural language. Unbound *ficelles* present clear danger, like that offered by the "fishwives" at the head of the barricades, or the female leaders in the storming of that royal house, Versailles. Their uncontained presence in James's art threatens to overturn the very foundations of his signifying practice, whose power—to compel, to adjudicate, to proscribe—resides, in part, in the logic of a higher consciousness finessed through the regulated distinction between female and male, passion and restraint, insight and blindness, sociality and withdrawal. The *ficelle* as figure thus aptly reveals the larger stakes of James's self-engenderment: in the *Portrait* Preface, he upholds his narrative of the craft of fiction even at the expense of misrepresenting his own images. To suppress the power of the female observer—who is, after all, yet another version of the "witness or reporter," the "substitute or apologist" for James's own "veiled and disembodied" creative "power"—is to authenticate the cultural presence of the master himself and his higher power to redeem the "muffled majesty" of "'authorship'" (23: v, vi; AN, 327, 328). Having secured an ironic authority in his designs of and on femininity, James can depart the *Portrait* Preface with a hugely *ficellesque* gesture of self-effacement and refusal; his own accession to London and a newly developing transatlantic audience, he tells us, "*is* another matter. There is really too much to say" (3: xxi; AN, 58).

III

In the simultaneity of its gestures of self-erasure and self-exposure, the *Portrait* Preface can usefully be taken to stand for the New York Edition as a whole: a text of self-representation inscribed, in its forms and its formalisms, its artistic flourishes and its artful dodges, with the motive of engendering a literary mastery that puts the social consequences of mastery at issue. Belying his own acute attention to the import of what we might call untold fictions of identity and difference, James's use of gender as a resource in the *Portrait* Preface and beyond tells some of the costs of an ironic cultural politics. With this "dramatise[d]" paradox at its unstable center, the New York Edition schools wary readers in the need for vigilance in explicating the language and fictions of cultural power. On these heuristic grounds, it remains one of those collections without which no imagination of the cultures of modernity can afford to "do" (3: 140).

PART II

"A Handsome Book":
Cultural and Publishing Contexts

Ambiguous Allegiances:
Conflicts of Culture and Ideology in
the Making of the New York Edition

Michael Anesko

Almost from the start of his writing career, Henry James provoked critical
censure by his ambiguous national allegiance. Influential American readers worried publicly over James's deliberate cosmopolitanism, an attitude
that seemed to assume the cultural inferiority of the United States. The
critical biography of Hawthorne (1879), with its notorious catalogue of
the items of high civilization found wanting in American life (no Epsom
nor Ascot!), helped to confirm the self-consciously patriotic suspicions of
James's enemies, whose charges of high treason quickly followed. The satiric nature of *The Bostonians* (1886) only made matters worse. For the rest
of his writing life, James's reputation in the United States was shadowed by
resentment of his alienation from his native land, an issue that attained renewed prominence in the wake of the author's celebrated return in 1904–
5.[1] James's deliberate identification of his life's work with the city of his
birth—he insisted that the collective issue of 1907–9 be called "The New
York Edition"—might be seen as an attempt to repair the novelist's esteem
among his native audience, a gesture of reconciliation. Indeed, the publisher's prospectus for the series proclaimed it as "the definitive edition of
the fiction of the first of American novelists."[2] The commercial failure of
the Edition might indicate, then, that American readers repudiated such
claims for James's specifically national value.

At the very end of his life, of course, James returned the favor, shrug-
ging off his American citizenship to ally himself with England's cause in
the Great War. Very few people at the time recognized James's renunciation
for what it was—a quintessentially American act of civil disobedience;
most simply viewed his choice as the terminal punctuation in a lifelong sen-

tence of betrayal. To the emerging generation of native literary craftsmen (expatriated Pound and Eliot notwithstanding), James had long since ceased to be an American writer; his dismissal by Van Wyck Brooks and Vernon Louis Parrington marked the nadir of his reputation in the United States. The collapse of James's American stature in the 1920's certainly encouraged his later revivalists to believe that even during his lifetime sympathetic readers were more likely to be found abroad than at home, that England had proved hospitable to the Master when America failed him. The American scene—hadn't James vociferously testified?—was culturally impoverished, morally and materially insufficient to the mature needs of the artist's imagination.

The presumption of estrangement and exile has had profound influence on subsequent critical assessments of James, with many voices raised to reclaim him as one of us. Surprisingly enough, however, the assumption of what might be called British clemency toward James remains largely unexamined and unquestioned, as if it were a given historical fact. The transatlantic publication and reception of the New York Edition call into question this received view and illustrate significant cultural differences between the English and American literary marketplace. Indeed, the curious fate of the Edition in London reveals a more precariously perched English James than one might otherwise have gathered from the standard sources. While the writer and his agent, James B. Pinker, fought many uphill battles before the Scribners could finally bring out the Edition in New York, securing an English publisher for the series was one of their most difficult obstacles. The historical reasons for this embarrassment, and their cultural significance, are the subject of this essay.

James's difficulties in arranging for the Edition in America were not unique. As early as 1882 *Publishers' Weekly* complained about the paucity of American writers who could present their work in uniform editions. The fundamental problem for living authors lay in the fact that their books often were distributed among a number of competing publishers. "Mr. Howells's writings are scattered about in a diversified form," the *Weekly* noted. "So are Henry James's."[3] Twenty-five years later that stubborn fact almost sank the New York Edition and, indeed, prematurely terminated the Harpers' work on the Library Edition of William Dean Howells.[4] To circumvent this obstacle, many collected editions were marketed by subscription only, a practice that kept them out of retail bookstores where they would compete directly with the ordinary trade editions of individual titles. Most trade publishers were only too well aware that, given the choice, consumers would naturally prefer to purchase volumes that could be displayed more attractively at home. Traditionally, however, subscription publishing in America had seldom been used to market books of outstanding quality. The typical provender were mass-marketed commodities: gargantuan illustrated books, encyclopedias, low-quality reprints of Dickens and other pirated fiction. The shift at the end of the nineteenth century toward a radically different market—one much more exclusive, to promote the sale of deluxe, limited editions—brought America's publishing practice much closer to that of Britain, where an older tradition of bibliographical connoisseurship was carefully nurtured by the literary establishment.

Even though the extent of James's textual revisions for the New York Edition alarmed and discomforted many of even his most dedicated American readers, nearly all of them were satisfied with the material presentation of his collected work. As an example of modern American book manufacture, the New York Edition largely fulfilled the author's yearning for a "*dignity* of aspect" which was, for this presentation of his books, his "dream & desire."[5] When the first two volumes were delivered to Lamb House on New Year's Eve 1907, James could not contain his pride. "They are in every way felicitous," he told his agent; "they do every one concerned all honour, & the enterprise has now duly to march majestically on."[6] As everyone knows, the enterprise was fated to march duly on into unmajestic oblivion, but not because the Scribners had cut corners or even from any want of everyday publicity. As successive volumes came from the press, reviewers in many parts of the country discussed James's extraordinary prefaces, the nature of his revisions, the principles of selection he seemed to be employing. As one critic approvingly noted, "Mr. James is no author for 'pocket' editions. He is to be read in the library, in all the dignity of large type and fair-margined pages. In the harmony of its outward seeming with its contents this edition is close to the line that precludes criticism."[7] A taste for James, then, was an unmistakable sign of literary discrimination, to which the Scribners catered by means of the Edition's discreet bindings; specially made, watermarked paper; and photogravure plates.[8]

How to preserve the book's cultural authority in an age of mass readership and mechanical reproduction was a problem not merely for James and the Scribners but for all the principal figures of the Anglo-American literary world. By the end of the nineteenth century, technological innovation and nearly universal literacy had created an ever expanding empire of

print and publicity; but such developments, while often profitable to authors and publishers alike, were not welcomed unhesitatingly. Even as they
poured from the presses, many periodicals decried the recent evidence of
literature's commercialization: the phenomenon of the best-seller, the pressure to advertise, the aggressive tactics of literary agents, the occasionally
stratospheric sums paid to writers of dubious merit. "The high prosperity
of fiction has marched, very directly, with another 'sign of the times,'"
James himself reported, "the demoralisation, the vulgarisation of literature
in general, the increasing familiarity of all such methods of communication. . . . If the novel, in fine, has found itself, socially speaking, at such a
rate, the book *par excellence*, so on the other hand the book has in the same
degree found itself a thing of small ceremony."[9] Very much aware of these
trends, publishers tried to maintain traditions of excellent craftsmanship,
especially in regard to their relatively sumptuous editions of standard authors. No thing of small ceremony, the New York Edition benefited not
merely from the Scribners' technical expertise but also from James's colla-
borative imagination, which worked to produce (in the words of the publisher's prospectus) "an elaborate edifice whose design and execution are absolutely unique in their kind owing to their complete unity of effect."[10]

But even while James was fondling his first volumes with almost "ri-
diculous pride," the publishers whom his agent had approached about marketing the series in England were ridiculing them. William Meredith of
Constable admitted that the book Pinker had sent was "quite attractive in
appearance"; nevertheless, it was still "only the ordinary American trade
Edition" and thus could not compare "as a piece of book production . . .
with our Edition of George Meredith, or the Edinburgh Stevenson, or the
Edition de Luxe of Kipling's works." Moreover, the Scribner prospectus
did not stipulate that the sale of James's edition would be in any way limited: this, from Meredith's point of view, was a very important point. Nor
was there anything to indicate that after the Edition was finished, the different volumes (printed from the same plates) would not be issued at a reduced price for a more popular market. As if this weren't bad enough, the
money Scribners wanted for sheets (2s. 6d. per volume, plus the cost of
folding) was simply outlandish. In light of the other marketing restrictions
connected with the Edition (the volumes to be sold in sets only, at a price
not less than the equivalent of the American retail tag of $2.00 per volume,
with the Canadian market reserved to Scribner's), "it was out of the question to pay anything like the price . . . asked for." As far as Meredith could

see, the case against publication was overwhelming, and he was "reluc-
tantly compelled to decline" Pinker's offer.[11]

If James and Pinker were surprised by this outcome, the Scribners
themselves had no reason to be. Nearly two years before, when preliminary plans for the Edition were first being made, Meredith had warned
Charles Scribner that marketing James's works in England would prove
burdensome. "You will realize," he advised, "that the difficulty here is that
so many different people have the copyright for so many different books
by this Author."[12] By this time Scribner himself had already gone through
months of tough negotiations with James's competing American publishers; Meredith's point was hardly lost upon him. "It is rather a long and
heavy undertaking," Scribner confessed about the Edition; he would need
several months before the firm would be ready to talk hard numbers as to
price and format.[13] What little enthusiasm Charles Scribner first had for
the project was clearly eroding.

Pinker's approach to Constable was logical, because that firm and
Scribner's had previously collaborated to produce other Editions de
Luxe—the Edinburgh Robert Louis Stevenson, for example, and the Library Edition of George Meredith (William's father). In fact, James had
these other projects in mind when envisioning a comparable standard by
which to judge his own work.[14] Meredith anticipated a similar arrangement for James, but he also recognized that unprecedented complications
could arise. Could purchasers be guaranteed, for example, that new works
by the author would automatically be added to the Edition? (Subscribers to
Kipling's Outward Bound Edition, jointly issued by Scribner's and Macmillan, had been assured of this.) From the very start, then, the British
publisher took it for granted that completeness would naturally be one of
the Edition's main attractions. But to persuade Scribner's to go ahead with
the New York Edition at all, James had been forced to be selective as well
as collective, and to omit a sizable number of titles. Many of these he sacrificed without qualm (*Washington Square*, most notoriously); but the dis-
crepancy of expectation as to the material dimensions of the Edition suggests that the cultural function of such an enterprise was conceived in much
different terms on opposite sides of the Atlantic.

At almost every point, James's publishers (even his would-be publishers) were working at cross-purposes. From Meredith's point of view, an
English Edition de Luxe necessarily would be textually comprehensive
and materially exclusive, produced in such a way as to preserve and mani-

fest a distinctive aura of authorial inscription. Curiously enough, however, the Scribners seem to have believed that James's following abroad would enable them to persuade a British publisher to take a half-interest in a more popularly styled edition. Their (mistakenly) generous estimate of James's transatlantic audience encouraged the Scribners' hope that the sale of foreign rights to the Edition would comfortably subsidize their own considerable investment in it. Apparently, the early note of warning from Constable did not dissuade them, even though Meredith had stipulated that selling the Edition was "not going to be an easy matter here"; he bluntly announced his intended preference for ordering the books only in sets of 10 or 25 at a time.[15] Almost like one of James's American protagonists, convinced of the possibilities of free expansion, the Scribners transferred an aggressively optative view of the marketplace to a culture that stubbornly refused to accommodate it. In fact, the product they hoped to dispose of was exactly the one least suited to the audience at which it was directed.

Scribner's planned to issue the New York Edition, like the other subscription editions they had recently produced, in two forms: a limited issue (which largely conformed to Meredith's description of a true Edition de Luxe); and an ordinary issue, printed from the same plates, but unlimited as to circulation. Perhaps because of Meredith's first discouraging report, Scribner's never even attempted to sell the limited issue of the New York Edition in Great Britain, even though *that* series might have been more successfully marketed abroad than at home. With only 156 copies available, the limited issue of the Edition was four times more expensive than the ordinary issue ($8 net per volume as opposed to $2); large, handmade paper was used in production; the national inscription ("New York Edition") was even omitted from the title pages. Outwardly, at least, the limited issue of the Edition seemed tailor-made for the upper end of the English market; perversely, it was never sold there.

In the wake of Meredith's ultimate refusal to take up the Edition, James's agent scrambled to find other buyers. Since one of Constable's objections concerned the problem of competing editions, Pinker shrewdly went to the house of John Murray, a firm that had never before published anything of James's; "from that point of view he is most desirable," Pinker reported to New York.[16] The novelist, too, was reinspired. "I greatly appreciate your news of the arrangement effected with Murray," James told Pinker,

& am glad indeed to hear of it. Much art had you doubtless to exercise to carry the matter so far. I infer in fact that your need for "art" isn't over, if there be any fear that the Scribner's may fail of accommodation in respect to quantity of sheets— which I devoutly trust they won't. One doesn't see why they should be positively disobliging—one would expect the contrary: though in all these matters I confess to a general sense of being surrounded with abysses.[17]

Quite unsuspectingly, James and Pinker and Scribner's had already fallen into another one. Like Constable, Murray was rather apprehensive about the prospects for the Edition, and he refused to take more than 25 sets to begin with. "I hope we may sell more than this," he reported, "but as we are not very confident, we do not want to risk more than this."[18] Now it was Scribner's turn to refuse, and they directed Pinker to turn elsewhere. "As you well know," the firm reminded him, "we have incurred a very heavy expense in the preparation of this edition and we expected to be able to sell an English edition of 250 or at the very least 100 sets."[19] To his own London agent, Charles Scribner himself was even more exasperatedly explicit: "25 is too small a lot on which to give the English market," he insisted; with "over $20,000" invested in plates and illustrations, "it seems absurd that an English publisher cannot be found to take 100 sets."[20]

This latest setback forced Scribner to recognize some errors of judgment. He now regretted leaving the disposal of English rights to the Edition in the hands of James's agent. But whose interests was Pinker commissioned to protect, after all: author's or publisher's? If, to James, Pinker had become "a blessing unspeakable,"[21] to Scribner he was probably just an unspeakable nuisance. Annoyed by Pinker's ineffective salesmanship, the firm pressured its official London agent, Lemuel Bangs, to intervene. By early June, Bangs got the desired result. His arrangement with Macmillan for the requisite order of 100 sets hugely gratified Charles Scribner, who announced himself "particularly pleased" by the order.[22] At least now the problem of selling the English Edition was in someone else's hands.

From James's point of view, however, there was still no Edition to sell. As in America, numerous other publishers had rights to his work, and permission was necessary to incorporate many of his most famous titles under Macmillan's imprint. While most were obliging, William Heinemann put up some resistance, and the correspondence that ensued between Scribner's partners in this venture reveals much about their view of the "Master." Anxious to recover the balance of James's royalty advances never earned back from sales of *The Spoils of Poynton*, *The Awkward Age*, and

other titles, Heinemann pressed Frederick Macmillan for details of his arrangement for the Edition. Macmillan responded in deprecating terms
"Scribners have asked us to purchase & put on the English market some
copies of the so-called 'New York Edition' of Henry James's Novels and
Tales," he wrote, "and we have agreed to do so though I am rather afraid
that we shall find them difficult to get rid of." As if to underscore the absur-
dity of the venture, Macmillan added: "The Edition is in 23 volumes at 8/
6 [8s. 6d.] net per volume!!"[23]

The double exclamation points did not discourage Heinemann from
grasping further. The next day he wrote again to Macmillan to claim a
share in the Edition's proceeds. Since his punctuation had not done the
trick, Macmillan now had to make more explicit his conservative estimate
of the Edition's probable sale. "There really is very little in this collected
Edition of Henry James's books," he confided, "of which Scribners apparently do not expect us to sell more than 250 sets at the outside." If Heinemann insisted on being compensated, Macmillan suggested that some portion of James's royalties be diverted to him ("but I am afraid the balances
against the books in your ledger will not be very much reduced thereby").
Heinemann was ticklish about making such an outright demand, which
might compromise the "rather intimate terms of personal friendship" that
he claimed to enjoy with James; instead he drafted a more modest proposal
concerning reparation, and asked Macmillan to pass it on to the novelist.
To console his out-of-pocket friend, Macmillan wryly confessed, "If it be
any satisfaction to you to know that you are not the only publisher who has
failed to make money out of the works of this novelist, I may tell you that
the debt against his works stands in our books at considerably over £950!!"
At last Heinemann was impressed—if not by the exclamation points, then
by the deplorably vivid numerals.[24]

Even though Heinemann and the unremunerative author eventually
came to terms, Macmillan insisted that the firm's contract with James in-
demnify the house against possible claims filed by his other English publishers. Such defenses were hardly necessary—not merely because Pinker
had preemptively settled the score, but also because any sums in question
were probably irretrievable. As Macmillan's responses show, he did not
anticipate hefty returns from the Edition because he could see no way to
market it effectively. At eight-shillings, six-pence (equivalent to the $2
American retail price), the volumes were too expensive to be considered
popular; but in material form the Edition was not exclusive enough to be-

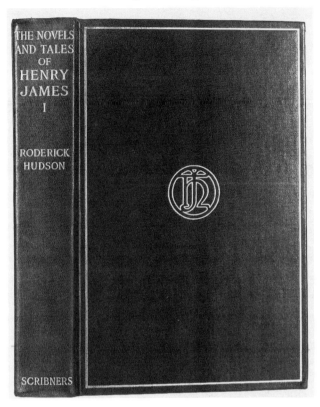

Figure 3. *Roderick Hudson*, volume I of *The Novels and Tales of Henry James*, the New York Edition, issued by Charles Scribner's Sons, New York (1907). Reproduced by permission of The Henry W. and Albert A. Berg Collection, The New York Public Library (Astor, Lenox, and Tilden Foundations).

come an object of connoisseurship. As if nervously aware of this fact, Macmillan's book designers overcompensated by embellishing the spines and covers of the James series with elaborate ornamental devices. Even the master thought "the gilding . . . perhaps a little heavy," especially when compared with the sleek modernity of Scribners' plum-colored binding (see figs. 3 and 4).[25] But from Macmillan's perspective, the books had to be gussied up in order to pass them off as an "Edition de Luxe," a phrase conspicuously used in the firm's paid advertisements and promotional literature.[26]

Despite his obvious misgivings, Macmillan did sell his hundred sets of the Edition—and then some. Contrary to discouraging assertions that

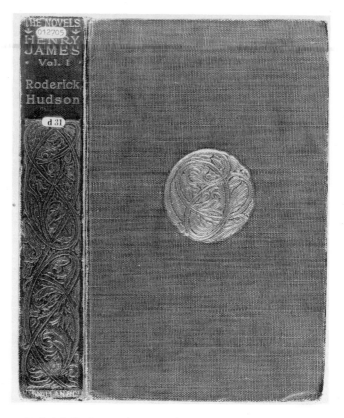

Figure 4. *Roderick Hudson*, volume 1 of *The Novels of Henry James*, issued by Macmillan & Company, London (1908). Even James thought "the gilding . . . perhaps a little heavy." Note too that, in contrast to Scribner's binding, the Macmillan spine omits any reference to James's tales, even though they constituted a third of the Edition's volumes. Reproduced by permission of the British Library.

unbound sheets of Macmillan's initial order were used as package wrapping during the Second World War,[27] documents in the Scribner archive at Princeton University show that the New York house exported additional sets of the Edition at least until the time of James's death in 1916, by which point nearly 300 were in circulation abroad. The repeated requests for relatively small numbers of sheets (usually 25 at a time) reflects the English firm's tight control over inventory and indicates that Macmillan ordered stock only as needed—that is, only when volumes already imported had been sold.[28] Even these revised figures suggest, however, that Frederick Macmillan was correct in assuming that the books would not find a sizable audience. A lifetime of publishing experience with James—and a cumulative deficit of £950—was hardly the prelude to a season of optimism.

From the English publisher's point of view, James's "so-called 'New York Edition'" (Macmillan's phrase) was tainted with a kind of bibliographical illegitimacy. Indeed, Macmillan would hardly have been surprised to hear William Meredith dismiss the English issue as a "so-called 'Edition de Luxe.'" But at the same time that the cost of ordinary English books (especially fiction) was falling drastically, James's volumes had to be maintained at an artificially high price. Even while the definitive series was in preparation, fairly lucrative requests came to the author to reprint some of his early titles in seven-penny editions. Because he was so deeply involved in revising those works (and redefining for himself what portion of his *oeuvre* he wished to perpetuate), James was in a curious bind. How could he reprint anything—now—without first revising? But how could he justifiably sell such work at seven-pence when the Edition would command a much higher price? James briefly flirted with the notion of giving *The Other House* (a work excluded from the Edition) to Thomas Nelson's Seven-Penny Library, but the author's troubled relations with Heinemann eventually ruled that out.[29] Two years later Nelson renewed his request, offering £150 up front; now James was willing to compromise. With his hopes for large returns from the Edition rapidly fading (a cheque for £7 14s. 2d. was all he had yet received), James begged Macmillan to allow Nelson to reprint the revised version of *The American*. ("I have written," James confided to his agent, "in a way that I hope will make my inquiry move him—even a Macmillan—to assent.")[30] By insinuating that his prolonged work on the Edition had plunged him into relative poverty ("It has been . . . & it will at the very best if any future profit from it remain, [be] the most expensive job of my life"),[31] James not only won Macmillan's assent but got an emphatic endorsement. "If [Nelson's reprint] has any effect on the sale of your 'Edition de Luxe,'" Macmillan bluntly affirmed, "it will be a good one."[32]

Whatever its effect on Macmillan's sales, within three years Nelson's cheap edition was earning money for James over and above the decent sum already advanced. Requests for other titles followed—and not only from Nelson. Pinker also received inquiries from Hugh Dent, who wanted James to appear in his Wayfarer's Library (forerunner to the Everyman series).[33] The outbreak of the First World War shelved most of these plans until after James's death, but the aggressive initiation of such proposals suggests that a "popular" market existed for James (or some part of him) that the relatively high-priced Edition de Luxe could not reach. Indeed, Macmillan was ultimately persuaded by Pinker and Percy Lubbock that a cheaper—and more inclusive—edition of James's works would find buyers, and plans were drawn up in 1919 for *The Novels and Stories of Henry James*, later issued (1921–23) in 35 volumes.

The British publication history of the New York Edition actually culminates in this later, more comprehensive series, which attempted to overcome the culturally defined liabilities inherent in its predecessor. Once Macmillan agreed to supplement the Edition by adding *The Bostonians* (which James had omitted only for want of space) and certain stories published later in *The Finer Grain* (1910), "the question may be raised," Lubbock noted, "whether it would not be well to include the other novels which did not appear in the New York Edition." Ironically, Macmillan was not even aware that such omissions had previously occurred: an edition was an edition, and if it was not complete, what was it? "I did not realise," he confessed, "that *The Europeans, Washington Square, Confidence*, and *The Sacred Fount*, as well as *The Bostonians*, were all omitted from the American edition." The only possible explanation for this—and here Macmillan accepted Lubbock's reasoning—was "the Procrustean methods" adopted by the Scribners.[34]

Both of them, of course, were wrong—but not entirely. James, too, had played the part of Procrustes, wanting to sift and select his works, "to quietly disown a few things by not thus supremely adopting them."[35] But his own disposition toward this end was shaped by very careful consideration of market imperatives in the American book trade. Working closely with the Scribners, James structured his Edition with the American market most clearly in view. "New York"—not Sussex—would grace its title pages. The "elaborate edifice" announced by the Edition's prospectus was reared by "the first of American novelists" whose work had "placed him in his present unrivalled position."[36] That position, as we have seen, was hardly uncontested. Undeniably complex—and frequently comic—the publication history of the New York Edition reveals with peculiar vividness how ambiguous James's cultural allegiances finally were. The curious transatlantic career of the Edition allows us to recognize that even the passage of international copyright (1891) could not wholly unify the practices and perspectives of the Anglo-American book trade. Latent within the Edition's "failure," differing and frequently incompatible ideologies of print culture can be discovered. Levin L. Schücking once observed, "The history of the development of publishing methods would be one of the most interesting, though not the most edifying, chapters in a history of literary taste."[37] The "chapter" devoted to James's New York Edition can claim, legitimately, to be both.

Figure 5. A. L. Coburn's "Henry James," frontispiece to *Roderick Hudson*, volume 1 of *The Novels and Tales of Henry James*. Reproduced by permission of the Harry Ransom Humanities Research Center, University of Texas at Austin.

Figure 6. A. L. Coburn's "Faubourg St. Germain," frontispiece to *The American*, volume 2 of *The Novels and Tales of Henry James*. Reproduced by permission of the Harry Ransom Humanities Research Center, University of Texas at Austin.

Figure 7. A. L. Coburn's "The English Home," frontispiece to the first volume of *The Portrait of a Lady*, volume 3 of *The Novels and Tales of Henry James*. Reproduced by permission of the Harry Ransom Humanities Research Center, University of Texas at Austin.

Figure 8. A. L. Coburn's "The Roman Bridge," frontispiece to the second volume of *The Portrait of a Lady*, volume 4 of *The Novels and Tales of Henry James*. Reproduced by permission of the Harry Ransom Humanities Research Center, University of Texas at Austin.

Figure 9. A. L. Coburn's "The Dome of St. Paul's," frontispiece to the first volume of *The Princess Casamassima*, volume 5 of *The Novels and Tales of Henry James*. Reproduced by permission of the Harry Ransom Humanities Research Center, University of Texas at Austin.

Figure 10. A. L. Coburn's "'Splendid Paris, Charming Paris,'" frontispiece to the second volume of *The Princess Casamassima*, volume 6 of *The Novels and Tales of Henry James*. Reproduced by permission of the Harry Ransom Humanities Research Center, University of Texas at Austin.

Figure 11. A. L. Coburn's "The Comédie Français," frontispiece to the first volume of *The Tragic Muse*, volume 7 of *The Novels and Tales of Henry James*. Reproduced by permission of the Harry Ransom Humanities Research Center, University of Texas at Austin.

Figure 12. A. L. Coburn's "St. John's Wood," frontispiece to the second volume of *The Tragic Muse*, volume 8 of *The Novels and Tales of Henry James*. Reproduced by permission of the Harry Ransom Humanities Research Center, University of Texas at Austin.

Figure 13. A. L. Coburn's "Mr. Longdon's," frontispiece to *The Awkward Age*, volume 9 of *The Novels and Tales of Henry James*. Reproduced by permission of the Harry Ransom Humanities Research Center, University of Texas at Austin.

Figure 14. A. L. Coburn's "Some of the Spoils," frontispiece to *The Spoils of Poynton*, in volume 10 of *The Novels and Tales of Henry James*. Reproduced by permission of the Harry Ransom Humanities Research Center, University of Texas at Austin.

Figure 15. A. L. Coburn's "The Cage," frontispiece to *In the Cage*, in volume 11 of *The Novels and Tales of Henry James*. Reproduced by permission of the Harry Ransom Humanities Research Center, University of Texas at Austin.

Figure 16. A. L. Coburn's "Juliana's Court," frontispiece to *The Aspern Papers*, in volume 12 of *The Novels and Tales of Henry James*. Reproduced by permission of the Harry Ransom Humanities Research Center, University of Texas at Austin.

Figure 17. A. L. Coburn's "The Court of the Hotel," frontispiece to *The Reverberator*, in volume 13 of *The Novels and Tales of Henry James*. Reproduced by permission of the Harry Ransom Humanities Research Center, University of Texas at Austin.

Figure 18. A. L. Coburn's "'On Sundays, now, you might be at Home?,'" frontispiece to "Lady Barbarina," in volume 14 of *The Novels and Tales of Henry James*. Reproduced by permission of the Harry Ransom Humanities Research Center, University of Texas at Austin.

Figure 19. A. L. Coburn's "Saltram's Seat," frontispiece to "The Coxon Fund," in volume 15 of *The Novels and Tales of Henry James*. Reproduced by permission of the Harry Ransom Humanities Research Center, University of Texas at Austin.

Figure 20. A. L. Coburn's "The New England Street," frontispiece to "Europe,"
in volume 16 of *The Novels and Tales of Henry James*. Reproduced by permission
of the Harry Ransom Humanities Research Center, University of Texas at Austin.

Figure 21. A. L. Coburn's "The Halls of Julia," frontispiece to "Julia Bride," in volume 17 of *The Novels and Tales of Henry James*. Reproduced by permission of the Harry Ransom Humanities Research Center, University of Texas at Austin.

Figure 22. A. L. Coburn's "By St. Peter's," frontispiece to *Daisy Miller*, in volume 18 of *The Novels and Tales of Henry James*. Reproduced by permission of the Harry Ransom Humanities Research Center, University of Texas at Austin.

Figure 23. A. L. Coburn's "The Doctor's Door," frontispiece to the first volume of *The Wings of the Dove*, volume 19 of *The Novels and Tales of Henry James*. Reproduced by permission of the Harry Ransom Humanities Research Center, University of Texas at Austin.

Figure 24. A. L. Coburn's "The Venetian Palace," frontispiece to the second volume of *The Wings of the Dove*, volume 20 of *The Novels and Tales of Henry James*. Reproduced by permission of the Harry Ransom Humanities Research Center, University of Texas at Austin.

Figure 25. A. L. Coburn's "By Notre Dame," frontispiece to the first volume of *The Ambassadors*, volume 21 of *The Novels and Tales of Henry James*. Reproduced by permission of the Harry Ransom Humanities Research Center, University of Texas at Austin.

Figure 26. A. L. Coburn's "The Luxembourg Gardens," frontispiece to the second volume of *The Ambassadors*, volume 22 of *The Novels and Tales of Henry James*. Reproduced by permission of the Harry Ransom Humanities Research Center, University of Texas at Austin.

Figure 27. A. L. Coburn's "The Curiosity Shop," frontispiece to the first volume of *The Golden Bowl*, volume 23 of *The Novels and Tales of Henry James*. Reproduced by permission of the Harry Ransom Humanities Research Center, University of Texas at Austin.

Figure 28. A. L. Coburn's "Portland Place," frontispiece to the second volume of *The Golden Bowl*, volume 24 of *The Novels and Tales of Henry James*. Reproduced by permission of the Harry Ransom Humanities Research Center, University of Texas at Austin.

Visual Culture:
The Photo Frontispieces
to the New York Edition

Ira B. Nadel

> Pictures, even extremely poor ones, have invariably
> some measure of attraction.
>
> —Alfred Stieglitz, 1899

Isabel Archer begins her education with the "uncontrolled use of a library full of books with frontispieces" (*3*: 29–30) in her grandmother's Albany home, the frontispieces actually guiding her choice of readings, formulating her decisions about texts. This detail suggests James's recognition of the interpretative power of frontispieces, a recognition reiterated by his inclusion of 24 photo frontispieces by Alvin Langdon Coburn in his New York Edition. James's role in directing Coburn concerning the subject matter of the photos, their shared exploration of London locales, and James's control over the final selection of images have been variously documented.[1] But the cultural function of the frontispieces has been neglected and their importance in providing a reality that validates James's fictional world overlooked. This "reading" of the frontispieces establishes them as central to the cultural discourse of an American writer aware of his rejection by a public impatient with serious literature, a fact confirmed by James's declining popularity and sales. One of the goals of the New York Edition, then, is the renewal of James's place in the literary culture of America; James, I shall argue, saw the new and exciting art of photography as one means of regaining the acceptance of the American audience he had lost.[2]

I

Why should not the camera also throw off the shackles of conventional
representation and attempt something fresh and untried?
—Alvin Langdon Coburn,
"The Future of Pictorial Photography" (1916)

At the very time Henry James was preparing his New York Edition and
instructing Coburn on where and what to photograph for his frontispieces,
photography itself was undergoing a radical change. Questioned as to its
documentary reliability and representational authority, despite its institu-
tionalization as the medium of record in such bureaucracies as prisons,
hospitals, and police departments, photography was claiming the status of
a fine art by 1901.[3] The emergence of the Photo-Secessionists in 1902, the
publication of *Camera Work* (1903–17), edited by Alfred Stieglitz, and
the establishment of the Little Galleries of the Photo-Secession at 291 Fifth
Avenue, New York, in 1905, confirmed a shift from an archival to an artistic interest in photography. Coburn, who in 1903 would be elected to the
prestigious avant-garde English photo group The Linked Ring, was also a
member of the Photo-Secessionists and in 1902 opened a studio at 384
Fifth Avenue, New York, not far from Stieglitz and his circle.

Accompanying these developments was a theoretical shift: the realization that photography had a cultural as well as an aesthetic function—that
what it photographed and how it photographed an object expressed and became the discourse of its culture. Photography altered from the art of imitation and illusion to one of self-authenticating images which sought to el-
evate the vernacular into the realm of high culture, while adding to that
culture as a new form of discourse. This new discourse of authenticity
sought to create not imitated works but works that were themselves real
things. Photography became the technical and artistic intermediary between the concreteness of the material object and its abstract existence expressed in its image.[4]

Photography moved from its archival to an artistic role through the
development of pictorialism, the effort of photographers to enhance the
pictorial elements of their prints by creating the look of a painting or drawing. Such pictorial photographs, made by retouching or manipulating a
print to create certain tones or shadings, or by using a soft-focus lens (first
employed by Coburn in 1901) to blur the images to create an atmospheric

quality, soon became the sign of art photography. This modernist version of pictorialism, distinguished from *fin de siècle* pictorialist impressionism, was also identified as "straight photography" by the Photo-Secessionists, who nevertheless had a pictorialist motive.[5] Altering printing techniques and angles in an effort to reinstate the clarity but not the sharpness of an image became the hallmark of the pictorialists, who sought to distinguish themselves from commercial and amateur photographers. The use of the telephoto lens to flatten perspective by placing the near and the far on the same plane, plus reliance on a triangular form of composition (two features of Coburn's work), advanced the originality of the pictorialists and early Photo-Secessionists. Their stress on the plasticity of the medium contributed to their efforts to establish the autonomy of art photography while consciously calling attention to the representational rather than mimetic nature of their images. By doing so, they also generated a cultural lexicon for their images, photographing not so much to record but to interpret their subjects.

Fundamental to this form of photography was composition, a point Coburn emphasized. Avoiding the "monotony of regularity and excessive repetition" became his goal because "exact equality of division lacks mystery."[6] The result for Coburn has been labeled his symbolist phase, referring to the 1905–10 period when he was principally photographing scenes for James's New York Edition. At this time Coburn believed that photography retained a middle ground between naturalism and abstraction, a ground summarized by his unifying of the representational image with an abstract pattern. The artist-illustrator protagonist of James's "The Real Thing" anticipates this aesthetic when he explains that he prefers "the represented subject over the real one." "I liked things that appeared; then one was sure. Whether they *were* or not was a subordinate and almost always a profitless question" (*18*: 317–18). But as Roland Barthes has more recently argued, "every photograph is somehow co-natural with its referent," although the power of authentication often exceeds the power of presentation.[7]

The photo frontispieces to the New York Edition confirm James's awareness that photography possessed the dual function of aesthetic object and cultural expression. Although his early attitude toward photography was critical because it seemed to be only the unimaginative record of experience, James often responded to its cultural and social importance.[8] Not only did he enjoy being photographed, but James valued the photographs

others sent to him. Beginning in August 1854 with Matthew Brady's da-
guerreotype of himself (age 11) and his father, and continuing through numerous snapshots—on the beach at Dunwich, Suffolk, or with his gar-
dener at Lamb house, or doffing his hat casually in front of the Palazzo
Borghese in Rome in 1899 or more formally in Alice Broughton's portrait
of him holding a copy of Meredith's *The Amazing Marriage*, or in the dual
portrait of himself and his brother in 1905—James consistently provided
a photographic iconography that belies his objection to the camera. To the
English journalist Theodore E. Child in 1888, for example, he expressed
thanks for two photographs, one a portrait of Flaubert which James hung
in his study at De Vere Gardens and later at Lamb House.⁹ In December
1905 he thanked Edith Wharton for a formal photograph she sent of herself seated at a desk "thoroughly in possession of [her] genius, fame and
fortune." The picture is to take a prominent place on his mantel, he adds.¹⁰

A letter from James to Hendrik C. Andersen written January 31,
1906, provides a glimpse of the intimacy generated by a photograph. After
praising several photos Andersen had sent of his latest statue, *The Kiss*,
James closes with an admiring yet concerned comment on a photograph of
Andersen himself: "I scan the so handsome fatigued face of the rabbit-
picture for signs reassuring and veracious. I don't know to what extent I
make them out: you're so beautiful in it that I only hope you're exempt
from physical woe. I take hold of you ever so tenderly and am yours ever
so faithfully."¹¹ At the end of a letter written in May 1906 James tells Andersen, "I look your kodaks (as I suppose them) over again, while I write
and they make me groan, in spirit, that I'm not standing there before the
whole company with you."¹²

James translated his early and sustained love of snapshots into a belief
that photographs would enact a cultural discourse for the reader which
would balance, if not enhance, the fictional world they suggest—contrary
to his view that photographs would be likely to compete with his prose, his
original objection to illustrations of his work expressed to Joseph Pennell,
a young American artist, in 1888 and restated in the Preface to *The Golden
Bowl*. To put his new belief in simple terms, photographs would provide a
concretization of the physical world presented in his verbal fictions, while
remaining independent works of art articulating a cultural discourse. The
explanation for James's explicit directions to Coburn may not be lack of
confidence in the 26-year-old photographer as much as his need to make
the selected images representative of an individual "marker" in the culture.

In addition, the representational quality of the images would mitigate the public's rejection of his writing by their immediate identifiability, enhanced by captions if not by their form.[13] The fiction would seem to possess a reality that the photographs, with their pictorial basis, anticipate. The attractiveness of the photo frontispieces would also enhance sales, since they would handsomely add to the format of the deluxe edition and represent the newest art at its most advanced stage—photography as a fine art—implicitly indicating the modernity of James's writing.

A collected edition redefines the value of its individual texts. Not only are the volumes uniformly presented, but their combination offers the *corpus* of the writer to the public. Physical design links one text with another, while the image of the author assumes a solidity and importance the publication of individual texts over a variegated period prevents. Uniformity establishes authenticity, a point James on several occasions made to Scribner's when celebrating the physical production of the series.[14] And as he explained in a letter to the novelist Robert Herrick, the *raison d'être* of his edition lay in its being "selective as well as collective . . . by the mere fact of leaving out certain things . . . I exercise a control, a discrimination."[15] Enhancing the edition with photographs immensely improved the appeal of the edition in the marketplace and acknowledged the commercial nature of its literary production. The commodity nature of James's texts redefined his authority as he capitalized on the general popularity of collected editions at this time. In addition, as he later explained to Scribner's in response to a specimen page for the New York Edition, "the *dignity* of aspect . . . was for this presentment of my books, my dream and desire."[16]

Among the many deluxe editions of the period were the Camden Edition of Whitman in 10 volumes, the Pathfinder Edition of James Fenimore Cooper, and the 8-volume illustrated edition of the works of Lincoln, all published by G. P. Putnam. Scribner's issued a 20-volume illustrated edition of the works of G. A. Henty, a 13-volume uniform edition of Ibsen, begun in 1905 but not finished until 1912, and, of course, the 24-volume New York Edition of James. The popularity of sets continued with Scribner's publishing of the deluxe Triton Edition of the Works of Santayana and the 8-volume Hampstead Edition of Keats. However, the set that especially appealed to James was the 25-volume pictorial edition of Kipling published by Scribner's between 1899 and 1910.[17] Illustrated frontispieces prefaced each volume. The technology that made possible the mechanical reproduction of art that replicated the real thing enhanced the accessibility of individual texts, although there is an irony in the fact that these finely printed and expensive sets were limited to a discriminating and largely wealthy audience.

James's decision to include photographs as frontispieces was not an aesthetic one alone, although he did find most engraved illustrations unsatisfactory for his work. Photography as art was new and controversial, and he realized that the appearance of photographs might enhance the edition because of the American interest in photography at the beginning of the century. Furthermore, the celebrity status conferred on an author by the appearance of his collected works in a deluxe edition consolidated his reputation and importance, and seemed to confirm the positive judgment of history even while the author was alive. James also followed the practice of having the first frontispiece be a portrait of the author, offering his image facing textward (i.e., looking to the right in anticipation of the words to follow) to provide an imprimatur for the work. And confirming his visual authorization of the edition is his hand, literally reproduced through his signature beneath his portrait (*1*: frontispiece [fig. 2]).

The presence of photography in the New York Edition announces James as a modern—or at least as an author sympathetic to the newest and most controversial visual art form. Furthermore, photographs act to transport his works from their original date of publication—whether it be 1875 (*Roderick Hudson*, vol. 1 of the New York Edition), 1877 (*The American*, vol. 2), or 1897 (*What Maisie Knew*, vol. 11)—into the present if not the future. James's fiction becomes part of a new and intriguing art that, despite Coburn's use of filters and success with soft-grained, suggestive images, never creates idealized photographic objects.[18] They are representational and readily identifiable, qualities that the captions, by James, confirm with their reference either to places or to texts. The referentiality of the images reinforces the physicality of the presented world and corroborates the reader's desire for a visual, almost tactile sense of the real. Collectively, they represent a theory of culture, one in which the photograph incorporates a physical reality counterbalancing the imaginary expressed in the fiction. Seeing becomes a visual as well as verbal experience for the reader of James's work. "Look, there is a locatable world in these fictions," the New York Edition seems to state.

Despite its swerve toward the fine arts at the turn of the century and Coburn's use of pictorialist techniques, photography was still largely perceived as the record of authentic experience by the public. The lens saw more than the eye and preserved the visual truth of a subject through detail and exactness. As a writer of the mid-nineteenth century remarked, "each photograph tells a *true* tale concerning a particular spot at a particular time."[19] Photography distorted the truth the least; it recorded the physical world with little interference, and although the artist-photographer always interpreted his image, the public was often unaware of this element. In addition, the photograph created and sustained immediacy. The photographer was always included in the action by virtue of his presence behind the camera at the scene, whereas the engraver or illustrator remained remote, most often reinventing the scene through memory and imagination from the vantage of the studio, not the street. The photographer was *there*, involving the viewer in a way the illustrator could not. No matter how accurate the engraving, it lacked the immediacy of the photograph, which nevertheless also possessed a certain distinguished "beauty," although this was partially lost for James in the necessary reduction of Coburn's photos for reproduction in the Edition (*23*: ix; *AN*, 331). The creation and placement of captions added another heuristic dimension to the content of the photos, although ironically, in composing these captions for Coburn's frontispieces, James precluded the photos from telling their own tales.

The function of Coburn's photographs in the New York Edition is to mitigate the American distrust of the literary and balance the negative response to James's complex fiction, a response centered in the public's rejection of his abstract style. The physical objects photographed in the frontispieces are the foundation of James's house of fiction, anchoring the New York Edition in a satisfying reality that is paradoxically enhanced by the fictional world that follows. The New York Edition, then, documents itself through its photo frontispieces, thus gratifying the wish expressed by an anonymous reviewer in the *Atlantic* for 1904: "I should like to own an illustrated edition of Henry James for my wife and children. The vague, interthreaded abstractions would, under the touch of a really great illustrator, solidify into visual actualities which any child could apperceive." As a postscript, the critic added that James's "style is so easy to write, but difficult to read."[20]

II

The essence of any representational work is of course
to bristle with immediate images.
—Henry James, Preface to *The Golden Bowl*

According to Leon Edel, James anticipated illustrated frontispieces for the
New York Edition from the beginning. James at first suggested hand-
drawn illustrations, possibly by the artist Albert Sterner.[21] But James rejected Sterner—"are twenty Albert Sterner's desirable or even thinkable???"[22]—expressing his preference for Coburn's photographs after
meeting with the photographer for a portrait session in New York in April
1905, viewing his first one-man show in London in February 1906, and
allowing Coburn to photograph him in London and Lamb House in May
and June 1906.[23] To Scribner's in June 1906, James explained that he did
not want the "common black-and-white drawing, of the magazine sort,"
but preferred a "scene, object or locality" associated with a tale "consummately photographed and consummately reproduced."[24]

James had, in fact, recently used photo frontispieces, but in the more
traditional form of the portrait. This was in his two-volume biography,
William Wetmore Story and His Friends (1903), which contains an oval
carte de visite portrait of Story taken by J. J. Waddington with Story's autograph reproduced beneath in volume 1 and a more informal portrait of
Story, also by Waddington and with an autograph, in volume 2. Whether
it was the decision of James or the publisher, the inclusion of the portrait
frontispieces for the biography illustrates the importance of photography
in confirming the presence of a subject. That confirmation is supported
here by the reproduction of Story's signature authorizing the image. It
reads "Yours faithfully, W. W. Story." This common practice James would
emulate in volume 1 of the New York Edition.

James's reputation before beginning work on the New York Edition in
1905/6 had slipped. Sales of his work had fallen not only because of the
public's rejection of his complex writing style but because of its reaction to
his adverse view of America from his 1904 trip, expressed in *The American
Scene* (1907), which appeared serially as early as April 1905 in the *North
American Review* and then in *Harper's Magazine* and the *Fortnightly Review*. But in an effort to reclaim his position and satisfy his financial needs
in his old age, as well as to see his works in a uniform and revised edition,

he pursued the project.[25] Photographs would enhance its appeal while ful-
filling the aesthetic needs of a deluxe edition and confirming James's link
with the modern. But economic news that early sales of the edition were not
going well forced Scribner's to advise James that he would have to consoli-
date and reorganize material for the remaining volumes.[26] Scribner's reported to James, "the volumes of tales [have] reach[ed] proportions destructive of almost all expectation of profitable publication."[27] James
would, therefore, have to redistribute and regroup the material he had
originally sorted, limiting volume 15 to five items and adding a new volume 16, resulting in 24 rather than 23 volumes. But the task in the end
was unprofitable: not only was the set expensive and each of the volumes
lengthy, but James's critical view of America, expressed in *The American
Scene*, made it difficult for readers to respond to him sympathetically. It
was easier, and perhaps fashionable, to spurn him, as he realized in a letter
to his agent, James B. Pinker. Declining an offer of a German translation
of his work, he remarks, "my late ones are things to be read in the original,
for proper appreciation—the appreciation of that very minor and 'cultivated' public to whom, alas, almost solely, my productions *appear* to address themselves."[28] Clearly, James's reputation of being a difficult, although important, writer limited his audience.

An additional and broader cause for the disappointing acceptance of the
New York Edition was the American distrust of the literary, a problem that
James recognized early in his own career and that he saw reflected in the
situation of Hawthorne, the subject of his 1879 critical biography. In "The
Custom-House," the preface to *The Scarlet Letter*, Hawthorne first mentions his rejection by his peers. Acknowledging his Salem identity as an
"idler," he adds that none of his ancestors would recognize his aims as
"laudable, no success of mine . . . would they deem otherwise than worth-
less, if not positively disgraceful. What is he? murmurs one gray shadow
of my forefathers to the other. 'A writer of story-books!' "[29] In his role as
surveyor of revenue in the Salem Custom House, Hawthorne learned how
little valued was the writer: "It is a good lesson—though it may often be a
hard one—for a man who has dreamed of literary fame, and of making for
himself a rank among the world's dignitaries by such means, as to step aside
out of the narrow circle in which his claims are recognized, and to find how
utterly devoid of significance, beyond that circle, is all that he achieves, and
all he aims at."[30] "Lettered intercourse"—the discussion of books as Hawthorne terms it—was rare, and above the collector's apartment in the Cus-

tom House a manuscript filled "with the thought of inventive brains and the rich effusion of deep hearts—had gone . . . to oblivion."[31] In reclaiming such texts, Hawthorne discovers the private documents that reveal local history and, most importantly, the scarlet letter and sheets that explain it.

In his study of Hawthorne, James acknowledges and identifies with the dislocated American writer. Criticizing the shortcomings of American culture, James remarks that "it takes a great deal of history to produce a little literature" and that literature "needs a complex machinery to set a writer in motion."[32] America was incapable of providing such a history or mechanism. America lacked a complex, stimulating society and disavowed a national literature and culture. The American character, he later stated, gave the impression of "a conscience grasping in the void, panting for sensations."[33] In the midst of James's criticism of "provincial" America comes the theme of the displacement of the American writer and the nation's distrust of literature:

It is not too much to say that even to the present day it is a considerable discomfort in the United States not to be "in business." The young man who attempts to launch himself in a career that does not belong to the so-called practical order . . . has but a limited place in the social system. . . . Fifty years ago . . . the literary man must have lacked the comfort and inspiration of belonging to a class.[34]

Hawthorne, James continues, "was one of, at most, some dozen Americans who had taken literature as a profession. The profession in the United States is still very young, and of diminutive stature."[35] Not surprisingly, in James's fiction the discovery by American "businessmen" of the value of imagination—a discovery that occurs almost exclusively in Europe—becomes one of his major answers to the question of how America can reclaim a lost spirit and artistic sensibility, whether the individual is Caspar Goodwood or Lambert Strether.

James's disillusionment with America finds later expression in *The American Scene*. While crisscrossing America in 1904, James found that the status of the writer had changed little. His journeys generated respect and attention but not the adulation or popularity he believed a writer of his stature deserved, and he returned to Europe with a renewed sense of belonging there. His decision in 1915 to become a naturalized British subject, sponsored by no less a personage than the prime minister, H. H. Asquith, confirmed his rejection of America, though he explained the naturalization as his acknowledgment of having lived in England for some

40 years and having gained literary recognition there. News of this act brought further criticism of James.

Henry Adams concurred with James's recognition of American uneasiness with culture and literature. Throughout the *Education*, Adams criticizes the uncomfortable disjunction of culture and the American experience. Commenting on his constant dislocation, Adams remarks, "the American character showed singular limitations which sometimes drove the student of civilized man to despair."[36] Americans "could not face a new thought. . . . They knew not how to amuse themselves; they could not conceive how other people were amused. Work, whiskey and cards were life." Adams admits that "even in America and in the twentieth century, life could not be wholly industrial." Nevertheless, culture only "amuses"; it never becomes serious or valued for itself. Adams's disaffection with America by 1892 reflected his conclusion that it "shunned, distrusted, disliked, the dangerous attraction of ideals, and stood alone in history for its ignorance of the past."[37]

Despite the American distrust of culture so painful to Adams, James persisted with the New York Edition, a work sponsored by an American publisher for an American audience. One irony, however, was his decision to eliminate the so-called "Scenes from American Life": *The Bostonians*, *Washington Square*, *The Europeans*, and his American short stories. Perhaps in his search for prominence, James wanted to be recognized as a cultural figure on the universal Eurocentric scale celebrated in an 1867 article in *Harper's*: "Homer, Shakespeare, Dante, Raphael, Michael Angelo, Handel, Beethoven, Mozart, they are the towering facts like the Alps or the Himalaya. They . . . are universally acknowledged. It is not conceivable that the judgment of mankind upon those names will ever be reversed."[38] Ironically, James's desire to be recognized *in* America as an American writer was premised, perhaps wrongly, on his self-identification as a European writer.

America's suspicion of literature and art stemmed from a Puritan fear of literature as an invitation to idleness, an idleness not only pernicious in itself but subversive to the practical goals and life of the country. This meant that many artists felt they could only survive elsewhere, most naturally (and cheaply) in Europe. Hawthorne, again, outlines the situation. At the close of the "The Custom-House," he rejects Salem, and although its memory lingers, he sadly but clearly concludes:

I am a citizen of somewhere else. My good townspeople will not much regret me; for—though it has been as dear an object as any, in my literary efforts, to be of some importance in their eyes, and to win myself a pleasant memory in this abode and burial place of so many of my forefathers—there has never been, for me, the genial atmosphere which a literary man requires, in order to ripen the best harvest of his mind. I shall do better amongst other faces; and these familiar ones, it need hardly be said, will do just as well without me.[39]

Henry Adams, whose view of America was similar, also revoked his past. "In thus sacrificing his heritage," he writes of himself, "he only followed the path that had led him from the beginning. . . . He had reckoned from childhood on outlawry as his peculiar birthright." He had to "educate himself over again" to survive, an aim he pursued first in Washington and then in Europe.[40]

III

The picture was . . . also completely to speak for itself.
—James, Preface, *The Golden Bowl*

James, who generally disliked illustrations, possessed a complex view of frontispieces, describing a successful one as an image that can "speak for its connexion with something in the book, and yet at the same time speak enough for its odd or interesting self" (*23*: xi; *AN*, 333). The photo is simultaneously attached to the text and separated from it. This, of course, requires the image to reflect a key aspect of the work yet possess enough aesthetic independence to be free of it. In a famous passage from the Preface to *The Golden Bowl*, James refers to the photographs as "optical symbols or echoes, expressions of no particular thing in the text" (*23*: xi; *AN*, 333). As an opening or aperture to the text, the image must delicately suggest the perceptions of the work while maintaining its own integrity.

The frontispiece to volume 10 of the New York Edition, containing *The Spoils of Poynton, A London Life*, and "The Chaperon," is a case in point. Captioned "Some of the Spoils," the image is that of Room 21 of the Wallace Collection, located in the eighteenth-century mansion of the marquesses of Hertford in London at Manchester Square. The third marquess, who died in 1842, was pilloried by Thackeray as Lord Steyne in *Vanity Fair*. The photograph (fig. 14) shows an ornate clock attributed to Boulle on an equally ornate fireplace; Sevres porcelain flanks the timepiece, balanced by two ornate candelabras. Paintings in the room are by Desportes, Lancret, and others. James particularly admired the "divine little chimney piece, with all its wonderful garniture, [and] . . . the pale green figured damask of the wall."[41] In front of the fireplace is what appears to be an embroidered screen; on either side is a chair. To the left are two paintings hanging on the damask-covered walls. Beautiful art objects, the currency of *The Spoils*, are the subjects of the photo—the result of James's conscientious efforts to gain permission to have the room photographed.

In a letter of December 7, 1906, James tells Coburn that it may not be necessary to leave for Venice as planned: "It will depend on Claude Phillips's [the curator] giving leave for Room 21 of the Wallace Collection. If he does so I can put 'Aspern Papers' in the same volume with *Spoils of Poynton*, and make *Spoils* plate serve . . . Take no step, therefore, till I hear about Room 21." Two days later James eagerly reports receipt of the Wallace Collection permit and provides an unusual degree of detail for the photograph and conduct of the photographer:

Here is the Permit for the Wallace Collection—perhaps you could go *tomorrow*. Please note the day and *hours*: *Mondays* 9–12. And Mr. Phillips, the Keeper, has asked me to tell you to ask the Attendant if he will *see* you, as he would like to do, if he is on the premises. (He probably doesn't get there till after 10.) And take the beautiful Subject *obliquely*, won't you?—and with as much of the damask on wall as possible. And, further, please give the attendant, as a tip, 2/6 [2s. 6d.] for me: (I will send you a postal order for same in the morning—I can't buy one today Sunday). I also enclose my own card.

And now, in spite of this, I think on further and intenser reflection, that you HAD better go to Venice and proceed as we have arranged. I *want* the Casa Capello, and will arrange (in order, purposely to *get* it) to change my order of combinations somehow—putting "In the Cage" with "The Spoils" and "The Aspern Papers" with something else where its picture will still be so valuable. The more *foreign* plates we have the better. . . . If you can't do Room 21 tomorrow, wait till you come back—though the Christmas holidays are a bad time generally. May every luck and success attend you!

Following this pressure to photograph Room 21 of the Wallace Collection as quickly as possible, James adds this postscript: "P.S. The 'January 31st 1906' [on the permit] must be a slip of the pen for 1907—as the date itself, of the Permit, proves."[42] Such detail, such concern and control over this picture, illustrates James's constant direction of Coburn's picture taking, whether in England, Italy, or America. What the photo demonstrates, however, is an objective scene equivalent not to a single moment in *The Spoils* but to its overall treatment and description of riches. It roots the novel in the physical and identifiable, even if few readers (and certainly fewer American readers) would recognize the subject as Room 21 of the Wallace Collection.

This balancing of the fictional with the physical occurs throughout the New York Edition's photo frontispieces. A small detail reinforcing their independence from the texts is the separation of the captions from the photographs. All captions appear on separate tissue-paper overleaves, which actually, when the pages are laid flat, read on the title pages rather than the photographs since they are rectos while the photos are all versos. The caption for the photo of *The Portrait of a Lady*, volume 3 of the Edition, illustrates this clearly. The photo of the magnificent English garden estate, taken from the lawn and looking up to the house (fig. 7), is placed sideways on the page in order to maintain its horizontal impact and grandeur. The book must actually be turned to view the image. But then it must be righted to read James's caption, "The English Home," which is printed on the separate tissue overleaf, superimposed on the title page when laid flat, thus creating a curious subtitle to the volume. The captions on the tissue guards all fall neatly between the lines of the double ruled border surrounding the title, author's name, ship-and-bridge device, publisher's name and date. More importantly, this separation reinforces the integrity of the images, for it allows each frontispiece to exist in its own space and frame *without a text*. In this physical way each image is permitted "completely to speak for itself" (23: xii; *AN*, 334), although the placement of the photos challenges the reader to puzzle out the relationship between the floating caption, image, title, and text. This underscores James's desire to maintain the photographs as "separate and independent subject[s] of publication" (23: x; *AN*, 332).

Volume 4 of the Edition, containing the second volume of *Portrait*, repeats the design of volume 3 with another sideways horizontal photograph and a separate caption. But in contrast to the strong horizontal lines of "The English Home," with its implied hierarchies of value and authority, the image of volume 4 is that of a half-circle, a span of the famous Ponte Sant' Angelo, which crosses the Tiber and connects the Vatican with secular Rome (fig. 8). Decorated with ten majestic sculptured figures of angels modeled by Bernini, each bearing a symbol of Christ's Passion, the narrow bridge leads from the old city of Rome to Castel Sant' Angelo, originally

Hadrian's tomb. In addition to designing the angels in response to Pope Clement IX's desire to modernize the bridge in 1667, Bernini remodeled the bridge itself by lowering the balustrades, allowing people to see the dome of St. Peter's to the west. Isolated in Coburn's image is the diminutive form of a single, shadowed individual in a boat caught almost exactly in the vertical plane created by two lamps virtually at the center of the bridge.

The second volume of *Portrait* begins with chapter 28, which is the second of two sections dealing with Roman architecture, the earlier chapter (27) ending with a visit by Isabel Archer, accompanied by Lord Warburton and others, to the "tesselated acres" (*3*: 424) of St. Peter's for vespers, the later chapter beginning with Warburton's visit to the opera theater where Isabel Archer and Gilbert Osmond watch a performance of Verdi (*4*: 1). Warburton and Osmond meet in chapter 27 for the first time and again in chapter 28 as England and Italy come into conflict, the horizontal encountering the curved. Osmond later reinforces the link between the circle and Italy when he remarks to Isabel, who has traveled round the world, "Don't put us in a parenthesis—give us a chapter to ourselves" (*4*: 14). And in the midst of his declaration of love for Isabel, Osmond extends the union of Italy and circles by turning "his hat, which he had taken up, slowly round with a movement which had all the decent tremour of awkwardness and none of its oddity" (*4*: 19). The Ponte Sant' Angelo allegorically introduces Isabel's "Passion," figuratively presented by the Bernini statues. It also suggests the difficult bridge Isabel must build between the secular and religious lives she faces, one represented by Warburton and England, the other by Osmond and life in Rome with Pansy. Circles are everywhere in Italy, and no less so than in the overall plot, which sees the return of Isabel to Pansy and Osmond after her visit to the dying Ralph. Not surprisingly, the Florentine villa taken by Mrs. Touchett is called Palazzo Crescentini, the house of the crescent (or half circle), while Isabel's last name contains, perhaps too obviously, the word "arch," a half circle evoked by Coburn's picture "The Roman Bridge."[43] But, of course, no direct correspondence to the text exists, since James insisted that illustrations should express "no particular thing in the text, but only . . . the type or idea of this or that thing" (*23*: xi; *AN*, 333). They are not intended "to keep anything like dramatic step with their suggestive matter" (*23*: x; *AN*, 333). Rather, the geometric contrast of images—the horizontality of "The English Home" and the half arch of "The Roman Bridge"—echoes the differences between England and Italy repeated in the novel.

Other photographs similarly resonate with their texts, but always in balance between representation and evocation, the former lending physical credence to the fiction, the latter generating an identity or association with the text. The illustration for volume 11, captioned on the recto tissue paper as "The Cage," demonstrates this double impulse well (fig. 15). The volume contains three stories: *What Maisie Knew*, *In the Cage*, and "The Pupil," although as James told Coburn in a letter dated December 9, 1906, he had had some difficulty in selecting the contents. Nevertheless, when he finally settled on the titles, he established a set of stories that involved entrapment and the conflict between hope and disillusionment.

In his letter of December 7, 1906, James reminds Coburn:

There will be then another thing that I haven't mentioned for "In the Cage": a London corner, if possible, with a grocer's shop containing a postal-telegraph office. This will be very good, and rather amusing to hunt for, if the right one be findable. It will all depend upon that, but a good deal of hunting may do it—all the more that I'm not sure the thing need absolutely be a corner. Look for grocer's shops with post-offices inside.[44]

The hunt was a success, as the photograph reveals. The bisected storefront divided into a post office and grocer's store has a huge mailbox intruding on the window space to the left. Identifying the building are the massive capitals which read "POST OFFICE," ironically footnoted with large advertisements for Sugar and Coffee, and then the smaller sign in the center of the divided windows reading "Post Office / for / money order savings bank / PARCEL POST TELEGRAPH / INSURANCE AND ANNUITY & / INLAND REVENUE STAMP BUSINESS." Across the grocery-store's front are the words "Mazawattee Tea."

Contrast strongly defines "The Cage," with the foreground of the patterned pavement and curb setting off and framing the divided black and white of the windows. The slit of the mailbox suggests an ingesting mouth, swallowing secrets, while the tea advertisement, supported by the packages and prices of the imported tea in the window, evokes the exotic and romantic. The patterning, in contrast to the severity of the building, suggests "*all* the dimensions" necessary to grasp reality. In the Preface to *In the Cage*, James speaks of "his love, when it is a question of a picture, of anything that makes for proportion and perspective, that contributes to a view of *all* the dimensions" (*11*: xviii; *AN*, 153; James's emphasis). The presence of the actual London post office / grocery store for the viewer intensifies the reality of the story for the reader; at the same time, it vivifies the image of

the experiences of the telegraphist while merging her private fancies—
what James calls her "winged intelligence" (11: xxi; *AN*, 157)—with the
commodity street-culture of the city, uniting the economic aspect of the
photographic reality with the fictional text. The photograph visually confirms James's absorption with "seeing 'through'—one thing through another, accordingly, and still other things through *that*" (11: xviii; *AN*,
153–54; James's emphasis). Characterizing all three of the stories included
in the volume, James writes, "the muddled state too is one of the very
sharpest of the realities, that it also has colour and form and character, has
often in fact a broad and rich comicality, many of the signs and values of
the appreciable" (11: xiii; *AN*, 149). This combination of the vague and
the detailed, the suggestive and the identifiable, is precisely the operation
and function of the photo frontispieces by Coburn.

The problem of rooting James's fiction in the real is partially resolved
by the process of "seeing 'through'" the actuality of the subjects in the photo
frontispieces to the texts they accompany. Photography between 1900 and
1910 was in a transitional stage, with the camera becoming an expressive
instrument for Coburn that could transform the immediate into the imaginary. Yet despite his later experiments with vorticism, his work for James
was largely literal, architectural, and exterior. To photograph objects in
their surroundings was Coburn's goal, while he altered impressions of life
into photographic reality. But this very reality served to stabilize and con-
cretize James's admittedly dense and indeterminate fictional world.

One mark of this reality is the incorporation of figures in the photographs. Coburn's pictures are *not* devoid of people, despite James's statement in the Preface to *The Golden Bowl* that they "were to remain at the
most small pictures of our 'set' stage with the actors left out" (23: xi; *AN*,
333). To the contrary, people appear in 10 of the 24 frontispieces, including "The Roman Bridge" of volume 4, with its solitary figure in a boat;
"'Splendid Paris, Charming Paris,'" in volume 6, with its numerous figures around the Arc de Triomphe; "The Comédie Français" of volume 7,
with figures both on the sidewalk and in the columns; "The Luxembourg
Gardens" of volume 22, peopled by the nurse and pram, individuals seated
on the benches, and the naked statue; and, finally, "Portland Place" of volume 24, with its cabmen.

Even when a scene is empty, the presence of individuals is imminent.
There is a constant sense of someone about to appear, especially behind
doors, whether the door is that of James's own at Lamb House, in the fron-

tispiece captioned "Mr. Longdon's" for volume 9, or the door in "Juliana's Court," frontispiece for volume 12. The elegantly set table for two, shown in "The Court of the Hotel" (fig. 17), the frontispiece of volume 13—containing *The Reverberator*, "Madame de Mauves," "A Passionate Pilgrim," "The Madonna of the Future," and "Louisa Pallant"—clearly renders the sense of imminent arrival found in several of the photographs. The incorporation in the New York Edition of such photographs containing actual figures and intimating others is a further defense against charges that James's fictional world lacks reality or solidity. By including the photographs, James and Scribner's were no doubt attempting to make the edition more attractive to readers.

IV

Necessary for the acceptance of James's work in America was the validation of its actuality—an actuality Coburn's representational photographs helped to confirm. Despite their fine-art quality, the frontispieces always present the identifiable, the concrete. They are images, first, of fact, and then of the imagination. James similarly acknowledges the claims of the real, and so counteracts charges of abstract and diffusive writing in his prefaces' repeated accounts of the sources of his fiction. He constantly identifies the origins of his stories to support their credibility, whether it is the narrative told to him by his American doctor friend (most likely Dr. W. W. Baldwin) in a dawdling Italian train during a summer's day which became the germ of "The Pupil" (*11*: xv; *AN*, 150–51), or the story reported to him by a Roman acquaintance in the autumn of 1877 of an American woman whose young daughter, "a child of nature and of freedom, . . . had 'picked up' by the wayside, with the best conscience in the world, a good looking Roman," which became the source of *Daisy Miller* (*18*: v; *AN*, 267). The need to provide such sources for his fiction is a further sign of his effort, evident in the photo frontispieces, to supply authenticity for his tales.

The photo frontispieces of the New York Edition reassert the link between James's fiction and the physical world. The carapace of reality they create helps defend his work from charges of abstraction while adding a visual dimension that complements his texts and fulfills the demands of the deluxe edition. Furthermore, Coburn's photographs visually formulate the cultural discourse of the Jamesian world as a record of images existing in a defined space and time. This role of the photographs enlarges their importance from aesthetic to cultural objects, paralleling the overall importance of the edition as a commodity produced to solidify James's acceptance in America through the renewal of his fiction's links with the actual. The photographs express James's desire to extend a deeper relation between his writing and the material world—and by so doing to reclaim an audience he believed might still value his work.

Revision, Rewriting, Rereading; or, "An Error [Not] in *The Ambassadors*"

Jerome McGann

In his Preface to the New York Edition of *The Golden Bowl* James reflects on his understanding of the idea of textual revision. It is a famous Jamesian text. Once daunted by "the grand air with which the term Revision had, to [his] imagination, carried itself," James has come to a new understanding of the matter:

> To revise is to see, or to look over, again—which means in the case of a written thing neither more nor less than to re-read it. I had attached to it, in a brooding spirit, the idea of re-writing. . . . I had thought of re-writing as so difficult, and even so absurd, as to be impossible—having also . . . thought of re-reading in the same light. . . . What re-writing might be was to remain—it has remained for me to this hour—a mystery. On the other hand the act of revision, the act of seeing it again, caused whatever I looked at on any page to flower before me as into the only terms that honourably expressed it; and the "revised" element in the present Edition is accordingly these terms, these rigid conditions of re-perusal, registered; so many close notes, as who should say, on the particular vision of the matter itself that experience had at last made the only possible one. (*23*: xvi; *AN*, 338–39)

For James, the textual changes in the New York Edition do not register a rewriting but a rereading. They are signs of an interpretive move, a commentary ("close notes") which he is making upon his own text—the signs of what his further "experience" has revealed to him about the meaning of his original writing. Like Chad and Strether and so many of James's other fictional characters, James's texts change under the pressure of events, but the changes are not essential alterations; they are revelations—clarifications—of what was always and originally true.

I shall shortly return to this important distinction between rewriting and rereading. For now I want to look at James's next set of comments:

What it would be really interesting, and I dare say admirably difficult, to go into would be the very history of the effect of experience; the history . . . of the growth of the immense array of terms, perceptional and expressional, that, after the fashion I have indicated, in sentence, passage, and page, simply looked over the heads of the standing terms—or perhaps, like alert winged creatures, perched on those diminished summits and aspired to a clearer air. (*23*: xxix; *AN*, 339)

"It would be . . . difficult" to "go into" such a history, for James, because to do so would entail proliferating an endless and regressive series of textual "revisions"—that is, interpretations of the interpretations, rereadings of the rereadings.

But it would not be difficult for James's *readers* to "go into" that history, especially if his readers were supplied with critical editions of his works. James's project anticipates the coming of, for example, the Norton Critical Edition of *The Ambassadors*.[1] To achieve the "clearer air" of a deepened understanding requires a dialectical vision, an interplay between the "standing terms" of the first writing and the "immense array of [new] terms" which are there to expose the latent meanings and secrets of the "standing terms." When James was revising his novel for the New York Edition he was able to gain, for a brief moment, that longed-for "clearer air" where his newly fledged "alert winged creatures" actually "perched" above their (now) "diminished summits." But in the Edition as published in 1909 that busy scene is entirely gone. The "alert winged creatures" are now leadenly fixed as "standing terms."

Happily for James, scholarship came to rescue his last "revisionary" imagination for his fiction. Archivists and libraries preserve the documents on which he worked and critical editors recover them for us in the texts they produce. And close readers have even come to "revise" James's physical texts! Who will ever forget that moment in 1950—41 years after James's New York Edition appeared—when a close rereading of *The Ambassadors* changed the text as we knew it.

HENRY: "A curious error which has no parallel in the annals of American literature appears in all [currently in print] editions of Henry James's novel, *The Ambassadors* . . . . : *chapters 28 and 29 are in reverse order*."[2]

JAMES: Yes—those were the very words with which that fateful essay began!

HENRY: I just made a statement of fact.

JAMES: Well, not exactly. You just *quoted* a statement of fact made in 1950 by Robert E. Young, in his famous essay "An Error in *The Ambassadors.*" Young's statement was correct in 1950, but now in 1995 it is no longer correct.

HENRY: Forty-five years later—in 1995—Mr. Young's statement remains accurate.

JAMES: It's true Young published his essay 45 years ago, but nothing else that you said is true. Now, 45 years later, Young's words express the opposite of what is the case. Now *all* the currently in print editions of *The Ambassadors* have put chapters 28 and 29 into their proper order. Criticism has intervened to revise and correct the text.

HENRY: As I said, I just made a statement of fact.

JAMES: What are you talking about!

HENRY: I mean simply that Young's famous statement was *in fact* not true in 1950. But it is true now, in 1995. And I hope that the statement will be untrue once again very soon.

JAMES: What are you saying—that chapters 28 and 29 as we read them in (for instance) the Norton Critical Edition of the novel "*are in reverse order*"?

HENRY: Exactly. And I think it's fair to say that this "curious error . . . [probably] has no parallel in the annals of American literature." And I would add—again quoting the prescient Mr. Young—that "perhaps the most astonishing feature of this curious matter is that it has gone unnoticed for so long a time despite the many readers and literary commentators (in and out of academic circles) who have delved into the work" (253).

JAMES: My friend, Young's 1950 essay showed that chapters 28 and 29 made no sense when read in the order of their appearance in the New York Edition or—its immediate source—the first American edition. And Young's argument has persuaded later editors and scholars—even those hostile and condescending to Young, like Leon Edel—to reverse the chapters and put them in their logically correct and necessary order.

HENRY: As I said, "*chapters 28 and 29 are in reverse order.*"

JAMES: No, now they are in *correct* order. They were in *reverse* order in the editions Young saw in 1950.

HENRY: You say that because you have accepted Young's views. I am saying Young was wrong, and to me it is indeed "astonishing" that Young's mistake "has gone unnoticed for so long a time" etc. etc.—exactly as long as the mistaken mistake Young imputed to James in 1950!

JAMES: So you're saying that there never was a mistake in the ordering of the chapters?

HENRY: Not exactly. There was a mistake, but it wasn't in the New York Edition of 1909 or its exemplar, the first American edition of 1903. Rather, it was in the first English edition of 1903—the only early text, according to received scholarly opinion, which preserves the "correct" ordering of chapters 28 and 29.

Let's recall the basic terms of the problem. First of all Robert Young published his notorious essay in 1950 arguing that the authoritative order of the chapters—that is to say, the order sanctioned by James in the 1909 New York Edition—presented certain problems of narrativity. The crux of the matter for Young involved apparent chronological anomalies. For example, in the (original) chapter 28, "we learn that Sarah is leaving that evening for Switzerland. Yet in chapter 29, Strether, meeting with Chad around midnight of that evening, speaks of his intention of seeing her again before her departure. . . . Neither mentions the fact that she has [already] left Paris, and therefore that it is no longer possible for him to do so" (247).

And again: "During this conversation, Chad tells Strether that he had talked with Sarah on the previous morning. . . . Yet though Sarah presumably called on Strether as a result of Chad's urging, her visit to Strether appears to have taken place the previous morning; that is, before Chad even talked with her. Obviously, the chronological sequence of events is out of joint" (248). Young points out other related problems, but these are the telling ones. His analysis of these cruxes leads him to the "contention that (the present) chapter 29 belongs properly before (the present) chapter 28. When this transposition is made, all discrepancies vanish" (248).

JAMES: And what is your point?

HENRY: That Young's words remain true to this day. The present chapter 29—for instance, in the Norton Critical Edition—belongs properly before the present chapter 28. When this transposition is made—when this return to the ordering of the New York Edition is made—all discrepancies vanish.

JAMES: What discrepancies? The only discrepancies seem to be those Young mentions, and they support *his* view about the reversed order in the New York Edition. So far as I can see, everyone now agrees that these narrative discrepancies exist in the New York Edition.[3]

HENRY: And also in its immediate exemplar, the first American edition of 1903—the edition James used to enter his corrections for the New York Edition when he was revising in 1908. The order is the same in both of those editions.

JAMES: Yes, of course. But that perpetuation of the error only served to support the second part of Young's argument: that the narrative anomalies arose because of the involutions of James's late prose style.

HENRY: In several later responses to Young, Leon Edel bristled at Young's suggestion that the narrative problem was the fault of the master's late prose style. According to Young, "there must be something radically wrong with a writing style that has managed to obscure an error of this magnitude for so many years from the probing eyes of innumerable readers, publishers, editors, critics, and even the author himself" (253). Edel's responses to Young challenged this attack on James's late fictional prose . . .

JAMES: But Edel did not challenge Young's main point: that the two chapters were in reverse order in the first American edition of 1903 and its descendant text, the New York Edition of 1909. Edel accepted that as fact, and so has everyone else ever since.[4]

HENRY: And everyone ever since has been mistaken. There is nothing wrong with the order of the chapters in the New York Edition.

JAMES: Start explaining. I've had enough of your paradoxes.

HENRY: All right, let's start with the discrepancies. Not the ones that Young saw in James's fictional narrative, but certain other problems that arise when we accept Young's historical narrative of the novel's composition history.

To accept Young's view means that we have to believe James himself twice missed seeing the reversed chapter ordering. On each occasion James was proofing, correcting, and revising his novel. The first occasion was in 1903 when he was preparing the first American and the first English editions for publication; the second was when he was doing the same for the New York Edition, in 1908.[5] Everyone agrees James carried out this kind of work with meticulous attention and thoroughness—everyone except

Edel, that is, who defended James's late style by impugning his late proof-
reading. How could James have blundered the chronology so badly as
Young has charged?

Young saw this historical and bibliographical problem but he did not
deal with it—indeed, was not equipped to deal with it. His interest was
fixed at the level of narrative chronology. Admittedly, he did address the
compositional and printing problems. But he did so obliquely, in his essay's
concluding polemic where he ventriloquized certain ideas of his mentor
Yvor Winters.[6] The novel's historical and bibliographical difficulties came
about, according to Young and Winters, not because James failed to proof-
read or correct with care but because—despite such efforts—his late prose
style was simply too byzantine even for its own author.

When Young published his essay, Edel was the undisputed living authority on the works of Henry James. It naturally fell to him to make a
response. What he wrote proved to be decisive. Making no challenge to
Young's literary-critical points, Edel moved to absolve James of responsibility for the supposed error in the chapter ordering. He pointed out a few
minor mistakes of fact in Young's bibliographical history, and from there
went on to narrate a theoretical history of the novel's composition and printing.

JAMES: You don't have to retell it again.

HENRY: Perhaps not, but one does want to recall that Edel's theoretical history was not only immensely influential on later editors and critics
but also quite wrong on several crucial points.

JAMES: What points?

HENRY: Edel told how *The Ambassadors* was first serialized in a
slightly abbreviated version in the *North American Review* (January–December 1903), in twelve numbered parts. This text lacked, among other
chapters and parts of chapters, the original chapter 29. The novel was then
issued as a book, with its full complement of chapters, in September 1903
as the first English edition, published by Methuen. As it happened, this
Methuen edition printed the problematic chapters in the order favored by
Young—a fact unknown to Young, but pointed out by James's champion
Edel. The novel's next printing was the first American edition, issued by
Harper's in November 1903, where the offending chapters were "re-
versed" from the Methuen order. Edel went on to show that the New York
Edition was printed from the first American edition—with the supposed

"incorrect" chapter ordering—and not from the first English edition, with the supposed "correct" ordering.

JAMES: Isn't that historical sequence accurate?

HENRY: Yes, so far as it goes. The problem is that Edel also supplied a microhistory of the English and American editions that was intended to shift the blame for the supposed "reversed" chapters to confused circumstances of publication and blunders by house editors. For Edel, the "correct" Methuen order shows that James knew what he was doing with his novel's chapters, that he got the sequence right for the first book publication. But things went awry in James's dealings with Harper's, according to Edel, and the supposed error of chapter sequence in the first American edition occurred because of what Edel calls "bad reading rather than bad writing (and of course careless printing)."[7]

JAMES: For Edel, James was one of those "bad readers," wasn't he?

HENRY: Yes, Edel is forced to concede two points on that score: that James, like his editor and/or printer at Harper's, missed the "error" of the reversed chapters in 1903; and that James once again failed to see the problem when he was revising in 1908 for the New York Edition. The latter happened, according to Edel, "because Scribner used the ['bad'] American edition [rather than the 'good' English edition] and James did not subject his late works to the close revision of his earlier writings" when he was correcting for the New York Edition.[8]

JAMES: That seems plausible enough.

HENRY: It has proved so for 45 years. But in fact this representation is partly wrong and wholly misleading. In the first place, the surviving documents for the New York Edition of *The Ambassadors* suggest that James was no less attentive to that text than he was to his earlier ones. That he made fewer changes to the text of *The Ambassadors* than to the text of (say) *Roderick Hudson* is no sign he didn't read the former with his usual care.

In the second place, we now know much more about the publishing history of the two book versions of his 1903 novel. This extended information tells us, quite unambiguously, that it is the first American edition, and not the first English edition, which is the text that James supervised and corrected with greatest accuracy and thoroughness. Indeed, much of the first English edition was printed from "defective" copy that James had no chance to correct, and this bad copy supplied the material for chapters 28 and 29.[9]

In short, the bibliographical history all argues that the chapter order in the first American edition, as well as the (corresponding and descendant) order in the New York Edition, are precisely what James intended the order to be. Furthermore, we know now that James wanted the first American edition and the first English edition "to be identical."[10]

JAMES: So?

HENRY: This means that if the sequence of chapters 28 and 29 got mixed up in either of the 1903 texts, it happened in the first English edition and not—as everyone, following Edel's lead, has always surmised—in the first American edition. And if it is right in the first American edition, it is still right in the New York Edition . . .

JAMES: . . . and wrong in the post-1950 editions which explicitly revert to the chapter sequence of the Methuen text.

HENRY: Right. And James's (unpublished) correspondence in late 1903 with Mrs. Humphrey Ward about *The Ambassadors* corroborates this view of the matter.

Mrs. Ward had evidently written to James, shortly after she obtained a copy of the Methuen edition (published September 24), that she was going to read the novel. On October 27 James wrote back to deprecate the book somewhat.[11] After finishing the novel, Mrs. Ward wrote an enthusiastic letter about it to James. James was of course very pleased, and after saying so when he wrote back on December 16, he made the following remarkable revelation (the full letter is printed in an appendix at the end of this essay): "the book is, intrinsically, I daresay, the best I have written in spite of a fearful though much patched over fault or weakness in it (which, however, I seem to see no one has noticed & which nothing will induce me *now* ever to reveal not at least till some one does spot it)."[12]

Three matters are especially important here. First, we must remember that James and Ward are corresponding about the Methuen text, not the Harper text.[13] Second, James's tone is extreme enough that the error he mentions would have to be serious—something as "fearful" as the reversed chapters. (When James revised his text for the 1909 New York Edition we find no correction which could reasonably correspond to a problem like the one he mentions in the letter.) Third, the letter tells us that James caught this error at the time it occurred, in 1903. This is something we would expect of a writer so scrupulous and even finicky as he was. James's letter therefore entirely disposes of the received view—which began with Edel and which has always been difficult to believe—that James simply missed the error.

James was embarrassed to reveal the problem with his text, and in fact he seems never to have told anyone else about it, not even his publishers. In the event he was able to deal with the problem without saying anything. In 1908, when revising for the New York Edition, he chose to work from a copy of the Harper rather than the Methuen. As *The Ambassadors* passed into what James saw as its perfected final condition, the "fearful" error was to be silently removed simply by avoiding the English text altogether, which alone contained the "reversed" chapters 28 and 29.

JAMES: But "reversed" into the order that Young thought was the "correct" order, and that is now universally regarded as "correct."

HENRY: Yes—but of course it is *not* the "correct" order. It is simply the order imposed upon James's novel by certain late-twentieth-century readers and editors.

JAMES: Where does this leave us, then?[14] Your historical and biblio-graphical narrative argues that we have had no textual call to be changing the original order of chapters 28 and 29. But one still has to deal with the novel's internal problems, its fictional chronology. After all, switching the order of the New York Edition chapters didn't happen because of pressure from editors and textual scholars; it happened because critics and readers found fault at the aesthetic level of the work.

HENRY: In situations like this one sometimes wants to say, simply: "what do readers and interpreters know about textual criticism and editing? They should leave such matters to experts, to people who have competence in such things."

JAMES: Like Leon Edel, I suppose, or the various scholars and editors who followed his lead?

HENRY: Ah, we all do make terrible blunders, don't we. But in textual matters, at any rate, there is an ancient rule that one violates only at great peril. It is the rule of *durior lectio*. It is the rule that says "do not tamper with the text unless you are forced to do so." It is the rule, specifically, which says that in cases where two or more readings are possible, one ought to choose the "harder" reading—especially if the harder reading carries the sanction of an authorized textual history. In the case of *The Ambassadors*, *durior lectio* tells us that, however anomalous the chronology of James's original text might appear, one is not licensed to alter that text without other, more compelling (and specifically *textual*) grounds.

JAMES: Do you intend simply to leave us in a quandary—impaled on the horns of this critical and textual dilemma?

HENRY: Not at all. But I want the significance of what I am about to say to be very clear.

First of all, Young's reading of the two chapters in James's novel seems to me a possible reading. One might even call it a *persuasive* reading, given the effect it has had on 45 years of literary criticism and scholarship. But it is *only* a possible reading. There is always another way of reading a text—and in the present case one would have to say that James, at any rate, must have read his text very differently indeed.

And *I* read it differently too. Is my reading the same as James's? I don't know. It's different from Young's reading, in any case, and is probably truer to James's reading since it's so much closer to James's original text.

To see this (new/old) reading we have first to *un*see the reading Young made authoritative in 1950. Young arrived at his reading because he perceived chronological anomalies in the narrative. Let me now briefly reconstruct that narrative.

Chapter 27 ends with the conclusion of a morning conversation between Lambert Strether and Sarah Pocock. The next two chapters deal with events that take place during the remainder of that same day and the next day. The key events—in chronological sequence—are an afternoon conversation between Strether and Maria Gostrey, an evening conversation between Strether and Chad, a second conversation on the next morning between Strether and Sarah Pocock, a second afternoon conversation between Strether and Maria Gostrey, and then the evening departure for Switzerland of Sarah, her husband, Mamie, Waymarsh, and Little Bilham.

Young's problems arose in his reading of (a) Strether's conversation with Chad, which occupies most of the original chapter 29, and (b) Strether's second conversation with Maria Gostrey, which occupies most of the original chapter 28. In each case Young saw events being referred to which seemed not to have happened yet, or which could no longer happen. Young's problems arose because he read the order of the fictional events as symmetrical with the order of textual presentation. Young, for example, clearly reads the conversation between Strether and Chad as if it took place around midnight of the second day, that is, after the departure for Switzerland of the Pocock party.

Young's reading depends entirely upon the meaning he assigns to one single word—the fourth word of the original chapter 29, the demonstra-

tive pronoun "that": "He [Strether] went late that evening to the Boule-
vard Malesherbes, having the impression that it would be vain to go early,
and having also, more than once in the course of the day, made enquiries of
the concierge. Chad hadn't come in and had left no intimation; he had affairs, apparently, at this juncture—as it occurred to Strether he so well
might have—" (Norton edition, chapter [28], 280). Young (correctly)
read "that" as a reference to the evening of the first day, the evening of the
day when Strether had his (first) morning conversation with Sarah (as presented in chapter 27). But in the edition read by Young this passage did not
appear in the book after the chapter 27 conversation; rather, it followed
(immediately) the end of the original chapter 28—which (mostly) involves
Strether's (second) conversation with Maria Gostrey on the second day.
(Their previous day's afternoon conversation is never reported in the
novel, nor—for that matter—is Strether's second meeting and conversation with Sarah.) Because the original chapter 28 ends at the close of their
conversation, when Young began reading the original chapter 29 he
(mis)took the phrase "that evening" to be a reference to the evening of the
second day. But it isn't. The phrase "that evening" is referring to the evening of the first day.

Of course Young's way of reading is natural enough. Nonetheless, it is
a reading that has neglected to see the exact narrative structure of the original chapter 28. That chapter's long conversation between Maria Gostrey
and Strether does not occupy the entirety of the text. Indeed, the conversation is a proleptically embedded event in the chapter—an event which has
not yet "happened" within the plot structure of the unfolding events. This
fact the reader is specifically told in the first paragraph of the chapter: "One
of the features of the restless afternoon passed by him after Mrs. Pocock's
visit was an hour spent, shortly before dinner, with Maria Gostrey, whom
of late . . . he had by no means neglected. And that he was still not neglecting her will appear from the fact that he was with her again at the same
hour on the morrow—" (Norton edition, chapter [29], 290). The chapter
then proceeds to give us this (second) conversation that Strether and Maria
Gostrey had together "at the same hour on the morrow" of the first (unre-
ported) conversation. In effect, James has constructed a kind of textual
flash-forward. The proleptic conversation is framed by a brief narrative
introduction where the sequence of events is described.

Thus, when the original chapter 29—which follows this chapter—
opens with a reference to "that evening," the novel is shifting from the

embedded narrative of the "morrow's" conversation back to the narrative position located in the opening sentences of the original chapter 28—the sentences I just quoted.

JAMES: Why be so recondite? What's to be gained by such a complex narrative move?

HENRY: That's up to the reader's imagination, isn't it? Or are you asking me to tell you what was in James's mind? I can't do that—no one can. And anyway, I think the business of criticism is to try to show as clearly as possible what the writer actually *did*, to show what he wrote and saw into print. The business of interpretation is to see that cities of meaning get built by those acts of writing.

JAMES: All right, give me a city of meaning.

HENRY: If we read the chapters in James's rather than Young's order, our attention is, I think, drawn more deeply into the dialectic of Strether's blindness and insight. In Strether's conversation with Maria Gostrey, for example, the reader is led to focus on two related emotional facts: that Maria is in love with Strether and that Strether—though Maria continually exposes her true feelings to him—fails utterly to register those feelings, let alone to respond.[15]

In the novel's plot-time this failure happens after Strether's midnight conversation with Chad, which is dominated by the subject of love and people's failed chances at a true emotional life. The reader will perceive this plot-time irony only after the events are over; it is an irony we gain by reflection, sometime after chapter 29.

Structured in this way, however—that is, structured as in James's 1909 text—the narrative provides another moment of irony that we may register as it were "immediately," a dramatic and experiential irony. This emerges as we move in reading-time from Strether's conversation with Maria to his (earlier) conversation with Chad. When we follow Strether's conversation with Chad in *that* textual sequence, we are forcibly confronted with the deep pathos of Strether's nuanced and sympathetic imagination. The insight he reveals to and for Chad is matched by an evil reciprocal—by the blindness (is it a willful blindness?) that he reveals toward his own situation, where real opportunities for love are lost.

The conversation with Chad shows as well, as so many readers have noticed, the ironic differential between the two men's characters. Crass and ultimately shallow, Chad worries about the financial problems Strether will have if he proves unsuccessful in his mission for Mrs. Newsome. Strether, on the other hand, dismisses such considerations as he tries to persuade Chad to make a choice for love and life beyond the suffocating world of Woollett. As the conversation proceeds, however, the future-perfect memory of the conversation with Maria Gostrey hovers over the text. Its presence generates as it were a reading from above, a revelation of the true extent of the disaster involved here. Both of these men are already, in their different ways, lost souls.

Those complex and interrelated effects are a function of the structure of the novel as James originally ordered it.

JAMES: And Young's reversed order presumably would yield other effects and emphases of meaning.

HENRY: Clearly. They might be very interesting effects and emphases. To secure them, however, means licensing the reader to restructure the novel that James passed on. Young altered the chapter sequence not because he had any documentary or historical call to do so but because he wanted to read the phrase "that evening" in a certain way. A desire for a certain kind of meaning—a reader's impulse—led him to reorder, to rewrite, James's novel. Ultimately what Young did was to treat James's modernist text as if it were a postmodern text—as if it were a text to be manipulated by the reader, like Cortazar's *Hopscotch*.

JAMES: Irony upon irony. As I recall, Young wanted to reorder chapters 28 and 29 because—like his mentor Yvor Winters—he found James's later prose altogether too loose, a prose in which the reader became lost in a cloud chamber of thick and immediate detail. Commenting exactly on the difficult prose of these two chapters, Winters lamented, "The virtues of expository prose have been abandoned: we must construct our own exposition of the story when the story is completed."[16] Winters did not want to place such authority, or responsibility, in the reader. Though "many . . . have decided that the thought of the conscious author is somehow unworthy . . . and should be eliminated," Winters took his stand for that conscious authority: "I prefer the complete thought of the great mind, and the structure that is proper to such thought."[17] In saying this Winters was simultaneously praising the work of his student Robert Young. In actual fact, however, what Young did was simply to "construct [his] own exposition of the story" that had already achieved the completeness of that (presumably) great mind's thought.

HENRY: So Young ended up—after all—treating the novel in the spirit of the later James rather than the spirit of Winters. Young executed what James praised, in the New York Edition's final Preface, as a "readerly revision" of the text.

JAMES: How lovely. And who now—in this postmodern age—would want to go back to 1909 and read *The Ambassadors* in the monumentality of its original, Jamesian text?

HENRY: Yvor Winters?

JAMES: Oh, that 'twere possible!¹⁸

APPENDIX

Letter from Henry James to Mrs. Humphrey Ward,
December 16, 1903

NOTE: The word included in angle brackets in the letter below is crossed out in the original.

Dec 16th 1903

Dear Mrs. Ward—

Please believe in the very great pleasure given me by your kind & generous letter. It belongs to the area of acts that touch deeply, & of which the remembrance abides. I felt a good deal of despair after "The Ambassadors" were launched, & said to myself "what ⟨can⟩ can be expected for a novel with a hero of 55, & properly no heroine at all?" But I have slowly felt a little better, & the book is, intrinsically, I daresay, the best I have written in spite of a fearful though much patched over fault or weakness in it (which, however, I seem to see no one has noticed & which nothing will induce me *now* ever to reveal not at least till some one does spot it.) It is in general meritorious for its conformation & composition—*that* I make bold to say. But it was written 4 years ago, & I feel myself rather away & "off" from it. What gives me particular pleasure is your feeling that one is in a fresh & a larger period which I really hope and believe (D. V., absit omen unberufen. etc. etc.!) may prove to be the case. Yet I find it all a too damnably difficult art & have so to pretend that it isn't. However, we pretend life isn't either & toward that such good friends as you exceedingly help. I rejoice to think of finding you before very long in town & I am, dear Mrs. Ward, yours very constantly,

Henry James

PART III

"Seeing It Again":
Lines of Revision

Reading James's Prefaces
and Reading James

Paul B. Armstrong

Whenever I teach a work from the New York Edition, I tell students not to read James's Preface until after they've finished the novel. That is unsurprising advice to anyone familiar with the prefaces, but it indicates how peculiar they are as texts—a peculiarity easily forgotten by expert readers because of the way the prefaces have been celebrated and monumentalized as models of criticism. The common reaction of the naive reader is a useful reminder of how bizarre the prefaces are as examples of their literary kind: "If this is an introduction, why doesn't it tell us what the novel is about?" J. Hillis Miller's striking description of the prefaces as "the 'translation' of the novels into criticism" is misleading (as Miller himself might agree) if the aim of translation is to make the foreign text comprehensible.[1] The opacity of the prefaces as reflectors of the novels brings to mind a speech from James's "The Figure in the Carpet" (1896): "Your description's certainly beautiful, but it doesn't make what you describe very distinct" (*15*: 230). Reading James's prefaces is a strange, often bewildering experience because they both invoke and frustrate the expectations that usually accompany authorial introductions. Prefaces can indeed be ambiguous affairs inasmuch as they often assume a prior understanding of the text they stand before even as they attempt to orient the reader's attitude toward it. James's prefaces call attention to this ambiguity by both raising and refusing to satisfy the reader's expectation that they will provide anticipatory structures of interpretation to help make sense of the works they introduce.

One could argue that the oddity of the prefaces as introductory texts is due to the fact that orienting the reader is not their primary intention. The prefaces typically give accounts of the production of the texts that follow, and the reproduction of a text in reading need not duplicate the processes of its original creation. A description of the creative act is not necessarily the best guide to how to appreciate the result. Furthermore, if James's prefaces are the result of his own rereading and reimagining of the works in the New York Edition, then it is only reasonable for him to assume readers who know his texts well enough to have points of reference as he reports what it meant for him to reencounter his *oeuvre*. For both of these reasons, the prefaces might seem more like epilogues than introductions and might more appropriately be situated after rather than before the main texts in the edition—or at least might with justice be recommended as follow-up reading.

Still, these arguments are not completely satisfying because they try to excuse the oddity of the prefaces instead of accounting for it by explaining its possible functions. A case can be made, I think, that the strangeness of these introductions is useful, justifiable, and perhaps even intentional. James is aware throughout the prefaces of the need to educate readers to the ideal of criticism he finds lacking in his world. I will argue that some of the peculiar features of the prefaces as introductory texts help provide the reader with a hermeneutic education that simulates modes of understanding appropriate for construing his fiction. A reader may be ready for this education only after at least one reading of the work the given preface discusses, but the reasons why James privileges rereading over the first reading are part of the explanation not only of the oddity of the prefaces but also of the difficult, even impossible mode of attention his fiction requires.

That James is aware of how a text standing before another text will orient the reader's expectations is evident from his comments about Alvin Langdon Coburn's prefatory photographs. As James explains in the Preface to *The Golden Bowl*, "anything that relieves responsible prose of the duty of being, while placed before us, good enough, interesting enough and, if the question be of picture, pictorial enough, above all *in itself*, does it the worst of services" (*23*: ix–x; *AN*, 332). Although the prefaces are not pictorial, they are, like Coburn's photographs, representations that stand before other representations to which they might similarly seem to provide the key. James's warning about the photographs might consequently apply just as well to the explanatory, introductory aims of the prefaces: "the reference . . . to Novel or Tale should exactly be *not* competitive and obvious, should on the contrary plead its case with some shyness" (*23*: xi; *AN*, 333; James's emphasis). Like the photographs, the prefaces might deflect attention from the main text unless they have an oblique, indirect reference to it—a reference that is suggestive without being too explicit, explanatory, or directive. Like an illustration that is too obviously a depiction of something in the text which readers need no longer imagine for themselves, a preface that is too clear and straightforward an introduction might diminish rather than enhance the attention directed toward the text that follows. The trick is to create an indirect relation between the prefatory document and the main text which suggests kinds of interpretive attitudes without closing off analysis and imagination as a definitive statement would.

In a sense this is the trick any good introduction must pull off—orienting readers to what follows without depriving them of possibilities of understanding they can develop themselves. But James structures the obliqueness of his prefaces to attain two goals, I think, which are characteristic of his project as a novelist and a critic. First, the indirectness of his prefaces to the texts they introduce encourages a kind of doubled reading that is concretizing and reflective at the same time (and not in alternation, as is customary in realistic fiction), a doubleness also invoked by his use of point of view in his fictions. Second, this obliqueness is part of an attempt to direct and even discipline the reader's attention without coercing or constraining it—a contradictory project that enacts a paradoxical ideal of criticism as a rigorous response to the text and an infinitely free act of imagination.

Doubled reading is one consequence of what James calls in his Preface to *The Golden Bowl* "the still marked inveteracy of a certain indirect and oblique view of my presented action"—his much discussed strategy of presenting "not . . . my own impersonal account of the affair in hand" but "my account of somebody's impression of it," including "the terms of this person's access to it and estimate of it" (*23*: v; *AN*, *327*). The prefaces are similarly screens that ask us to attend simultaneously to what they present and to the way they regard it. They are thus an extension of James's habit (he calls it an "addiction") of "seeing 'through'—one thing through another, . . . and still other things through *that*" in order to attain "a certain fulness of truth—truth diffused, distributed and, as it were, atmospheric" (*11*: xviii; *AN*, *153–54*; James's emphasis). Whether "fulness" is the result of this strategy is debatable, not only because "seeing through" defers and displaces the object it presents, but also because the doubled act of attention it calls for from the reader can interfere with immersion in a represented world. Reading *The Ambassadors* or *The Golden Bowl* entails the impossible double act of concretizing a represented world while at the same time observing and criticizing the interpretive acts of another consciousness perceiving and reflecting about that world. The dilemma for James's readers is that one cannot simultaneously observe something and observe oneself observing it. You can go back and forth between these attitudes, but you can't do both at the same time.[2] Reading James can be an uncanny experience precisely because his use of point of view demands this sort of impossible doubled attention—immersing oneself in an imaginative world even as one reflects about the conditions of its apprehension.[3]

James's interpretive attitudes as the author of the prefaces are as much on display and as much an object for the reader's scrutiny as the impressions of a Lambert Strether or a Maggie Verver. This doubleness is in a way self-evident inasmuch as the prefaces are not only accounts of the fictions they introduce but also recollections of James's experiences writing them, explanations of his aesthetic principles, and reflections about his reactions on reencountering earlier works. What may not be so obvious, however, is that this doubleness calls for acts of attention on the part of the reader which simulate and reproduce the characteristic structure of response invoked by his fictions. Although the prefaces are not simply transparent reflectors of the texts they introduce, there is a mirroring effect in the parallel between the kinds of double reading required by the critical texts and those required by the fictional texts. The prefaces should be read like the fictions they introduce, and the fictions should be read like the prefaces—both requiring an impossibly doubled attention to the object represented (novel or tale, character or event) and to its mode of apprehension (James's critical consciousness, the attitude of the central registering intelligence).

The status of the author of the prefaces as a problematic, not perfectly transparent screen may first become apparent to the reader through the seeming eccentricity of some of James's concerns. Although the prefaces have been praised as models of criticism, they are often quirky and idiosyncratic in what they single out for attention. I think it is fair to say, for example, that one of the first matters of concern to most readers of *Roderick Hudson* would *not* be whether the hero's hometown of Northampton, Massachusetts, is adequately rendered. Yet this is the first aspect of the novel James dwells on in his first preface (see *1*: ix–xii; *AN*, 8–10). The obligation to thorough, detailed representation incurred by naming a location is of course an important issue for James because, as he himself notes, it raises the ghost of Balzac (see *1*: xi; *AN*, 9), and this always influential figure may have been much on James's mind if collecting an edition of his works seemed to him to mean emulating the author of the *Comédie Humaine*.[4]

As understandable as this concern might be, it is distinctly James's, not the reader's. Examining critically the rendering of Northampton may raise interesting general questions about the role of specification and blanks in representation. It may also provide the attentive, reflective reader with guides to understanding both James's evolving manner of representation (how he changes from *Roderick Hudson* to *The Ambassadors*, for example, where so much about Woollett is not told) and his place in the history of the novel (the differences between his indirection and Balzac's directness may stand out all the more strikingly because of James's invocation of this father figure). Nevertheless, giving such prominent and early mention to a relatively minor feature of this novel suggests that a private preoccupation has overridden James's sense of audience. Here and elsewhere, the consequence of the peculiarity of James's concerns is to make him seem like one of his registers—like a Fleda Vetch or a Lambert Strether whose eccentric ways of seeing are themselves a matter of interest in their own right and compel criticism of the screen through which things are observed in order to see them adequately.

The need to scrutinize critically James's perspective as author of the prefaces may help to make sense of their notorious mistakes. Some of these errors may be unintentional lapses in memory or simple misreadings— such as his odd claim that "The Altar of the Dead" endorses the humanity of George Stransom's "individual independent effort" to honor the dead (see *17*: vii–ix; *AN*, 244–45), where the story suggests that this worship gets in the way of life and love; or James's strange oversimplification of the alternation and diversity of point of view in *The Golden Bowl* when he wrongly asserts that the prince "virtually represents to himself everything that concerns us" in the first volume and that the princess does likewise in the second (*23*: vi; *AN*, 329).[5] We can't know whether James knows he's wrong in these instances, but the need to read against his perspective to arrive at the truth requires a healthy sense of the fallibility of a central intelligence, a fallibility that any reader of *The Ambassadors* would find familiar.

Some of James's observations and judgments seem to cry out, if not for correction, at least for reconsideration—as when he condemns Maria Gostrey's "false connexion" with Strether's story (*21*: xxi; *AN*, 324) or finds that "we have indubitably too much" of Henrietta in *Portrait of a Lady* (*3*: xix; *AN*, 55). These are controversial claims about which not all readers will agree, and the modesty of James's self-criticism might seem like the kind of polite gesture of self-deprecation that makes an interlocutor jump in and say "Oh no, you don't do yourself justice." That sort of reaction implies a doubled reading of James's self-commentary which constantly compares his perspective on his works with the reader's own independent assessment of them in much the same way as readers must double a reading of a registering consciousness's interpretations with an ongoing evaluation of them. We must read through and against James's reading of himself just as we must see through a Jamesian screen while simultaneously studying its idiosyncrasies as a mediator.

The requirement to undertake curiously doubled acts of attention in order to read the prefaces is reinforced by their complex temporal structure. As prefatory texts, standing before other texts that await reading (or rereading) afterwards, the governing tense of the prefaces would seem to be the future. Prefaces can provide clues to change one's understanding of the texts they introduce because of their futurity as instruments for orienting the reader's expectations. What Heidegger calls the "fore-structure" (*Vorstruktur*) of understanding—the circular relation between anticipation and discovery—is the epistemological foundation of the critical power of prefaces as "fore-texts."[6] A central paradox of James's prefaces, however, is that the way they show to the reader's future is through the author's past. The very first words of the Preface to the first work in the New York Edition make clear the dominance of the past:

"Roderick Hudson" was begun in Florence in the spring of 1874, designed from the first for serial publication in "The Atlantic Monthly," where it opened in January 1875 and persisted through the year. I yield to the pleasure of placing these circumstances on record, as I shall place others, and as I have yielded to the need of renewing acquaintance with the book after a quarter of a century. This revival of an all but extinct relation with an early work may often produce for an artist, I think, more kinds of interest and emotion than he shall find it easy to express, and yet will light not a little, to his eyes, that veiled face of his Muse which he is condemned forever and all anxiously to study. (*1*: v; *AN*, 3)

As these initial sentences suggest, the prefaces are not only history and autobiography—records of the circumstances of the initial writing and publication—but also accounts of what it meant to James in the recent past of rereading and revising to revisit earlier versions of himself (the "veiled face of his Muse" peeking through a past production). Doubled relations proliferate in the various temporal screens deployed by these complex acts of recollection—consciousness doubling back on itself in the memory of earlier events and intentions, revision doubling back on the original creation it preserves by changing, or the consciousness of the writer of the prefaces doubling back on the experiences of rereading and revising by reflecting on these recent but still past events.

The reader's relation to these temporal screens is not the same as the writer's. What we see through them is not only James's past but also the work of fiction we will read differently as a result of what we learn from these recollections. We see a future reading or rereading through James's reflections on his past. There is a persistent disjunction between the orientation to future interpretation of the reader who uses the prefaces as introductions and the play of their author with the relations among various versions of his past in his autobiographical reflections. The difficulty of the prefaces for first readers is at least in part a consequence of this disjunction, inasmuch as they are asked to share recollections about works toward which they still need to have their expectations oriented. If the anticipated new reading is a rereading, this disjunction may be more manageable, but the reader's consciousness will still be a temporally double structure that looks ahead and back in time. In both cases, reading the prefaces is, oddly, a simultaneously anticipatory and retrospective activity.

This oddity is perhaps characteristic of any authorial introduction in which a writer offers recollections about a work the reader may not yet have experienced. The peculiarity of James's prefaces is in part a matter of the degree to which he accentuates this disjunction because the urge to follow the trail of his own memories and impressions is so powerful. The elaborate temporal doublings of James's prefaces also seem uniquely a product of his fascination with the epistemology of consciousness and self-consciousness. In his fictions James repeatedly invokes an analogous kind of temporal double vision to explore and play with the epistemological structure of time. One of his recurrent strategies of representation couples future and past by depicting a character's present perception of a scene through an anticipatory account of how he or she will later remember it (a famous example is how James portrays Strether's encounter with Chad and Madame de Vionnet on their country outing by rendering his recollections of its probable meanings as he sits lost in thought later that night on his bedroom sofa).[7] Throughout his fictions James frequently doubles tenses so as to compel the reader not only to see a scene but also at the same time to reflect about it, an act of reflection that can only occur in a future where the perception it takes as its object is already past.

The prefaces similarly demand that the reader hold different tenses together which are epistemologically distinct, and one purpose of such coupling is to foreground and thematize the temporality of self-consciousness. This doubleness calls attention to how the act of "seeing through" sets up not only spatial but also temporal displacements. For the reader as well as the writer (although in different ways), screening involves both spatial and temporal doubling because viewing one thing through another means that they are not simultaneously present. The displacement of "seeing through" defers what it presents, a deferral that can lead either into future acts of interpretation (as it does for the reader of the prefaces) or into acts of recollecting the past (as it does for their author). The different positions of the reader and the writer of the prefaces display different possibilities of temporal deferral. The implication of these various kinds of doubling, displacement, and deferral is that neither consciousness (the activity of "seeing through") nor self-consciousness (reflecting on that process of screening) is unified, self-sufficient, or stably centered in itself.[8] Learning that lesson is valuable education for reading both the prefaces and the fictions they introduce.

The double reading that the prefaces require indicates that their author cannot always be taken as a reliable narrator of his own actions and intentions as a fiction writer. James's explicit remarks about the importance of authorial intention are curiously ambiguous. On the one hand, he clearly states that his justification for giving the history of his creations is that knowledge of the author's intention is essential for understanding and evaluating his work: "What matters, for one's appreciation of a work of art, however modest, is that the prime intention shall have been justified—for any judgment of which we must be clear as to what it was" (*10*: xix; *AN*, 134). On the other hand, he frequently discounts the value of intention as a guide to appreciating what it produced: "one's plan, alas, is one thing and one's result another" (*19*: xiii; *AN*, 296), and an artist's "triumph . . . is but the triumph of what he produces" (*7*: xxi; *AN*, 96). Indeed James claims, "it is dreadful to have too much, for any artistic demonstration, to dot one's i's and insist on one's intentions" (*3*: xx; *AN*, 56). Such explanations hint that the plan has not been successfully realized, and they also unburden the reader of the responsibility to analyze and project what the writer may have been trying to do. James both *is* and *is not* an intentionalist because he insists on taking the highest responsibility for his work even as he believes that artistically embodied intentions transfer that responsibility to the reader: "I am responsible for my work: it means. But that requires you as reader to become responsible for it: you must make it mean."[9]

The prefaces convey this double message to the reader by both invoking and refusing the authority of the writer to define and control the meaning of his works. James's repeated recollections about the origins of a work or his aims in writing it claim to give definitive guidance about how it should be taken, and a large part of the authority that the prefaces have accrued as magisterial documents of James's artistic intentions is a recognition of this ambition. But when critics turn to the prefaces to resolve an interpretive dispute, they typically find that James is silent or ambiguous on crucial matters. The prefaces are curiously unhelpful when it comes to settling some of the most notorious interpretive conflicts that his works have inspired: whether Isabel's return to Osmond deserves praise or blame, whether Maisie develops a "moral sense" or is depraved by her surroundings, whether Maggie Verver is "saint" or "witch," whether the governess in *The Turn of the Screw* is crazy.[10] At one point, in the Preface to *Daisy Miller*, James curiously sets hares in motion in opposite directions by telling two stories with contradictory implications about the proper attitude to take toward his heroine: one suggesting that his unflattering depiction presents "an outrage on American girlhood," and the other indicting him for expending "too much imagination" on a romanticized portrait that falsifies "the real little Daisy Millers" (*18*: v, vii; *AN*, 268, 270). In all of these cases, the impossibility of deciding James's intention duplicates for the reader a dilemma familiar from his fictions, where a central intelligence is clearly the originator of meanings but where evaluating and interpreting those meanings may lead to endless disagreement. For James, consciousness has the power to originate meanings, but it is not necessarily authoritative even when it is their source, and this is just as true of the author of the prefaces as it is of a character's point of view.

The doubleness of an invoked but questioned authority over meaning puts the reader in a doubled situation that is crucial to the educational project of the prefaces. On the one hand, James's readers are called upon to attend rigorously and carefully to meanings not their own. Reading therefore requires the discipline and responsibility of recognizing and acceding to otherness. On the other hand, the limits of that Other's authority over his own meanings leave readers free to imagine and create interpretations and evaluations that cannot be coerced or restricted by their origin, and this freedom gives us a responsibility to imagine and create which paradoxically does not negate our responsibility to listen to and respect the author.[11]

This doubleness in the reader's role re-creates in different form the doubleness of James's own relation to the "germs" from which he got the inspiration for many of his fictions. In both instances it is important to be responsible to but also free from the controlling influence of an originating authority. Some of the best-known passages in the prefaces are the places where James describes and illustrates "that odd law which somehow always makes the minimum of valid suggestion serve the man of imagination better than the maximum" (*12*: vii; *AN*, 161). James acknowledges the importance of the "tiny nugget" of suggestion that gives his imagination "the prick of inoculation" in the various anecdotes he relates to explain the source of a novel or tale (*10*: vi, vii; *AN*, 120, 121). But as many readers have noted, the point of these anecdotes again and again is that the germ would be nothing without the transformative power of James's imagination. His point is not only that "clumsy Life again at her stupid work" (*10*: vii; *AN*, 121) lacks any sense of economy or of aesthetically satisfying relationships but also that "the modern alchemist" in pursuit of "the secret of life" can discern "the positive right truth" contained in a germ only by ignoring the "muddle of wrong truths" cloaking it (*10*: ix; *AN*, 123). In insisting on his independence from his sources, then, James does not disown his responsibility to them but instead, in a curious dialectic, claims that he can only respond rigorously and insightfully to their challenge—can only reveal the hidden meanings of his inspiring germs—if he does not allow them to restrict the play of his imagination.

The relation of the reader to James's recollections about his sources and the circumstances of the original writing reenacts this dialectic. For a writer who, in "The Death of the Lion" (1894) and elsewhere, derides the curiosity of the public about "the scene of an author's labours," it is odd how much time James devotes in the prefaces not only to recounting where he got the idea for a fiction but also to describing where he wrote it (*15*: 118). James indulges again and again in largely private associations about the place of composition, even if only to complain that some sites (like Venice, where he worked on *Portrait*) stifle the imagination because "they are too rich in their own life and too charged with their own meanings merely to help him out with a lame phrase" (*3*: v; *AN*, 41). The apparent uselessness of these recollections to the reader seeking guidance about how to interpret James's fiction seems at times to demonstrate "the fatal futility of Fact" (*10*: vii; *AN*, 122). If there is anything to be gained for the reader's understanding of Isabel Archer from such reflections on how "romantic and historic sites . . . offer the artist a questionable aid to concentration" (*3*: v; *AN*, 40–41), such insight will come only from the work of the reader's own transformative imagination seeking out connections between the novel and this germ of suggestion. There are connections to be discovered in this particular case, I think (by comparing, for example, Isabel's response to Europe and James's own reactions). But my argument is that those connections can only be made if the reader duplicates the uses James makes of his germs—like him, undertaking a dialectical action in which we respond attentively to suggestions emanating from an origin even as we also indulge the liberty to imagine freely about them.

It is as if James is playing a complex game with us for our benefit. Setting aside his scruples about invasions of authorial privacy, he pretends to lead readers to the promised land of the artist's innermost consciousness, the sanctuary where his meanings and values had their origins. But what that trip dramatizes is that this sphere is not the end of interpretation it would be if it held the secret key to a work's meanings. If James is offering "an earnest invitation to the reader to dream again in my company and in the interest of his own larger absorption of my sense" (*23*: xxii; *AN*, 345), then our imaginings will have to take a different course from the original act of creation precisely because James's recollections are largely inconclusive as programs for reading. Readers must participate in their own way in what James calls "the felt fermentation . . . that enables the sense originally communicated to make fresh and possibly quite different terms for the new employment . . . awaiting it" (*17*: xii; *AN*, 249). The metaphor of "fermentation" implies that a meaning can be preserved in a new context only by transforming it, as James did his sources and as readers must his texts, by employing it for different purposes not anticipated by the founding intention originally (but not finally, conclusively) responsible for it.

What James does to his germs, transforming them beyond recognition, bespeaks the necessary indeterminacy of criticism as a quest for origins. By inviting readers to come with him back to those origins, James asserts his own authority over works whose history he alone is privileged to know, even as the inconclusiveness of his private associations tells the reader that, for us as for the author, the responsibility for discovering and creating meaning is one's own. James can tell his tales of origin because he exercised that responsibility, but the particulars of those anecdotes are of limited help to us as readers for the very reason that we must reenact the general lesson they hold of the need for interpretive intelligence and imagination to analyze and transform a text in order to do it justice.

Some of the most useful aspects of the prefaces are their theoretical observations not only about the structure of James's narratives (his use of a "central consciousness," for example, or his alternation of "picture" and "scene") but also about the novel as a genre (his famous definition of "romance" versus realism, or his metaphor of the "house of fiction"). The usefulness of these theoretical notions lies precisely in their generality, their lack of specificity. They are not inextricably tied to a single text or commentary, and their broad range of possible reference leaves it to the reader to figure out how best to apply them as instruments for understanding and appreciation.

The unpredictable potential breadth of their applicability also gives the prefaces a degree of independence which is unusual for introductions. This independence is what enables R. P. Blackmur to collect the prefaces as documents that can stand alone and offer an account of "the art of the novel." Blackmur's edition has become such a classic that one tends not to notice how strange a text it is inasmuch as it separates what would seem inseparable. Because of their generality and indeterminacy as theoretical statements, however, the prefaces are not purely parasitic on the texts they introduce. Their openness and lack of specific reference manifest yet again their peculiarity and distinctiveness as examples of their literary kind. If the prefaces are characterized by the kind of indeterminacy, the absence of concrete specification, inherent in conceptual abstractions, this structure of negativity results once more from the fact that the prefaces are *not* simply exegetical commentaries on the fictions they introduce.

But also as before, this very negativity is functional (it helps educate the reader) and typical of James's larger project (he is a writer who, after all, "glor[ied] in a gap").[12] What James said of *The Turn of the Screw* could apply just as well to the prefaces and to much of the rest of his fiction: "my values are positively all blanks" (*12*: xxii; *AN*, 177). In yet another curious twist, then, the ability of the prefaces to stand alone is a consequence of the most powerful, effective education they offer to readers of James in search of an introduction to his fiction: the development of theoretical knowledge about the construction of fiction. The final paradox of the prefaces is that they provide the most useful preparation for reading James to the extent that they are independent of the texts they introduce. This paradox is once again evidence of the contradictory educational project the prefaces undertake, disciplining the reader's attention (as rigorous theoretical conceptualization can) while encouraging its free, unpredictable exercise (by leaving open the application of the theory and the exploration of its precise, concrete implications). James's prefaces are at their best as introductions to James when they refuse to specify what his fiction means.

The "Grafted" Image:
James on Illustration

J. Hillis Miller

"I am for—no illustration," said Stéphane Mallarmé, "everything a book evokes having to pass into the mind or spirit of the reader" ("tout ce qu'évoque un livre devant se passer dans l'esprit du lecteur").[1] The words on the page have a performative power of evocation. They make present in the spirit something otherwise absent. If that power is distracted, drawn off in a detour, diverted into an illustration (presumably after passing first into the mind of the illustrator), it will then not operate where it ought, on the spirit of the reader. It will pass into the picture and be present there. The text will be impotent to work its magic effect of evocation on the mind of the reader, calling forth spirits within it. A book, it seems, has only so much magic energy. An illustration will drain this power off, leaving the book a dead letter, short-circuited by the superior power of the illustration to make something present. The book has always been no more than a dead letter, since its power is the power of evocation, a raising of the dead. The word evokes. The illustration presents.

Mallarmé, with however much or little irony, follows his rejection of graphic illustration for books with the remark that if you substitute photography for the traditional illustration in etching or engraving, why not go all the way to cinematography. Cinema, in its unrolling along a temporal axis of narration, will to advantage replace both the texts and the illustrations of many a volume: "que n'allez vous droit au cinématographie, dont le déroulement remplacera, images et texte, maint volume avantageusement."[2] This comment is a prophecy, accurate enough, of the power cinema has had to displace the illustrated book. What Mallarmé says is also an ironic recognition that there are many books that in no way exploit the particular evocative power of the printed word and therefore might as well be replaced by the "movies." The key word in Mallarmé's formulation is "replace." Photographs were in Mallarmé's time replacing the older graphic arts as the medium for book illustration. Photographs are replaced in turn by cinematography, one form of graphing or graving rapidly substituting for another, leaving the power of the written word further and further behind. Finally, words are present only as the subsidiary remnant of subtitles in silent movies. Even these were no longer necessary when the talkies were developed, in the final triumph, so it seems, of the visual and auditory over the written word. Just as John Ruskin (in *Ariadne Florentina*, for example) expressed his hatred of the photograph in the name of the superior representative power of engraving, so Mallarmé makes his ironic tribute to the obliterating power of illustration over text in the name of something only the written word can do, something all his own work attempts to exploit in its naked purity.

Henry James took a different view, as is evident in his correspondence with Alvin Langdon Coburn about the photographic frontispieces for the New York Edition of his novels and in the discussion of these photographs in the Preface to *The Golden Bowl*. He saw photographs as acceptable illustrations because they were "in as different a 'medium' as possible" from the text (*23*: x; *AN*, 333). Nevertheless, James shares Mallarmé's fear that illustrations will usurp or darken the illuminating power of the text. The words on the page, in James's view as in Mallarmé's, have as their prime gift the ability to evoke images, to conjure them into being: "The essence of any representational work is of course to bristle with immediate images"; it "put[s] forward illustrative claims (that is, produce[s] an effect of illustration) by its own intrinsic virtue" (*23*: ix; *AN*, 331). The reader is sometimes reduced to "such a state of hallucination by the images one has evoked" that he cannot rest until he has made a "semblance of them in his own other medium." But those illustrations of what is already, if it has any value, sufficiently illustrative on its own are entirely alien to the text and should stand off from it, keep out of its light.

The images James uses for the danger posed by the graphic to the verbal are obliquely illustrative themselves. They are taken, oddly enough, from gardening and eating. Gardening is like illustration in that in both cases something comes into the light out of an obscure ground. The elucidation of the graphic would interfere with the free growth of the verbal illustration, shade it, stunt it. So it must be kept at a distance: "his [the author's] own garden, however, remains one thing, and the garden he has prompted the cultivation of at other hands becomes quite another; which means that the frame of one's own work no more provides place for such a plot than we expect flesh and fish to be served on the same platter" (*23*: x; *AN*, 332). A novel with pictures is like a garden growing two incompatible crops. It is a frame enclosing not only its own shapely design but also an alien parasitical plot, plot as garden and plot as artistic design or story. Or it is a plate offering two inharmonious foods, or, in a final variation, it is a plant on which is grafted a foreign stock: "I, for one, should have looked much askance at the proposal, on the part of my associates in the whole business, to graft or 'grow,' at whatever point, a picture by another hand on my own picture—this being always, to my sense, a lawless incident" (*23*: ix; *AN*, 331–32). "Graft" and "graphic" of course have the same root, Greek "graphein," to write. Grafting relates to the Greek concept through the pencil-like shape of the sharpened shoot inserted under the bark of the parent stock. A grafted tree producing both yellow and red apples is "lawless," a monster or *lusus naturae*.

Why, if he so fears the alien power of illustration, does James show such "inconsistency of attitude in the matter of the 'grafted' image" as to share with Coburn in the delightful search for appropriate scenes to photograph for the frontispieces for the New York Edition? The photographs must simultaneously be as separate from the text as possible, echoing it at a distance, and slavishly dependent on it. And all the while they must also assert their own power of bringing to light something not in the text but out there in the real world. James's idea was that the photographs were "not to keep or to pretend to keep, anything like dramatic step with their suggested matter" (*23*: x; *AN*, 333). They would be rather "images always confessing themselves mere optical symbols or echos, expressions of no particular thing in the text, but only the type or idea of this thing or that thing" (*23*: xi; *AN*, 333). They were to be "pictures of our 'set' stage with the actors left out" (ibid.).[3] An example of this procedure is Coburn's photograph of a curiosity shop as an illustration for *The Golden Bowl* (fig. 27). The photograph shows neither people nor that sunlike half sphere, with its hidden crack, that is James's prime symbol of the secretly flawed relations among his characters.

As James's gingerly comments indicate, he knew he was playing with fire, the fire of a possible excess of visual image over text, a "competition" of the one with the other. In *A Small Boy and Others* he observes that when he was a child, *Oliver Twist* for him meant more the powerful etchings by Cruikshank than Dickens's text. The illustrations, for him, obliterated the words.[4] James tries to avoid this danger in the New York Edition by thinking of the photographs as in no way pictures of specific passages in the text. Moreover, the people are to be entirely left out. Photographs can present settings or background, such as the curiosity shop, but not minds, feelings, persons in their interaction. The latter are the business of words. The photographs are "optical symbols" not of the text but of "types" or "ideas," which stand above both image and text as something each points toward in its own special way. Image and text echo each other at a safe distance. Their resonance is guaranteed by their equal relation to a third thing that they bring to light in different ways. Each photograph illustrates, makes visible, not this or that detail in the text but a general type or idea that the text magically evokes, as Mallarmé says. Each photograph would thereby be kept subsidiary to the text, posing no danger of overwhelming it. The photograph imitates the text at a double remove. It represents neither its signs nor its referent, but its significance, its impalpable "signifié."

Another passage in the Preface to *The Golden Bowl* expresses James's wavering, his double theory of photographic illustrations. On the one hand he holds that the photographs echo at a distance something in the novel. On the other hand he holds that they speak for something in the objects they picture, thereby making present within the covers of the book something alien to the text. His idea, he says, held up as a "light" to the city of London for Coburn's illumination, was "of the aspect of things or combinations of objects that might, by a latent virtue in it, speak of its connection with something in the book, and yet at the same time speak enough for its odd or interesting self" (*23*: xi; *AN*, *333*). An example of this is the other photograph for *The Golden Bowl*, "Portland Place" (fig. 28). The "latent virtue" is not in the photograph but in what the photograph copies, in the visible aspect of real things. This virtue brings into the open both something exposed in another way by the words of the book and something separate, something proper to itself. All James's work, it could be shown, turns on the undecidable question (which nevertheless urgently needs deciding) of whether the type or idea preexists its representation in picture or word, or is present in something the representation copies, or is generated by the representation. Much is at stake in his not wholly consistent attempt to adjudicate the relation between picture and dramatic word in the New York Edition of his novels.

Doctoring the Text:
Henry James and Revision

Julie Rivkin

The two most extensive treatments of revision in Henry James—Hershel Parker's *Flawed Texts and Verbal Icons* and Philip Horne's *Henry James and Revision*—take opposite stands on the criteria for determining which versions of the works James revised for the New York Edition are the aesthetically superior and authoritatively definitive ones. Parker, who favors the original versions, argues for a "creative process" with a definitive closure and sees authorial intervention beyond a legitimate "polishing" as tampering that ought to be outlawed. He objects to "the termless legal authority of the author" and regards the author as without legitimate property rights in his work once the creative process is over.[1] Horne, on the other hand, while he does consider notions of the "creative process" that "preclude returns and rehandlings," sees James's authority as exercised most characteristically in the text revised to his satisfaction.[2] What he ultimately celebrates, indeed nearly fetishizes, is not the original process but the last word, the last *revised* word, that is. Horne's book ends with a chapter entitled "Last Words," and his project is to turn attention away from James's deathbed dictation—those painfully hasty and incoherent "last words"—and toward the last published text that James was able to revise.[3] Original conceptions or last words: the difference between Parker and Horne can be taken as emblematic of the two versions of literary authority called forth by the practice of revision. In the case of Henry James, which version of literary authority should receive our credence, and which text should we read?

This mode of staging the issue of revision—as a debate between the advocates of original conceptions and those of last words—might be precisely what James is attempting to avoid when he addresses the subject in the Preface to *The Golden Bowl*. Yet if James does not take the same direction as either of his authoritative readers, his discussion of revision could nonetheless be said to open the way for both of them. Revision, which he initially explores as a matter of how authority is exercised over time, quickly turns into an affair of reading, and in granting certain liberties to himself as a rereader, James finds himself doing the same for those readers who will follow him. James may or may not have anticipated the particular debate that rages between these two contemporary readers, but he did know that the practice of revision, while it might seem to extend the jurisdiction of the author over his or her text, also has the contradictory effect of licensing the reader.

That these two readers use that power to attempt to stabilize James's authority by freezing it in time—for such is the strategy they both adopt, whether a notion of origins or of conclusions governs their temporal model—is ironic but not surprising; one might say they show a greater respect for authority than the "Master" they serve. That is, while James the author of the New York Edition clearly favors the revised versions of his work and thus would seem to stand with Horne rather than Parker, his own analysis of the representational consequences of revision undermines a univocal defense of "last words."

My project here, then, is to explore James's own representations of revision, and in particular to pursue the logic that leads to the scenario of reading enacted by Parker and Horne. The central theoretical text for any discussion of revision in the New York Edition is, of course, the Preface to *The Golden Bowl*. But I also will be working with a Jamesian fictional text in which revision plays a central role. In the tale "The Middle Years" not only does revision figure as the very signature of authority, but also the role of the reader becomes a matter of life and death.

I

When James first turns to the subject of "re-perusal" and "re-representation" in the second half of the Preface to *The Golden Bowl*, his emphasis is on the easy coincidence between potentially different versions of his texts (*23*: xiii; *AN*, 335). Rather than open up the debate between the virtues of one text or another, one concept of authority or another, he eases his way out of conflict by suggesting there really is no difference. More exactly, he speaks of the "docile reader" he "consentingly" becomes for the "historian of the matter," that earlier author he once was (23: xiii; *AN*, 336). "His vision, superimposed on my own as an image in cut paper is applied to a sharp shadow on a wall, matches, at every point, without excess or deficiency" (ibid.). The author of the New York Edition finds his conception of authority served by portraying himself not only as docile and subject to the impositions of an earlier authorial design (the image in cut paper) but also as insubstantial or shadowy. For the sake of sustaining the authority of his earlier vision, the returning author seems willing to render himself surprisingly without force.

But this metaphor that seems to grant so little to the revisionist, the author of the New York Edition, actually grants him an important resource. The representation of artistic vision as a shadow invokes a Platonic theory of representation, and in doing so, leads James to a conception of the literary work that can accommodate the practice of revision without any loss of mastery or authority. Further, if this Platonic metaphor is useful in the cases where those two moments of "vision" fall into easy coincidence, it is even more useful when the two "visions" do not match. In fact, James introduces the most Platonic of his metaphors to represent just this phenomenon of difference:

It was, all sensibly, as if the clear matter being still there, even as a shining expanse of snow spread over a plain, my exploring tread, for application to it, had quite unlearned the old pace and found itself naturally falling into another, which might sometimes indeed more or less agree with the original tracks, but might most often, or very nearly, break the surface in other places. (*23*: xiii–xiv; *AN* 336)

In this passage, James separates the "matter" of his work—figured in the "shining expanse of snow"—from any specific textual representations— whether the "original tracks" or the ones that deviate from them. In other words, there is an ideal form of the literary work that preexists, exceeds, and transcends any textual embodiments. Whether James calls that ideal form his "matter" as he does here or his idea or intention as he does elsewhere in the prefaces, he is drawing on a similar Platonic model.

This image is thus not the only one that depends on a Platonic conception of revision. The metaphor of dress, which James uses several times, also suggests that there is an essential body, much like that "shining expanse of snow," which may be dressed more or less appropriately in different editions, but which will remain fundamentally the same under its various textual cloaks. When James treats revision as the "twitching, to a better effect, of superannuated garments" (*23*: xiv; *AN*, 337) or apologizes for a "subject bristling with a sense of over-prolonged exposure in a garment misfitted, a garment cheaply embroidered and unworthy of it" (*23*: xxi; *AN*, 344), his figures presuppose a stable self that endures the foibles of tailoring and fashion, the fits and misfits of textual representation.

These metaphors describe not only an ideal literary form that transcends its particular versions but also a unity that subsumes difference. Interestingly, when James actually comes to define the practice of revision in the Preface, his preoccupation is with translating potential pluralities into unities:

To revise is to see, or to look over, again—which means in the case of the written thing neither more nor less than to re-read it. I had attached to it, in a brooding spirit, the idea of re-writing—with which it was to have in the event, for my *conscious* play of mind, almost nothing in common. I had thought of re-writing as so difficult, and even so absurd, as to be impossible—having also indeed, for that matter, thought of re-reading in the same light. But the felicity under the test was that where I had thus ruefully prefigured two efforts there proved to be but one—and this an effort but at the first blush. What re-writing might be was to remain—it has remained for me to this hour—a mystery. On the other hand the act of revision, the act of seeing it again, caused whatever I looked at on any page to flower before me as into the only terms that honourably expressed it; and the "revised" element in the present Edition is accordingly these terms, these rigid conditions of re-perusal, registered; so many close notes, as who should say, on the particular vision of the matter itself that experience had at last made the only possible one. (*23*: xvi; *AN*, 339)

A reader whose understanding of James's revisions in the New York Edition derived from this passage might well be surprised that he made changes at all. If "re-writing . . . remained for [James] to this hour—a mystery," as he claims, then how are we to account for two versions of so many of his texts? What curious bookkeeping is the author performing here, in order to represent his activity in this fashion?

In fact, his bookkeeping is precisely what is at issue in the above passage; he is doing something here with his figures such that two things repeatedly appear as if they are one. That is, while one would expect the activity of revision to be associated with various kinds of doublings, in his representation of revision, multiplication amounts to unification. First, re-reading and rewriting: "where I had thus ruefully prefigured two efforts there proved to be but one." Then, revision, the singular act that replaces the twin acts of rereading and rewriting, produces a similarly singular effect, it causes the object of the reviser's vision to "flower before [him] as into the only terms that honourably expressed it." The "flowering"—a metaphor that lends to this activity the authority of a natural process—presumably produces terms that differ from as well as terms that match the original ones, but the phrase emphasizes their singularity—"the only terms"—and concludes by reinforcing the natural category of growth with the social category of honor. Finally, even the plural "terms" is subordinated to a singular: "the 'revised' element in the present Edition"—a phrase in the singular—may be defined as "terms," "conditions registered," and "notes"—all plurals—but they are terms for, conditions of, and notes on "the particular vision of the matter itself that experience had at last made the only possible one." The sentence and the paragraph conclude with emphatic singular expressions, the last of which—"the only possible one"—is singularly absolute. The antecedent for that final pronoun is "vision," which suggests how completely James has moved from the potential doublings of "revision" to the strict and restrictive economy of a singular vision. The docile reader and the dictatorial author become hard to distinguish from one another; as James follows out his definition of revision as rereading, he is drawn to the conclusion that revision confirms the one real right thing.

James invests his authority in a more inclusive unity in this passage, much as he does in the metaphor of the snowy expanse that transcends the varying tracks of particular passages. But even while he claims to have discovered the essential unity that underlies all textual representation, he is able to accomplish this covertly coercive unification only through representation. That is—to shift to a more technical vocabulary—his signifiers are the only things that are singular, yet they suggest that what they signify—the essential meaning of the text—is the source of the singleness. Interestingly, the same kind of argument can be made about his Platonic metaphor of tracks in the snow; there too the unity he claims to be a transcendent essence is a product of the signifier. The image of a snowy expanse tracked by footprints bears a notable resemblance to the revised page it is supposed to represent. The snowy expanse is very much like the white paper, and those footprints the alphabetical characters of a particular "passage" (a crucial pun). To propose that James's metaphor for a Platonic theory of representation derives from the tracks of alphabetical signifiers is to question the premises of his argument. Indeed, if James's figure for the transcendent "matter" or idea derives from the blank page, one could argue in classic deconstructive fashion not only that a transcendental signified is conjured out of a signifier but also that this signifier of absence, the blank page, is being asked to endorse a theory of presence that it simultaneously disqualifies.

I Iui iic iiotcs how frequently the look of the revised page provides James with his metaphors for the process of revision.[4] Not only does the "snowy expanse" derive from the blank page, but an even more curious figure derives from the writings that fill the margins of James's revised text. James speaks of how revision leads to "the growth of the immense array of terms, perceptional and expressional, that, after the fashion I have indicated, in sentence, passage and page, simply looked over the heads of the standing terms—or perhaps rather, like alert winged creatures, perched on those diminished summits and aspired to a clearer air" (23: xvi–xvii; *AN*, 339). As Horne observes, James's figure here can be traced back to the actual look of the revised pages, in which revised text in the author's hand was suspended balloonlike in the margins of the printed page, attached only by lines or cables to the passages they emended or displaced (fig. 29).[5] Those winged words that float above the diminished summits of his old prose and aspire toward the clearer air of the ideal text can also be described as a form of transcendence that derives from the signifier. But in this case James's model of revision is less Platonic than Derridean. What rises, after all, is not the transcendent ideal of the eternally same literary work but the supplementary text. Reading between the lines may conform to the Platonic theory in that it means reading an intention that is not expressed; writing in the margins, on the other hand, is a Derridean figure because it acknowledges the supplementary status of representation.

James's theory of revision seems even less Platonic and more Derridean in another metaphor that he uses for those occasions of textual difference. This metaphor draws attention to the economic dimensions of representation, and it suggests that textual deviation or difference might augment value rather than diminish it. Noting his "fascination, at each stage of [his] journey, on the noted score of that so shifting and uneven character of the tracks of [his] original passage" (23: xix; *AN*, 341), he then characterizes his suspense: "What would the operative terms, in the given case, prove, under criticism, to have been—a series of waiting satisfactions or an array of waiting misfits? The misfits had but to be positive and concordant, in the special intenser light, to represent together (as the two sides of a coin show different legends) just so many effective felicities and substitutes" (23: xix;

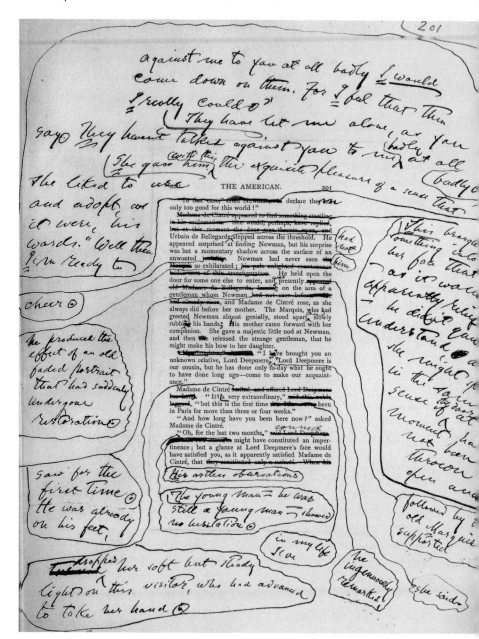

Figure 29. An example of James's revisions for *The American* in the New York Edition, revised from the 1883 version. Reproduced by permission of the Houghton Library, Harvard University.

AN, 341–42). Although one might presume that the writer would derive greater benefits from the "satisfactions" than from the "misfits," James's metaphor adumbrates a different economy. The two versions of a passage offer a double "legend" that works like the two sides of a coin to register value. The authorial economy benefits not from exact matches or harmonies, in this account, but from mismatches or differences. Indeed, those differences "represent together" a new relationship of substitution that offers a third legend derived from the difference between the first two. Rather like those winged words that transcend the prose supporting them, the coin images doubling and difference as an increase in value and a multiplication rather than a unification of texts.

A similar dislocation of the Platonic model occurs when James considers how rare the practice of revision is:

"People don't do such things," we remember to have heard it, in this connexion, declared; in other words they don't really re-read—no, not *really*; at least they do so to the effect either of seeing the buried, the latent life of a past composition vibrate, at renewal of touch, into no activity and break through its settled and "sunk" surface at no point whatever . . . or else they have in advance and on system stopped their ears, their eyes and even their very noses. (*23*: xx; *AN*, 342–43)

Revision is figured here as a kind of resurrection, a return of the Platonic original, but again the look of the revised page gives shape to the image. The "settled and 'sunk' surface" is the printed page, and what breaks its surface is the writing that rises above it into the margins and between the lines. The "settled and 'sunk' surface" is also presumably a grave, and James's figure not only equates the text with death but also makes the reanimation produced by reading both vital and ghostly. Reading must disrupt the settled published text to qualify as genuine reading, but it does so through a figure that links stability to death and vitality to ghostliness.

James's metaphor may derive from the appearance of the emended text, but it also speaks to those cases in which the supplemental writing makes no visible imprint, in which the different passage makes no permanent mark. In other words, reading is always a process of revision even if it leaves no traces, and the effect is to make James's rereading a prototype for the activity of the readers who will follow him. Just as the writer coins new value in the doubled legends produced by his revisions, so too does the reader:

What has the affair been at the worst, I am most moved to ask, but an earnest invitation to the reader to dream again in my company and in the interest of his own

larger absorption of my sense? The prime consequence on one's own part of re-
perusal is a sense for ever so many more of the shining silver fish afloat in the deep
sea of one's endeavor than the net of widest casting could pretend to gather in. (*23*:
xxii; *AN*, 345)

In the Platonic model, the value of the ideal form (that "shining expanse of
snow") preexists and survives any particular limited textual embodiments.
But in this metaphor, a different economy governs the production of value.
Re-casting, to adapt James's figure, expands the sea of possibility; it's not
that the revisionist captures more of the original fish than he was once able
to do but that he expands that shoal of "shining silver" through the very
renewal of his efforts. And the effect of revision extends to the reader,
whose capacity for seeing more value resembles the revisionist's own.

James's own Preface offers a model of how revision expands the resources of the writer when he discusses the effect of his marginal additions.
Marveling at "the immense array of terms" that fill in the once blank peri-
pheries of his text, he finds his interest turning to yet another immensity
revealed by these changes—the "history . . . of the growth of [those]
terms" (*23*: xvi; *AN*, 339). This "history"—untold but beckoning—is revealed to the writer as an effect of the supplementary process of revision
itself; "what it would be really interesting, and I dare say admirably difficult, to go into," the revisionist comments, "would be the very history of
this effect of experience"—the history of the revisionary process itself
(ibid.). If James's prefaces tell the "story of the story," he speculates here on
telling the story of the *revision* of the story. That this untold story remains
a hypothetical one—as the conditional verbs emphasize—does not detract
from its value; this added value is like the third legend created by the different legends on the two sides of the coin. If revision is a supplementary
process, then, it creates the need to tell more stories in the very process of
attempting to fill in the blanks. Writing in the margins reveals more margins yet to be filled, more "shining expanses" yet to be marked, more revised texts yet to be revised.

The unwritten stories summoned up by the process of revision do not
always seem like novelistic resources, though; James is also acutely sensitive to the deficits revealed by the process of revision. Interestingly, the
same conditional mood used to mark possibility is used to mark regret;
speaking now about the inadequacies revealed by his second passage
through certain texts, he laments: "If only one *could* re-write, if only one
could do better justice to the patches of crude surface, the poor morsels of

consciously-decent matter that catch one's eye with their rueful reproach for old stupidities of touch!" (*23*: xxi; *AN*, 344). Here his "would's" have been replaced by "*could*'s" to mark inadequacy rather than possibility; revision reveals the need for more revision. The image of the misfit returns, not as value, the coin with two legends, but as indebtedness; the revisionist encounters "the long-stored grievance of the subject bristling with a sense of over-prolonged exposure in a garment misfitted, a garment cheaply embroidered and unworthy of it" (ibid.). Faced with this complaint, he cannot help but hear the "sharpness of appeal, the claim for exemplary damages, or at least for poetic justice" (ibid.). These economic and legal metaphors draw attention, above all, to the compensatory nature of revision, its promise to provide "redress." But just as the Platonic theory of representation lingers in that image of dress, so too it can be felt in the image of "redress." That is, the perfect fit of subject to representation is as much a Platonic fiction as the economic balance promised by the concept of "poetic justice." Whatever the resources called into being by the process of revision, they can never simply balance the books and provide poetic justice. Instead, the resources are forever too great and too little, inexhaustible and yet inadequate to cover the subject. Such a recognition can produce regret or marvel, but what it can never provide is unity or closure.

In renouncing closure, James's logic of revision must give up both original conceptions and last words. The supplemental chain initiated—or perhaps only extended—by his revisions in the New York Edition has neither an origin nor a termination to anchor it. Authority cannot be stabilized around a concept of original conception because such conceptions are always vulnerable to "last words"; similarly, because last words are themselves supplementary to first words, they are equally provisional, never in themselves fully authoritative. Indeed, no words can be "last" because the very addition of any revisionary words means that each version is part of a series of possibilities. "Firstness" and "lastness" alike lose their meanings as markers of the identity of the text; instead, the text is always in the middle, in the process of being revisited and revised.

To say that James is a defender of neither original conceptions nor last words is not to relieve his readers of making choices about which texts to read. Indeed, the reader's need to choose seems to follow logically from those choices the author makes in the process of revision. It is simply that the reader cannot ground his choices on a theory of authority and revision that James refuses to grant himself, that his very texts undermine. Instead, what James offers the reader is a theory of revisionary reading that extends his own logic of revisionary writing. Another way to put this is that the economy that governs the production of texts also governs their consumption. James might wish to control that process of consumption by treating it as a form of reading between the lines, of taking in more of the writer's unexpressed intention—after all, he proffers "an earnest invitation to the reader to dream again in my company and in the interest of his own larger absorption of my sense" (*23*: xxii; *AN*, 345). But in spite of the possessive—"*my* sense" (emphasis added)—the logic that regulates the production of meaning implies that he cannot own the further meanings generated in the process of reading. The potential for dispossession might be a cause for anxiety, but it is inseparable from the economy that promises an extension of value. Indeed, how is the author different from the reader except in a legal sense? James's possessive pronoun, his "my," speaks a fantasy of protection from de-authorizing consumption, but he cannot own the meanings that the text produces in its potentially infinite revisions.

II

If the Preface to *The Golden Bowl* evokes the unstable relation between writer and reader, James's tale "The Middle Years" makes the logical connection between the practice of revision and the role of the reader its very subject. Published in 1893, over a decade before James wrote the Preface to *The Golden Bowl*, "The Middle Years" anticipates James's situation in preparing the New York Edition not by treating revision as a specific project undertaken at a certain point in a literary career but instead by seeing it as intrinsic to the activity of writing itself. The tale characterizes revision as the hallmark of literary authority, but it also treats revision as a source of authorial vulnerability; in fact, the heightened role of the reader in this tale derives directly from the needs created by revision. However, reading proves to be no escape from the vulnerabilities of revision; both are situated within an economy of textual consumption that makes evident the fears as well as the hopes that James only hints at in the Preface to *The Golden Bowl*.

The tale's cast of four—an ailing writer, a doctor who is also an admiring reader, a patient who rivals the writer for the doctor's attention, and the patient's paid companion—enact a drama that reveals James's intense ambivalence toward both the revision and the reception of literary texts. The

tale's protagonist is Ralph Dencombe, a writer whose failing health is a
particular anguish because he feels himself only now on the verge of writing his own best work. Dencombe finds consolation if not a cure in the
ministrations of Doctor Hugh, a young medical man whose professional
devotion to the writer follows from his personal admiration for Den
combe's literary genius. But Dencombe must compete for Doctor Hugh's
attention with another patient whose claim on the doctor is as urgent as his
own and who constitutes a threat to any fantasy of the ideal reader. In the
figure of the Countess—and her companion Miss Vernham—the tale reveals the author's nightmare of an unsympathetic reception from the reading public, a nightmare that cannot be fully separated from its companion
dream of the ideal reader Doctor Hugh. Doctor Hugh may represent the
authorial relief derived from a fantasy of relinquishing authority to a benign reader, a reader who can, in the words of James's Preface, "dream
again in my company and in the interest of his own larger absorption of my
sense," but the Countess and her companion reveal the fears attendant on
that same relinquishing of control. If the tale seems to muffle the Countess
and celebrate the doctor-reader, it does not entirely succeed in quieting the
anxieties she represents. What readers tend to remember in reading "The
Middle Years" is the celebration of art—vulnerable yet somehow triumphant—with which the tale closes. But the tale is actually more ambivalent
than its conclusion indicates, and therefore the narrative middle—and the
full cast of four rather than the celebrated twosome—are crucial to an interpretation of James's allegory of revision and reading.

Dencombe, the writer whose health fades just as he feels himself coming into possession of his own literary powers, sees the source of his mastery
in the source of his fallibility; because of his dedication to revision, the
work that he is able to complete is meager to the very degree that his time
has been filled with so many reworkings. If Dencombe's obsessive revising
expresses his sense that the work could always be improved by some supplementary attention from the "master," the tale also explores another supplementary practice that can take the place of revision. Reading becomes
the necessary supplement to writing, and the tale raises the possibility that
the literary text might find its completion not in the marginal penciling of
the ailing author but in the admiring responses of the devoted reader.

The writing practices of the tale's protagonist—which is to say practices of revision—initially establish an oppositional relationship between
writing and reading. As "a passionate corrector, a fingerer of style," Den-

combe finds it difficult to reveal his less than perfect text—and thereby give
up some portion of his authority—to a reading public: "The last thing he
ever arrived at was a form final for himself. His ideal would have been to
publish secretly, and then, on the published text, treat himself to the terri-
fied revise, sacrificing always a first edition and beginning for posterity and
even for the collectors, poor dears, with a second" (*16*: 90). An appropriate
emblem of supplementarity, this imaginary text without a first edition is
seen as particularly a problem for those who fetishize "originality," the collectors. Theoretically, of course, the habit of revision that leads Dencombe
to favor a second over a first edition would lead him to favor a third over a
second; in other words, the process of revision is potentially endless. Dencombe's difficulty in arriving at a "form final for himself" can be described
as his unwillingness to cease being an author, to relinquish his text to a
reading public.

   The first effect of his writing practice is to prolong his authority, ex-
tending his authorial control over his text at the very moment that he would
otherwise release it for publication. Yet his recognition in this tale is that
the practice that extends his authority paradoxically restricts it; having
spent so long revising each of his works, he has not the time to produce
enough of them. In his late years he has only arrived at his "Middle Years";
thus, his present lament that his creative life has been cut short can also be
viewed as an effect of revision:

His development had been abnormally slow, almost grotesquely gradual. He had
been hindered and retarded by experience, he had for long periods only groped his
way. It had taken too much of his life to produce too little of his art. The art had
come, but it had come after everything else. At such a rate a first existence was too
short—long enough only to collect material; so that to fructify, to use the material,
one should have a second age, an extension. (*16*: 82)

The textual economy of revision is in fact the existential economy that governs his life's work. Just as Dencombe finds that a first economy necessitates
a second, here he finds that a "first existence" demands "a second age, an
extension."

   As if to counter this sense of restricted resources and potentially infinite
labors, Dencombe finds his attention drawn toward a scene that seems both
to extend his future as a novelist and to bring revision to an end. What
engages Dencombe's attention is not the work already complete, the novel
in its packet from the publisher, but a novel as yet unwritten, a story being
performed on the beach below him. A trio of figures—a gentleman with

two ladies—immediately begins to generate a story: "Where morcover was the virtue of an approved novelist if one couldn't establish a relation between such figures? the clever theory for instance that the young man was the son of the opulent matron and that the humble dependent, the daughter of a clergyman or an officer, nourished a secret passion for him" (16· 79) As Dencombe develops this hypothetical drama out of the lives before him, ignoring the published text at hand, he notices a curious reversal: the young man he observes is, in exact contrast to Dencombe, engaged in reading a book while "the romance of life [stands] neglected at his side" (ibid.). The inverse symmetry is striking, even before the book is identified as the one in Dencombe's lap. What the contrast highlights is the paired displacements of reading by writing and of writing by reading. For Dencombe, drawn to images that mark his extended career as a writer, this substitution of the completed text for the text as yet unwritten, of the act of reading for the act of authorship, has a surprising appeal. Just as the book's cover appears "alluringly red" (16: 78), the book's reader is "an object of envy to an observer from whose connexion with literature all such artlessness had faded" (ibid.). The effect, then, of Dencombe's turn toward future "material" and further composition is a return to the book at hand. Presumably the same color as the book Dencombe possesses, it appears "alluringly red" because it is "alluringly read."

Reading replaces writing and completes it; with reading, revision finally comes to an end. The figure who seemed to provide Dencombe with material for future texts provides him instead with a desire to read what he has already written. To his surprise, when he turns to his own novel his reading produces something entirely unexpected: he experiences "a strange alienation" (16: 80). "He had forgotten what his book was about" (ibid.). This forgetting he attributes to "the assault of his old ailment," and it thereby anticipates a greater loss: "He couldn't have chanted to himself a single sentence, couldn't have turned with curiosity or confidence to any particular page. His subject had already gone from him, leaving scarce a superstition behind. He uttered a low moan as he breathed the chill of this dark void, so desperately it seemed to represent the completion of a sinister process" (ibid.). He forgets what he has written because the book has figuratively passed into the hands of a reader and is out of his authorial control and beyond his revisionary power. The end of revision—appropriately, given its existential parallel—is death.

But this "strange alienation" from his own work also has another effect;

if it figures his death as an author it also signals his birth as a reader. Becoming other to himself provides gains as well as losses. If he had turned to his completed text simply for refuge, what he now discovers in it gives back more than he can remember having put into it. "Everything came back to him, but came back with a wonder, came back above all with a high and magnificent beauty" (*16*: 81). Reading feels like a wondrous seduction; he finds himself "drawn down, as by a siren's hand" into the "dim underworld of fiction" (ibid.). This self-division or self-doubling occasioned by reading can feel like a death—the death of a singular authority with the power to revise endlessly—but it can also mark the escape from death, the extension of the life of the writer in the life of the reader. Even the images double one another: the "chill of the dark void" is transformed into "the dim underworld of fiction."

What Dencombe experiences in his own act of reading—this "othering" of himself—is reenacted in less solipsistic terms with the tale's other reader, Doctor Hugh. From the episode of the matched book that marks his first encounter with the older man, Doctor Hugh doubles Dencombe, intimating another form of extension from the one Dencombe had originally envisioned—the prolonged life of the single author. Indeed, Doctor Hugh's own multiple roles—potential character, reader, doctor, even surrogate family—suggest a variety of ways in which he might act as supplement and extension to the ailing author.

The contrast between a fatally depleting economy associated with authorship as opposed to a potentially renewing economy associated with reading emerges again in the first scene between the two men. The distinction between the two economies is emphasized by the structure of the scene, since it takes as its point of departure Dencombe's pretense of being merely another reader and as its conclusion the revelation of his identity as the author of *The Middle Years*. The two men are initially drawn to one another as two readers of the same book; in fact, Doctor Hugh leaves his copy of the book beside Dencombe as a pledge of his intention to return. Moreover, Dencombe's identity as the book's author first emerges because of the difference between the two men's copies. When Doctor Hugh mistakenly picks up Dencombe's copy of *The Middle Years* instead of his own and discovers that their texts are different, Dencombe both literally and figuratively reveals his hand through precisely the signs of his most characteristic writing practice—revision. Doctor Hugh notes the small penciled changes in Dencombe's text with reproach and then wonder; the man before him is neither reader nor reviewer but the author in person. There is a noticeable mirroring in their physical responses to this recognition: as Doctor Hugh guesses Dencombe's identity the doctor "change[s] color" (16: 90), a response that is doubled and intensified in this response of Dencombe himself: "Through a blur of ebbing consciousness [he] saw Doctor Hugh's mystified eyes. He only had time to feel he was about to be ill again—that emotion, excitement, fatigue, the heat of the sun, the solicitation of the air, had combined to play him a trick, before, stretching out a hand to his visitor with a plaintive cry, he lost his senses altogether" (16: 91). Dencombe loses consciousness at the moment his reader Doctor Hugh discovers his authorial secret—revision. His loss of consciousness indicates the anxiety reading represents, an anxiety revision attempts to waylay. Doctor Hugh discovers Dencombe's weakness, his lack of a sense of completion and his fear of what it means to have his art pass out of his control and into the arena of consumption.

If Dencombe loses consciousness in revealing his identity to Doctor Hugh, he regains it with a generous reassurance from the young doctor: "You'll be all right again—I know all about you now" (16: 92). Doctor Hugh's equation of Dencombe's recovery with his own knowledge suggests his own intuitive sense of himself as Dencombe's extension. As their earlier mirrored responses to the revelation intimate, the two men supplement one another in needs and talents. Not only is Doctor Hugh Dencombe's ideal reader, but his medical expertise seems precisely designed for Dencombe's rescue. Moreover, Doctor Hugh is eager to offer his own professional services in recompense for the tremendous literary gifts he has received from Dencombe. "I want to do something for you," the young man proclaims. "I want to do everything. You've done a tremendous lot for me" (ibid.). Even his practice of reading is the ideal counterpart to Dencombe's practice of writing: if Dencombe's "signature" is his penciled revision, Doctor Hugh distinguishes the works of his admired author by describing them as "the only ones he could read a second time" (16: 86). Doctor Hugh too is a "revisionary" reader, one who returns to the text repeatedly—not as in Dencombe's case out of feeling of doubt regarding the writer's authority but for converse reasons—out of a feeling of respect for a complete and unrevisable authority. Indeed, Doctor Hugh reminds us, through this interdependence of writing and reading, that revision restores and extends as well as exhausts vitality and value. With his declaration to Dencombe—"You *shall* live!" (16: 96)—Doctor Hugh insists on the restorative side of this revi-

sionary economy, his faith that he can use his life as doctor-reader to allow
Dencombe to write again.

But this benign vision of relations between admired author and admiring reader does not tell the whole story, for Doctor Hugh does not come
alone. When Dencombe makes himself dependent on the ministrations of
the young doctor, he also renders himself subject to the women who accompany—and indeed employ—Doctor Hugh. Moreover, if Doctor Hugh
represents the restorative possibilities associated with reading, the two
women represent the dangers, dangers most associated with the author's
lack of control. This loss of control can be traced in the spatial reposition-
ing of these four figures; if at the tale's outset, the solitary author sat above
the trio, looking down and exercising his control in his ability to imagine
"combinations," he later finds himself on their level and "combined" with
them in relations he never would have chosen. When Doctor Hugh climbs
to Dencombe's level on the cliff, he not only brings the reader to the same
level as the writer but brings what had been the author's material—those
two less than cooperative women—up to the ground occupied by the author. This spatial change figures the change in relations that accompanies a
turn to the readerly economy; the master mind who controls the world
through observation must submit his body and his text to the same conditions that assail his characters. Reading submits the textual body to the attentions of another—an acknowledgment that the author is not capable of
doing everything to doctor the text. But he ends up relinquishing his body
to a treatment he never would have chosen, at the hands not of the devoted
specialist but instead of the competing women.

Dencombe's resistance to the Countess and Miss Vernham is expressed
in part as a critique of the terms according to which the older woman exercises a hold over Doctor Hugh, terms that are implicit in the Countess's
personal history. The Countess is "the daughter of a celebrated baritone,
whose taste *minus* his talent she had inherited" and also "the widow of a
French nobleman and mistress of all that remained of the handsome fortune, the fruit of her father's earnings, that had constituted her dower" (16:
88). The story told by the Countess's fortune is that the male artist is the
origin of wealth, both literal and figurative. Moreover, "the fruit" of those
artistic earnings goes to furnish a dowry, the form of payment that seals a
woman's claim on a man and grants it institutional legitimacy. The death of
men—both father and husband—releases that fortune to a woman who has
no power to create one herself, since she has "taste without . . . talent." The
fortune allows her to make "terms" with a new man—Doctor Hugh—that

render his attention legitimate, while leaving another artist—Dencombe—without the resources that would allow him to continue his creative career. The Countess is, in other words, not only a consumer of art but a consumer of artists, with her parasitical mode of survival on her father's fortune and husband's title. Her relations with Doctor Hugh and Dencombe repeat and extend her earlier relations with the father and husband from whom she inherited her resources.

The Countess's physical condition becomes the emblem of her identity as a consumer. Her excessive size, grand fortune, and ill health seem of a piece; she is the appetitive self carried to a precarious extreme. One of her first remarks to Doctor Hugh emphasizes this association with physical appetite: "I find myself horribly hungry. At what time did you order luncheon?" Doctor Hugh's response—"I ordered nothing to-day—I'm going to make you diet" (16: 83)—suggests the best treatment for the Countess's disorder is a restriction of her appetites. If Dencombe's ill health can be seen as an excess of revisionary production, the Countess's can be seen as excess of absorption or consumption; she is a monstrous bloated parody of the reader as consumer, the one who inherits the artistic fortune and whom the law thereby favors to make legitimate claims, but who performs no labor and creates no value herself. Her power to purchase, like her appetite for food and her taste for art, becomes just another symptom of her unbridled consumption; moreover, her most extravagant purchase, the medical attention of Doctor Hugh, is so important to her that she cannot live without it: "She paid so much for his fidelity that she must have it all: she refused him the right to other sympathies, charged him with scheming to make her die alone" (16: 97–98).

Recognizing that the Countess's legal claim on Doctor Hugh is ultimately a financial one, Dencombe displays metaphoric resources that surpass the Countess's. Further, unlike the Countess, he is no mere inheritor of wealth created by another; he is instead the source of treasure himself:

[Dencombe] found another strain of eloquence to plead the cause of a certain splendid "last manner," the very citadel, as it would prove, of his reputation, the stronghold into which his real treasure would be gathered. . . . Even for himself he was inspired as he told what his treasure would consist of; the precious metals he would dig from the mine, the jewels rare, strings of pearls, he would hang between the columns of his temple. (16: 98–99)

Dencombe's choice of figures not only makes creative genius the source of all value, the mine from which all treasure comes, but it also makes that creative genius a distinctly male possession. Dencombe's metaphor—"jew-

els rare . . . hang[ing] between the columns of his temple"—has become a
cultural commonplace, the all too familiar "family jewels." He resists the
older woman's claim on the young man—legitimate yet parasitical—with a
display of his resources that leaves the young man "pant[ing] for the combinations to come" (*16*: 99). The effect is a promise that supplants Doctor
Hugh's commitment to the Countess: he "renewed to Dencombe his guarantee that his profession would hold itself responsible for such a life"
(ibid.).

The resolution of the tale is to give Doctor Hugh the choice of these
two models of artistic creation and consumption—he gets to choose which
economy to endorse, which inheritance to claim. Neither patient can survive without him, but he selects the idealized relation between author and
reader embodied in Dencombe. When Dencombe discovers that the
Countess has died and left the young man "never a penny"—presumably
the fortune will go to Miss Vernham—Doctor Hugh interprets his choice:
"I chose to accept, whatever they might be, the consequences of my infatuation. . . . The fortune be hanged! It's your own fault if I can't get your
things out of my head" (*16*: 104–105).

Dencombe's displacement of the Countess—and of Miss Vernham—is
central to any account of the tale's allegory of revision. Dencombe now has
what the Countess attempted to contract for—"the whole of [Doctor
Hugh's] attention"—but more importantly, Dencombe has also taken the
place of a younger woman the doctor might have wed. This alternative
union depends for its value on the renounced legacy of the Countess (which
gives Dencombe the measure of how much Doctor Hugh cares) and for its
representation on the displaced relationship with Miss Vernham. The language here—Doctor Hugh's "infatuation," his declarations in a voice that
has "the ring of a marriage-bell"—derives from the heterosexual union
with which such a story might have closed (*16*: 105). Whatever contrac-
tual power the Countess once exerted over Doctor Hugh, that power has
been displaced in this image of a wedding of male writer and male reader.
It is an image not simply of love but of matching and legal sanction. That
is, Dencombe finds in his ideal reader Doctor Hugh such a mirroring and
confirmation of his authority that he is finally cured of the need to revise.

The medium of Doctor Hugh's cure is the tightly echoing dialogue
with which the tale concludes, the responses of the reader seconding, confirming, and thereby completing the writer's words. What is often ex-
cerpted from this dialogue is Dencombe's passionate definition of the writ-

er's activity; it is an account of art as fraught with doubt, as nothing more in fact than the need to revise: "A second chance—*that's* the delusion. There never was to be but one. We work in the dark—we do what we can— we give what we have. Our doubt is our passion and our passion is our task. The rest is the madness of art" (*16*: 105). But this definition is transformed by its context in the dialogue of voices; the presence of the ideal reader assures Dencombe that revision is in fact unnecessary. The danger of the consuming women is removed, and instead Dencombe hears the voice of a reader so like himself that he need no longer fear his words going astray, his texts being misunderstood. The doubt that drove his revisionary practice is turned, in this repetition, into the very stuff of his accomplishment, the confirmation of his fully achieved authority.

"If you've doubted, if you've despaired, you've always 'done' it," his visitor subtly argued.

"We've done something or other," Dencombe conceded.

"Something or other is everything. It's the feasible. It's *you*!"

"Comforter!" poor Dencombe ironically sighed.

"But it's true," insisted his friend.

"It's true. It's frustration that doesn't count."

"Frustration's only life," said Doctor Hugh.

"Yes, it's what passes." Poor Dencombe was barely audible, but he had marked with the words the virtual end of his first and only chance. (*16*: 106)

It is hard to distinguish the source from the echo, the author from his reader, in that Dencombe repeats Doctor Hugh's phrases as often as Doctor Hugh does Dencombe's. This echoing dialogue between Dencombe and Doctor Hugh relieves Dencombe of the very anxiety that constituted his art as revisionary; Dencombe is saved here from the potential danger of reading, of a deviation from the author's sense that would undermine his authority. Instead, what Doctor Hugh returns to Dencombe is a sense of the same, an assurance of a unified and single meaning shared by author and reader. As a supplement, Doctor Hugh completes Dencombe's deficiency, ministering to both his bodily life and his text. Dencombe need no longer doctor himself. Not surprisingly, this exchange is able to provide for Dencombe's *The Middle Years* what it does for James's "The Middle Years"—closure, an end to the interminable need to revise.

The strangely similar male voices that conclude the tale must, however, be heard against the female voices they silence. The tale is haunted not just by the prospective death of the author but by the excluded figures of the

textual consumer embodied in the Countess and Miss Vernham. In the figure of the Countess, the supplement appears in its debased and dangerous
form; it is the excessive appetitive body, the avaricious purchaser, the
threatening female sexual other. It is also the cause that makes interminable
revision necessary, thus depleting the author's life and his creative possibilities. Now the Countess is dead, Doctor Hugh announces, and her final
words have been to curse him and divest him of an inheritance. But although Dencombe might seem to have succeeded at getting Doctor Hugh
alone, and although Doctor Hugh may provide Dencombe with the idealized image of the reader as authorial echo, as repetition without danger of
deviation, still the very necessity of such absolute assurance testifies to the
danger against which it operates. There would be no need for so singular a
model of authority, purged entirely of the artistic doubt and the need to
revise, if there were no ghosts at the margins, no haunting possibilities of
a different kind of textual reception. What the tale cannot help but reveal
is the author's lack of control in its other ghost, the Countess. Present at the
end only in her lost legacy, she shows that textual effects are no ethereal
echo that reverberate exclusively to the author's controlling voice but ex-
cesses and fallibilities beyond the anticipation of even the most foresightful
of authors, the most doctored of texts.

III

If in the Preface to *The Golden Bowl* James argues that revision is rereading, in "The Middle Years" James reveals just how potent a force the reader
is. What we might call a Platonic theory of reading, following those metaphors of ideal essence in the Preface to *The Golden Bowl*, provides one way
of countering and containing the power of the reader. However much the
reader might deviate from the particular textual representations, those deviations will always serve the interest of a larger grasp of the writer's sense.
The Platonic reader's passage through the text would resemble the travel-
er's passage through that "shining expanse of snow"; even if his tracks differed from those of his author, they would be other marks on the field of
the writer's more generous intention. Doctor Hugh might figure as this
Platonic version of the reader, giving back what the writer designs, but
with an extension. That he has the Countess in tow, however, suggests that
one cannot have one kind of reader without the other. The Countess, expansive, errant, and irreverent toward the writer, could be seen as a decon-

structive supplement who fails to remain under authorial control. Bloated like those balloons suspended above the printed text on James's revised page and compared to a broken down flying machine, she reminds us of the material origins of signification, the physical body that sustains all flights of fancy. Although James's tale rejects her version of artistic inheritance in favor of the idealized relationship between the ailing writer and his healing reader, her presence in the tale confesses what James's Preface to *The Golden Bowl* cannot quite address: the writer's own revisions are the signature both of possession and of dispossession, and the writer will never know all that will be written in the ever expanding margins of his own revised text.

PART IV

Representing Henry James

The Emotional Aftermath of the New York Edition

Carol Holly

Henry James received the first royalty statement from the New York Edition in October 1908, while the final volumes were still being prepared. The figures came as a shock. James's "four years of unremunerated labor, the gathering in of his work of a lifetime," writes Leon Edel, "showed signs of being a complete failure." Writing to his agent, James claimed that he felt "a great, I confess, and bitter, grief." His amanuensis wrote in her diary that the master was feeling depressed. Eventually the depression was complicated by an obscure physical illness, "some palpitations" of the heart, says Edel, and "a little shortness of breath." James thought he was suffering from heart disease, like his brother, William, but his heart specialist called attention to James's anxieties instead. "It is the mystery that is making you ill," the fear that "you have got angina pectoris" and should "die suddenly," Sir James Mackenzie pronounced. He advised James, "if you be more judicious in your living, and give your heart less work to do, there is no reason why you should not reach the ordinary span of human life."[1]

But Mackenzie did not attend to the mystery that fueled James's preoccupation with his health—his anxieties about his work—and, after several months of improvement, James's condition became worse. His letters in the fall of 1909 conveyed a renewed concern for his health. In October he received another disappointing royalty statement for the Edition. Shortly thereafter he burned his private papers. Early in January he tried to recover his spirits by appealing in his notebook to "all the powers and forces and divinities to whom I've ever been loyal and who haven't failed me yet."[2] But a few days later he collapsed. "There was nothing for me to do," wrote William's son, Harry,

but to sit by his side and hold his hand while he panted and sobbed for two hours until the Doctor arrived, and stammered in despair so eloquently and pathetically that as I write of it the tears flow down my cheeks again. He talked about Aunt Alice and his own end and I knew him to be facing not only the frustration of all his hopes and ambitions, but the vision looming close and threatening to his weary eyes, of a lingering illness such as hers. In sight of all that, he wanted to die. . . . He didn't have a good night and the next day the same thing began again.[3]

"What happened," Henry later explained to William, "was that I found myself at a given moment more and more beginning to fail of power to eat through the daily more marked increase of a strange and most persistent and depressing stomachic crisis: the condition of more and more sickishly *loathing* food." He was suffering, he wrote to a friend, from "a digestive crisis making food loathsome and nutrition impossible—and sick inanition and weakness and depression permanent."[4] Leon Edel observes that James "blamed his condition on his having for so long 'Fletcherized' his food—the fad involving lengthy mastication." But James's doctor was treating him as a "case of 'nerves,'" and, by viewing James's illnesses as "delayed" reactions to the financial failure of the Edition, Edel also treats the master as a nervous "case" whose problems are distinct from his nutritional program.[5] I would like to propose that in a sense both James and Edel were right: a psychological condition or "case of 'nerves,'" the digestive crisis *was* linked to James's practice of controlling his eating. For the history of James's Fletcherizing not only points to a problem inherent in the enthusiasm with which he embraced the chewing fad in the first place; it also indicates that an increasingly problematic reliance on Fletcherizing was set in motion between 1908 and 1910 by James's need to manage his painful feelings of failure and loss. Eventually his Fletcherizing resulted in symptoms of what the medical experts in James's time called anorexia hysteria or anorexia nervosa: "abhorrence of or aversion to food, symptomatic of certain mental afflictions."[6]

What was "Fletcherizing," and how did it come to play such a central role in James's life after the financial failure of the Edition? These questions call for an inquiry into both the origins of James's Fletcherizing and the circumstances under which this practice became increasingly compulsive and self-destructive. They require as well an inquiry into the relationship among James's attitudes towards his work, his concerns for his health, and his need for emotional control. And finally, I believe, they demand an exploration of James's emotional difficulties within the context of James family psychology, as interpreted in recent years through the lens of what Howard Feinstein calls "family therapy theory."[7]

I

Named after its originator, Horace Fletcher, the practice of Fletcherizing one's food was one of the most popular developments in the nutrition and hygiene movements of the late nineteenth century. After 1890, writes Harvey Green, "public awareness of nutrition grew as newspapers and magazines reported the finds of scientists and physicians, as well as the often rancorous sectarian arguments between meateaters and vegetarians." Horace Fletcher's contribution to this growing interest in the relationship between health and nutritional management was his theory of chewing. "Fletcher reasoned that by chewing food so thoroughly that all the flavor was extracted and the remains involuntarily swallowed, people would eat less, digest their food more easily, and more efficiently use the food they ate."[8] Fletcher had begun his career as an expert in self-improvement by writing books on "menticulture," the cultivation of mental and emotional health.[9] His interest in dietary reform arose from the "discovery that the best mental results could not be accomplished in a body weakened by any indigestion, any mal-assimilation of nutriment, any excess of the waste of indigestion."[10] Fletcherism, then, was a program of both dietary reform and "Physiologic Optimism," and accordingly Fletcher claimed it could produce benefits ranging from an "increase of 50% to 200% in physical endurance" and "immunity from sickness" to "renewal of normal confidence and laudable ambition" and "optimism, usefulness and happiness."[11]

Within the James family, it was William who first became aware of Fletcher's writings. In the Gifford lectures he delivered in 1901–2, William twice quoted Fletcher to illustrate the "healthy-minded" or "mind-cure" philosophy that had gained popularity in late-nineteenth-century America.[12] In 1905 William went on to characterize Fletcher as "one of the most original and 'sympathetic' personalities whom Massachusetts in our day has produced."[13] A year earlier, William had sent Henry a copy of Fletcher's early treatise on dietary management, *The New Glutton or Epicure* (1903), with "certain passages marked" for Henry "to read." "Every word is true about it," William maintained. "You are in a very favorable

situation for learning his art of chewing, which he says it takes a good three
months for a man to acquire automatically. . . . I advise you to give it your
most respectful attention. I am quite sure it meets my case to a T, and I am
going to try to become a muncher, as he is."[14] William never specified his
reasons for recommending the "art of chewing" to Henry, but it appears
from their correspondence that he believed Fletcherizing might serve as a
cure for Henry's gout, indigestion, and weight problems.

As William put it, Henry's reaction to Fletcher was "instantaneous."
The day after receiving *The New Glutton*, Henry wrote to acknowledge
that a

mere dip into it made me sit up so straight that I failed, under the consequent excitement, almost entirely of my night's sleep. I don't know who H.F. is . . . but
his treatise somehow speaks to me on the spot, and I have been breakfasting this
morning wholly in the light of it. This single experiment has seemed to me illuminating—but I'm fairly afraid to commit myself to rash hope. I have all the same
a sneaking confidence, engendered in these few hours. I've read the book already
almost twice over, and I shall certainly give its doctrine the most patient and reso-
lute trial.

Promising to keep William informed of the results—"I'm so sure you'll be
interested," he declared—Henry went on to ask for "one or two" more of
the "delightful creature's other books. That is I mean mainly, one other
copy of 'The New Glutton,' and one of the 'A.B.–Z of Our Own Nutrition.' I'm sure I shall have good use for them."[15]

Having received the volumes by March, Henry wrote to William that
he was using Fletcher "to work out . . . my salvation," and in May he reported: "I continue to found my life on Fletcher. He is immense—thanks
to which I am getting much less so." By the following year, he was writing
to friends that he was "*fanatic*" about Fletcher, and to Fletcher himself that
his dietary regime was "my conversion and redemption": "I Fletcherize—
and that's my life, I mean it makes my life possible, & it has enormously
improved my work." Because of his "salubrity" and "serenity," Fletcher
himself became an "object-lesson" to James; "two or three days" after returning from a meeting with Fletcher to the "quiet living & sane nutrition" of Lamb House, James is so full of "the measure of what" he owes the
nutritionist that "my existence scarcely affords room for the operation of
further benefits."[16] In Rye, moreover, he became a proselytizer for Fletcher's methods: "'You must chew,' he would tell his neighbours in Rye, insisting that every disorder could be cured by chewing, and he would give

them copies of Mr Fletcher's book *The New Glutton or Epicure*, which he would inscribe, begging them 'to try the same cure.'"[17]

In one of the several letters he wrote to Fletcher during this time, however, James identified a drawback to the food faddist's program of nutrition control: the inclination "to make Fletcherism perhaps a little *excessively* reduce" the "quantity" of food one eats. Fletcherism "legitimately & triumphantly" reduces one's intake of food, he explains, "when this virtue in it is not made an over-ridden horse." For several years, accordingly, James was careful to observe the "difference between Fletcherizing on really *enough* (of quantity) & on too little," and, as a result, he was able to claim to William in 1909 that "the past 6 years of Fletcherizing—with no shadow of *strain* or overdoing"—had been responsible for "the best period of health I have had in my life." But the 1905 letter to Fletcher nonetheless hints at a prior history of eating problems, a history that can help us to understand the risks James incurred not only by adopting the program in the first place but also by pursuing it for six years with such regularity and zeal. "I find I must be on my guard," he acknowledges, "against real *under*-feeding—into which I tend rather easily to fall—as the result of an old hatred of the whole act & business of eating, the source for me, in the past, of so much misery—black to look back upon. That underfeeding fixed in me at one time certain very bad, quite horribly bad, *weakened* abdominal conditions, & I find that these tend to lie in wait for me again unless thoroughly due nourishment keeps them at bay."[18]

II

When he speaks in this letter of a period in which he experienced "weakened abdominal conditions," James most likely refers to the late 1860's and the early 1870's when, like several of his siblings, his passage from adolescence to adulthood was hampered by a number of physical ailments, chief among them his back problems, digestive complaints, and costiveness.[19] Biographers have argued that these digestive complaints were symptomatic of the "intense inner malaise" James was experiencing at the time.[20] James was uncertain whether, through his travels and his efforts to write, he could work his way into health, action, and productivity or, through the collapse of these efforts, he would become an invalid doomed to a life of illness and inactivity. This uncertainty, in turn, was related to a fear that to become an invalid was to succumb to a family legacy of illness, ineffectuality, and failure, was to become, in particular, like his lame and emotionally dependent father [21] His physical ailments, by this account, expressed his struggle to assert his will and achieve a measure of autonomy within a family that unconsciously attempted to keep him emotionally enmeshed. They were also a way to express emotions—anger and shame, for example—that were forbidden in a family committed to the Victorian ideal of familial devotion and harmony. [22]

James's 1905 letter to Horace Fletcher now invites us to consider yet another factor in our interpretation of his youthful ailments: the possibility that his digestive crises were themselves caused by or related to some kind of eating disorder, the symptoms of which were his loathing of food and his "real *under*-feeding." Perhaps the young James was suffering from what one nineteenth-century physician described as a frequent source of anorectic behavior in young women: "hysteric apepsia" or "nervous stomach condition." [23] Perhaps James regulated his eating to gain control over aspects of his life that had heretofore been controlled by his family, including his sense of identity. Perhaps his "real *under*-feeding" was an attempt to manage the painful emotions and troubling desires he was experiencing during this transition from youth to adulthood. [24]

Whatever the explanation—and all of these possibilities are intertwined—the young James's near obsession with his digestive problems and his "hatred of the whole act & business of eating" are clearly related to disturbing patterns of behavior evident in other members of his family. His father admitted to having been "hopelessly addicted" to alcohol and other stimulants in his early years, and during a period in his later years Henry, Sr., subjected his family to an almost compulsive pattern of relocation and travel. [25] James's younger brother Robertson likewise suffered from alcoholism—as did their cousin Robert Temple—and Alice's diary repeatedly suggests that her chronic invalidism stemmed from her emotional difficulties within her family. [26] The entire family, in fact, lived by an emotional system which, according to family psychologists, gives rise to compulsive or addictive behaviors in its members.

Focused around and perpetuated by the senior Henry James's "negative identity" or shame, and rigorously maintained by his wife, Mary James, the rules of this system not only demanded a high level of dependence upon and loyalty to the family but also created within the family a sense of emotional fusion or entanglement. Negative affect was to be repressed and shameful secrets (father's in particular) were to be carefully guarded by everyone in the family, even by the children who had but a vague, uneasy awareness of their existence.[27] At all costs, a positive image of the family was to be maintained outside the family circle, and within the family it was crucial to maintain a sense of harmony and order. By thus insisting on the rigorous control of emotions, yet fostering within its system a wide range of emotions to be repressed, the James family unintentionally encouraged the alternative and, all too often, unhealthy means of self-expression and control that we see in William's depression, Alice's chronic invalidism, Robertson's alcoholism, and the young Henry's tendencies toward "real *under*-feeding," among other symptoms. It encouraged a means of self-expression, moreover, that would become increasingly debilitating when, 50 years later, James believed his Edition had failed and his career had ended.

Following the pattern inaugurated by Saul Rosenzweig in his 1934 essay, "The Ghost of Henry James," most biographers of James, including Edel, have based their psychological analysis of the novelist on traditional psychoanalytic theory as it "developed through the study of individual patients" and have viewed the family "only as a collection of relatively autonomous people, each motivated by his or her own particular psychological mechanisms and conflicts"—or in the case of James biography, driven by conflicts between James and other family members, his father and elder brother in particular.[28] Beginning with Howard Feinstein's groundbreaking biography *Becoming William James*, however, James family biography has seen a shift away from the traditional psychoanalytical model toward what Michael Kerr calls the "family systems" model.[29] On the basis of "family systems theory," Feinstein interprets the psychology of James family members—William in particular—in the light of an emotional system that grows out of the family as a whole, often in response to the needs of the parents, and shapes the psychology of its individual members. He identifies a number of concepts taken from his work in family therapy—the family secret, the multigenerational hypothesis, and so on—that he found particularly useful in his "three-generation, biographical study of the family of William James."[30] Feinstein draws extensively on the work of family psychologists who explore the dynamics of highly enmeshed families with multigenerational histories of psychosomatic illness, patterns of emotional conflict, and repeated incidents of addictive behaviors.

Feinstein justifies his approach on the basis of the James family's highly developed level of self-consciousness: "All of the family were talented correspondents," he notes, "and their letters and journals have attracted many biographers. Keen observers of themselves and even keener of each other, they invite psychological study."[31] But my reading in the Victorian family in general and the James family in particular suggests that we can take Feinstein's rationale for this approach one step further. For the patterns of psychological dependencies, intense family relationships, psychosomatic illnesses, and the silencing of unacceptable emotions—the patterns that psychologists now see as characteristic of troubled families—had their roots in the changes in child-rearing techniques, assumptions about marriage, approaches to emotional conflict, and other middle-class family patterns that developed in England and America during the nineteenth century. The keen lens that James family members trained on one another and on their dynamics as a family was thus a manifestation of a culturally and privately sanctioned system that fostered a high level of psychological dependence and emotional enmeshment. (As James said of his family in *A Small Boy and Others* [1913], "We were, to my sense, the blest group of us . . . *so fused and united and interlocked*.")[32] The point is not only that the James family and its members invite psychological study because they were self-conscious and "keen observers of themselves" and each other. The point is that the self-conscious James family—and the highly self-conscious second son Henry—invite psychological study tailored to their complex, multigenerational patterns of emotional behavior.

How does a family psychology model apply to this consideration of James's problems with eating, both early and late? To believe, as R. D. Laing explains, that the *"family as a system* is internalized" in individuals as "an introjected set of relations"—and, I would add, as introjected emotional patterns—is to believe that the behaviors James learned from his family in his youth were to be lived out in various forms and, as many critics and biographers maintain, expressed in his writings throughout his career.[33] I have already argued that the James family fostered an emotional climate that gave rise to depression, invalidism, alcoholism and, in Henry James's case, digestive difficulties and tendencies towards "real *under-*feeding." So, too, did the effect of this climate on his emotional life inform the process by which the elderly James responded to debilitating feelings of professional failure: Focusing largely on bodily complaints, he turned to Fletcherizing as an emotional resource and a physical cure. Let us look briefly at the middle years of James's career—the period between the 1870's and the year of his breakdown, 1910—to begin our examination of this process.

III

Apparently James's youthful problems with eating did not continue beyond the early 1870's. By the end of the decade, he was dining out so regularly and eating so well that he boasted to his family of his bulky and ruddy appearance—and of the literary success of which this ample appearance was a sign.[34] What did not change was the need for emotional control that he had learned in his family; and as he matured, an increasingly intense commitment to work and professionalism became his means of both repressing and escaping from the fears of weakness, worthlessness, and failure that had threatened to cripple him in his early years. Feinstein has argued that in William's case, such feelings were the result of Henry, Sr.'s, failure to acknowledge his own sense of vocational worthlessness and his attempts to work out his problems on his eldest son.[35] But like William, Henry inherited a sense of the powerful paternal identity that permeated the family and dictated its emphasis on repression and control: the negative identity of failure and shame. Accordingly, he carefully cultivated his "ferocious ambition" as a way of holding his father's identity at bay, and he rigorously defined success in opposition to the failure he wished to avoid.[36] "I must make some great efforts during the next few years, however," he wrote in 1882, "if I wish not to have been on the whole a failure. I shall have been a failure unless I do something *great*." What is more, working itself became a means of avoiding depression and doubt. As he writes in his notebook in 1881, it was only during periods of "forced idleness" that he experienced moments of "unspeakable reaction" to or "melancholy reflections" on his lapses and deficiencies. "When I'm really at work, I'm happy," he writes, "I feel strong, I see many opportunities ahead."[37]

   I do not want to suggest, by this account, that James's vocation as a writer was no more than a means of escape from painful emotion, and his fiction nothing more than the outpourings of a compulsive personality. But I do want to show that James carefully adhered to a philosophy of emotional control and, in expressing this philosophy, often hinted at the surfeit of emotions that needed such control. "Only sit tight . . . *and go through the movements of life*," he wrote to Edith Wharton in 1908; "the deeper and darker and the unapparent, in which things *really* happen to us, learns, under that hygiene, to stay in its place. Let it get out of its place and it swamps the scene."[38] Moreover, James himself saw his work as an escape from crippling emotions and self-preoccupation. Writing to Antonio de Navarro in 1902, he claims: "I pity you for being without some practicable door for getting out of yourself. We all need one [a commanding occupation], and if I didn't have mine I should—well, I shouldn't be writing you this now. . . . One must do everything to invent, to force open, that door of exit from mere immersion in one's states."[39]

When James expressed his philosophy to de Navarro and Wharton, he was at an age in which his profession had assumed an especially crucial role in routing his doubts and depression. For compounding the fears that drove his ambition in the early years was the pain and discouragement of his failures in the novel in the late 1880's and in the theater in 1895. Edel's argument to the contrary is well known: James worked through the depression of the "treacherous years" by writing a series of fictions about victimized children. In "returning to earlier, to earliest experience," says Edel, "he rediscovered the means by which he had long before armed himself for life. He healed his wounds, and recovered his strength, finding new sources of power within himself."[40] But as William Veeder claims, Edel's case for the therapeutic benefits of the fiction about adolescent children is overstated. The fact that James experienced a nervous breakdown in 1910 indicates that the work of the late 1890's "at best restored James to function." It was a very high level of functioning indeed, but it did not cure his problems or heal the wounds that had "plagued him from childhood."[41] To maintain that James used his fiction to rediscover the means by which he had long before armed himself is to argue against the therapeutic value of the fiction, for to rediscover the means by which he armed himself as a boy is to reaffirm his lifelong need for strategies of repression and control.

Supporting this argument is a notebook entry written in 1895, shortly after the humiliating failure of *Guy Domville*. "I only have to *face* my problems," writes James in a moment of reckoning. But he goes on to say, "all that is of the ineffable, too deep and pure for any utterance. Shrouded in sacred silence, let it rest."[42] Here a decision to confront the issues that are troubling him is immediately followed by a decision not only to let his "problems" rest "shrouded" in "silence" but also to idealize as "ineffable" and "sacred" both the problems and the process of repressing them. By this account, all that was "shrouded in silence"—all the pain of the treacherous years, and the earlier emotional conditions that made this pain so acute—was left to be contained and managed by James's faith in his art and the "beneficent act of doing." The "commanding occupation" he celebrates in his letter to de Navarro, in other words, both represses and compensates for the feelings of failure and humiliation that he expresses time and again in his writings through the 1890's.

Around the time he discovered the benefits of Fletcherizing, in fact, James had been working with "unremitting intensity" on the novels of the major phase: *The Wings of the Dove* had been published in August 1902; *The Ambassadors* appeared a year later; and in May 1904, he reported to his agent that he had been working tirelessly on a third novel, *The Golden Bowl*, "the whole of every blessed morning since I began it, some thirteen months ago." To a certain extent, this professional regularity was nothing new. "He admitted that he worked *every* day, dictated every morning," wrote Arthur Benson in 1904, "and began a new book the instant the old one was finished." James's household servants related numerous anecdotes about James's impatience with interruptions in his work, and one of his amanuenses, Mary Weld, described a day in which James, being "too ill to dictate," required her to return to Lamb House at regular intervals in case "he should recover quickly" and be able to work.[43] But James's letters to family and friends during this period reveal that his well-established routine was fueled by a particular sense of urgency about his career. He rejected the idea of traveling with William in 1900, for example, because he didn't want to "sacrifice any present and immediate period of production . . . that I can stiffly (*and* joyously!) keep in its place." He didn't want to sacrifice any opportunity to further the "New Career"—and the new chances at success—that his agent James B. Pinker was now making possible. He rejected an offer to join a friend in Paris for the same reason. But this time he expressed his concern in a fashion reminiscent of the comments he once made on his father's lack of public recognition, suggesting the fears of failure and oblivion that haunted him: "I *am* face to face . . . with every successive lost opportunity (wait till you've reached it!) and with the steady, swift movement of the ebb of the great tide—the great tide of which one will never see the turn."[44]

When James turned to Fletcherizing in 1904 there was no question of using the chewing fad itself as a means of controlling the uncontrollable. Nor was there a problem with eating too little. But the possibility existed that, with its promise of physical health and emotional well-being, Fletcherizing would facilitate James's already intense commitment to focused professionalism. Not only did it make "my life possible," as James said, but it also "enormously improved" his work. Not only did it keep the 61-year-old author in good health, but it also enhanced his chances to develop his "New Career" and stem the tide of failure and oblivion. No wonder James was willing to regulate his meals as carefully—and as enthusiastically—as he controlled his work. "Here I spend fifty minutes (I spent 'em tonight)," he wrote to a fellow Fletcherizer, "over a cold partridge, a potato (three potatoes) and a baked apple—all with much bread (indispensable with soft things); which means that I munch unsociably and in passionate silence, and that it is making me both unsociable and inhospitable (without at the same time making me in the least ashamed of so being. I brazenly glory in it.)"[45] Because it enhanced his ability to work, dietary control once again had become intertwined with James's feelings of self-esteem. It had become part of the psychological economy that linked his emotional well-being, his ability to work, his hopes for his profession, and his unresolved and recently aggravated feelings of failure and shame.

IV

The good health James attributed to Fletcherizing in the years prior to his nervous breakdown saw him through a period of production that, if possible, was more important than the "New Career" initiated by Pinker and the novels of the major phase. For his painstaking labor on the New York Edition that began in 1906 was intended to gain an audience for the work of a lifetime and, as such, to redeem his career from a condition of insufficient recognition and himself from the fears of failure and oblivion that haunted him. We recognize these motives in the eagerness with which, as Michael Anesko points out, James tried to "assist the public" in its efforts to read and value him anew. "James was eager to embellish his Edition with prefaces and frontispieces and to rework his earlier fictions. To captivate a publisher and the public, James was prepared to frame his artistic goals in distinctly marketable form."[46] Indeed, writing to Scribner's in 1905, James was very definite about his desire to package his writings so that they would "gain in significance and importance" in the public's eyes. His prefaces, too, "might count as a feature of a certain importance in any such new and more honorable presentation of my writings." To insist on an "honorable presentation," James explains, is to ensure that many of his fictions will enjoy "for the first time . . . a form and appearance, a dignity and beauty of outer aspect, that may seem to bespeak consideration for them as a matter of course. Their being thus presented, in fine, as fair and shapely will contribute, to my mind, to their coming legitimately into a 'chance' that has been hitherto rather withheld from them, and for which they have long and patiently waited."[47]

The final pages of his Preface to *The Golden Bowl* also show the extent to which James believed that the revision of his fiction would contribute to the act of redeeming his honor. At one point he imagines his works as mussy children who need to be spruced up before being displayed to the bright lights and the peering eyes of the drawing room. Later he extends the metaphor of dress to explain that, in some of his early works, there is the "long-stored grievance of the subject bristling with a sense of overprolonged exposure in a garment misfitted." He imagines these works, *The American* in particular, making "claim for exemplary damages, or at least for poetic justice, for wanting their just deserts." Soon after, he describes the mistakes in his earliest texts as the "old catastrophes and accidents, the old wounds and mutilations." Thus his process of revision has served not only to "hang about" or "gild" about his fictions "the finer air of the better form" but also, in the process, to spruce up their appearance, correct the accidents, undo the catastrophes, and heal the wounds. In a remark that interprets his personal investment in this process, James explains that revision has thus "doubtless" been a way of "remaining unshamed," of protecting himself from the shame that would accrue to his work and to its author were he to let his fictions appear in their original form. But given what he has already said about the mistakes of the past, given the language of mussiness, catastrophes, and mutilations, the claim that he desires to "remain unshamed" is deeply ambiguous. For the desire to spruce up mussy fictional children or to correct past accidents indicates that the shame is already there to be covered over, compensated for, or healed (*23*: xiv–xv, xxii; *AN*, 337, 344–45).

The entire history of his "operative consciousness" in the prefaces, moreover, constitutes an additional effort to rescue his career from the shame of its smudges, mutilations, and mistakes. Not only does James avoid mention of texts that would tarnish his "honorable" presentation of his *oeuvre*—*The Bostonians*, for example—but he often makes obvious or explicit efforts to defend his choice of subject matter or technique. He justifies his attraction to the form of the ghost story in his Preface to "The Altar of the Dead," for example; he defends his interest in the "poor, sensitive gentlemen" of his fiction in the same place and in his Preface to "The Lesson of the Master" (*17*: ix; *AN*, 246); he justifies his use of the seemingly unpromising subject of "Flickerbridge" in his Preface to *Daisy Miller*; and, in the same Preface, he goes to some length to defend his decision not to use the *nouvelle* form to treat the world of American business. "To ride the *nouvelle* down-town, to prance and curvet and caracole with it there— that would have been the true ecstasy. But a single 'spill'—such as I so easily might have had in Wall Street or wherever—would have forbidden me, for very shame, in the eyes of the expert and the knowing, ever to mount again; so that in short it wasn't to be risked on any terms" (*18*: xii; *AN*, 274).

James admits in this passage that the fear of shame—the shame of failing before "the eyes of the expert and the knowing"—motivated his decision to avoid the world of business in his fiction. His prefaces reveal that a similar fear informed his expectations for the New York Edition, and that, given the nature and scope of the project, this fear made the prospect of failure all the more perilous for James. To take a "spill" with the Edition, after all, is to do more than fail at a *nouvelle* about Wall Street; it is to do more than fail, as he did in 1895, at writing for the stage. To "spill" with the Edition would be to fail at a full-scale presentation of the literary forms—the short story, the *nouvelle*, and the novel—in which he had invested a lifetime of effort and expertise. It would be to fail at giving these fictions the final "chance" for the recognition he believed they deserved. It would be to fail at the attempt—at his greatest, most ambitious attempt of all—to lay to rest his deepest fears: that he is weak and ineffective like his father and that his voice, like his father's, will be swept into silence and oblivion. This failure would come, moreover, in spite of a deliberate effort to invite the reader to see his work as James believed it deserved to be seen. "What has the affair been at the worst," he wrote, "but an earnest invitation to the reader to dream again in my company and in the interest of his own larger absorption of my sense?" (*23*: xxii; *AN*, 345). It would come, in other words, after a massive effort of self-justification which, when ignored, would further intensify James's feelings of exposure and shame. James wrote to Pinker that he had tried, really tried, to subdue his hopes for the Edition.[48] But the extraordinary amount of time, energy, and emotion he invested in a project intended to blot out his shame and bolster his honor bespeaks hopes that were impossible to subdue.

V

Sometime in 1908 James began to practice the excessive dieting that he had previously identified as a potential drawback to the nutritionist's chewing program. A letter to William remarks that this "long & protracted (systematic) . . . *underfeeding*" began after a renewal of his "thoracic worry" or gout, the result, he claims, of too much "meat & . . . port-wine" in his diet. Another letter suggests that it either began or became more rigorous several months later, around the time of the first royalty return from the New York Edition. Yet a third letter points to the likelihood that, by the time he experienced his obscure illness in February 1909, James had been overdoing, possibly abusing, his hygienic program for several months.[49] I have already proposed a connection between the emotional turmoil of James's early years and the serious "underfeeding" he described in his letter to Horace Fletcher. Now with the renewal of painful emotion in his life, indeed with the renewal of feelings of failure and shame that were deeply rooted in his childhood, James returned to a practice abandoned years before. For a time at least, his "commanding occupation" had failed him, and Fletcherism became the "hygiene" used to keep in place "the deeper and darker" feelings James expresses in his letters to Pinker in October 1908, his "bitter" disappointment and "grief" over the failure of the Edition, and his sense of feeling "sickened and poisoned" by the postponement of creative work.[50]

Within months, James's sense of feeling grieved and sickened by the failure of the Edition gave rise to an obscure set of symptoms and a palpable sense of anxiety about his health. He cabled his brother in February 1909 that he had discontinued his Fletcherizing.[51] But shortly thereafter he consulted Mackenzie, and as a result James reported that what was needed to restore him to health was, among other things, a continuation of his eating regime. Himself a Fletcherizer, Mackenzie had "the highest opinion of its virtue and has practised complete mastication and insalivation himself and disseminated it systematically . . . for a long time past." Thus he held "strongly that Fletcherism had nothing to do with the matter" of James's anxious irregularities of the heart. What James was suffering from, he believed, was too little exercise and "too great increase of fat," in addition to a great deal of anxiety, and he advised the novelist to resume his old habit of walking, "*superabundantly and up to the limit of exhaustion*," and to continue his Fletcherizing, "to practise it just as I *have* been doing (thank the powers)."[32]

In a letter to William in July 1909, Henry claims that his condition improved after his February visit to Mackenzie. "I am really better—ever so much better—than I have been at any time since I began to grow too fat & move too little," he exclaimed; "my clothes hang loose upon me, & I must soon begin to have some of them 'taken in.'" Clearly James had continued to Fletcherize regularly and, it appears, to reduce his intake of food. What is more, he had recently and "renewedly" met with Fletcher in London to thrash "things out together in a way that will have really been of great use to me for the rest of my days." Not only did James feel he was "more full of resource, on a more intimately understood Fletcher basis" than ever before, but he also claimed to be "pegging away" on a number of plays for which people had recently "applied."[53] The crisis of the fall and winter appeared to be well behind him, in other words, and he appeared to feel secure in his hygienic routine and his prospects for work.

What the July letter to William fails to mention, however, is that other professional discouragements had surfaced in recent months. And more discouragements were to surface in the months ahead. In May, he had written to Edith Wharton that because "two American 'high-class (heaven save the mark!) periodicals' declined" his story "The Velvet Glove," what he "infinitely need[ed] and yearn[ed] for" was to "believe a little in myself."[54] Three days after his letter to William, James wrote to his agent, "clearly I have written the last short story of my life—which you will be glad to know." In August he reports that he is "having a very good & propitious working time & deep in my theatrical jobs—deeper and more interested, & really with more horizon, I think, than ever in anything"—a sentiment he repeats in the fall.[55] But in early October he received yet another discouraging royalty statement from Scribner's. "James told his agent," says Edel, "that in no year had he so 'consummately managed to make so little money as this last.'"[56]

Not surprisingly, a letter written on October 31 reports that, sometime in August or September, James's health had begun to fail him again: although the "heart trouble" is "distinctly & confirmedly better & better," he wrote to William, the experience of the "last 3 months" has nonetheless been "very trying." Now he was experiencing digestive difficulties, and the Fletcherizing was proving a "*cul de sac.*" But, he adds, "I am worrying out my salvation." Once again obscure physical symptoms coincided with explicit professional setbacks; once again the capacity of Fletcherizing to remedy his problems was a central concern. But in this case, the possibility that Fletcherizing had failed him became a source of anxiety for James, and he emphasizes this anxiety when, in writing to William, he crosses out the phrase "*working out* my salvation" and replaces it with "*worrying out*" (my emphasis).[57]

Instead of abandoning his Fletcherizing at this point, however, James began to Fletcherize to the point of self-starvation and to exercise to the point of exhaustion. When he collapsed in January 1910, his secretary wrote to William, his "own method" had been "to eat little or nothing and go for immense walks."[58] That both his Fletcherizing and his exercising had become somewhat extreme suggests that he had begun to respond to his emotional distress by increasing his reliance on hygienic control.[59] That his Fletcherizing resulted in "the condition of more and more sickishly *loathing* food" and eventually in a total inability to eat indicates that he was suffering from something like what we now think of as an eating disorder. Far more serious than the brief period of undereating in his youth, James's severe loss of appetite gave rise to the physical weakness and heightened state of emotionality described so eloquently by his nephew Harry.

Conscious of the emotional problems at work in Henry's condition, William maintained that his brother had experienced a "nervous breakdown," a diagnosis that, initially at least, Henry was unwilling to accept. Later William acknowledged to his wife that the local physician Dr. Skinner had been treating his brother's symptoms as a "hysteric imitation."[60] This diagnosis does not mean that Dr. Skinner understood his patient to be suffering from anorexia hysteria, as defined in the medical literature of the day. But it does suggest that Skinner believed James to be patterning his condition on or mimicking the symptoms of a mental affliction that, like anorexia, was generally attributed to women. His treatments of rigid two-hour feedings likewise demonstrate that he understood how closely James's hysterical symptoms were bound up with his compulsive attempts at self-starvation.[61]

It is possible that by imitating the afflictions of Victorian women and identifying directly with his sister Alice, James was expressing what many critics have defined as the "feminine" core of his personality.[62] It is also possible that by aligning himself with the gender most Victorians associated with weakness and dependency, James unconsciously expressed his feelings of helplessness and shame over the failure of the Edition and the illnesses

that followed. But the fact is that Victorian men were known to have suffered from forms of hysteria, including anorexia hysteria, and the men in
the James family were known to have experienced breakdowns similar to
the tearful collapse described in the letter from Harry: Henry, Sr., in
1842; Uncle Augustus James in 1866; and William in 1874.[63] Like Henry's, each of these breakdowns occurred during periods of vocational uncertainty or crisis, and, like Henry's, his father's breakdown was associated
(metaphorically at least) with the ingestion of food and with abdominal distress.[64] Shaped by his shame-based family, and tormented by fears of ineptitude and failure, James expressed through his compulsive Fletcherizing
and emotional collapse an anxiety about the relationship among vocational
integrity, physical health, and psychic wholeness that permeated his entire
family. Through these symptoms he voiced an anxiety about his own integrity as a writer who, try as he might, was unable to keep in place "the
deeper and darker and the unapparent" fears of failure and deficiency that
haunted him. The New York Edition had been intended to allay these
fears. Thus, James's supreme expression of his artistic confidence and serenity also constitutes a supreme attempt to compensate for the "wounds
and mutilations" of a lifetime.

New York Monumentalism and
Hidden Family Corpses

Alfred Habegger

In Henry James's early "The Story of a Masterpiece," a youthful artist utters the powerful boast "*Exegi monumentum*" after completing a particularly happy painting.[1] By July 30, 1905, however, when the 62-year-old James sent Scribner's a memorandum setting forth his projections for a grand collected edition, he was aware he had not yet imposed his monument on the world. If his writings were ever to have their "chance," they needed an ample and distinguished presentation, something combining the imperial grandeur of a triumphal arch with the skyscraper's modern bravado. It was particularly important that the whole enterprise refer "explicitly to my native city—to which I have had no great opportunity of rendering that sort of homage."[2] "New York" was the only name that would do for the monument James was ready to assemble.

Monuments, as James admitted in calling Paul Bourget's collected edition his "mosaic sarcophagus,"[3] tend to be tombs. They may celebrate the great dead, as does Grant's Tomb, but they may equally well recall the anonymous dead, or even the defeated. Many imperial monuments turn out, though not by intention, to be memorials to the obscure. There is a good example of this in Ivo Andrić's novel, *The Bridge on the Drina*, where a Bosnian rebel is impaled by Turkish authorities and left to die a lingering death. In this work, the bridge marks the site where the assertion of imperial will stimulates the aspiration to self-rule in the act of defeating it. James's New York Edition memorializes in both respects, glorifying the author's greatest deeds but also interring—and preserving—the unnamed dead.

Thus James's prefaces alternate somewhat irresolutely between brazen commemoration and dark concealment. The brazen mode is much in evidence, particularly where James evokes the scenes of his early compositional labors. These scenes provide a vivid image of the author at work in his private space in some great city, ardently projecting his new work of art while absorbing the sounds and sights of a nearby public square. Similarly, when he records the anecdote that caused some work of fiction to germinate, the original story is inevitably some shapeless public thing that undergoes a major alteration once it reaches the inner sanctum of James's imagination. The prefaces frequently disclose the historical operations of this imagination—the use of Gyp in working up *The Awkward Age*, the intended compositional role of Kate Croy's father, the way Turgenev's quoted speech encouraged James to build *The Portrait of a Lady* on the heroine's own sense of herself. James's 1905 memorandum to Scribner's announced a determination finally to go public. Immediately after declaring that the prefaces would be "freely colloquial and even, perhaps, as I may say, confidential," he pointed out that they would represent a kind of scoop for his publishers: "I have never committed myself in print in any way, even so much as by three lines to a newspaper, on the subject of anything I have written."[4]

All the same, James's historic commemorations are thoroughly ambiguous, as one would expect of a writer who guarded his privacy so jealously. His memory of the rise and development of his works of fiction is so penetrated by strong purpose—the will to be great, a desire for fame and wealth, a wish to instruct critics in their neglected craft—that the historical accuracy of what James recovers as he "remounts the stream of time" is always to be questioned. His original notebooks often belie his recollections. Some have doubted that Turgenev said exactly *that*.

The question of frankness was always a particularly trying one for James, and often brought his contradictions to the surface. It so happens that the two most openly autobiographical passages in his entire output of fiction, both of which refer to his life in New York, do not appear in the New York Edition. In *Washington Square* James, or his unusually discursive narrator, supposed that it might be "owing to the tenderness of early associations" that he was so fond of the park he took for his title. Recollecting his widowed maternal grandmother, Elizabeth Walsh, who resided at 19 Washington Square until her death in December 1847,[5] when James was still only four and a half years old, he indulged in a "topographical parenthesis":

It was here that your grandmother lived, in venerable solitude, and dispensed a hospitality which commended itself alike to the infant imagination and the infant palate; it was here that you took your first walks abroad, following the nursery-maid with unequal step, and sniffing up the strange odor of the ailanthus-trees . . . ; it was here, finally, that your first school, kept by a broad-bosomed, broad-based old lady with a ferule, who was always having tea in a blue cup, with a saucer that didn't match, enlarged the circle both of your observations and your sensations.[6]

The north side of Washington Square was definitely an upscale area, Mrs. Walsh's house being assessed in 1844 at $15,500 (compared to the $9,500 valuation ten years later of the James' comfortable West 14th Street home).[7] Even so, James's brief sketch of the mismatched china, the woman's amusing figure, and the unpleasant-smelling ailanthus (which some Americans call "stink tree") emphasized the lack of urbane amenity.

In this respect, the topographical parenthesis in *Washington Square* forms a striking companion piece to the uncharacteristically detailed notation of Basil Ransom's shabby neighborhood on what was at that time upper Second Avenue. Here, after acting as a sort of naturalistic tour-guide through the odors and sights of an untidy street scene and calling our attention to the "fly-blown card" in a boardinghouse window and the heaped-up produce of a Dutch grocery, James airily admits the irrelevance of the whole scene: "I mention it not on account of any particular influence it may have had on the life or the thoughts of Basil Ransom, but for old acquaintance sake and that of local color; besides which, a figure is nothing without a setting, and our young man came and went every day, with rather an indifferent, unperceiving step, it is true, among the objects I have briefly designated."[8] Both passages call attention to urban disorders the local inhabitants take for granted—bad smells, untended vegetation, objects that don't belong together, and other disagreeable effects.

Without pretending to explain why James kept *Washington Square* out of the New York Edition or why he did not push harder for the inclusion of *The Bostonians*, we can see that James's vivid sense of New York's rank though fruitful confusion was in conflict with his monumentalizing intention. (The fact that James as narrator more or less apologized for introducing the two passages shows that the same conflict was present in the original embedding narratives.) The author's homely memories of New York's sights and sounds had to be excluded from the distinguished collection dedicated to the city. This exclusion recalls James's chronic anxiety about his relation to American life, or, in another register, the always problematic function of sharp local detail in his prevailingly bland narrative surface. It also admonishes us to keep alert for what is missing, to try to let nothing that is buried beneath the surface be lost on us.

Twice James calls our attention to the sources of his fiction in James family annals and then refuses to name names. In the Preface to *The Portrait of a Lady* he tells us that he had possessed the image of a certain kind of young woman "for a long time," but then he draws the curtain, announcing that the manner in which he acquired this image is "not here to be retraced" (*3*: xi; *AN*, 47). He never did retrace it, as it happened, not even in the chapter commemorating Minny Temple in *Notes of a Son and Brother*. If it were not for private letters that happen to be extant, such as the one he sent Grace Norton on December 28, 1880,[9] we would not know for sure that James's image of Minny helped prompt his conception of Isabel. Similarly, in the Preface to *The Wings of the Dove*, James informs us that the basic idea of a fortunate but doomed person had been with him so long he could "scarce remember" when it had not been "vividly present" to him, and he hints that when he made Milly Theale the last descendant of "an 'old' New York stem," he was drawing on a "fine association" and "happy congruities." These presumably personal matters, however, he "may not now go into." Their exposition "shall yet elsewhere await" him. Interestingly, when the time comes to tell this story, the difficulties are such as "rather to defy than to encourage exact expression" (*19*: v,viii–ix; *AN*, 288, 292)—a phrase that nicely evokes the nervousness with which James approached the task of historical narration. The difficult trick, for him, was to combine truth-telling with ennobling monumentalization. His worry lest a full and frank telling detract from narrative dignity remained one of the fundamental impulses operating in his writing.

Thus, to effectively commemorate a life's productive work in writing fiction, the people and events in James's personal history that inspired his imaginative activity had to be obscured. Their existence would have to be alluded to, and then they would be forgotten, *publicly* forgotten. The New York Edition announces itself as both a monument to the author's long compositional labors and a cryptic memorial to others who must remain nameless. We are advised that there are bodies present under the grand arch which are not to be inquired about, let alone dug up.

To be a biographical critic, however, is to violate such imperatives—to be a shamelessly speculative prospector, perhaps even a grave-digger.

James resembled Milly Theale in deriving from an "'old' New York stem,"
and at the time he conceived of his grand collected edition, he was beginning to feel like a surviving remnant. His parents were long dead, and a
younger brother and sister, Wilky and Alice, had died at the ages of 38 and
43. Numerous cousins had died young—not only Minny Temple but her
sterling older brother William, Gus Barker, John Vanderburgh James,
and many others whom James had known in his youth. Most conspicuously, many of his paternal uncles and aunts had proved extraordinarily
fragile. Of his father's ten siblings who reached adulthood, seven died between the ages of 23 and 40. Four of these deaths took place after James was
old enough to take notice.[10] It is not too much to say that the father's generation was scattered and smashed, and that when Senior and his children
looked back, they saw a catastrophic die-off. Many of James's readers have
not grasped this.

As one would expect, James's two completed volumes of memoirs, *A
Small Boy and Others* and *Notes of a Son and Brother*, are not as frank about
the individual family tragedies as they might have been. We get a general-
ized image of a glamorously wild group. In the stories that James and his
brother William passed on privately to William's oldest son, Henry III,
the paternal aunts and uncles formed "a richly colored social kaleidoscope,
dashed, as the patterns changed and disintegrated, with amusing flashes of
light and occasional dark moments of tragedy."[11] The one tragedy in his
father's generation that James wrote about with any specificity involved
Minny Temple's mother, Catharine, who, already dying from tuberculo-
sis, had to be forcibly separated from her dying husband.[12] About the other
deaths, at least one of which, as we shall see, might be regarded as even
more bitter and catastrophic, James did not go into detail. Instead he
turned his father's kin into a collective legend, as he did in *The Wings of the
Dove* with Milly Theale's doomed ancestry.

Underneath James's New York monument lies the author's own disas-
ter-ridden New York lineage. The New York Edition is an artful structure
erected on a place where something closely resembling a fatal family curse
had worked itself out.

I

One of the family ghosts about whom James felt sorest was that of his father, Henry James, Sr. (whom I will call "Senior" for convenience). The

eight-year period from 1847 to 1855, when Senior and his wife and children resided in New York, marked the peak of his success as lecturer and writer. The almost weekly essays Senior contributed to the *Harbinger* in 1848, its last full year, attracted much interest and comment. He was friends with Ralph Waldo Emerson and several influential editors and publishers, and his lectures, essays, and books got long, attentive, sympathetic notices in the *New York Tribune*. This was the most influential reform Whig (and then Republican) newspaper in the country, and after 1851, when Senior put $10,000 into it,[13] its pages were open to his lengthy essays on spiritualism, American democracy, marriage, and other topics. The series of six lectures he delivered at New York City's Stuyvesant Institute was so well received that he was sure he had at last found his calling: "I hear every day of profound impressions having been made in this quarter and that, and of one thing at all events no doubt remains, that my business is lecturing. All parties unite in telling me that I must do nothing else for a living, but disseminate the gospel of the divine humanity now henceforth and forever."[14] For a few brief years, Senior was reputed to be a daring new intellectual luminary, someone it was obligatory to pay attention to if you wanted to keep up. In 1852, the year his first big book appeared, *Lectures and Miscellanies*, the *Tribune* named him and Emerson as "the two profoundest and most sweeping radicals of our time."[15] When Thackeray visited the United States, it was Senior who wrote the *Tribune*'s glowing announcement on the opinion page,[16] and when a newly elected mayor of New York, Fernando Wood, seemed to be seriously interested in closing the city's many gambling houses, Senior contributed two or three supportive editorials. By the time he moved to Europe in 1855, Senior had enjoyed several years' access to a great New York daily, he was moving with some of the powerful currents of the day, and he had won widespread recognition.

Then he became disconnected, his early success was gradually forgotten, and, although he achieved a definite comeback in Boston and Cambridge after 1864, it is fair to say that Senior did not fulfill the promise of his early maturity. He was marginalized by the passing of the utopian reformism of the 1840's, so that while he continued to harp on his confusing views on marriage and divorce,[17] he had absolutely nothing to say about the great issue that dominated the 1850's, the expansion of slavery to the territories. In addition, he marginalized himself. During the three years in Europe in 1855–58 he made few productive contacts with important Eu-

ropean social or religious thinkers. Although his writing continued to de-
nounce all sectarian allegiances, it often seemed aimed at small groups of
Swedenborgians or others out of the mainstream. By the time his children
reached the age where they could begin to take their father's measure as a
thinker, Senior was for the most part repeating his message to the world in
long, strident books that were ignored, harshly dismissed, or fervently
studied by a tiny number of scattered true believers. He spent long hours
at his desk expounding his system to his devoted disciples or engaging in
strenuous contention. Meanwhile, the family would never again take up
residence in New York City, which, in the mind of Henry James, Jr., became an isolated hoard of rich, vulgar, and astonishingly detailed memories.

Senior's children seem never to have understood that their father had
once been illuminated by New York's bright publicity apparatus and that it
was partly his own doing that he passed into repetitious obscurity, and they
tended to come up with strange excuses for his failure. William proposed
that Senior was a victim of history, a theologian fated to live in an age of
positivistic science.[18] Henry saw his father as a great thinker—great in his
way, of course—who never got his chance. He was passionate, devoted,
and hardworking, and the recognition he deserved never materialized.
This image of his father as a writer who failed abysmally with the public
had an enormous, formative influence on James, who, in contrast with Senior, fully appreciated the importance of building a career, working in the
marketplace, avoiding the parochial. One of the lessons Senior inadvertently taught his son was the importance of traveling first-class, literarily
speaking. You fraternized with those at the top or in the center; you preferred New York to Boston, and London and Paris to New York. Yet even
though (or is it because?) James emphatically did not follow his father's career path, he felt an unappeasable soreness about his father's failure to win
public recognition.

Although James generally kept this soreness to himself, rather like his
many characters who endure unjust treatment in silence, there was a moment when he openly expressed it. In the summer of 1884 William selected some of Senior's uncollected writings and arranged with James R.
Osgood for the publication of *The Literary Remains of the Late Henry James*;
this would be the last chance for recognition and distinction. Hurling himself into the editorial project with all his filial piety, William wrote a long
introductory essay that attempted to render his father more palatable to

contemporary readers. Instead of going back to Senior's daring controversial and speculative essays from the late 1840's and early 1850's, or attempting a retrospective view of the growth of his thought, William regarded his father's final writings as representative of his entire life's work and gave most of the volume over to the treatise he had been preparing at his death, *Spiritual Creation*, a not particularly fresh restatement of his views on the origins of selfhood. This left room for only two shorter pieces, the popular lecture (and essay) on Carlyle and the memoir of Stephen Dewhurst, a work of anomalous genre that was simultaneously a work of fiction and Senior's closest approach to autobiography. Somewhat naively, William presented the Dewhurst narrative as disguised autobiography rather than as didactic fiction drawing on autobiographical materials. Thus, to Dewhurst's declaration that his father emigrated from "his native Somerset County, with its watery horizons, to settle in Baltimore," William misleadingly provided corrective footnotes: "County Cavan, Ireland," and "Albany, N.Y."[19] All in all, the editing of the *Remains* was too devoted, amateurish, and tendentious to restore Senior's reputation.

In the lengthy acknowledgment Henry sent William three days after receiving the book, he showed no recognition of its deficiencies as a final gathering and presentation of a writer's lifework. Instead, Henry assumed that the volume fairly represented his father's thought. The Introduction, the only part he had read so far, was "admirable, perfect," and William's extracts from father's writings were "beautiful and extraordinarily individual." James's reaction was not as extreme as that of Alice, who broke into tears and exclaimed, "How beautiful it is that William should have done it! isn't it, isn't it beautiful? and how good William is, how good, how good!"; but it is clear he was no more able to bring his critical intelligence to bear on the book than she was. He bounced between a fancy Victorian melancholy—he and Alice "talked of poor Father's fading away into silence and darkness, the waves of the world closing over this System which he tried to offer it, and of how we were touched by this act of yours which will (I am sure) do so much to rescue him from oblivion"—and the abrupt announcement that he still saw no reason to take the system seriously. Far from confronting the system, James could not even give a perfunctory account of it. His confession that he couldn't "be so theological nor grant [Senior's] extraordinary premises, nor through [*sic*] myself into conceptions of heavens & hells, nor be sure that the keynote of nature is humanity"[20] made Senior sound even more stultifying than he was. Perhaps one of the

reasons James thanked William for his Introduction was that his interpretation of Senior as an anachronism gave Henry the excuse he needed to
waste no more time on him. Yet he wanted the world to waste time on him.

Henry loved his father, but, like many modern Jamesians (understand-
ably), he could not bring himself to focus on his father's writing or to be at
all precise, *conscious*, in describing his own response to it. "I can enjoy
greatly the spirit, the feeling & the manner of the whole thing (full as this
last is of things that *dis*please me too,) & feel really that poor Father, struggling so alone all his life, and so destitute of every worldly or literary ambition, was yet a great writer."[21] Everything in this sentence—the sentimental and inaccurate picture of Senior's solitary struggle, the vague
analytical lexicon ("spirit," "feeling," "manner"), the simple declaration of
unexamined liking and disliking, the loose invocation of the powerful
phrase "a great writer"—manifest a critical slackness quite uncharacteristic
of Henry James. We know from elsewhere how much this writer believed
in the importance of having a grasping imagination, in really facing one's
artistic problems, in looking ideas in the face, in not letting go of the
thread. Here, however, where nothing has been thought through, the writer's mind seems scattered and distracted, as if compelled to rehearse certain
obligatory sentiments without pausing to reflect lest their mutual contradictions lead him to examine his real feelings.

James's letter to William puts into action James's basic strategies for
living with the metaphysical madman who was his father—maintaining a
stiff dignity, never explaining himself, always keeping his own literary
work in a separate compartment from his father's, operating *on his own* in
the literary marketplace. Unfortunately for James's peace of mind, William had inadvertently threatened the last of these strategies by arranging
for his brother in London to receive several review copies of *The Literary
Remains* for distribution to potential reviewers. This chore worried James.
It was one thing to predict glibly that William's editorial labors "will (I am
sure) do so much to rescue [Senior] from oblivion" but a very different
thing to promote the book in the tough literary marketplace in which he
himself was trying to swim. He confessed he was "embarrassed as to what
to do with so many" copies of the book. He thought he could get rid of five
or six, and he came up with the names of four potential reviewers, but he
clearly wanted nothing to do with the practical difficulties of securing public honors for his father's writing—of arranging for its reception "in a
manner which will entail some prospect of decent consideration & cour-

tesy." The press was "so grim & philistine & impenetrable, & stupid"[22] that he was afraid his father would be savaged. James had long ago learned the trick of honoring his father without paying much attention to his ideas, but his instincts told him that the London press would not be so indulgent.

In fact, *Literary Remains* was not reviewed in London, and the only important American journal that picked it up, *The Nation*, curtly dismissed it: "Except for students of philosophy, this [William's introductory] essay does away with the necessity, if there ever was any, of reading Mr. James."[23] The only things this anonymous reviewer found of interest were Senior's account of Emerson and his narrative of his collapse in 1844. The review prompted James to send two letters to the magazine's editor, E. L. Godkin. The second of these confessed to "a certain wounded feeling" at the reception given his father's posthumous collection, which had "a real literary importance." Once again, James cranked up his most lugubrious tone as he pictured a person sinking beneath the waves:

I have a tenderness for my poor Father's memory which is in direct proportion to the smallness of the recognition his work was destined to obtain here below and which (in spite of my own personal inability to enter into that work save here and there, or accept most of the premises on which it rests) fill[s] me with a kind of pious melancholy in presence of the fact that so ardent an activity of thought, such a living, original, expressive spirit may have passed into darkness and silence forever, the waves of time closing straight over it, without one or two signs being made on its behalf.[24]

The year in which James wrote this, 1885, proved to be a year of bitter failure for him. The realization that no one cared for his father's last book came to him in the same months that the serialized *Bostonians* turned into a disaster. Not only did his own and his father's books prove monumentally unpopular, but the publisher who had contracted for both books, James R. Osgood, went bankrupt, costing the novelist most of his anticipated earnings for that year.[25] James's reflections on these disappointments reveal his deep identification with his father. In a letter to William complaining (inaccurately) that he had not heard "a word, echo or comment on the serial" since the two opening installments, he recalled the lack of interest in his father's last work:

But how can one murmur at one's success not being what one would like when one thinks of the pathetic, tragic ineffectualness of poor Father's lifelong effort, and the silence and oblivion that seems to have swallowed it up? Not a person to whom I sent a copy of your book, in London, has given me a sign or sound in consequence, and not a periodical appears to have taken the smallest notice of it. It is terribly touching and, when I think of the evolution of his production and ideas, fills me with tears.[26]

Beneath the monumental New York Edition lies a corpse that haunted James, the *Remains* of Henry James, Sr. (William not only selected the book's funerary title but passionately defended "the *morbid* view" in his Introduction.)[27] This was a saint's corpse, one of the cherished dead for whom James burned a votive candle.

All the same, James was determined not to be like his father. *He* would not be ineffective, provincial, ridiculed. *His* collected works would be an unprecedentedly deliberate creation, selective, rationalized, definitive, dignified, a self-carved tomb that would re-present and interpret the labors of a lifetime. Instead of leaving the job to someone else, who would undoubtedly bungle it, he himself would see to it that his culminating edition was an *artist's* self-presentation. He would exhibit his work in the best possible light, with due piety and self-celebration but at the same time with a degree of confession and frank, evaluative commentary. In writing his prefaces, he would even apply his old artistic credo—*dramatize, dramatize*—to the narrative of his various compositional struggles, making a new series of stories out of his old labors.

Thus, at their best, James's prefaces repeatedly brought forward insights and admissions that had not yet seen print in any of his public writings. Repeatedly he demonstrated, as in his treatment of *The Wings of the Dove*, that his original plans had proved strangely irrelevant to the work as written. He expatiated on his inveterate habit of concentrating on a gifted perceiver, of running out of space near the conclusions of his narratives (a tendency visible in every line of his handwriting, which slopes down at the end of each line in order to avoid running off the page). He even admitted to what is for many writers an obscure and embarrassing matter, the effort to avoid always retelling the same basic story, the "need to cultivate almost at any price variety of appearance and experiment, to dissimulate likenesses, samenesses, stalenesses" (*18*: xiv; *AN*, 277). Coming from a writer with James's hermetic tendencies, passages like these seem extraordinarily confidential. At his best, he looks at himself in his prefaces with a keen, critical eye, and without piety, self-exculpation, special pleading. He also looks at the "cold Medusa-face"[28] of the past without turning to stone—that is, without refusing to see, feel, and think (as he tended to do in the letter to William). In more senses than one, James buried his father in the New York Edition.

The father's book had been a sort of Boston Edition—provincial, religious, haphazardly retentive, forgettable. The son's book would be a New York Edition—world-class, secular, undismissable. But also, unlike the retrospective passages about New York in *Washington Square* and *The Bostonians*, without trash or bad smells.

II

There were other remains besides Senior's buried deep beneath the monument.

From 1847 to the summer of 1855, when Senior took his family to Europe, James spent eight crucial years in New York City. The evocation in *A Small Boy and Others* of his experiences there from age four to twelve seems considerably richer in feeling and detail than is his recollection in *Notes of a Son and Brother* of the roughly equal number of years he spent in Boston and Cambridge, where he became a man and writer. Even so, James omitted a great deal from his account of his early years in New York. Indeed, much of his experience there remains terra incognita to this day. The remainder of this essay will attempt to excavate what was perhaps the gravest New York tragedy in the James family annals.

There is no evidence, and thus no point in arguing, that the body I am about to exhume was on James's mind when he conceived of the New York Edition. I mean only for this death to suggest the dark, private New York memories that James barely opened the door to, and did so only near the end of his life when writing some of his last works of fiction—here I am thinking in particular of the extravagantly nightmarish tales, "The Jolly Corner" and "A Round of Visits." The story of John Barber James may remind the reader as well of Susan Stringham's references to Milly Theale's family history—the opaque evocation of "lurid uncles" and the statement "it was New York mourning, . . . it was a New York history" (*19*: 105).

Chapter 14 of *A Small Boy and Others* contains a powerful and cryptic epitaph:

They make collectively their tragic trio: J.J. the elder, most loved, most beautiful, most sacrificed of the Albany uncles; J.J. the younger—they were young together, they were luckless together, and the combination was as strange as the disaster was sweeping; and the daughter and sister, amplest of the "natural," easiest of the idle, who lived on to dress their memory with every thread and patch of her own perfect temper and then confirm the tradition, after all, by too early and woeful an end.[29]

Frederick W. Dupee's index to James's *Autobiography* correctly identifies J.J. the elder as John Barber James, Senior's next younger brother and the father of John Vanderburgh James (J.J. the younger, or Johnny, as he was known) and Mary Helen James.[30] If the impassioned diction—"most loved, most beautiful"—can be taken literally, and I think it can, it tells us that among all the paternal uncles John was preeminent in the boy's affection and imagination. John resided in Albany during the period in question, but he was often in New York City, where he was a welcome addition to fashionable society. In 1851, according to a boasting letter from James's father, John "took a distinguished part in a series of grand tableaux at Mrs John Stevens," his performance as Richard III being "encored three times."[31] Among James's uncles, John was one of the two most "familiar" (the second being Edward, whose death in 1856 remains completely unexplained). With their hats tipped forward and their casual geniality, these two were "the most splendid as to aspect and apparel," and young James was sure they numbered among "the principal men of their time." It was when John returned from Vevey, where he had placed his misbehaving boy in school, that Senior became seriously interested in providing William and his brothers with a Swiss education.[32]

Although James's epitaph in *A Small Boy* memorialized John as "sacrificed," the word was euphemistic. A page from the family notes compiled by Henry James III informs us that this uncle committed suicide: "John James was much beloved by his brothers and sisters and was spoken of as the handsome man of the family. . . . What my mother remembers hearing about him would indicate that he was a spendthrift and gambled too freely for the good of his fortune. Ultimately he killed himself."[33] That was on May 22, 1856, in Chicago, soon after James's thirteenth birthday.

Absolute confirmation that John took his own life has not been found— the Cook County Coroner's records were destroyed by the Chicago fire, all known newspaper obituaries are silent on the cause of death, and I know of no extant James family letters announcing the bad news. Nonetheless, my own opinion is that Henry James III got the facts right. As the self-appointed archivist of James family documents, he understood the value of an accurate record; he meticulously sorted and, in most cases, preserved letters; he helped Katharine Hastings compile a fine genealogy in the early 1920's; and he disapproved of the liberties his uncle Henry took with historical fact in composing his memoirs.[34] His notation of John's suicide indicates that he did not think it necessary to keep this tragic act covered up. Perhaps, as an insurance man (he was both chairman of the board and president of TIAA from 1932 to 1943),[35] he was professionally opposed to concealment.

Two of the other key details in Henry James III's report, that John was
a spendthrift and a gambler, *can* be confirmed. The New-York Historical
Society has a few of his letters to James King, his lawyer, accountant, and
brother-in-law, and these documents show that John was as anxious about
raising money to meet debt obligations as he was helpless to engage in any
productive activity himself.[36] When he drew up his will ten months before
his death, the terms in which he arranged for a trustee to redeem his unse-
cured notes suggest that even then John knew he was in financial trouble:
the trustee was to pay all "debts not secured by liens upon my estate, but
justly due by me, out of the income of said estate as soon after my decease
and burial as may be."[37]

Soon after John's death, his trustee, a respected Albany lawyer named
James Dexter, set aside two leather-bound account books—a ledger and a
cash book—for John's estate. First, Dexter listed some of the real property
in Albany, Syracuse, and New York which John had owned at his death (all
of it probably inherited from his father, William James of Albany). As the
months and years passed, Dexter entered the income from John's stocks,
shares, and rental properties along with disbursements for such items as
the funeral ($57), his son's stay in the Bloomingdale Asylum ($130 semi-
annually), and "preparations for Voyage to Europe" for Mary Helen
($81). This daughter, twenty years old when she sailed in 1860, received a
yearly allowance of $1,500.[38] John Vanderburgh, or Johnny,[39] proved a
good deal less expensive, for he apparently killed himself in 1858, two
years after his father's death. Most of the disbursements speak for themselves, but in 1858 and 1859 Dexter made several large and unexplained
payments to two men whose names do not appear in the Albany city directories of the time, Charles H. Hileman and P. L. Hearne. Hileman was a
dapper New York gambler with an "unexceptionable"[40] establishment and
a clever system for attracting bettors. Hearne, who ran one of New York's
biggest gambling houses, was so notorious that a verse in a traditional
hymn was modified for his sake:

> Ye Saints rejoice, give cheerful thanks,
> For Awful Gardner's joined your ranks.
> And, while the lamp holds out to burn,
> There still is hope for *Patrick Hearne*.[41]

John's improvidence had been so spectacular that it was not until three
years after he died that Dexter was able to pay Hearne off in full. On
March 9, 1859, John's estate received its quarterly dividend, $2,124.34,

from the Syracuse Coarse Salt Company. The very next day Dexter began
tending to Hearne: "$1500. John J. Olcott on acct. P. Hearne's note
against J. B. James, assigned to him." Hearne's bill collector belonged to
the family that ran Albany's highly politicized Mechanics and Farmers
Bank, which had close affiliations with Tammany Hall and Martin Van
Buren's Democratic Party. The fact that the Jameses had always steered
clear of this bank and these political interests shows how seriously John had
betrayed certain James family traditions.

Two weeks later Dexter judged that it was safe to make a second payment: "$500. John W. [*sic*] Olcott on a/c Note of J B. James to P L
Hearne, assigned to him." Hileman had proved willing to "compromise,"
but the amount of the third and final payment tells us that Hearne held out
for every last cent he had coming to him: "$481.32. John J. Olcott in full
of note given by John B James decd to P. L. Hearne."[42]

Hearne had a particular motive for demanding his pound of flesh. In
January 1855, more than a year before John's death and not long after Fernando Wood was elected mayor of New York, the police raided several
gambling houses and made some arrests. A few days later a long letter appeared in the *New York Tribune* over a signature its readers had seen before,
H.J.:

I notice in your columns that among the gamblers arrested . . . [was] Patrick
Hearne. . . . Who would have thought that these huge and impudent gambling
establishments were ever going to be assailed . . . ? The chief of them are situated
in Broadway . . . [and] furnished in the most luxurious and seductive manner
. . . ; they are fed and fattened and pampered on the tears of broken-hearted fathers
and mothers, on the anguish of wives, on the sighs of kindred, on the desolation
of all the virtues and pleasant charities that sweeten home.[43]

It would have been a simple matter for Hearne to find out who H.J. was,
if only because the letters from Europe that Senior began dispatching to the
Tribune that autumn were followed by the same initials.[44] The directness
and ferocity of Senior's attack on Hearne hint at a private source of outrage.
Perhaps John Barber James was by this time deep in Hearne's debt. It may
even be that what Senior called "the desolation of all the virtues" of home
had begun to tell on nineteen-year-old Johnny. Yet if Hearne already had
John's check or IOU in his possession, Senior's public denunciation was
imprudent to the point of foolhardiness.

Two years earlier, in 1853, John had been appointed to the board of
inspectors at Sing-Sing Penitentiary.[45] It may have been soon after this that

a large number of the James clan were given a tour of the prison, where young Henry's attention was arrested by a "refined and distinguished" prisoner paring his nails.[46] By 1855 or 1856 John must have been worried about—possibly even threatened with—a civil action.[47] He owed at least $7,000 to New York's roughest crowd, one of whom, Hearne, had every incentive to seek revenge for his own humiliations. As if all this were not enough, John was entangled in a liaison with a Mrs. Little—whose husband he considered a friend.[48] What made his situation all the more intolerable was that he continued to play the part of a fine gentleman and a trusted and loved member of the James clan. When his mother, Catharine Barber James, added a codicil to her will in September 1854, she kept John on as her sole executor.[49] He was the son who bore her maiden name. He had made her Albany home his residence since the death of his wife in 1846. The man who had once played Richard III seems to have been living a dangerously double life.

John's mother may have been kept in the dark about her son's troubles, but other members of the family were worried. Judging from a fascinating scene in *A Small Boy*, young James seems to have detected the general anxiety without understanding what it was about. His memoirs recall how his father took him more than once to a conspicuously refined shop that sold men's "pockethandkerchiefs, neckties, collars, umbrellas" and also provided "furnished apartments for gentlemen." He even recalled that the place was near Fourth Street in the "labyrinth of grave bye-streets westwardly 'back of' Broadway," and that its proprietor was named Mrs. Cannon. If one checks city directories and recorded deeds, one finds that James's recollections were right on the money: Mrs. Anne C. Cannon lived on the corner of Mercer Street and Waverley Place—a good address, and quite close to Mrs. Elizabeth Walsh's Washington Square home—and supported herself by "boarding" and selling "made linen."[50] As she and her employees, Maggie and Susie, sat in their rocking chairs with their "poised needles," the talk always seemed to turn to the "remarkable Uncles," John, Edward, and Howard—"where they at the moment might be, or as to when they were expected, or above all as to how (the 'how' was the great matter and the fine emphasis)." Something more than drinking seemed to be involved, and there was a fine Jamesian mystification in the air: "If I didn't understand, however, the beauty was that Mrs. Cannon understood . . . and my father understood, and each understood that the other did, Miss Maggie and Miss Susie being no whit behind. It was only

I who didn't understand."[51] It was in this fashion that James hovered on the sidelines of John's tragic denouement, much as Maisie Farange haunts her parents' and stepparents' adulteries without understanding about sex.

Senior's next communications to the *Tribune* consisted of two or three editorials, which, following standard practice, did not carry his signature. Because they constitute his one foray into the rough-and-tumble realities of civic reform, these editorials afford an invaluable sidelight on the nature of Senior's thought. The first of them, "Our Best and Worst Society," seems even more intemperate than the letter on the arrest of gamblers: If the law does not root out professional gambling in New York, "the awful form of Judge Lynch" will soon establish its "sovereign and merciful jurisdiction."[52] The second editorial, inspired by a further raid on Hearne's parlors, not only singled him out once again for reprobation but provided his address, as if to inform "Judge Lynch" of the malefactor's whereabouts: "No. 587 Broadway, in the house next north of John Jacob Astor's old residence."[53] This was between Prince and Houston streets.

In addition to reflecting their author's anguish at what was happening to a much-loved younger brother, these editorials mark the one moment in Senior's life when he seemed to be moving in sync with large public events. He had reason to believe that his side was winning, that Gotham's municipal leaders were seriously interested in cleaning up the city, and he assailed the forces of vice and corruption with extraordinary rhetorical energy. But then, in late spring or summer 1855, it became clear that Mayor Wood was not seriously interested in reform and was only playing a complicated game. In the end he proved to be one of New York's sleaziest mayors, leaving office a good deal richer than he entered it.[54] Hearne apparently continued to prosper at his trade. His brick dwelling on Broadway was valued at $16,000, and when the state census marshal made his official visit in the summer of 1855, Hearne gave his profession as "gentleman."[55] Although he got swept up in another gambling raid early in 1856, he was released on a promise to close his gambling establishment.

The lawyer who got Hearne off was Daniel Sickles, a big-time sachem in Tammany Hall and a New York State senator. Sickles was later sent to Congress by New York's strongly Democratic third district, and while serving in Washington he shot and killed the son of Francis Scott Key, whom he suspected of being his wife's lover. That was in 1859, and when Sickles was brought to trial and found innocent, against the evidence, Senior once again wrote some lengthy and intemperate letters to the *Tribune*.[56]

Judging from the fact that a few years later William sent Sickle's photograph to Alice as an example of a bully's physiognomy,[57] the James children
had some knowledge of their father's entanglement with this powerful and
dangerous New Yorker.

The defeat of Senior's high hopes for Mayor Wood's anti-gambling
campaign furnishes an additional and very important motive for the James
parents' determination to reside in Europe for three years and never to return to New York. It also explains Senior's sudden disillusionment with
American democracy and the astonishing preference that shows up in his
letters of 1856–57 for the dictatorial rule of Napoleon III.[58] It is not too
much to say that John's misadventures in Broadway's gaming houses and
Senior's intense involvement in a reform movement that turned out to be
phony were two of the primary forces that shaped young Henry James's
boyhood, leaving him with a lasting awe of the "splendid monumental reference" of "the shining second Empire."[59] Behind the future novelist's
three-year transplantation to Europe, his swerve away from the American
scene (a swerve that was coerced, not chosen, in spite of all his later claims),
and his early fondness for imperial display, stable hierarchies, and artistic
grandeur—behind all these initiations that helped make James the man and
artist he was stood the gentlemanly and "sacrificial" figure of John Barber
James.

Exactly how John committed suicide is not known. His motives for
traveling to Chicago to consummate the act would be a complete mystery if
it were not for a faint hint preserved in the cash book kept by his trustee
after his death. Having inherited some of his father's vast landholdings in
Illinois, John evidently turned the deeds over to the Chicago firm of
Moore, Morton, & Co. on April 22, 1856, one month before his death,
to be converted into cash. Although numerous parcels were sold, bringing
in amounts ranging from $25 to $667, the money did not reach John's estate until June 1857,[60] a year after his death. Perhaps he was finally led to
kill himself by the apparent failure of his last-ditch plan to raise money. If
so, and if Henry James ever learned of his desperate effort—and these are
two very big ifs—then it seems more than likely that John's tragic end inspired the narration in *Watch and Ward*, James's first novel (later dis-
owned), of Nora's father's desperate attempt to borrow $100 before shoot-
ing himself.

The news of John's death must have reached Senior's family just before
or after they moved into an elegant house at 44 Champs-Elysées, taken for

a month beginning June 3.[61] Temporarily installed in what was then Paris's
most fashionable street,[62] James never forgot the house's mirrorlike floors,
white and gold paneling, "tense red damask" upholstery, and "perilous
staircase."[63] In such surroundings, the circumstances of John's life and
death may have seemed particularly sordid. The one thing that is clear is
that the story was effectively hushed up. There is only one extant 1856 document from any member of the James clan that so much as mentions John's
death, and that is Senior's September 14, 1856, letter to his close friend,
Edmund Tweedy:

> I don't think I had ever such a shock as the news of his death. I had been used too
> to say he will soon die unless he stops; but I always supposed that he *would* stop.
> And when at last I heard that he had actually been hurried away into that distant
> and dishonoured grave, when I thought of his youth and his beauty and his wit and
> his generosity and his genial feeling for all that was noble or manly under the sun,
> I felt as if my heart must break within me, or that madness would be a relief. He
> was inexpressibly dear to me: I was proud of him, I was full of hope that with
> maturity of intellect would come serene and beneficent action: but he has gone, and
> I have already ceased to complain.[64]

Senior was not one to keep his feelings hidden from his family. His
inability to keep secrets, together with the intensity of his grief, suggests
that young Henry probably picked up some circumstantial information
about John's death—the gambling debts, the fact of suicide. But we must
also remember that some deaths in the extended James family were followed not by explanations but by "unfathomed silences and significant
headshakes."[65] On balance, it seems best to suppose that John's story was
imparted to the children in a heavily mystified version, and that the thir-
teen-year-old boy was left with a good deal of pain, uncertainty, and confusion.

The man who may have been Henry's favorite uncle had done away
with himself and been buried in what Senior called a "dishonoured grave."
The boy's immediate reaction can only be conjectured, but the long-term
impact on his imagination may be inferred from Nora's father's suicide in
Watch and Ward, Isabel's loyalty to the improvident father her other rela-
tives disapprove of, the sympathetic presentation of Newton Winch in "A
Round of Visits," and the basic conception and fate of Hyacinth Robinson.
John's suicide casts a new light on some of James's settled views, particu-
larly his conviction that gentlemen of leisure were out of place in America.
My hunch is that James came to see his uncle's death not as a consequence

of his character and circumstances but as a sign of the defects of a society that made no provision for cultivated but careerless men, and that this ex planatory strategy was linked to James's deep-seated need to defend himself from certain common American ways.

III

The moment when James's parents brought his New York childhood to an abrupt and effective end may be regarded as the critical turning point of his life. Certainly, James's own memoirs insist on the momentous implications for his future development of this turning point, though without treating its painful and unarticulated aspects as I am doing in this essay. In spite of his serious European illnesses (suffered while traveling from London through Paris to Geneva and later while wintering at Boulogne), James presents his sojourn in Europe as a stay in the promised land and not at all as an expulsion from Eden. But a writer's account of his own formation is always necessarily suspect, and James's capacity for rationalization was truly extraordinary. One of the things I think he forgot, and in fact had to forget, was that his discovery of the Old World splendor of Paris coincided with the announcement that his most loved, most beautiful uncle had been sacrificed to the New World's disorders. Within the obscure economy of James's imagination, these two discoveries became related, the first being required by the second. James's conversion to Europe was a way for him to leave his New York childhood safely behind, along with the murderous New York world he had loved. Yet his handsome uncle's unburied body pressed on his imagination for 50 years and more, showing up in his first novel, his last story ("A Round of Visits"), his treatment of the dead father of his most important heroine, and his most tragic hero, Hyacinth Robinson.

During the years in which James saw the New York Edition through to completion, his autobiographical recollections of New York had not yet been committed to paper. When he composed the prefaces to *The Portrait of a Lady* and *The Wings of the Dove*, the terms in which he glanced at their sources in family history imply that he knew he would have to revisit all that, "retrace" it, "go into" it—some of it. He could not know whether he would live long enough to transform the past and all its tragic waste into his kind of art, which labored to redeem life, to silver it, sprinkle it with gold dust, ennoble it. Autobiography lay in the vague and difficult future. The present task was monument building. Bringing back the treasures of

his long expatriation and enshrining them in the great, lethal city that had
destroyed his charming uncle, and from which he himself had been torn
away in his thirteenth year, and where his family's richly remembered past
was being built over and built over again by new and monstrous buildings,
was one way to try to settle a restless mob of uneasy old ghosts.

Back in 1856, a couple of months after learning of his brother's suicide, James's father had written an essay, "The Order in American Disorder," which was published in a progressive London weekly, *The Leader*.[66]
Some such title, say "The Order in New York's Disorder," could serve as
the willed inner meaning of James's New York Edition, and of *A Small Boy
and Others* as well. In James's memory and imagination New York was a
place of tremendous chaos, ranging from the mismatched table settings he
remembered in *Washington Square* through the overspilling Dutch grocery
of *The Bostonians* all the way to John Barber James's terrible, threatening
fall. And yet, not only had young James been perfectly at home in New
York, solemnly observing and storing it all up, but he and his James and
Walsh relatives and the schools he attended and the plays he was taken to
were all small parts of the chaotic whole. Then it was all swept away and
treated to a drastic inner revaluation and made subservient to the more august European order (the word "order" acquiring an overwhelmingly massive new meaning). The earlier time and place became one with the James
family's, and James's own, losses, defeats, disasters, collapses, and failures.
All of it was put away, becoming the unseen ground his English life was
constructed on. It was only as James approached the end, after revisiting
the United States and of course New York in 1904–5, that he resolved to
go back in another sense as well, back in time, like a salmon remounting
the stream. The moment had come to try once and for all to wrest a definitive and lasting success from that terrible array of wasted life—his father's,
his uncle John's, all the other poorly explained James and Walsh family
deaths and disasters, and of course his own inexplicable failure to achieve
the greatness he had been aiming at for so long. First he made the New
York Edition, which cost him a good four years of what little life remained,
and, in a commercial sense, turned out to be yet one more failure, and then
he remounted the stream of time for real, writing his two great autobiographical volumes. With them at last he produced the monuments he had
been dreaming of, whose greatness was a consequence of his brave and belated though not always successful effort to look all that wasted life square
in the face without turning to stone.

Shame and Performativity:
Henry James's
New York Edition Prefaces

Eve Kosofsky Sedgwick

I don't remember hearing the phrase "queer performativity" used before, but it seems to be made necessary by, if nothing else, the work of Judith Butler in and since her important book *Gender Trouble*. Inevitably, as any theory of cultural consumption would suggest, the iteration, the citation, the *use* of Butler's formulations in the context of queer theory will prove to have been highly active and tendentious. Probably the centerpiece of Butler's recent work has been a series of demonstrations that gender can best be discussed as a form of performativity. But what that claim, in turn, "means" is performatively dependent on the uses given it. Its force so far has been in pressing the anti-essentialist account of gender toward a radical extreme of interrogation; in ratifying the apparently unique centrality of drag performance practice as—not just the shaping metaphor—but the very idiom of a tautologically heterosexist gender/sexuality system, and the idiom also of the possibility for its subversion; in broadening the notion of parody and foregrounding it as a strategy of gender critique and struggle; and more generally, in placing theater and theatrical performance at front and center of questions of subjectivity and sexuality.

There is a lot to value in all this. But as a reader I do find that the magnetism exerted on me by the notion of performativity emanates from some different places than these—also queer ones, and also, I believe, resonant with at least some concerns in Butler's writing that have proven less easy to attend to so far. I'd single out especially the relation between systemic melancholia—the melancholia she describes so suggestively as being instituted by the loss, not of particular objects of desire, but of proscribed desires themselves—the relation between that systemic melancholia and performativity. But I'm also very interested in how central the concept of *exposure* is to her own and other anti-essentialist projects: *exposure* of hidden assumptions, *exposure* of contradictions. If this exposure is a purely epistemological project, then from where is its political or motivational efficacy, its *performative* force, supposed to derive?

But where then, I must ask to begin with, are we to look for performativity itself? I would like the question of performativity to prove useful in some way for understanding the obliquities among *meaning, being,* and *doing,* not only around the examples of drag performance and (its derivative?) gendered self-presentation, but equally for such complex speech acts as coming out, for work around AIDS and other grave identity-implicating illnesses, and for the self-labeled, transversely but urgently representational placarded body of *demonstration.*

To begin with: the divided history, hence the divided reach across present and future, of this term "performativity." In many usages I am currently hearing, it seems to be affiliated *only* with, motivated only by, the notion of a performance in the defining instance theatrical. Yet Butler's work constitutes an invitation to, in her words, "consider gender . . . as . . . an 'act,' as it were, which is both intentional and performative, where 'performative' itself carries the double-meaning of 'dramatic' and 'non-referential.'"[1] "Performative" at the present moment carries the authority of two quite different discourses, that of theater on the one hand, of speech-act theory and deconstruction on the other. Partaking in the prestige of both discourses, it nonetheless, as Butler suggests, means very differently in each. The stretch between theatrical and deconstructive meanings of "performative" seems to span the polarities of, at either extreme, the *extroversion* of the actor, the *introversion* of the signifier. Michael Fried's opposition between theatricality and absorption seems custom-made for this paradox about "performativity": in its deconstructive sense performativity signals absorption; in the vicinity of the stage, however, the performative is the theatrical. But in another range of usages, a text like Lyotard's *The Postmodern Condition* uses "performativity" to mean an extreme of something like *efficiency*—postmodern representation as a form of capitalist efficiency—while, again, the deconstructive "performativity" of Paul de Man or J. Hillis Miller seems to be characterized by the *dis*linkage precisely of cause and effect between the signifier and the world.[2] At the same time, it's worth keeping in mind that even in deconstruction, more can be said of performative speech-acts than that they are ontologically dislinked or introversively nonreferential. Following on de Man's demonstration of "a radical estrangement between the meaning and the performance of any text,"[3] one might want to dwell not so much on the nonreference of the performative as on (what de Man calls) its necessarily "aberrant"[4] relation to its own reference—the torsion, the mutual perversion as one might say, of reference and performativity.

"Performativity" is already quite a queer category, then—maybe not so surprising if we consider the tenuousness of its ontological ground, the fact that it begins its intellectual career all but repudiated in advance by its originator, the British philosopher J. L. Austin, who introduces the term in the first of his 1955 Harvard lectures (later published as *How to Do Things with Words*) only to disown it somewhere around the eighth. He disowns or dismantles "performativity," that is, as the name of a distinct category or field of utterances (that might be opposed to the "constative"); and indeed the use that deconstruction has had for "performativity" begins with the recognition of it as a property common to all utterance.[5] Yet, as Shoshana Felman points out in *The Literary Speech Act*, Austin's own performance in these texts is anything but a simple one; and one of their sly characteristics is a repeated tropism toward—an evident fascination with—a particular class of examples of performative utterance.[6] Presented first as pure, originary, and defining for the concept; dismissed at the last as no more than "a marginal limiting case" of it if indeed either the examples or the concept can be said to "survive" the analytic operation of the lectures at all;[7] nonetheless reverted to over and over as if no argument or analysis, no deconstruction or dismantlement could really vitiate or even challenge the self-evidence of their exemplary force—these sentences are what Austin's work installs in the mind *as* performativity *tout court*, even while rendering nominally unusable the concept *of* performativity *tout court*. Famously, these are a cluster of sentences in the first-person singular present indicative active, about which "it seems clear that to utter the sentence (in, of course, the appropriate circumstances) is not to *describe* my doing [a thing] . . . or to state that I am doing it: it is to do it."[8] Examples include "I promise," "I bet . . . ," "I bequeath . . . ," "I christen . . . ," "I apologize," "I dare you," "I sentence you . . . ," and so on. But the first example Austin offers remains both his own most inveterately recurrent and his most influential: "'I do (sc. take this woman to be my lawful wedded wife)'—as uttered in the course of the marriage ceremony."[9]

The marriage ceremony is, indeed, so central to the origins of "performativity" (given the strange, disavowed but unattenuated persistence of *the exemplary* in this work) that a more accurate name for *How to Do Things with Words* might have been *How to Say (or Write) "I Do" About Twenty Million Times Without Winding up Any More Married than You Started Out.* (Short title: *I Do—Not!*) This is true both because most of the "I do"'s (or "I pronounce thee man and wife"'s) in the book are offered as examples of the different ways things can go *wrong* with performative utterances (e.g., "because we are, say, married already, or it is the purser and not the captain who is conducting the ceremony");[10] but even more because they are offered *as* examples in the first place—hence as, performatively, voided in advance. *How to Do Things with Words* thus performs at least a triple gesture with respect to marriage: installing monogamous heterosexual dyadic church- and state-sanctioned marriage at the definitional center of an entire philosophical edifice, it yet posits as the first heuristic device of that philosophy *the class of things* (for instance, personal characteristics or object choices) *that can preclude or vitiate marriage*; and it constructs the philosopher himself, the modern Socrates, as a man—presented as highly comic—whose relation to the marriage vow will be one of compulsive, apparently apotropaic repetition and yet of ultimate exemption.

So, as Felman's work in *The Literary Speech Act* confirms, the weird centrality of the marriage example for performativity in general isn't exactly a sign that this train of thought is doomed to stultification in sexual orthodoxy. Nevertheless I am struck by the potential interest that might also lie in speculation about versions of performativity (okay, go ahead and call them "perversions"—or "deformatives") that might begin by placing some different kinds of utterance in the position of the exemplary. Austin keeps going back to that formula "first person singular present indicative active," for instance, and the marriage example makes me wonder about the apparently natural way the first-person speaking, acting, and pointing subject, like the (wedding) present itself, gets constituted in marriage through a confident appeal to state authority, through the calm interpellation of others present as "witnesses," and through the logic of the (heterosexual) supplement whereby individual subjective agency is guaranteed by the welding into a cross-gender dyad. Persons who self-identify as queer, by contrast, will be those whose subjectivity is lodged in refusals or deflections of (or by) the logic of the heterosexual supplement; in far less simple associations attaching to state authority; in far less complacent relation to the witness of others. The emergence of the first person, of the singular, of the present, of the active, and of the indicative are all questions, rather than presumptions, for queer performativity.

That's why I like to speculate about a performative elaboration that might begin with the example, not "I do," but, let us say, "Shame on you." "Shame on you" has several important features in common with Austin's pet examples: most notably, it names itself, it has its illocutionary force (the conferral of shame) in and by specifying its illocutionary intent. Then, like Austin's examples, it depends on the interpellation of witness. And like them too it necessarily occurs within a pronoun matrix. Unlike the "I do" set of performatives, though, its pronoun matrix begins with the second person. There is a "you" but there is no "I"—or rather, forms of the inexplicit "I" constantly remain to be evoked from the formulation "Shame on you." They can be evoked in different ways. The absence of an explicit verb from "Shame on you" records the place in which an I, in conferring shame, has effaced itself and its own agency.[11] Of course the desire for self-effacement is the defining trait of—what else?—shame. So the very grammatical truncation of "Shame on you" marks it as the product of a history out of which an I, now withdrawn, is *projecting* shame—toward another I, an I deferred, that has yet and with difficulty to come into being, if at all, in the place of the shamed second person. The verblessness of this particular performative, then, implies a first person whose singular/plural status, whose past/present/future status, and indeed whose agency/passivity can only be questioned rather than presumed.

Why might "Shame on you" be a useful utterance from which to begin imagining *queer* performativity? Appearances are strongly against it, I admit. What's the point of accentuating the negative, of beginning with stigma, and for that matter a form of stigma—"Shame on you"—so unsanitizably redolent of that long Babylonian exile known as queer childhood? But note that this is just what the word "queer" itself does, too: the main reason why the self-application of "queer" by activists has proven so volatile is that there's no *way* that any amount of affirmative reclamation is going to succeed in detaching the word from its associations with shame and with the terrifying powerlessness of gender-dissonant or otherwise stigmatized childhood. If "queer" is a politically potent term, which it is, that's because, far from being detachable from the childhood scene of shame, it cleaves to that scene as a near-inexhaustible source of transformational energy. There's a strong sense, I think, in which the subtitle of any truly queer (perhaps as opposed to gay?) politics will be the same as the one Erving Goffman gave to his book *Stigma: Notes on the Management of Spoiled Identity.*[12] But more than its management: its experimental, creative, performative force.

"Shame on you" is performatively efficacious because its grammar—admittedly somewhat enigmatic—*is* a transformational grammar: both at the level of pronoun positioning, as I've sketched, and at the level of the relational grammar of the affect shame itself. As best described by the psychologist Silvan Tomkins, who offers by far the richest theory and phenomenology of this affect, shame effaces itself; shame points and projects; shame turns itself skin side outside; shame and pride, shame and dignity, shame and self-display, shame and exhibitionism are different interlinings of the same glove: shame, it might finally be said, transformational shame, *is performance.* I mean theatrical performance. Performance interlines shame as more than just its result or a way of warding it off, too, though importantly it is those things. Recent work by theorists and psychologists of shame locates the proto-form (eyes down, head averted) of this powerful affect—which appears in infants very early, between the third and seventh months of life, just after the infant has become able to distinguish and recognize the face of its caregiver—at a particular moment in a particular repeated narrative. That is the moment when the circuit of mirroring expressions between the child's face and the caregiver's recognized face (a circuit which, if it can be called a form of primary narcissism, suggests that narcissism from the very first throws itself sociably, dangerously into the gravitational field of the other) is broken: the moment when the adult face fails or refuses to play its part in the continuation of mutual gaze; when, for any one of many reasons, it fails to be recognizable to, or recognizing of, the infant who has been, so to speak, "giving face" on the basis of a faith in the continuity of this circuit. Michael Franz Basch explains:

The infant's behavioral adaptation is quite totally dependent on maintaining effective communication with the executive and coordinating part of the infant-mother system. The shame-humiliation response, when it appears, represents the failure or absence of the smile of contact, a reaction to the loss of feedback from others, indicating social isolation and signaling the need for relief from that condition.[13]

The proto-affect shame is thus not defined by prohibition (nor, as a result, by repression). Shame floods into being as a moment, a disruptive moment, in a circuit of identity-constituting identificatory communication. Indeed, like a stigma, shame is itself a form of communication. Blazons of shame, the "fallen face" with eyes down and head averted—and to a lesser

extent, the blush—are semaphores of trouble and at the same time of a desire to reconstitute the interpersonal bridge.

But in interrupting identification, shame, too, makes identity. In fact
shame and identity remain in very dynamic relation to one another, at once
deconstituting and foundational, because shame is both peculiarly contagious and peculiarly individuating. One of the strangest features of
shame—but perhaps also the one that offers the most conceptual leverage
for projects like ours—is the way bad treatment of someone else, bad treatment *by* someone else, someone else's embarrassment, stigma, debility, bad
smell, or strange behavior, seemingly having nothing to do with me, can
so readily flood me—assuming I'm a shame-prone person—with this sen-
sation whose very suffusiveness seems to delineate my precise, individual
outlines in the most isolating way imaginable.

What most readily distinguishes shame from guilt is that shame attaches to and sharpens the sense of what one *is*, while guilt attaches to what
one *does*. One therefore *is something*, in experiencing shame: though one
may or may not have secure hypotheses about what. In the developmental
process, shame is now widely considered the affect that most defines the
space wherein a sense of self will develop (Francis Broucek: "shame is to
self psychology what anxiety is to ego psychology—the keystone affect").[14]
Which I take to mean not at all that shame is the place where identity is
most securely attached to essences but rather that it is the place where the
question of identity arises most originarily, and most relationally.

At the same time, shame both derives from and aims toward sociability.
Basch writes:

The shame-humiliation reaction in infancy of hanging the head and averting the
eyes does not mean the child is conscious of rejection, but indicates that effective
contact with another person has been broken. . . . Therefore, shame-humiliation
throughout life can be thought of as an inability to effectively arouse the other person's positive reactions to one's communications. The exquisite painfulness of that
reaction in later life harks back to the earliest period when such a condition is not
simply uncomfortable but threatens life itself.[15]

So whenever the actor, or the performance artist, or, I could add, the activ-
ist in an identity politics, proffers the spectacle of her or his "infantile" narcissism to a spectating eye, the stage is set (so to speak) for either a newly
dramatized flooding of the subject by the shame of refused return; or the
successful pulsation of the mirroring regard through a narcissistic circuit
rendered elliptical (which is to say: necessarily distorted) by the hyperbole

of its original cast. Shame is the affect that mantles the threshold between introversion and extroversion, between absorption and theatricality, between performativity and—performativity.

What links the currently hot topic of shame to a high-cultural figure like Henry James? Those of you who have paid attention to the recent, meteoric rise of shame to its present housewife-megastar status in the firmament of self-help and popular psychology—along with that of its ingenue sidekick, the Inner Child—may be feeling a bit uneasy by this point. So, for that matter, may those used to reading about shame in the neoconservative framework that treasures shame along with guilt as, precisely, an adjunct of repression and an enforcer of proper behavior. In the ways I want to be thinking about shame, the widespread moralistic valuation of this powerful affect as *good* or *bad*, *to be mandated* or *to be excised*, according to how one plots it along a notional axis of prohibition/permission/requirement, seems distinctly beside the point. It seems to me that the great usefulness of thinking about shame comes, by contrast, from its potential *distance* from the concepts of guilt and repression, hence from the stressed epistemologies and bifurcated moralisms entailed in every manifestation of what Foucault referred to as the repressive hypothesis. Surely then I can't appeal to *Toxic Shame*, *Healing the Shame that Binds You*, or *Guilt Is the Teacher, Love Is the Lesson* for my very methodology? Am I really going to talk about Henry James's inner child? But I am. My sense of the force and interest of the affect shame is clearly very different from what is to be found in the self-help literature, but there it is: Henry James and the inner child it must be.

I

Henry James undertook the New York Edition (a handsome 24-volume consolidation and revision, with new prefaces, of what he saw as his most important novels and stories to date) at the end of a relatively blissful period of literary production ("the major phase")—a blissful period poised, however, between two devastating bouts of melancholia. (The connection between melancholia and performativity, derived from Butler, with whose invocation I began this essay, needs to open out, I think, into a full-scale discussion of the connections among melancholia, mourning, dis/identification, and shame—but this is a project for the future.) The first of these scouring depressions was precipitated in 1895 by what James experienced as the obliterative failure of his ambitions as a playwright, being howled off the stage at the premiere of *Guy Domville*. By 1907, though, when the volumes of the New York Edition were beginning to appear, James's theatrical self-projection was sufficiently healed that he had actually begun a new round of playwriting and of negotiations with producers—eventuating, indeed, in performance. The next of James's terrible depressions was triggered not by humiliation on the stage but by the failure of the New York Edition itself: its total failure to sell, and its apparently terminal failure to evoke any recognition from any readership.

When we read the New York Edition prefaces, then, we read a series of texts that are in the most active imaginable relation to shame. Marking and indeed exulting in James's recovery from a nearly fatal episode of shame in the theater, the prefaces, gorgeous with the playful spectacle of a productive and almost promiscuously entrusted or "thrown" authorial narcissism, yet also offer the spectacle of inviting (that is, leaving themselves open to) what was in fact their and their author's immediate fate: annihilation by the blankest of nonrecognizing responses from any reader. The prefaces are way out there, in short (and in more than a couple of senses of "out").

In them, at least two different circuits of the hyperbolic narcissism/shame orbit are enacted, in a volatile relation to each other. The first of these, as I've suggested, is the drama of James's relation to his audience of readers: in using the term "audience" here, I want to mark James's own insistent thematization of elements in this writing as specifically theatrical, with all the implications of excitement, overinvestment, danger, loss, and melancholia that the theater by this time held for him.[16] The second and related narcissism/shame circuit dramatized in the prefaces is the perilous and productive one that extends between the speaker and his own past. James's most usual gesture in the prefaces is to figure his relation to the past as the intensely charged relationship between the author of the prefaces and the often much younger man who wrote the novels and stories to which the prefaces are appended—or between either of these men and a yet younger figure who represents the fiction itself.

What undertaking could be more narcissistically exciting or more narcissistically dangerous than that of rereading, revising, and consolidating one's own "collected works"? If *these*, or their conjured young author, return one's longing gaze with dead, indifferent, or even distracted eyes, what limit can there be to the shame (of him, of oneself) so incurred? Equal to that danger, however, is the danger of one's own failure to recognize or to desire them or him. Failure to recognize: here is a place—a vitally important one, I think—where *epistemological* issues of cognition and recognition can be seen to mesh deeply with a crux of affect and motivation. Tomkins, for example, places shame at one end of the affect polarity *shame-interest*, suggesting that the pulsations of cathexis around shame, of all things, are what either enable or disable so basic a function as the ability to be interested in the world:

> Like disgust, [shame] operates only after interest or enjoyment has been activated, and inhibits one or the other or both. The innate activator of shame is the incomplete reduction of interest or joy. Hence any barrier to further exploration which partially reduces interest . . . will activate the lowering of the head and eyes in shame and reduce further exploration or self-exposure. . . . Such a barrier might be because one is suddenly looked at by one who is strange, or because one wishes to look at or commune with another person but suddenly cannot because he is strange, or one expected him to be familiar but he suddenly appears unfamiliar, or one started to smile but found one was smiling at a stranger.[17]

To consider interest itself a distinct affect, and to posit an association between shame and (the [incomplete] inhibition of) interest, makes sense phenomenologically, I think, about depression, and specifically about the depressions from which James had emerged to write his "major novels"— novels that do, indeed, seem to show the effects of a complicated history of disruptions and prodigal remediations in the *ability to take an interest*. Into such depressions as well, however, he was again to be plunged.

The James of the prefaces revels in the same startling metaphor that animates the present-day literature of the "inner child": the metaphor that presents one's relation to one's own past as a relation*ship*, intersubjective as it is intergenerational. And, it might be added, almost by definition homoerotic. Often the younger author is present in these prefaces as a figure in himself, but even more frequently the fictions themselves, or characters in them, are given his form. One needn't be invested (as pop psychology is) in a normalizing, hygienic teleology of *healing* this relationship, in a mawkishly essentialist overvaluation of the "child"'s access to narrative authority at the expense of that of the "adult," or in a totalizing ambition to get the two selves permanently merged into one, in order to find that this figuration opens out a rich landscape of relational positionalities—perhaps especially around issues of shame. James certainly displays no desire whatever to become once again the young and mystified author of his early productions. To the contrary, the very distance of these inner self-figurations

from the speaking self of the present is marked, treasured, and in fact eroticized. Their distance (temporal, figured as intersubjective, figured in
turn as spatial) seems, if anything, to constitute the relished internal space
of James's absorbed subjectivity. Yet for all that the distance itself is prized,
James's speculation as to what different outcomes might be evoked by different kinds of overture across the distance—by different sorts of solicitation, different forms of touch, interest, and love between the less and the
more initiated figures—provides a great deal of the impetus to his theoretical project in these essays. The speaking self of the prefaces does not attempt to merge with the potentially shaming or shamed figurations of its
younger self, younger fictions, younger heroes; its attempt is to love them.
That love is shown to occur both in spite of shame and, more remarkably,
through it.

   Not infrequently, as we'll see, the undertaking to reparent, as it were,
or "reissue" the bastard infant of (what is presented as) James's juvenilia is
described simply as male parturition. James also reports finding in himself
"that finer consideration hanging in the parental breast about the maimed
or slighted, the disfigured or defeated, the unlucky or unlikely child—
with this hapless small mortal thought of further as somehow 'compromising'"(7: vi; AN 80–81). James offers a variety of reasons for being embarrassed by these waifs of his past, but the persistence with which shame accompanies their repeated conjuration is matched by the persistence with
which, in turn, he describes himself as cathecting or eroticizing that very
shame as a way of coming into loving relation to queer or "compromising"
youth. In a number of places, for example, James more or less explicitly
invokes *Frankenstein* and all the potential uncanniness of the violently disavowed male birth. But he invokes that uncanniness in order to undo it, or
at least do something further with it, by offering the spectacle of—not his
refusal—but his eroticized eagerness to recognize his progeny even in its
oddness. "The thing done and dismissed has ever, at the best, for the ambitious workman, a trick of looking dead if not buried, so that he almost
throbs with ecstasy when, on an anxious review, the flush of life reappears.
It is verily on recognising that flush on a whole side of 'The Awkward Age'
that I brand it all, but ever so tenderly, as monstrous" (9: v–vi; AN, 99).
It is as if the ecstasy-inducing power of the young creature's "flush of life,"
which refers to even while evoking the potentially shaming brand of mon-
strosity, is the reflux of the blush of shame or repudiation the older man in
this rewriting *doesn't* feel. Similarly, James writes about his mortifyingly

extravagant miscalculations concerning the length of (what he had imagined as) a short story: "Painfully associated for me has 'The Spoils of Poynton' remained, until recent re-perusal, with the awkward consequence of
that fond error. The subject had emerged . . . all suffused with a flush of
meaning; thanks to which irresistible air, as I could but plead in the event,
I found myself . . . beguiled and led on."

"The thing had 'come,'" he concludes with an undisguised sensuous
pleasure but hardly a simple one; "the flower of conception had bloomed"
(*10*: x; *AN*, 124). And he describes his revision of the early fictions both as
his (or their?) way of "remaining *unshamed*" and in the same sentence as a
process by which they have "all joyously and *blushingly* renewed themselves" (*23*: xxii; *AN*, 345, my emphasis). What James seems to want here
is to remove the blush from its terminal place as the betraying blazon of a
ruptured narcissistic circuit, and instead to put it *in* circulation—as the
sign of a tenderly strengthened and indeed now "irresistible" bond between
the writer of the present and the abashed writer of the past; between either
of them and the queer little *conceptus*.

You can see the displacement at work in this passage from James's most
extended description of his process of revision:

Since to get and to keep finished and dismissed work well behind one, and to have
as little to say to it and about it as possible, had been for years one's only law, so,
during that flat interregnum . . . creeping superstitions as to what it might really
have been had time to grow up and flourish. Not least among these rioted doubtless
the fond fear that any tidying-up of the uncanny brood, any removal of accumulated dust, any washing of wizened faces, or straightening of grizzled locks, or
twitching, to a better effect, of superannuated garments, might let one in, as the
phrase is, for expensive renovations. I make use here of the figure of age and in-
firmity, but in point of fact I had rather viewed the reappearance of the first-born
of my progeny . . . as a descent of awkward infants from the nursery to the drawing-room under the kind appeal of enquiring, of possibly interested, visitors. I
had accordingly taken for granted the common decencies of such a case—the responsible glance of some power above from one nursling to another, the rapid flash
of an anxious needle, the not imperceptible effect of a certain audible splash of
soap-and-water. . . .

"Hands off altogether on the nurse's part!" was . . . strictly conceivable; but
only in the light of the truth that it had never taken effect in any fair and stately
. . . re-issue of anything. Therefore it was easy to see that any such apologetic
suppression as that of the "altogether," any such admission as that of a single dab of
the soap, left the door very much ajar. (*23*: xiv–xv; *AN*, 337–38)

The passage that begins by conjuring the uncanniness of an abandoned, stunted, old/young Frankenstein brood (reminiscent of the repudiated or abused children in Dickens, like Smike and Jenny Wren, whose deformed bodies stand for developmental narratives at once accelerated and frozen by, among other things, extreme material want) modulates reassuringly into the warm, overprotected Christopher Robin coziness of bourgeois Edwardian nursery ritual. The eventuality of the uncanny child's actual exposure to solitude and destitution has been deflected by an invoked domesticity. Invoked with that domesticity, in the now fostered and nurtured and therefore "childlike" child, is a new, pleasurable form of exhibitionistic flirtation with adults that dramatizes the child's very distance from abandonment and repudiation. In the place where the eye of parental care had threatened to be withheld, there is now a bath where even the nurse's attention is supplemented by the overhearing ear of inquiring and interested visitors. And in the place where the fear of solitary exposure has been warded off, there's now the playful nakedness of ablution, and a door left "very much ajar" for a little joke about the suppression of the "altogether."

This sanctioned intergenerational flirtation represents a sustained chord in the New York Edition. James describes the blandishment of his finished works in tones that are strikingly like the ones with which, in his letters, he has also been addressing Hendrik Anderson, Jocelyn Persse, Hugh Walpole, and the other younger men who at this stage of his life are setting out, with happy success, to attract him. Note in this passage (from the *Ambassadors* Preface) that "impudence" is the glamorizing trait James attributes to his stories—impudence that bespeaks not the absence of shame from this scene of flirtation but rather its pleasurably recirculated afterglow:

[The story] rejoices . . . to seem to offer itself in a light, to seem to know, and with the very last knowledge, what it's about—liable as it yet is at moments to be caught by us with its tongue in its cheek and absolutely no warrant but its splendid impudence. Let us grant then that the impudence is always there—there, so to speak, for grace and effect and *allure*; there, above all, because the Story is just the spoiled child of art, and because, as we are always disappointed when the pampered don't "play up," we like it, to that extent, to look all its character. It probably does so, in truth, even when we most flatter ourselves that we negotiate with it by treaty. (*21*: xii–xiii; *AN*, 315)

To dramatize the story as *impudent* in relation to its creator is also to dramatize the luxurious distance between this scene and one of *repudiation*: the conceivable shame of a past self, a past production, is being caught up and recirculated through a lambent interpersonal figuration of the intimate, indulged mutual pressure of light differentials of power and knowledge.

James writes about the writing of *The American*, "One would like to woo back such hours of fine precipitation . . . of images so free and confident and ready that they brush questions aside and disport themselves, like the artless schoolboys of Gray's beautiful Ode, in all the ecstasy of the ignorance attending them" (2: x; *AN*, 25). (Or boasts of *The Turn of the Screw*: "another grain . . . would have spoiled the precious pinch addressed to its end," *12*: xv; *AN*, 170.) Sometimes the solicitude is ultimately frustrated, and "I strove in vain . . . to embroil and adorn this young man on whom a hundred ingenious touches are thus lavished" (7: xxi–xxii; *AN*, 97). The wooing in these scenes of pederastic revision is not unidirectional, however; even the age differential can be figured quite differently, as when James finds himself, on rereading *The American*, "clinging to my hero as to a tall, protective, good-natured elder brother in a rough place" (2: xxiii; *AN*, 39), or when he says of Lambert Strether, "I rejoiced in the promise of a hero so mature, who would give me thereby the more to bite into" (*21*: viii; *AN*, 310). James refers to the protagonist of "The Beast in the Jungle" as "another poor sensitive gentleman, fit indeed to mate with Stransom of 'The Altar [of the Dead]'"—adding, "my attested predilection for poor sensitive gentlemen almost embarrasses me as I march!" (*17*: ix; *AN*, 246). The predilective yoking of the "I" with the surname of John Marcher, the romantic pairing off of Marcher in turn with the equally "sensitive" bachelor George Stransom, give if anything an excess of gay point to the "almost" embarrassment that is however treated not as a pretext for authorial self-coverture but as an explicit source of new, performatively induced authorial magnetism.

James, then, in the prefaces is using reparenting or "reissue" as a strategy for dramatizing and integrating shame, in the sense of rendering this potentially paralyzing affect narratively, emotionally, and performatively productive. The reparenting scenario is also, in James's theoretical writing, a pederastic/pedagogical one in which the flush of shame becomes an affecting and eroticized form of mutual display. The writing subject's seductive bond with the unmerged but unrepudiated "inner" child seems, indeed, to be the condition of that subject's having an interiority at all, a spatialized subjectivity that can be characterized by absorption. Or perhaps I should say: it is a condition of his *displaying* the spatialized subjectivity that can be characterized by absorption. For the spectacle of James's performative absorption appears only in relation (though a most complex and unstable relation) to the setting of his performative theatricality; the narcissism/shame circuit between the writing self and its "inner child" intersects with that other hyperbolic and dangerous narcissistic circuit, figured as theatrical performance, that extends outward between the presented and expressive face and its audience.

I am working here with the hypothesis that James's reflections on performativity will appear most interestingly in his ways of negotiating the intersection between absorption and theatricality, between the subjectivity-generating space defined by the loved but unintegrated "inner child" on the one hand and the frontal space of performance on the other. James works in the prefaces on developing a theoretical vocabulary for distinguishing (in the structure of his novels) between what Austin will provisionally come to call the constative and the performative, and between different senses of performativity. None of this differential vocabulary, however, retains its analytic consistency as it gets recruited into the scenarios of the prefaces' performance. Among the diacritical pairings that get more or less mapped onto differentials around performativity—and, that accomplished, get more or less explicitly deconstructed there—are romance versus reality (e.g., *2:* xiv–xv; *AN,* 30–31), substance versus form (e.g., *9:* xxi–xxii; *AN,* 115–16), anecdote versus picture (e.g., *10:* xxiv; *AN,* 139), anecdotal versus (and note the shift here) developmental (*16:* v–vi; *AN,* 233).

An example of the more or less explicit self-deconstruction of these differentials: Each scene of *The Awkward Age,* precisely because it "abides without a moment's deflexion by the principle of the stage-play," is said to

help us ever so happily to see the grave distinction between substance and form in a really wrought work of art signally break down. I hold it impossible to say, before "The Awkward Age," where one of these elements ends and the other begins: I have been unable at least myself, on re-examination, to mark any such joint or seam, to see the two *discharged* offices as separate. They are separate before the fact, but the sacrament of execution indissolubly marries them, and the marriage, like any other marriage, has only to be a "true" one for the scandal of a breach not to show. (*9:* xxi–xxii; *AN,* 115–16)

Seemingly, the theatrical performativity of *The Awkward Age* is supposed to mesh with its speech-act performativity, *as* its substance is supposed to mesh with its form, *as* man and wife are supposed to be "indissolubly" unified in the exemplary speech act of marriage. But one hardly has to look to

The Awkward Age itself (though of course one could)—nor need one look ahead to the sly deflations in Austin—to see that the indissoluble unity of marriage offers no very stout guarantee for the stability of this chain of homologies. Bad enough that marriage is a sacrament of *execution*; bad enough that, only a score of words after it has been pronounced indissoluble, marriage turns out to be efficacious not in preventing a breach, not even in preventing the scandal attending a breach, but only, for what it's worth, in keeping the scandal of a breach from *showing*. But the worst news is that in order to guarantee even these limited benefits, the marriage "has" ("only") "to be a 'true' one." The Jamesian scare-quotes call attention to how weaselly the qualification is. In what sense must a marriage be "a 'true' one" in order to guarantee that the scandal of a breach not show? Perhaps it must be true in the sense that its parties are "true" to each other, or to their vows, or that the marriage "takes" at some ineffable level—in the sense, that is, of partners' rendering their vows constatively precise descriptions of their behavior. Thus there's no occasion for a breach, and the guarantee is guaranteed unnecessary—that is to say, as a guarantee, meaningless. To bring in the truth qualification at all is to suggest that a speech act may be performatively efficacious only to the degree of (which is to say, only *through*) its constative validity.

The most sustained of the differentials through which James works out the meanings of performativity is the nearly ubiquitous opposition between drama itself (or the "scenic") and "picture." The high instability and high mutual torsiveness of the terms of this opposition are occasions for both shame and excitement:

I haven't the heart now, I confess, to adduce the detail of so many lapsed importances; the explanation of most of which, after all, I take to have been in the crudity of a truth beating full upon me through these reconsiderations, the odd inveteracy with which picture, at almost any turn, is jealous of drama, and drama (though on the whole with greater patience, I think) suspicious of picture. Between them, no doubt, they do much for the theme; yet each baffles insidiously the other's ideal and eats round the edges of its position. (*19*: xiv; *AN*, 298)

Beautiful exceedingly, for that matter, those occasions or parts of an occasion when the boundary line between picture and scene bears a little the weight of the double pressure. (*19*: xvi; *AN*, 300)

Characteristically, James's aesthetic asseveration of the *beauty* of the "double pressure" between picture and scene is embedded in psychological narrative at several textual levels. It adheres to a pederastic relation be-

tween characters, and equally again to the one between the author and the
anthropomorphized novel, the attaching character. Rereading *The Ambassadors*, James notes there "the exquisite treachery even . . . the straightest
execution may ever be trusted to inflict even on the most mature plan" (21:
xxii; *AN*, 325). He locates this lapse, which is a lapse in authorial technique, a lapse, he says, from the "scenic" into "the non-scenic form"
(ibid.), at a particular foundational crux of the novel: the scene in which
Strether, whom James as we've already seen finds lovable for his maturity,
suddenly becomes infatuated with a young man, Chad Newsome. Chad
however is destined to disappoint in turning out to be quite an ordinary,
self-ignorant young heterosexual, incapable of responding to Strether's intensities even as he is incapable of doing real justice to the love he evokes in
women. "The exquisite treachery even . . . the straightest . . . may ever be
trusted to inflict even on the most mature" is at once something Chad inflicts on Strether; something the novel (or its characters) inflicts on James;
and something that "picture," as a descriptive or propositional principle of
composition, inflicts on "scene" as a performative one. At each level, in a
characteristic locution, it represents "deviation (from too fond an original
vision)" (21: xxii; *AN*, 325). The author's fond, mature original vision of
an uncontaminatedly "scenic" technique suffers the same fate as his mature
hero's fond first vision of Chad, and is destined equally to be "diminished
. . . compromised . . . despoiled . . . so that, in a word, the whole economy
of his author's relation to him has at important points to be redetermined"
(21: xxiii; *AN*, 325–26). But note again that the treachery is described,
however ambiguously, as "exquisite," and the certainty of treachery is
something in which one is invited, however ironically, to "trust." It is the
very instability among these relations, and in particular, I infer, their ability to *resist* clear representation at any given, single level, that confers
value. "The book, however, critically viewed, is touchingly full of these
disguised and repaired losses, these insidious recoveries, these intensely redemptive consistencies" (21: xxiii; *AN*, 326). In James's theorizing of the
novel, consistency is the name, not for any homogeneous purity of the
speech act at a given level, but rather for the irreducible, attaching heterogeneity and indeed impurity with which each meets the "touch" of another.

II

What should also be specified is the imaged sexual zoning and sexual act in
which these relations repeatedly dramatize themselves in the prefaces. In a

footnote to a previous essay on James, "The Beast in the Closet," I quoted a passage from James's notebooks—written during a visit to California only a few months before he started on the New York Edition—which still seems to me the best condensation of what these prefaces press us to recognize as his most characteristic and fecund relation to his own anal eroticism:

I sit here, after long weeks, at any rate, in front of my arrears, with an inward accumulation of material of which I feel the wealth, and as to which I can only invoke my familiar demon of patience, who always comes, doesn't he?, when I call. He is here with me in front of this cool green Pacific—he sits close and I feel his soft breath, which cools and steadies and inspires, on my cheek. Everything sinks in: nothing is lost; everything abides and fertilizes and renews its golden promise, making me think with closed eyes of deep and grateful longing when, in the full summer days of L[amb] H[ouse], my long dusty adventure over, I shall be able to [plunge] my hand, my arm, *in*, deep and far, up to the shoulder—into the heavy bag of remembrance—of suggestion—of imagination—of art—and fish out every little figure and felicity, every little fact and fancy that can be to my purpose. These things are all packed away, now, thicker than I can penetrate, deeper than I can fathom, and there let them rest for the present, in their sacred cool darkness, till I shall let in upon them the mild still light of dear old L[amb] H[ouse]—in which they will begin to gleam and glitter and take form like the gold and jewels of a mine.[18]

At the time, I quoted this as a description of "fisting-as-*écriture*"; I am sure it is that, but the context of the prefaces brings out two other saliences of this scene of fisting equally strongly—saliences related to each other and, of course, also to the writing process. These involve, first, wealth, and second, parturition. One of the most audible intertexts in the passage is surely "Full fathom five thy father lies"—with the emphasis, perhaps, on "five," the five of fingers. The other important intertext seems to be from Book IV of *The Dunciad*, the passage where Annius describes the Greek coins he has swallowed to protect them from robbers and anticipates their being delivered, in the course of nature, from "the living shrine" of his gut to the man who has bought them from him:

> this our paunch before
> Still bears them, faithful; and that thus I eat,
> Is to refund the Medals with the meat.
> To prove me, Goddess! clear of all design,
> Bid me with Pollio sup, as well as dine:
> There all the Learn'd shall at the labour stand,
> And Douglas lend his soft, obstetric hand.[19]

In the context of *The Dunciad*, the obstetric hand feeling for wealth in the rectum seems meant to represent the ultimate in abjection and gross out, but under the pressure of James's brooding it has clearly undergone a sea change to become a virtually absolute symbol of imaginative value.

Sharply as this thematic emphasis may differ from a received understanding of James's aesthetic preoccupations, any reader interested in Henry James's bowels is, as it turns out, in fine company. "I blush to say," William James writes to Henry in 1869, "that detailed bulletins of your bowels . . . are of the most enthralling interest to me."[20] Maybe it seems— to some—an odd site for such captivation, but I would nonetheless argue that to attend passionately or well to much of James's strongest writing is necessarily, as it were already, to be in thrall to what had long been his painful, fussy, immensely productive focus on the sensations, actions, paralyses, accumulations, probings, and expulsions of his own lower digestive tract. The recent publication of the two brothers' early correspondence, including pages upon pages about Henry's constipation ("what you term so happily my moving intestinal drama")[21] begins to offer an objective correlative—startling in its detail and intimacy, if not in its substance—for what had before been inferential readings of the centrality of an anal preoccupation in James's sense of his body, his production, and his pleasure.[22]

Even from these early letters, it is evident that there is no such thing as the *simple* fact of James's constipation: it informs not only his eating, exercise, and medical attendance but also his travel destinations (during a part of his life defined by travel), his reading, his family relations, and the composition and circulation of his writing. The need to discuss his condition with the brother at home, for instance, mobilizes a drama of secret complicity (William: "It makes me sick to think of your life being blighted by this hideous affliction. I will say nothing to the family about it, as they can do you no good, and it will only give them pain")[23] that both mimics Henry's internal blockage and seemingly invokes the atmosphere of a sexual secret. William advises Henry, for instance: "A good plan is for you to write such on separate slips of paper marked private, so that I may then give freely the rest of the letter to Alice to carry about & re-read. . . . If you put it in the midst of other matter it prevents the whole letter from circulation. Sur ce, Dieu vous garde."[24] The organizing question in the brothers' long consultation is, What available technology (chemical, electric, thermal, hydraulic, manual) can best be mobilized to reach into and disimpact Henry's bowel? William advises:

Inject . . . as large & hot an enema as you can bear (not get it, *more tuo*, scalding) of soap suds & oil. . . .—Electricity sometimes has a wonderful effect, applied not in the piddling way you recollect last winter but by a strong galvanic current from the spine to the abdominal muscles, or if the rectum be paralysed one pole put inside the rectum. If I were you I wd. resort to it.[25]

And from Henry:

The diet here is good—both simple & palatable. But the only treatment for my complaint is the sitzbath. I was disappointed not to find here some such mechanism (i.e. that injection-douche) as you found at Divonne.[26]

I may actually say that I can't get a passage. My "little squirt" has ceased to have more than a nominal use. The water either remains altogether or comes out as innocent as it entered. For the past ten days I have become quite demoralized & have been frantically dosing myself with pills. But they too are almost useless & I may take a dozen & hardly hear of them. . . . Somehow or other I must take the thing in hand.[27]

What I have called the "crisis" was brought on by taking 2 so-called "anti-bilious" pills, recommended me at the English druggist's. They failed to relieve me & completely disagreed with me—bringing on a species of abortive diarrhoea. That is I felt the most reiterated & most violent inclination to stool, without being able to effect anything save the passage of a little blood. . . . Of course I sent for the . . . Irish physician. . . . He made me take an injection, of some unknown elements, which completely failed to move me. I repeated it largely—wholly in vain. He left me late in the evening, apparently quite in despair. . . . Several days have now passed. I have seen the doctor repeatedly, as he seems inclined (to what extent as a friend & to what as a doctor & [c] I ignore) to keep me in hand. . . . He examined [my bowels] (as far as he could) by the insertion of his finger (horrid tale!) & says there is no palpable obstruction. . . . I find it hard to make him (as I should anyone who hadn't observed it) at all understand the stubbornness & extent—the length & breadth & depth, of my trouble.[28]

From this intense, acutely unhappy relation of a young writer to a part of his body were also to emerge, however, pleasures and riches. In particular, the valences attaching to digestive accumulation and to manual penetration were to undergo a profound change. Let 30 years elapse, and more, in the career of this deeply imagined erotic and writerly thematic. The early letters' accounts give particular point (the point of distance and imaginative transmutation, as much as the point of similarity) to a passage like the 1905 notebook entry with which I began this section.

By the time of the writing of the prefaces, the images of the obstetric

hand, the fisted bowel, materialize as if holographically in the convergence
of two incongruent spatialities: the spatiality of inside and outside on (as it
were) the one hand, and on the other the spatiality of aspects ("aspects—
uncanny as the little term might sound," *9*: xvi; *AN*, 110), of presented and
averted, of face and back. They go together like recto and rectum.

The condensation of the two spatialities, frontal and interior, adheres
insistently to invocations of the medal or medallion, perhaps through an
association with the *Dunciad* passage quoted above. In the Preface to *The
Wings of the Dove*, for instance, James suggests that the novel's two plots
are the sides of an engraved and fingered coin:

> Could I but make my medal hang free, its obverse and its reverse, its face and its
> back, would beautifully become optional for the spectator. I somehow wanted
> them correspondingly embossed, wanted them inscribed and figured with an equal
> salience; yet it was none the less visibly my "key," as I have said, that though my
> regenerate young New Yorker [Milly], and what might depend on her, should
> form my centre, my circumference was every whit as treatable. . . . Preparatively
> and, as it were, yearningly—given the whole ground—one began, in the event,
> with the outer ring, approaching the centre thus by narrowing circumvallations.
> (*19*: xi; *AN*, 294)

To make any sense of how a geography of the concentric, involving a "key"
and the penetration of rings inner and outer, supervenes in this passage on
a flat, two-sided geography of obverse and reverse virtually requires that
obverse and reverse be read as recto and verso—and that "recto" as the
(depthless) frontal face be understood as opening freely onto "rectum" as
the (penetrable) rear. Concerning *What Maisie Knew*, James writes of "that
bright hard medal, of so strange an alloy, one face of which is somebody's
right and ease and the other somebody's pain and wrong" (*11*: viii; *AN*,
143). If indeed "face" and "back" "beautifully become optional for the
spectator," that is because recto and verso, the straight or "right" and the
"turned" or perverted or "wrong," converge so narrowly onto what is not a
mere punning syllable but rather an anatomical *double entendre* whose interest and desirability James (and I can only join him in this) appears by this
time to have experienced as inexhaustible.

Hard to overstate the importance of "right" and some other words ("direct," "erect") from the Latin *rect* in mediating for James between, as it
were, recto and verso of the presented and enjoyed body.

> For the dramatist always, by the very law of his genius, believes not only in a pos-
> sible right issue from the rightly-conceived tight place; he does much more than
> this—he believes, irresistibly, in the necessary, the precious "tightness" of the

place (whatever the issue) . . . so that the point is not in the least what to make of it, but only, very delightfully and very damnably, where to put one's hand on it. (*21*: ix; *AN*, 311–12)

"A possible right issue from the rightly-conceived tight place": a phrase like this one can refer at the same time to the "straight" (proper or conventional) avenue of issue from the "straight" place of conception—yet also at the same time the rectal issue from the rectal place of conception, "strait" only in the sense of pleasurably tight. *Whatever* the "issue," "nothing is right save as we rightly imagine it."

This family of words, insisted on as in these constructions, positively swarms in James's late writing (the novels as well as the prefaces), as if such syllables enjoyed some privileged access to "the raw essence of fantasy": "This is the charming, the tormenting, the eternal little matter *to be made right*, in all the weaving of silver threads and tapping on golden nails; and I should take perhaps too fantastic a comfort—I mean were not the comforts of the artist just of the raw essence of fantasy—in any glimpse of such achieved rightnesses" (*5*: xiv–xv; *AN*, 69). Nor, as we'll see, is the associated invocation of the hand at all less frequent.

Considering that *The Art of the Novel*—R. P. Blackmur's title for the collected prefaces—is taken (when discussed at all) as the purest manifesto for the possibility of organic form and the power of the organizing center of consciousness in fiction, it is striking how much of it constitutes a memorandum of misplaced middles. There is nothing unproblematic about centers or circumferences in any of the prefaces. James speaks of

a particular vice of the artistic spirit, against which vigilance had been destined from the first to exert itself in vain, and the effect of which was that again and again, perversely, incurably, the centre of my structure would insist on placing itself *not*, so to speak, in the middle. . . . I urge myself to the candid confession that in very few of my productions, to my eye, *has* the organic centre succeeded in getting into proper position.

Time after time, then, has the precious waistband or girdle, studded and buckled and placed for brave outward show, practically worked itself, and in spite of desperate remonstrance, or in other words essential counterplotting, to a point perilously near the knees. . . . These productions have in fact, if I may be so bold about it, specious and spurious centres altogether, to make up for the failure of the true. (*7*: xi; *AN*, 85–86)

"Center" is clearly being used in a multivalent way in passages like these, as much as when it had conjured the impossible orifice by which a flat round medallion opens out into depth. Here it offers a pretext for the com-

ically explicit anthropomorphization of the novel as a body, a body celebrated for its way of being always more than at risk of "perverse" reorgan-
ization around a "perilously" displaced and low-down zone. But,
confusingly, these spatial metaphors refer to the interrelation among characters' points of view (e.g., as "centers of consciousness"), but also (and
quite incommensurably) to the relation between the first half and the latter
(or, anthropomorphically, the lower and/or back) half of each novel. As
when James in the Preface to *The Wings of the Dove* diagnostically probes
"the latter half, that is the false and deformed half" of the novel, maintaining his "free hand" for "the preliminary cunning quest for the spot where
deformity has begun" (*19*: xviii–xix; *AN*, 302–303). Incoherent as it is,
however, the relation between the halves is one whose very perils can be
pleasures, and whose pleasures have the rhythm of climax: James celebrates
in *The Tragic Muse* "a compactness into which the imagination may cut
thick, as into the rich density of wedding-cake. The moral of all which indeed, I fear, is, perhaps too trivially, but that the 'thick,' the false, the dis-
sembling second half of the work before me . . . presents that effort as at
the very last a quite convulsive, yet in its way highly agreeable, spasm" (*7*:
xiii; *AN*, 88).

And over the anthropomorphic mapping of these relations there constantly hovers the even more incommensurable image of the theater. "The
first half of a fiction insists ever on figuring to me as the stage or theatre for
the second half," James writes for instance, "and I have in general given so
much space to making the theatre propitious that my halves have too often
proved strangely unequal" (*7*: xii; *AN*, 86). Or, in a very different kind of
mapping: "The novel, as largely practised in English, is the perfect para-
dise of the loose end. The play consents to the logic of but one way, mathe-
matically right, and with the loose end [a] gross . . . impertinence on its
surface" (*9*: xx; *AN*, 114).

To trace the ramifications of these images through the prefaces would
involve quoting from literally every single page of them. A more efficient
approach would be, perhaps, to offer something brief in the way of a lexicon of a few of the main words and semantic clusters through which the
fisting image works in these prefaces—since the accumulated and digested
redolence of particular signifiers is one of the delights James most boasts of
enjoying in "my struggle to keep compression rich, if not, better still, to
keep accretions compressed" (*16*: v; *AN*, 232).

But in advance of offering this lexicon, I suppose I should say some-

thing about what it is to hear these richly accreted, almost alchemically imbued signifiers in this highly sexualized way—and more generally, about
the kinds of resistance that the reading I propose here may offer to a psychoanalytic interpretive project. In her psychoanalytic essay on James, Kaja
Silverman declares herself (for one particular passage in one particular
preface) willing to "risk . . . violating a fundamental tenet of James criticism—the tenet that no matter how luridly suggestive the Master's language, it cannot have a sexual import."[29] I'm certainly with her on that
one—except that Silverman's readiness to hear how very openly sexy
James's prefaces are is made possible only by her strange insistence that he
couldn't have *known* they were. James's eroticized relation to his writings
and characters, in her reading, is governed by "unconscious desire rather
than an organizing consciousness"; and "armored against unwanted self-
knowledge," James is diagnosed by Silverman as having his "defenses" "securely in place against such an unwelcome discovery."[30] I am very eager
that James's sexual language be heard, but that it not be heard with this in-
sulting presumption of the hearer's epistemological privilege—a privilege
attached, furthermore, to Silverman's uncritical insistence on viewing sexuality exclusively in terms of repression and self-ignorance. When we tune
in to James's language on these frequencies, it is not as superior, privileged
eavesdroppers on a sexual narrative hidden from himself; rather, it is as an
audience offered the privilege of sharing in his exhibitionistic enjoyment
and performance of a sexuality organized around shame. Indeed, it is as an
audience desired to do so—which is also happily to say, as an audience desired.

Though any reader of even these few passages could undoubtedly generate a list of other repeated, magnetic, and often enigmatic signifiers needing to be added to this little lexicon, the terms that seem to me to clamor
for inclusion are these: fond/foundation, issue, assist, fragrant/flagrant,
glove or gage, half, and, as we have already seen, right and a group of
words around *rect*, center/circumference, aspect, medal. I pick these
words out not because they are commonplace "Freudian" signifiers in the
conventional phallic mode, a mode that was scarcely James's, but instead
because each underwent for him "that mystic, that 'chemical' change . . .
the felt fermentation, ever interesting, but flagrantly so in the example before us, that enables the sense originally communicated to make fresh and
possibly quite different terms for the new employment there awaiting it"
(*17*: xii; *AN*, 249). Each opens onto—as it condenses—a juncture between

the erotic fantasy-localization per se and some aspect or aspects of its performative dimension.

"Fond," for example, is one of James's most cherished words, especially
when used self-descriptively: whether applied to the young author's "first
fond good faith of composition" (*1*: xv; *AN*, 13), to the older "fond fabu-
list" (*21*: xvi; *AN*, 318), or to the "fond . . . complacency" (*2*: v; *AN*, 21)
of a personified fiction. It marks the place of the author's pleasure in dramatizing himself as all but flooded with self-absorbed delusion and embarrassment, but equally with pleasure. When he speaks of himself as having
had a "fond idea," you don't know whether you're therefore meant to see it
as having been a *bad* idea or whether you're hearing, in James's phrase, the
still-current "exhibit" of "an elation possibly presumptuous" (*2*: xiv; *AN*,
30). But the self-absorbing "fond" marks him, by the same token, as all
but flooded with transitive, *cathectic* energy, the energy of interest, fond *of*
. . . someone—in particular as lovingly and interestedly inclining toward
the other, usually younger male figurations in this inter/intrapersonal
drama, loving and interested "all sublimely and perhaps a little fatuously"
(*2*: xiii; *AN*, 29). The fatuous "fond" notation of delight and self-delight
already notable in the California journal passage is warp and woof of the
prefaces. "Inclined to retrospect, he fondly takes, under this backward
view, his whole unfolding, his process of production, for a thrilling tale"
(*1*: vi; *AN*, 4).

Or, with a different use of emphasis: "Inclined to *retro*spect, he fondly
takes, *under* this *backward* view, his whole unfolding, his process of production, for a thrilling tale." That "fond" is also the French word for bottom may explain its affinity with the "retrospect," the "backward view,"
even with the "thrilling tale." The fondness of the artist, as James para-
phrases it in one preface, may lie in his "willingness to pass mainly for an
ass" (*7*: viii; *AN*, 83).

The association between fondness and the fundament extends, as well,
to James's interest in the foundation, in the highly (and always anthropomorphically) architectural image with which he describes his ambitions for
the structure of his works:

Amusement deeply abides, I think, in any artistic attempt the basis and ground-
work of which are conscious of a particular firmness. . . . It is the difficulty produced by the loose foundation . . . that breaks the heart. . . . The dramatist strong
in the sense of his postulate . . . has verily to *build*, is committed to architecture, to
construction at any cost; to driving in deep his vertical supports and laying across

and firmly fixing his horizontal, his resting pieces—at the risk of no matter what vibration from the tap of his master-hammer. This makes the active value of his basis immense, enabling him, with his flanks protected, to advance. (*9*: xv–xvi; *AN*, 109)

"Fond," then, is a node where the theatrics of shame, affection, and display are brought together with a compositional principle and at the same time lodged firmly, at the level of the signifier, in a particular zone of the eroticized body. (See also—if this were a completer lexicon—James's quasi-architectural, quasi-anthropomorphic use of the terms "arch," "brace," "pressure," "weight.") Another thing it makes sense to me to speculate about regarding "fond": that this syllable provides the vibratory bass note in the "fun" that James was so fond of putting in flirtatious scare quotes. "For the infatuated artist, how many copious springs of our never-to-be-slighted 'fun'!" (*21*: xxi; *AN*, 324). "It all comes back to that, to my and your 'fun'" (*23*: xxii; *AN*, 345). *Au fond*.

"Issue" and "assist" are an important pair of pivot words in the prefaces. Each is significantly charged by allusion to the obstetric scene, as when the injunction "Hands off altogether on the nurse's part!" (though "strictly conceivable") is said to render impossible "any fair and stately . . . re-issue of anything" (*23*: xv; *AN*, 337–38). Each, too—like "brood" and "conceive," which deserve separate lexicon entries but won't get them just here—is also specific to the compositional or dramatic scene. I've remarked on how the reissue cum revision of the books and the, so to speak, reparenting process of the prefaces seem to come together in the signifier "issue." The "issue" is not only the edition and the child or other emitted matter but also the birth canal, the channel by which the issue issues, the "possible right issue from the rightly-conceived tight place" (*21*: ix; *AN*, 311). And as with the "backward view" of the fond "retrospect," as also with the novels' "latter" halves, the temporal can be mapped anthropomorphically as the spatial, the past issue becoming the posterior issue: "When it shall come to fitting, historically, anything like *all* my many small children of fancy with their pair of progenitors, and all my reproductive unions with their inevitable fruit, I shall seem to offer my backward consciousness in the image of a shell charged and recharged by the Fates with some patent and infallible explosive" (*12*: xxiii; *AN*, 178; James's emphasis).

"Assist," like "issue," seems to begin by alluding to the scene of birthing; it links the obstetric hand with the applauding one, the childbed with—not publication—but the theater. In the Preface to *The Wings of the Dove*, James seems both to assume the attending position of the novel's master physician Sir Luke Strett and at the same time, through a chain of suggestive semantic choices, to rewrite Milly Theale's fatal illness as a pregnancy at which "one would have quite honestly to assist": her illness is designated as "the interesting state," with intensities that "quicken" and then "crown"; her part in the matter is "the unsurpassable activity of passionate, of inspired resistance. This last fact was the real issue, for the way grew straight . . ." (*19*: vi; *AN*, 289).

But it is less easy to say which sense of "assist," the obstetric or the theatrical, is operative in this account of the play of point of view in *The American*:

At the window of [Newman's] wide, quite sufficiently wide, consciousness we are seated, from that admirable position we "assist." He therefore supremely matters; all the rest matters only as he feels it, treats it, meets it. A beautiful infatuation this, always, I think, the intensity of the creative effort to get into the skin of the creature; the act of personal possession of one being by another at its completest. . . . So much remains true then on behalf of my instinct of multiplying the fine touches by which Newman should live and communicate life. (*2*: xxi; *AN*, 38)

"Assist" is in scare-quotes here, and it's not easy (it hardly ever is in James) to see why—unless to point to the word's double meaning (obstetric/theatrical); or unless to signal flickeringly, as the scare-quotes around "fun" do, that a not quite legitimate French pun is slipping about in the background—in this case the association between being *seated* at the window and, "from that admirable position," *assist*ing. *Assister* (attending, as at childbed or theater) and *s'asseoir* (to sit) aren't actually related, even in French, but they do sound alike via the resonant syllable *ass-*. And firm though it may be with an architectural firmness, the unexpectedly dramatic associations of the seat, in particular of the relished ample seat, the "immense" "basis," "wide, quite sufficiently wide," are well attested in the prefaces. At one of the windows, for instance, at which James has done his writing,

a "great house" . . . gloomed, in dusky brick, as the extent of my view, but with a vast convenient neutrality which I found, soon enough, protective and not inquisitive, so that whatever there was of my sedentary life and regular habits took a sort of local wealth of colour from the special greyish-brown tone of the surface always before me. This surface hung there like the most voluminous of curtains—it masked the very stage of the great theatre of the town. To sit for certain hours at

one's desk before it was somehow to occupy in the most suitable way in the world
the proportionately ample interests of the mightiest of dramas. (*14*: xviii; *AN*,
212)[31]

One set of associations for all this seated labor has of course to do with
the process of digestion and its products; no feasible amount of quotation
could offer a sense of how fully these perfume the language of the prefaces.
"[Art] plucks its material . . . in the garden of life—which material elsewhere grown is stale and uneatable. But it has no sooner done this than it
has to take account of a *process* . . . that of the expression, the literal squeez-
ing-out, of value. . . . This is precisely the infusion that, as I submit, completes the strong mixture. . . . It's all a sedentary part" (*21*: ix–x; *AN*, 312;
James's emphasis). The most available language for digestion is that more
or less ostensibly of cooking, each "thinkable . . . —so far as thinkable at
all—in chemical, almost in mystical terms":

We can surely account for nothing in the novelist's work that hasn't passed through
the crucible of his imagination, hasn't, in that perpetually simmering cauldron his
intellectual *pot-au-feu*, been reduced to savoury fusion. We here figure the morsel,
of course, not as boiled to nothing, but as exposed, in return for the taste it gives
out, to a new and richer saturation. In this state it is in due course picked out and
served, and a meagre esteem will await. . . . If it doesn't speak most of its late
genial medium, the good, the wonderful company it has, as I hint, aesthetically
kept. It has entered, in fine, into new relations, it emerges for new ones. Its final
savour has been constituted, but its prime identity destroyed. . . . Thus it has become a different and, thanks to a rare alchemy, a better thing. (*15*: xvii–xviii; *AN*,
230)

The products of cooking and of digestion seem interchangeable—and
equally irresistible—because each is the result of a process of recirculation
described as if it could go on endlessly, only adding to the richness of (what
James usually calls) the "residuum," the thing "picked," "plucked" (*11*: xx;
AN, 155) or, as in the California passage and many others, "fished" out.
("The long pole of memory stirs and rummages the bottom, and we fish up
such fragments and relics of the submerged life and the extinct consciousness as tempt us to piece them together" (*2*: xi; *AN*, 26).) In the artist's
intellectual life, James says,

the "old" matter is there, re-accepted, re-tasted, exquisitely re-assimilated and re-
enjoyed. . . . The whole growth of one's "taste," as our fathers used to say: a blessed
comprehensive name for many of the things deepest in us. The "taste" of the poet

is, at bottom and so far as the poet in him prevails over everything else, his active sense of life; in accordance with which truth to keep one's hand on it is to hold the silver clue to the whole labyrinth of his consciousness. He feels this himself, good man. (*23*: xvii; *AN*, 339–40)

To trace the career of the word "fragrant" (possibly including its more explicitly, indeed flamingly performative variant "flagrant") through the prefaces would be to get at least somewhere with the digestive plot. One culminating usage:

The further analysis is for that matter almost always the torch of rapture and victory, as the artist's firm hand grasps and plays it—I mean, naturally, of the smothered rapture and the obscure victory, enjoyed and celebrated not in the street but before some innermost shrine; the odds being a hundred to one, in almost any connexion, that it doesn't arrive by any easy first process at the *best* residuum of truth. That was the charm, sensibly, of the picture . . . ; the elements so couldn't but flush, to their very surface, with some deeper depth of irony than the mere obvious. It lurked in the crude postulate like a buried scent; the more the attention hovered the more aware it became of the fragrance. To which I may add that the more I scratched the surface and penetrated, the more potent, to the intellectual nostril, became this virtue. At last, accordingly, the residuum, as I have called it, reached, I was in presence of the red dramatic spark that glowed at the core of my vision and that, as I gently blew upon it, burned higher and clearer. (*11*: vi; *AN*, 142; James's emphasis)

I don't want to make the prefaces sound too much like *The Silence of the Lambs*, but James does have a very graphic way of figuring authorial relations in terms of dermal habitation. As we've seen, he considers "the intensity of the creative effort to get into the skin of the creature" to be "a beautiful infatuation," indeed "the act of personal possession of one being by another at its completest" (*2*: xxi; *AN*, 37). All the blushing/flushing that marks the skin as a primary organ for both the generation and the contagion of affect seems linked to a fantasy of the skin's being entered—entered specifically by a hand, a hand that touches. Some words James favors for this relation are "glove," "gage," and French *gageure*. "That was my problem, so to speak, and my *gageure*—to play the small handful of values really for all they were worth—and to work my . . . particular degree of pressure on the spring of interest" (*23*: viii; *AN*, 330–31). Indeed the glove or gage is, for James, the prime image of *engagement*, of interest, motivation, and cathexis *tout simple*—of the writerly "charm that grows in proportion as the appeal to it tests and stretches and strains it, puts it powerfully to the touch" (*9*: xvii; *AN*, 111). Even more powerfully, it offers a durable image for the creation (which is to say: the entering of the skin) of personified characters. As when James sees "a tall quiet slim studious young man, of admirable type," who offers habitation to a character whom James had before barely so much as imagined: "Owen Wingrave, nebulous and fluid, may only, *at the touch*, have found *himself* in this gentleman; found, that is, a figure and a habit, a form, a face, a fate" (*17*: xxii; *AN*, 259–60; first emphasis mine).

And, of course, the animation of character by reaching a hand up its backside has a theater of its own: in this case the puppet theater. "No privilege of the teller of tales and the handler of puppets is more delightful, or has more of the suspense and the thrill of a game of difficulty breathlessly played, than just this business of looking for the unseen and the occult, in a scheme half-grasped, by the light or, so to speak, by the clinging scent, of the gage already in hand" (*21*:ix; *AN*, 311). The scent that clings to glove, to hand, to puppet may not seem particularly inexplicable by this time. It is the smell of shit even as it is the smell of shame. It is the smell of a cherished identity performed through a process of turning-inside-out.[32]

Clearly, there are more lexicon entries that could be shown to work in comparable ways in the prefaces; I'd mention only the following terms: bristle, interest, use, basis, uncanny, treatment, strain, express, elastic, the high/free hand, handsome, bear (v.), conceive, touching (adj.), rich, spring (n. and v.), waste/waist, postulate, preposterous, turn (n.), passage, and foreshorten. The variety of these signifiers answers to, among other things, the range of sexual aims, objects, body parts, and bodily fantasies and pleasures clustering however loosely around the fisting phantasmatic: there are flickers of the phallus, the womb, the prostate, as well as the bowel and anus; flickers between steady and climactic rhythms, between insertive and receptive, between accumulation and release, between the allo- and the auto-erotic. I hope it's evident enough that the prefaces do respond to this way of reading, "whenever the mind is, as I have said, accessible—accessible, that is, to the finer appeal of accumulated 'good stuff' and to the interest of taking it in hand at all":

For myself, I am prompted to note, the "taking" has been to my consciousness, through the whole procession of this re-issue, the least part of the affair: under the first touch of the spring my hands were to feel themselves full; so much more did it become a question, on the part of the accumulated good stuff, of seeming insistently to give and give. (*23*: xviii; *AN*, 341)

The simplest truth about a human entity, a situation, a relation . . . on behalf of which the claim to charmed attention is made, strains ever, under one's hand, more intensely, *most* intensely, to justify that claim; strains ever, as it were, toward the uttermost end or aim of one's meaning or of its own numerous connexions; struggles at each step, and in defiance of one's raised admonitory finger, fully and completely to express itself. (*18*: xv; *AN*, 278)

Yet however richly the text responds to it, this cumulative and accumulative, lexicon-driven reading remains a particular, hence a partial *kind* of reading—not so much because it is organized around "sexuality" as because it is organized around the semantic unit. To say that it is tethered to the semantic and thematic is perhaps also to say that it is unsublimatably (however unstably) tethered to the intensively zoned human body. Hardly the worse for that. Yet, obviously enough, the argumentational momentum of the prefaces is impeded as much as facilitated by a reading that indulges or honors James's investment in the absorptive or (as he generally puts it) the "rich" (or strange) signifier. The clumsy, "fond" rhythm of reading enforced by any semantic absorption or adhesion seems necessarily to constitute a theoretical deviance.

III

To gesture at a summing up: The thing I *least* want to be heard as offering here is a "theory of homosexuality." I have none and I want none. When I attempt to do some justice to the specificity, the richness, above all the explicitness of James's particular erotics, it is not with an eye to making him an exemplar of "homosexuality" or even of one "kind" of "homosexuality," though I certainly don't want, either, to make him sound as if he *isn't* gay. Nonetheless I do mean to nominate the James of the New York Edition prefaces as a kind of prototype, not of "homosexuality" but of *queerness*, or queer performativity. In this usage, "queer performativity" is the name of a strategy for the production of meaning and being, in relation to the affect shame and to the later and related fact of stigma.

I don't know yet what claims may be worth making, ontologically, about the queer performativity I have been describing here. Would it be useful to suggest that some of the associations I've been making with queer performativity might actually be features of all performativity? Or useful, instead, to suggest that the transformational grammar of "shame on you" may form only part of the performative activity seen as most intimately related to queerness, by people self-identified as queer? The usefulness of thinking about shame in relation to queer performativity, in any event, does not come from its adding any extra certainty to the question of what utterances or acts may be classed as "performative" or what people may be classed as "queer." Least of all does it pretend to define the relation between queerness and same-sex love and desire. What it does, to the contrary, is perhaps to offer some psychological, phenomenological, thematic density and motivation to what I described before as the "torsions" or aberrances between reference and performativity, or indeed between queerness and other ways of experiencing identity and desire.

But I don't, either, want it to sound as though my project has mainly to do with recuperating for deconstruction (or other anti-essentialist projects) a queerness drained of specificity or political reference. To the contrary: I'd suggest that to view performativity in terms of habitual shame and its transformations opens a lot of new doors for thinking about identity politics.

It seems very likely that the structuring of associations and attachments around the affect shame is among the most telling differentials among cultures and times: not that the entire world can be divided between (supposedly primitive) "shame cultures" and (supposedly evolved) "guilt cultures," but rather that, as an affect, shame is a component (and *differently* a component) of all. Shame, like other affects, is not a discrete intrapsychic structure but a kind of free radical that (in different people and also in different cultures) attaches to and permanently intensifies or alters the meaning of—of almost anything: a zone of the body, a sensory system, a prohibited or indeed a permitted behavior, another affect such as anger or arousal, a named identity, a script for interpreting other people's behavior toward oneself. Thus, one of the things that anyone's character or personality *is* is a record of the highly individual histories by which the fleeting emotion of shame has instituted far more durable, structural changes in one's relational and interpretive strategies toward both self and others.

Which means, among other things, that therapeutic or political strategies aimed directly at getting rid of individual or group shame, or undoing it, have something preposterous about them: they may "work"—they certainly have powerful effects—but they can't work in the way they say they work. (I am thinking here of a range of movements that deal with shame variously in the form of, for instance, the communal *dignity* of the civil rights movement; the individuating *pride* of "Black is Beautiful" and gay pride; various forms of nativist *ressentiment*; the menacingly exhibited *ab-jection* of the skinhead; the early feminist experiments with the naming and foregrounding of *anger* as a response to shame; the incest survivors' movement's epistemological stress on *truth-telling* about shame; and, of course, many many others.) The forms taken by shame are not distinct "toxic" parts of a group or individual identity that can be excised; they are instead integral to and residual in the processes by which identity itself is formed. They are available for the work of metamorphosis, reframing, refiguration, *trans*figuration, affective and symbolic loading and deformation; but unavailable for effecting the work of purgation and deontological closure.

If the structuration of shame differs strongly between cultures, between periods, and between different forms of politics, however, it differs also simply from one person to another within a given culture and time. Some of the infants, children, and adults in whom shame remains the most available mediator of identity are the ones called (a related word) shy. ("Remember the fifties?" Lily Tomlin asks. "No one was gay in the fifties; they were just shy.") "Queer," I'd suggest, might usefully be thought of as referring in the first place to this group or an overlapping group of infants and children, those whose sense of identity is for some reason tuned most durably to the note of shame. What it is about them (or us) that makes this true remains to be specified. I mean that in the sense that I can't tell you now what it is—it certainly isn't a single thing—but also in the sense that, *for them*, it remains to be specified, is always belated: the shame-delineated place of identity doesn't determine the consistency or meaning of that identity, and race, gender, class, sexuality, appearance, and abledness are only a few of the defining social constructions that will crystallize there, developing from this originary affect their particular structures of expression, creativity, pleasure, and struggle. I'd venture that queerness in this sense has, at this historical moment, *some* definitionally very significant overlap—though a vibrantly elastic and temporally convoluted one—with the complex of attributes today condensed as adult or adolescent "gayness." Everyone knows that there are some lesbians and gay men who could never count as queer, and other people who vibrate to the chord of queer without having much same-sex eroticism, or without routing their same-sex eroticism through the identity labels lesbian or gay. Yet many of the performative identity vernaculars that seem most recognizably "flushed" (to use James's word) with shame-consciousness and shame-creativity do cluster intimately around lesbian and gay worldly spaces: to name only a few, butch abjection, femmitude, leather, pride, SM, drag, musicality, fisting, attitude, zines, histrionicism, asceticism, Snap! culture, diva worship, florid religiosity, in a word, *flaming*. . . .

And activism.

Shame interests me politically, then, because it generates and legitimates the place of identity—the *question* of identity—at the origin of the impulse to the performative; but does so without giving that identity-space the standing of an essence. It constitutes it as to-be-constituted, which is also to say, as already there for the (necessary, productive) misconstrual and misrecognition. Shame—living, as it does, on and in the muscles and capillaries of the face—seems to be uniquely contagious from one person to another. And the contagiousness of shame is only facilitated by its anamorphic, protean susceptibility to new expressive grammars.

These facts suggest, I think, that asking good questions about shame and shame/performativity could get us somewhere with a lot of the recalcitrant knots that tie themselves into the guts of identity politics—yet *without* delegitimating the felt urgency and power of the notion "identity" itself. The dynamics of trashing and of ideological or institutional pogroms, like the dynamics of mourning, are incomprehensible without an understanding of shame. Survivors' guilt and, more generally, the politics of guilt will be better understood when we can see them in some relation to the slippery dynamics of shame. I would propose that the same is true of the politics of solidarity and identification; perhaps those, as well, of humor and humorlessness. I'd also—if parenthetically—want to suggest that shame/performativity may get us a lot further with the cluster of phenomena generally called "camp" than the notion of parody will, and more too than will any opposition between "depth" and "surface." And can anyone suppose that we'll ever figure out what happened around "political correctness" if we don't see it as, among other things, a highly politicized chain reaction of shame dynamics?

It has been all too easy for the psychologists and the few psychoanalysts working on shame to write it back into the moralisms of the repressive hypothesis: whether "healthy" or "unhealthy," shame, as I've pointed out, can be seen as *good* because it preserves privacy and decency, *bad* because it colludes with self-repression or social repression. Clearly, neither of these valuations is what I'm getting at; I want to say that *at least* for certain ("queer") people, shame is simply the first, and remains a permanent, structuring fact of identity: one that, as the example of Henry James suggests, has its own, powerfully productive and powerfully social metamorphic possibilities.

The Excluded Seven:
Practice of Omission,
Aesthetics of Refusal

Martha Banta

Why do we have what we have in the New York Edition? Chapter 8 of Michael Anesko's study of Henry James's often taut relationship with the marketplace provides a compelling argument for the manner in which James, his agent James Brand Pinker, and the Scribner's editor W. C. Brownell worked laboriously through a "Push-Me-Pull-You" situation to arrive at the twenty-odd volumes that constitute the edition we know.[1] The evidence Anesko mounts reveals both James the Practical and James the Indecisive; a writer who began with modest plans for a sixteen-volume edition, then experienced moments of flushed aspiration for a larger, grander collection, and finally "simply collapsed into the arms of his editor" in weary acknowledgment that "publisher's arithmetic and artistic intention would not always square."[2]

As we pace through Anesko's outline of the quiet little dramas that took place between 1905 and 1908, we discover that of all James's novels only *Watch and Ward* was decisively off James's list from the start. Fairly quickly James excised three more titles because of the demands of rewriting he believed they would involve: *Confidence*, *Washington Square*, and *The Europeans*. Neither *The Other House* nor *The Sacred Fount* appears to have come under serious consideration for inclusion, but the fate of *The Bostonians* dangled during 1905 and 1906 until James finally let go. By December 1908 James wrote to Scribner's that he was ready to yield altogether to the publisher's need to·hold back on the number and size of the volumes.

If James felt he was simply too tired to continue the distracting and self-depleting push-pull of these negotiations, the language of his letter to Brownell is prime James in its use of payment metaphors. James describes himself as "completely *spent!*" The project "has cost me a more intense expenditure of diligence and ingenuity" than can be expressed. "Almost as much economically as artistically 'spent,'" he feels "pretty well finished and voided" by the experience. It is now entirely up to Scribner's to make the final "subdivision and extension" in whatever seems "the simplest and most obvious way."[3]

We have here a convincing account of the give-and-take most authors go through in confronting the frictions of the marketplace. In no way do I wish to counter the facts that Anesko's research underscores. What this essay seeks to do, rather, is to offer a meditation, a speculation, on what *we as readers* would have confronted if the seven novels left out of the New York Edition had been incorporated within its sanctioning imprint as well as what manner of author we are offered as the consequence of these excisions: excisions not restricted to matters of structure (whether from the psychological motives delineated by Leon Edel or from the commercial needs argued by Anesko), but excisions compelled by attentiveness to matters of style on the part of the self-stylized "Master" whom James wrote into being in the Edition's prefaces.

I have no intention of arriving at final answers as to why James disengaged from his *magnum opi* those creations never to be enclosed within the multivolume spread. Nor do I pretend that the following remarks can pin down the "real" cause-effect relations that led to his (however hesitant) "decisions." The remarks will, however, deal with the "reality" of the New York Edition that emerges from our acknowledgment that absences indeed affect whatever is present.[4]

Three points will be pressed home: (1) An increased sense of the continuity and weight of James's ruling themes would have been ours if the seven novels had been left in, available for telling juxtapositions not only against the novels he in fact included but also against one another. That is, the effect that results when "the others" are added to the present texts we "know" expands our sense of what is *stylistically possible*, as much as of what is substantively feasible. (2) Our sense of *the style of author* James represents in the New York Edition is altered once the narrator of the prefaces is set in contrast to the authorial role portrayed or implied by the seven novels he excised (exorcised). That is, our sense changes, at least in degree, when what we "know" (the persona in the prefaces) is supplemented, even supplanted, by yet another type of author. (3) Our understanding of the nature of the famed and infamous "renunciation" theme grows once we take notice

of how absences become *the stylistic strategy* that shapes an artistic reputation.

Self-censorship, denial of immediate gratification, mastery of the art of
inaction: these terms are frequently applied to James himself and to the
characters who people his fictive creations. But perhaps it can be demonstrated that James—however "spent" and "voided" he was by the costly "expenditure" of having to be both James the Practical and James the Indecisive while wheedling the New York Edition into being—was committed to
a practice of omission and *an aesthetics of refusal* that yielded positive gain,
not negative depletion, in forwarding the forms of high art he gave over
his life to perfecting.

I

The Edition's final format is not merely the product of the mature craftsman who decides to banish apprentice work lest it distract attention from
more polished achievements. If James omitted *Watch and Ward* and *Confidence*, he retained *Roderick Hudson* and *The American*, novels published
prior to the works he dismissed.[5] Inclusion and exclusion on the basis of
dates of publication was not necessarily the ruling principle; winnowing
the perpetually weak from the potentially strong was.

James took pains to revise *Roderick Hudson* and *The American* but was
unwilling to devote himself to their near cousins in composition. He continued to prize *Roderick Hudson* over the years because he viewed it as his
first attempt at "a long fiction with a 'complicated' subject" (*1*: vi; *AN*, 4),
whereas *Watch and Ward* was "something slight." Although he *had* hoped
to make *Watch and Ward* "a work of art," he soon acknowledged it could not
grow beyond a piece that was "pretty enough" yet "very thin and as 'cold' as
an icicle," lacking the resonance ever to do more than emerge "demurely"
into print.[6]

During the ten years between 1871 (when *Watch and Ward* first tip-
toed into view) and 1881 (when *The Portrait of a Lady* imposed itself upon
the literary scene), James was closely monitoring his career. In 1881 James
assessed the wisdom of taking up the offer made by his friend Thomas Sargent Perry to write an extended review-essay that would survey all James's
writings through *Confidence* and *Washington Square*. James advised Perry to
hold off until *The Portrait of a Lady* was out. In 1905–6, when once again
sizing up what he wanted to be known for, he again dismissed what might

come across as stylistically thin—the pretty, the cold, and the demure—while retaining the "complicated" pleasures of *Roderick Hudson*.

Nor was the warmth of *amor* to be set aside, however early its examples might have made their appearance in James's professional career. Although *The American* caused James all kinds of trouble decades later once he decided to revise it for inclusion in the New York Edition, he never left off being "enamoured" of the impulses that lay behind his 1877 account of Christopher Newman's vicissitudes.[7] However youthful its flavor, if James could remain in love with the idea of an early work, he would not discard it merely for the sake of careful career management that privileges late over early. But one constant remained as an abiding criterion for continuing tenderness: the piece had to be a thing *to be taken seriously*. Seriousness, however, did not mean the sterile sobriety of aspirations to static perfection; it meant having the capacity to be alive—*not to be dead*.[8]

Piling flesh upon flesh (warm as it may be) does not guarantee the presence of life. Novels published early or late that are simple accumulations of those themes and character types that stimulated James's creativity almost from the start could not solely for that reason remain on his list of beloved things. It is easy enough to find "the man of hesitation" in *Watch and Ward*, "betrayal" in *Confidence*, "renunciation" in *Washington Square*, "possession" in *The Bostonians*, "the international theme" in *The Europeans*, "freedom and fatality" in *The Other House*, and "the ordeal of consciousness" in *The Sacred Fount*. In truth, James's oft-reiterated themes are present from first to last, whether or not given final sanctuary within the New York Edition. What matters instead are the stylistic spins developed in each of the excluded texts, and what it means that those spins were allowed to escape from the orbit of the Edition.

Readers devoted enough to James to have troubled themselves with his entire *oeuvre* have the smug satisfaction of placing Nora Lambert of *Watch and Ward* alongside Maisie Farange (or Mrs. Keith with Madame Merle); Rose Arminger of *The Other House* over against the governess of Bly; or Catherine Sloper of *Washington Square* next to Milly Theale. But the New York Edition itself apparently sees no need to encourage readers to establish an informed cross-referencing between the novels in the Edition and those left out; nor does such a task seem of great moment to the overall "James project" of confirming his reputation. One must wonder why. Did James believe he would be hurt more than helped if the abundance of examples pulled from the absent novels was let loose? Did he sense that the expected audience for the New York Edition might feel cloyed rather than delighted by new slants on off-repeated themes? Was he excessively sensitive to the inclusion of notation that might convert narrative concerns into self-parodies and lend the look of flab to what might otherwise pass as lean solidity? Perhaps he did not wish to risk making the Edition appear to diminish rather than enhance that *significance* James took as his constant aim.

Let us briefly test some parallel passages to see if we should really be cross with the New York Edition for not affording easy access to absent material, let alone allowing it to be fully possessed. (What Jamesian doesn't count *Washington Square*, *The Bostonians*, *The Europeans*, and *The Sacred Fount* as basic critical equipment; but how many fully "possess" *Watch and Ward*, *Confidence*, and *The Other House*?)

Watch and Ward is a filing cabinet of tropes and types: suitors hovering around a "free" young woman who wants to be able to "choose" even as she is being packaged as "property" to be bought.[9] We catch gleams of Morris Townsend from *Washington Square* in Nora's feckless cousin, Fenton, both charming young men given to "falsity, impudence, and greed."[10] Nora, like Verena Tarrant of *The Bostonians*, emerges from a lurid, theatrical past, though apparently untouched by its taint. There is the Daisy question to be asked of Nora (just as it is asked of Blanche Evers in *Confidence*): is she pure angel or outrageous flirt? Finally, there is the prototype of many Jamesian males to come in Roger Lawrence, the wealthy young man who lives in his imagination and hesitates to act; but it is Rowland Mallet in *Roderick Hudson*, not Lawrence, whom James places at the head of the line of his sensitive ditherers with Volume I of the New York Edition.

The test case I wish to highlight here, however, does not involve the character types just itemized—types, it might be argued, which were eliminated in order that their fictional cousins who stayed the course into the New York Edition would have no competition in looking like the best of their kind. I want instead to lay side-by-side three quotations drawn from three of the excluded novels,[11] each of which utilizes lock-and-key metaphors suggestive of relations between knowledge and innocence. From *Watch and Ward*:

Nora came in. Her errand was to demand the use of Roger's watch-key, her own having mysteriously vanished. . . . Roger's key proved a complete misfit, so that she had recourse to Hubert's. It hung on the watch-chain, and some rather intimate fumbling was needed to adjust it to Nora's diminutive timepiece. It worked admirably, and she stood looking at him with a little smile of caution as it creaked on the pivot.

From *The Europeans*:

Forming an opinion—say on a person's conduct—was with Mr. Wentworth a good deal like fumbling in a lock with a key chosen at hazard. He seemed to himself to go about the world with a big bunch of these ineffectual instruments at his girdle. His nephew, on the other hand, with a straight turn of the wrist, opened any door as adroitly as a house-thief.

Finally, from *The Bostonians*:

[Ransom] kept talking about the box; he seemed as if he wouldn't let go that simile. He said that he had come to look at her through the glass sides and if he wasn't afraid of hurting her he would smash them in. He was determined to find the key that would open it, if he had to look for it all over the world; it was tantalizing only to be able to talk to her through the keyhole.

When *Watch and Ward* is mentioned at all, it is usually to call readers' attention to the knowing sophistication they share with the critic who is pointing out the embarrassing naïveté and the pre-Freudian prurience of the scene cited above.[12] It is more productive, I think, to watch James working out the image (admittedly one that teeters on the edge of the silly) three times over. On the one hand, these passages can be used to support the "psychological" notion that James in his thirties and forties was too ignorant and clumsy to deal expertly in metaphors sexual in nature but referring to knowingness in general; this ability would emerge only in his final decades of life, when self-acknowledgment of his homoerotic feelings finally released him to set down an effective variation on the theme found in the purse-of-gold passage from *The Golden Bowl*.

[Prince Amerigo] knew . . . the perfect working of all her main attachments, that of some wonderful finished instrument, something intently made for exhibition, for a prize. He knew above all the extraordinary fineness of her flexible waist, the stem of an expanded flower which gave her a likeness also to some long loose silk purse well filled with gold-pieces, but having been passed empty through a finger-ring that held it together. (23: 47)

On the other hand, the preceding three passages can be employed in the "aesthetic" argument that James was, relatively speaking, both ignorant and clumsy in stylistic matters until he learned to heed his own admonition to "let himself go." Whatever the explanation of the differences in quality between the key-turnings in the excluded works and the purse in *The Golden Bowl*, readers need to consider whose advantage is served when writers keep the unspeakable out of sight until they learn how to say it very well. Does it not make a difference for us to know what was there all along, struggling for expression but hidden away by being denied the final laying on of hands?

The Europeans is filled with characters dedicated at all costs to being unhappy, devoted to renunciation, self-discipline, and submission to duty, virtues whose imaginative sparseness the narrator is out to mock. The New England obligation to refuse enjoyment and to shrink back from opportunities makes up the thin, pure, febrile atmosphere of the Wentworths' world. The narrator can, however, be relatively mild in his remarks since this is but "a little history" of "gentle, generous people" given to "the simple, serious life," though he still holds the Wentworths and their kind accountable for their fear of taking life on its own impure terms, an act that might actually result in "enjoyment."[13]

In recognizing the lack of passion in the abstinence practiced by those who are not "Europeans," James-watchers ought to realize that it is not the skimmed-milk caution of the elder Wentworth that receives the most attention, or the way Mr. Brand, who likes cake, keeps large morsels within reach but refuses to do more than finger them. No, it is Acton—the man whose "national consciousness had been complicated by a residence in foreign lands"[14]—who is made to appear most at fault by this genial account. A blandly passive man who keeps his hands in his pockets as a sign of fear of commitment (without the good reasons Ralph Touchett has for this pocket-clenching posture), Acton inspires us to liken him to the passive Frederick Winterbourne (who gets into the Edition by courtesy of Daisy Miller's vibrant presence, not his own), rather than to Lambert Strether, who will later be written up to say "no" with passionate high style.[15]

Washington Square shows that James already has at hand an insight about the failings of his own sex that he will further elaborate over the course of the next decades. Morris Townsend merits recognition as one of the first of the Jamesian males who see to it that women do everything for them, including suffering, but Chad Newsome and Prince Amerigo are far more stylish about it. There is also Catherine Sloper, who sets up another dynasty of response: a line of women (including Verena Tarrant and Isabel Archer) marred by the debilitating impulse to please.[16] Catherine's attempt to "express" herself by means of an outrageously ornate dress of red satin trimmed with gold fringe[17] is instructive, as is the fact that her father, by limiting himself to a reading of clothes, only partially comprehends what lies beneath her bedizened exterior; but it takes the intensity of Isabel Archer's retort to Madame Merle that she refuses to be known by the clothes she wears to make us really care about the metaphysical import of James's "clothes philosophy."

Almost from the moment of the genesis of James's world, to know only partially is to misread entirely. When observing the narrator of *The Portrait of a Lady* as he carefully counsels readers to consider the pros and cons of his willful heroine's inner nature, one might review how James sorts out diverse opinions about the antiheroine of *Washington Square*. Whereas Isabel Archer is an endless stimulation to discussion and speculative "ado" on the part of both narrator and the characters surrounding his lady—their asides clearly affecting the "Who is Isabel?" question—in Catherine's case, the narrator plays close to his chest, restricting himself to recording what "they" said: "A dull, plain girl she was called by rigorous critics—a quiet, lady-like girl, by those of the more imaginative sort."[18] Whereas Isabel's critic/mentor directly appeals to the readers to treat his heroine with tenderness, Catherine's chronicler elicits sympathies that remain underinscribed. The moistness of *Portrait* stands next to the dryness of *Washington Square*, and the contrast is highly instructive: especially, as we shall see, in illuminating the kind of author/narrator figure James allows entry into the New York Edition and the figure he shuts out.

The connections between minute details and overarching motifs embedded in the novels both in and outside the canonizing edition are many. Who hasn't picked up on the description of Rose Arminger from *The Other House* that replicates the apparition of Miss Jessel from *The Turn of the Screw?*—but it is also useful to notice that the standoffs that take place in *The Other House* between Jean Martle and Rose are not unlike those enacted by Fleda Vetch and Mona Brigstock in *The Spoils of Poynton* over the beautiful young man both women wish to possess. In the one account about brutal contests over "spoils," the bad heroine uses murder, whereas in the other version, written at the same time, the bad heroine (Mona) operates with far greater effectiveness by using sexual coercion to advance her slaughter of innocents.

As for *The Sacred Fount*, the mark of its success as a fascinating failure (figuring in James's canon as *Pierre* does in Melville's) is the way it serves as a wastebasket anthology for major themes from James's major phase: having to pay for what one gets; meddling in what is none of one's business; the "wondrous new fashion" of pairs of lovers who happen not to be married to each another; an all-consuming physical passion whose deprivation sweeps over the male with palpable sensations of sickness.

All these motifs and more lie outside the cloth covers of the New York Edition, though hardly outside everything Henry James was most about. To get at them, we must re-create a phantom edition that includes what he excluded. But once we do this, the result is, after all, but a supplementation, an ornamentation, to what we already know. Cross-referencing establishes connections between scattered materials, yet affirms materials already in existence. It is difference in degree we deal with here, not difference in kind: difference centered upon the "clothes" with which James dresses his texts—as well as the costuming he assumed as appropriate to his self-appointed role as the Master.

II

At the time James was coming to terms with Scribner's, his concerns were not over the future need to keep on the good side of F. R. and Queenie Leavis or to woo undergraduates by continuing in the vein of his early, "social realist" writings characterized by straightforward style and concise representations of contemporary mores and manners. But with George Bernard Shaw singling out Mark Twain as America's Voltaire, would the mature James have wished to be viewed for posterity as the nation's Molière or the thinking man's P. G. Wodehouse? as the master of comic portrayals of twits and coquettes? It was Percy Lubbock who actually lowered the mantle of the Master upon the aging shoulders of the novelist, but no one imagines James objecting to the enrobing he helped to initiate.

One of the most striking consequences of the New York Edition as it is finally constructed is the portrait of the artist set forth by the novels it sanctions and by the appended prefaces through which James presents both the craft and the craftsman. Let us therefore consider what type of artist James suppressed by leaving out the novels he did.

The monumental back of the author bent over his desk viewed in chiaroscuro retrospect by the meditative narrator of the prefaces is one of the masterly strokes by which we are caught up within the special world created by the collection of volumes launched in 1907. Anxieties experienced decades before by the younger author are passed through the scrim of memory, softened by golden lights and soothing shadows. Guided by the voice in the prefaces, we are assured that all is well after all. Nagging problems of organization, of characterization, of thematic detail that once disturbed the struggling author's imagination have either been met or been forgiven by a fond shrug. *Ficelles*, foreshortening, centers of consciousness—strategies somehow conjured out of the mists of Florence or Venice or Paris—have resolved old uncertainties; they emerge as touchstones for the craft of fiction to be followed for the generations of artists to come.

Stay with the James of the prefaces as he looks back over "the continuity of an artist's endeavour, the growth of his whole operative consciousness," and you meet the "veiled face of his Muse." But although that Muse may remind him that "he is condemned forever and all anxiously to study" what came before, the Preface writer appears no more threatened than if his Muse were the Spirit of Christmas Past who beckons Scrooge backwards through time (*1*: v–vi; *AN*, 3–4).[19] The prefaces are composed by the master in charge of stage-managing the tableaux we watch at his side. Little dramas are set up by his use of phrases such as "ache of fear," "going to pieces," "go under" (*1*: vi, viii, xiv, xv; *AN*, 4, 6, 13), but we sense deeply that these prefaces and the narratives they introduce are part of the same "thrilling tale." In the prefaces James takes pleasure in looking back with the assured safety and triumph of one who has come to harbor after taking the most dangerous of voyages.[20]

James's prefaces convey the image of the ship's master who, with the completion of each novel, has arrived at the spice islands whose smell once lured him and frightened him at the thought of the stretch of ocean (the passage through long and complicated plots) that lay ahead.[21] The prefaces also insist (in their own engagingly insidious manner) that the captain on this never-ending voyage is the master of his craft because he possesses a particular kind of well-bred authority: mellow, a little avuncular, potentially vulnerable to teasing by Beerbohm's caricatures or Wharton's anecdotes of the long-winded, portly elder of Rye, but a major figure nonetheless, characterized both by godlike good nature and unassailable high seriousness.

Consider the quite different figure struck by the artist which would have demanded our attention if at least five of the missing novels[22] had been brought into the New York Edition: witty, cool, tough, urbanely (almost foppishly) attired, not too nice when viewed in the conventional terms that publishers and public like to exact of their sanctioned authors. Serious, but always at risk of not being taken seriously because what he writes is so amusing, with more than a touch of the flaneur. Out to needle the world's vulgarians but liable to be regarded as somewhat of a vulgarian because of the means he used to gain his critical ends; vulgar in the sense James himself employed when referring to the manners of lesser folk—a style of speech, deportment, and dress more casual and familiar than mysterious and genius-touched.[23]

Very clever, brash young men are often vulgar, especially in the impudent way they call attention to the failings of their betters or their elders. Even a mature man of style and sophistication who turns his wit wickedly upon others approaches vulgarity. As a physician and man about Old New York, Dr. Sloper is an impeccably attired gentleman; as a father who mocks the follies that besiege him within his own household in the figures of his sister, Mrs. Penniman, and his daughter, Catherine, he is given to the lancet-sharp words that, if not quite vulgar, are just barely genteel—paradoxically, since social satirists are self-defined as being superior to the mob. Let us say that the type of the satirist who kills by means of wit lies somewhere between the common folk who feel at home with exactly those conditions the satirist seeks to expose and the aristocrats who exist comfortably by choosing not to notice what underlies their faith in their own superiority.

Henry James elected in the New York Edition to be the Master. To do so he had to wipe out lingering traces of those decades during which he was the brash young man with comic talent and the keen eye of the journalist. Well through the 1880's he had skewered social foibles as if he were that other brash boy, Randolph Miller, puncturing flower beds and scattering gravel with his alpine stick wherever he went. True, James concealed his likeness to his satiric countryman by jabbing Randolph with his own pointed stick, but it would not be as easy to distance himself completely from the figure of Dr. Sloper. His narrator might insist that he had a larger view of Washington Square and of Catherine Sloper's role in it than did the doctor, but his indecorous tongue had no less bite.

The James who appears in the New York Edition—both in the declared fictions and in those other fictions, the prefaces—is hardly lacking in the art of deft assaults. But the narrator's darts directed at Jim Pocock or Waymarsh are cuffed in cotton; they seem almost as genial on contact as if Lambert Strether himself had aimed them. The comments upon the social scene in the novels of the major phase that dominate the edition are devastating, but their scorn is somehow softened by the tragic tone that simultaneously underscores how terrible things are and how compassionate the Master can be toward the fools we all are. The attacks sanctioned within the New York Edition are no longer those of a satirist who is full of himself and thus a bit of a vulgarian; they come from the mature man of profound vision, sadder, wiser, and infinitely more "acceptable." Being "good" is better than being merely "clever"; it also means being more desirable to the public at large.[24]

Take *Confidence* for contrast. It is filled with marvelous portraits of silly asses like Captain Lockwood and the lightness of being evidenced by Blanche Evers.[25] Here is the Captain talking at full tilt, commenting upon the impressions of New York garnered by the visiting Englishman:

I hope you don't mind my saying anything about America? You know the Americans are so deucedly thin-skinned—they always bristle up if you say anything against their institutions. The English don't care a rap what you say—they've got a different sort of temper, you know. With the Americans I'm deuced careful—I never breathe a word about anything. While I was over there I went in for being complimentary. I laid it on thick, and I found they would take all I could give them. I didn't see much of their institutions, after all; I went in for seeing the people. Some of the people were charming—upon my soul, I was surprised at some of the people. I dare say you know some of the people I saw; they are as nice people as you would see anywhere. There were always a lot of people about Mrs. Wright, you know; they told me they were all the best people.

And here is Blanche Evers Wright caught up in the midst of her own non-stop prattle:

I haven't the least idea what's the matter with me, and neither has any one else; but that doesn't make any difference. It's settled that I am out of health. One might as well be out of it as in it, for all the advantage it is. If you are out of health, at any rate you can come abroad. It was Gordon's discovery—he's always making discoveries. You see it's because I'm so silly; he can always put it down to my being an invalid. What I should like to do, Mrs. Vivian, would be to spend the winter with you—just sitting on the sofa beside you and holding your hand. . . . I am sure I should be happy if I never went out of this lovely room. You have got it so beautifully arranged—I mean to do my own room just like it when I go home. And you have such lovely clothes. You never used to say anything about it, but you and Angela always had better clothes than I. Are you always so quiet and serious—never talking about *chiffons*—always reading some wonderful book? I wish you would let me come and stay with you. If you only ask me, Gordon would be too delighted. He wouldn't have to trouble about me any more.

In truth, James is up to more serious moves here than pinning a social butterfly to the mat. As he was doing at almost the same moment in *Daisy Miller*, he lightly conceals behind this lightweight chatter a breaking heart. The assertion he places in the foreground with Daisy—that hearts with the capacity to be hurt, even if possessed by young things with silly heads, should receive our tender attention—he places to the side with Blanche. One "problem" with *Confidence* is that it focuses upon the serious young people—Bernard, Gordon, and Vivian—sober-sided characterizations that have not yet achieved the stylistic mastery with which James brings aesthetic and moral seriousness to his elegant later portraits of heartbreaking relations. *Daisy Miller* works wonderfully as a piece worthy of inclusion in the New York Edition because it gives itself up to Daisy herself. In contrast, there seemed to be no justification for including *Confidence* based on its lead characters—solemn, tiresome, inadequately sketched.

Confidence could not be carried solely by the brilliance of its send-up of Captain Lockwood (the type of the ass James kept returning to, Captain Sholto in *The Princess Casamassima* being but one primary example), or by the perfection of its rendering of the poignant, rattle-brained Blanche: not if James were to place himself before the public as an artist of far more weight than that attributable to an author from whom readers could only expect endless comic repetitions of the International Theme that focused upon the transoceanic follies of its social nitwits. The time and effort James put into revising *Roderick Hudson*, an expenditure he denied to *Confidence*, is not proof that the former is a "better" piece of literature—only that its original text allowed James sufficient leeway for translation from its juvenile somberness into juvenilia reclaimed by the aura of high style introduced three decades later by the Master.

Watch and Ward has more wrong with it than jejune sobriety. However touching its awkwardnesses, James's first novel is demonstrably unredeemable because strung along a series of sagging middles. Compare the firm, lucid organization and the absence of adolescent Wertherism of *The Europeans* or *Washington Square*, virtues that set them clearly apart from *Watch and Ward* or *Confidence*; but they were doomed to exclusion because they are perhaps too perfect for their kind: perfect by way of *fitting exactly* within the limited scope James chose for them.[26]

If novels had to be discarded that were "too small" to be taken seriously by an author who had come to crave the elaborate lighting and costuming of the big show, what about *The Bostonians?* Ambitious enough, certainly; but flawed perhaps to James's way of thinking by 1906 because of a damnable cleverness that jabs at every social target in sight, somewhat too revealing of its emotional meagerness and stylistic parsimony.

It is ironic that *The Bostonians* is currently receiving a great deal of serious attention: by feminist critics who hasten to express how much they dislike James's dislike of the ardent women of Boston, and by those who rush to defend the novel by insisting that James was actually quite sympathetic with his women characters and disparaging of his Mississippi chauvinist, Basil Ransom. Agreed that those rare moments when consideration of any kind is granted to anyone are moments descriptive of Miss Birdseye's autumnal passing or of the agonies suffered by Olive (a far more tragic New England type than any within the Wentworth clan). But such compassionate touches are withdrawn almost as quickly as they are made, fearful as the novel's narrator appears to be over any betrayal of his program of questioning an entire age and its depleted society.

As a man of his times, James abhorred the thought of women voting or ever entering into the ranks of the male world. As a novelist, he is rather too successful at conveying his distaste for the women and men alike who make up a diminished society marked by "the feebler passions of the age."[27] The narrator of *The Bostonians* would be as unhappy for being misread as backing Basil Ransom's antediluvian views as for being misread as sharing sympathy with Olive Chancellor's cause. He would certainly not deny himself the pleasure of incising such marvelous lines as the following:

1. Olive's smile "might have been likened to a thin ray of moonlight resting upon the wall of a prison."

2. Mrs. Tarrant's "husband's tastes rubbed off on her soft, moist moral surface."

3. Encountering the guests at Mrs. Burrage's (unidentified bodies who "pushed each other a little, edged about, advanced and retreated, looking at each other with differing faces—sometimes blandly, unperceivingly, sometimes with a harshness of contemplation, a kind of cruelty, sometimes with sudden nods and grimaces, inarticulate murmurs, followed by a quick reaction, a sort of gloom"), Ransom is "absolutely certain that he was in the best society."

4. "Mr. Burrage was successful . . . not perhaps as having a com-

manding intellect or a very strong character, but as being rich, polite, handsome, happy, amiable, and as wearing a splendid camellia in his buttonhole."

We know from James's letters that he was personally upset because few readers liked the novel with which he had so brilliantly excoriated an unlikable society.[28] When it came time to authorize his career, James seems to have yielded to the desire to please (a trait he formerly displaced with care upon his heroines) and the need to be liked for the compassionate, "large" vision he brilliantly developed in the monumental novels of his final two decades. Detestable types remain in the writings of the major phase that claim space in the New York Edition. Selah Tarrant of *The Bostonians* is resurrected as Lionel Croy of *The Wings of the Dove*, but a cosmic touch has been added to the comic slash at Croy's amoral irresponsibility. Tarrant can be contained within the realm of the bad jokes that society plays on itself; Croy is of a piece with the underlying meanness of the universe. Just as much to the point: the self-limiting comic style and the expansive cosmic style literally make *a world of difference* in the quality of the two novels.

Before taking leave of the novels of which James himself took leave, consider the ways in which *The Bostonians* and *The Sacred Fount* play off certain of the qualities that James as author might wish to deny as being too directly applicable to his own approach to the narrative act.

Would James want to be associated with the dominant voice of *The Sacred Fount*? Caught up in the "tragedy" of predicament and the "comedy" of situation, this man attempts to be "a providence" who knows all and thus risks being a "bore" to everyone else. The people surrounding the narrator further resent him for having "spoiled their unconsciousness." In revenge, they will use the consciousness he has forced upon them to be "effectively cruel" to him.[29] Precisely what the James whom we find in the prefaces *does do* is to take the risk of being viewed as a bore and of spoiling the readers' unconsciousness to the point that they may inflict upon him the talent for cruelty to which he has introduced them. But he limits the extent of this risk—by excluding those fictive records that explicitly inscribe the satirist's role; by insuring that the despot of the prefaces is benevolent in manner, not mordant of wit; and by finding the right style for the words and deeds of the Master imaged therein.

If *The Sacred Fount* could be viewed as an unfortunate giveaway to the less pleasant aspects of the narrator's role, it would be just as dangerous to leave lying about similar clues to the lies, deceptions, and other questionable practices on view in *The Bostonians*, traits that could be laid at James's door. Olive Chancellor takes things too hard; so does James, however much he tries to disguise this fact throughout his life. Verena is said to have the "gift" that drives Basil Ransom to mockery in order to retain control of the situation; James wants such a gift, may fear he does not possess it, yet must not seem to care too much about what might be "humbug" after all. Like Ransom, James wants to be in control, but the prefaces oscillate between showing him in the "Verena" position (ease of performance, spontaneity, the "it's not me" way of denying concerted effort that it pleases "geniuses" to affect) and the stance that admits the everyday difficulties of composition that the professional only overcomes through hard work. Lying becomes a necessity to the lives of Olive, Verena, and Ransom; lying is a necessary part of the authorial act, required to protect precious secrets and hide gross errors of judgment. Wiser, therefore, to suppress the nontranscendent nature of narrative acts constantly exposed by *The Bostonians*, thereby allowing precedence to the counterversion of the prefaces that, by pretending to transparency, achieves the high style that is a masterly composite calling simultaneous attention to easy perfection and minute care over detail.

III

If the New York Edition is an intaglio (with what is absent carving out space for what is present), what exactly are the principles of omission it follows? What ethic and aesthetic of renunciation does it take as its model for doing without?

It is Olive Chancellor, not James, who seizes upon the admonition of Goethe, "Thou shalt renounce, refrain, abstain," as the means of possessing greatness through the act of "giving your life."[30] The German Idealists never tempted Henry James to the kind of passionate commitment he saw fit to undercut in *The Bostonians*, but several scholars have noted certain affinities between James's working philosophy and that of the Stoics.[31] There are even more provocative connections between James's practices and the tenets of medieval asceticism which Geoffrey Galt Harpham brilliantly sets out under the labels "cenobitic" and "eremitic" art.[32]

The cenobitic artist fights against self-indulgence in heightened subjectivity. Seeking self-negation, he "disappears" into the anonymity of his art, "leaving no trace of self," in order to separate the suffering man and the creative artist. In contrast, the "eremitic artist" "fills an aesthetic form with symbolic representations of self." Although both modes of asceticism are intended to "resist temptation," cenobitic art decries "distinctiveness, glamour, self-assertion," whereas eremitic art rejects the submission to "order and uniformity, to mundanity and mediocrity." There are many indications that James *as the narrator within the texts he chose to canonize* in the New York Edition (because they were worthy enough, holy enough) obeyed the principles of the cenobitic, but that James *as the figure that appears in the prefaces* is clearly the type of the "genius" abhorred by the cenobitic artist but embraced by the eremitic.

There is still another field of reference besides those provided by the classic Stoics and the medieval ascetics, one that is much closer to home regarding the years during which Henry James was working his way through the formulation of the New York Edition. This is the aesthetic of absent things practiced by Madame Paquin, Paul Poiret, and Elsie de Wolfe in a society in which the decoration of one's body and one's house was being revised away from previous standards for correctness. What the *haute couture* of the final decades of James's life created is paralleled by what James designed for his exhibition of style. It anticipates Coco Chanel's declaration that to play "the part of the revolutionary" one must be sure "to do away with all the things [one] didn't like," and Diana Vreeland's conviction that "elegance is refusal," however unaware these fashion mavens were that Nietzsche and Foucault believed that "this refusal *is* what we are."[33]

Elegance as refusal is, of course, an elitist position grounded on an extravagant austerity that is quite in keeping with the modernist spirit in art for which James's prefaces serve as an important manifesto. It means commitment to an aesthetics of the kind that made it necessary for James to do away with the vestiges of a premodernist mode by leaving out whatever novels contained them. Authority was James's final aim; gaining more in terms of presenting himself as the Master before the world. Thus he had to delete any evidence of what others might construe as weakness or ending with less. Any one or any part of the seven novels under question that invited the aspersion that this was an author given to triviality, parochialism, or vulgarity must be sacrificed. The works of the clever young man, or of the mature but self-limited satirist, or of one who settles for too little, had to be viewed as part of "all the things [one] doesn't like" that one does away with.

What in brief was the nature of the revolution in women's fashions and house decoration that leads to the perhaps *outré* suggestion that there are provocative affinities between the aesthetics of refusal practiced by James and that practiced by the men and women of the *haute couture* of the same era? What is there about an attitude toward fashion that subscribes to an aesthetics—shared by James's late manner and by Paquin, Poiret, and de Wolfe—that is simultaneously "beflounced" and "denuded"?[34] that is ascetic yet voluptuous? that holds to a naturalism of bodily shapes and to material spaces that nevertheless abstract themselves from nature? If we agree with Poiret that "the style of women's clothes and the style of interior decorations, are the two dominant features of an epoch's concrete physiognomy,"[35] what links them to the "physiognomy" of the texts James placed before his public in 1907?

With "In Praise of Make-Up" (from his *L'Art Romantique* of 1868), Charles Baudelaire pronounced: "Fashion is a symptom of a craving for the ideal [that] soars irresistibly to the top of our thoughts, leaving far below it the accumulation of the gross, the mundane and the despicable that are fundamental to everyday life. Fashion is a sublime deformation of nature."[36] One generation's "deformation of nature" is, however, the succeeding generation's everyday life, what it must "refuse" in the name of a new manner of correcting "the gross, the mundane and the despicable." Madame Paquin (née Jeanne Becker) first opened her shop in 1891; between 1902 and 1908 her loosely hung empire silhouette repudiated the bodily constrictions and overblown draperies of the previous mode.[37] Poiret became Paquin's major competitor in 1904 by adopting "Greek" shapes that also freed women from the "tyrannies" of high collars and stiff corsets and by reducing costume ornamentation to the minimum. By 1910, avant-garde fashion took further inspiration and delight from the exotic, fantastic "Orientalism" introduced by Léon Bakst's designs for the Ballets Russes and the influential Munich exhibition of Art Deco design.[38] Poiret's design expressed his belief that "the inherent mystery and charm of a woman should be evoked by suggestion and understatement,"[39] but he also launched the look that Fanny Assingham took as her own which "seemed to present her insistently as a daughter of the South, or still more of the East, a creature formed by hammocks and divans, fed upon sherberts and waited upon by slaves" (*23*: 34).

The distance between Mrs. Newsome's Elizabethan ruche, Maria Gostrey's red-ribbon neckband, and Madame de Vionnet's wristful of discreet but extravagant gold bracelets traces the curriculum in taste in which Lambert Strether must enroll upon arriving in Paris circa 1903.[40] The route taken in the years 1897 to 1907 by James's compatriot Elsie de Wolfe, an actress who lived out Isabel Archer's worst nightmare of being a woman known only by her clothes (albeit the best of Worth, Doucet, and Paquin, while featured in the theater productions of Charles Frohman), also suggests the ways in which "experimentation" in the theater world, in the *haute couture*, and in the arts of house decoration coincides with the theories of literary technique developed by James during that same decade.[41]

In 1897, inspired by Edith Wharton and Ogden Codman's *The Decoration of Houses*, a book that honored the ascetic beauties they maintained were the glory of eighteenth-century French decor, de Wolfe eased her way out of her theater career as a stylish mannequin. She made the important transition by her redecoration of Irving House, the establishment near Gramercy Park she shared with Bessie Marbury, internationally successful theater agent and the indispensable link of "the Boston marriage" that bound the two women together for decades.[42] The Irving House enterprise was the start of de Wolfe's fabled career in which she "became famous not for what [she] added, but for what she had removed."[43] De Wolfe replaced darkness with lightness, clutter with open spaces, jumbled patterns with carefully designed color and figure harmonies: all as the right setting for parties with guests ranging from Henry Adams, Isabella Stewart Gardner, and Ethel Barrymore to Edith Wharton and J. P. Morgan. Had James not been self-exiled into the English house-party scene of late Edwardian society, he might have had an early look at an aesthetic that he would be carrying over into his own writings.[44]

It was in 1907, however, the year the first volumes of the New York Edition appeared, that Elsie de Wolfe transposed the private triumph of her experimentations in the aesthetics of refusal into her public entrance into the profession of interior decoration. 1907 was the year she decorated the Colony Club, the newest and most exclusive of New York's women's clubs. Given the commission at the insistence of Stanford White, designer of the building's exterior, de Wolfe spent the years 1905 and 1906—the same years Henry James was worrying through "the architecture" and design of the Scribner's edition—gathering together ideas on how to present this radically "barren" interior to the high society public.[45] Both de Wolfe and James wished, according to Poiret's prescription for his own artistry, to move past the dictates of "a general consensus of opinion" and to "escape from majority styles"[46]—and at the same time to find favor with the discriminating elite who had the authority to recognize artists with "seriousness" of intent and "success" of achievement.

The making of the New York Edition involves more than the marketing concerns so carefully probed by Michael Anesko, and more than the need for self-therapy out of which Leon Edel constructs his theories of why James wrote what he did. External decisions forced upon the author by the economic constraints of the Scribner's project, and emotional factors imposed by James's relations to his family, are obviously to be taken into account, but the project calls for further analysis of the possible reasons why James followed the way of the aesthetics of refusal. It was a way taken toward the kind of greatness he envisioned for the works lovingly presented within the covers of the Edition, at the sacrifice of other novels that finally found no justification for inclusion.

On the closing page of the closing Preface he contributed to the New York Edition, James summed up the differences between life and art. They constitute two areas of dress-performance, the one over which we have no real control, the other over which we do. The first area comprises those "social performances" that we as private individuals are often forced "to abandon and outlive, to forget and disown and hand over to desolation." The second, contrasting area is the artist's realm, where, with "incomparable luxury," he has the power to decide "not to break with his values, not to 'give away' his importances." The first is where life's acts are "done," dead, renounced through no choice of one's own. The second is where art's acts are "always doing," exhibiting "conduct with a vengeance" out of choice. Life as lived outside the New York Edition, as it were, is the exposed area where "noted behaviour . . . may show for ragged, because it perpetually escapes our control; we have again and again to consent to its appearing in undress." Life as presented within the Edition obeys the "one sovereign truth" that art is "exemplary," care is "active," and "finish nothing if not consistent" (23: xxv; *AN*, 348).

There is always the possibility that the image an artist painstakingly creates for himself and the novels he selects to represent his achievements will be rejected by the reading public. In its effort to be taken seriously, James's late manner has been viewed by many more than just the Leavises as having moved away from the moral seriousness of the early works; to those readers, the fictions featured in the New York Edition would be seen as having been tainted by the frivolous nature of a *haute couture* quickly dated by its fantastic embellishments. A pity, then, if James's intention to be true to the life of the imagination becomes ludicrous when judged as being "the abstract [that] disguises and denies"—its texts deforming nature, just as Poiret was said to have done by making "women look like embroidered velvet eggs."[47]

Asceticism and aestheticism make strange partners indeed. But then there is little that can match the strangeness of the entire New York Edition enterprise, especially when it comes time to assess that enterprise according to our incisive consideration of what Henry James left out in the name of high style.

Appendixes

Bibliography and Publication History of the New York Edition

The Novels and Tales of Henry James. New York Edition. 24 [26] volumes. New York: Charles Scribner's Sons. The edition was published two volumes at a time between December 1907 and July 1909 in 24 volumes, and was issued in Great Britain by Macmillan & Company beginning in 1908. Besides the regular issue of the New York Edition of the *Novels and Tales,* a limited edition of 156 numbered sets was also isssued by Scribner's. In 1917, after James's death, Scribner's issued the unfinished novels *The Ivory Tower* and *The Sense of the Past* in volumes uniform with the original 24, thereafter marketing the Edition in 26 volumes. The Edition was reprinted in 1971, minus the Coburn frontispieces, by Augustus M. Kelley Publishers of New York.

Each volume consists of: a photographic frontispiece by Alvin Langdon Coburn; a tissue-paper overleaf with caption for the frontispiece, overlaid on the title page (overleaf captions in the list below are here followed by the title of the work illustrated in instances where volumes contain more than one title); title page; and copyright information on works included in the volume. Eighteen of the 24 volumes contain prefaces.

Contents of New York Edition Volumes

Vol. I (1907): frontispiece, "Henry James" [facsimile signature]; title page, "Roderick Hudson"; Preface (v–xxiii).

Vol. II (1907): frontispiece, "Faubourg St. Germain"; title page, "The American"; Preface (v–xx).

Vol. III (1908): frontispiece, "The English Home"; title page, "The Portrait of a Lady, Volume I"; Preface (v–xxii).

Vol. IV (1908): frontispiece, "The Roman Bridge"; title page, "The Portrait of a Lady, Volume II."

Vol. V (1908): frontispiece, "The Dome of St. Paul's"; title page, "The Princess Casamassima, Volume I"; Preface (v–xxiii).

Vol. VI (1908): frontispiece, "'Splendid Paris, Charming Paris'"; title page, "The Princess Casamassima, Volume II."

Vol. VII (1908): frontispiece, "The Comédie Français"; title page, "The Tragic Muse, Volume I"; Preface (v–xxii).

Vol. VIII (1908): frontispiece, "St. John's Wood"; title page, "The Tragic Muse, Volume II."

Vol. IX (1908): frontispiece, "Mr. Longdon's"; title page, "The Awkward Age"; Preface (v–xxiv).

Vol. X (1908): frontispiece, "Some of the Spoils" (*The Spoils of Poynton*); title page, "The Spoils of Poynton, A London Life, The Chaperon"; Preface (v–xxiv).

Vol. XI (1908): frontispiece, "The Cage" (*In the Cage*); title page, "What Maisie Knew, In the Cage, The Pupil"; Preface (v–xxii).

Vol. XII (1908): frontispiece, "Juliana's Court" (*The Aspern Papers*); title page, "The Aspern Papers, The Turn of the Screw, The Liar, The Two Faces"; Preface (v–xxiv).

Vol. XIII (1908): frontispiece, "The Court of the Hotel" (*The Reverberator*); title page, "The Reverberator, Madame de Mauves, A Passionate Pilgrim, and Other Tales"; Preface (v–xxi); also includes "The Madonna of the Future," "Louisa Pallant."

Vol. XIV (1908): frontispiece, "'On Sundays, now, you might be at home?'" ("Lady Barbarina"); title page, "Lady Barbarina, The Siege of London, An International Episode, and Other Tales"; Preface (v–xxii); also includes "The Pension Beaurepas," "A Bundle of Letters," "The Point of View."

Vol. XV (1908): frontispiece, "Saltram's Seat" ("The Coxon Fund"); title page, "The Lesson of the Master, The Death of the Lion, The Next Time, and Other Tales"; Preface (v–xviii); also includes "The Figure in the Carpet," "The Coxon Fund."

Vol. XVI (1909): frontispiece, "The New England Street" ("Europe"); title page, "The Author of Beltraffio, The Middle Years, Greville Fane, and Other Tales"; Preface (v–xii); also includes "Broken Wings," "The Tree of Knowledge," "The Abasement of the Northmores," "The Great Good Place," "Four Meetings," "Paste," "Europe," "Miss Gunton of Poughkeepsie," "Fordham Castle."

Vol. XVII (1909): frontispiece, "The Halls of Julia" ("Julia Bride"); title page, "The Altar of the Dead, The Beast in the Jungle, The Birthplace, and Other Tales"; Preface (v–xxix); also includes "The Private Life," "Owen Wingrave," "The Friends of the Friends," "Sir Edmund Orme," "The Real Right Thing," "The Jolly Corner," "Julia Bride."

Vol. XVIII (1909): frontispiece, "By St. Peter's" (*Daisy Miller*); title page, "Daisy Miller, Pandora, The Patagonia, and Other Tales"; Preface (v–xxiv); also includes "The Marriages," "The Real Thing," "Brooksmith," "The Beldonald Holbein," "The Story in It," "Flickerbridge," "Miss Medwin."

Vol. XIX (1909): frontispiece, "The Doctor's Door"; title page, "The Wings of the Dove, Volume I"; Preface (v–xxiii).
Vol. XX (1909): frontispiece, "The Venetian Palace"; title page, "The Wings of the Dove," Volume II."
Vol. XXI (1909): frontispiece, "By Notre Dame"; title page, "The Ambassadors, Volume I"; Preface (v–xxiii).
Vol. XXII (1909): frontispiece, "The Luxembourg Gardens"; title page, "The Ambassadors, Volume II."
Vol. XXIII (1909): frontispiece, "The Curiosity Shop"; title page, "The Golden Bowl, Volume I"; Preface (v–xxv).
Vol. XXIV (1909): frontispiece, "Portland Place"; title page, "The Golden Bowl, Volume II."

The complete prefaces were reprinted in *The Art of the Novel: Critical Prefaces by Henry James*, ed. Richard P. Blackmur (New York: Charles Scribner's Sons, 1934; reprint, Boston: Northeastern University Press, 1984). They are also available in Henry James, *Literary Criticism: French Writers, Other European Writers, the Prefaces to the New York Edition*, ed. Leon Edel and Mark Wilson (New York: Library of America, 1984), 1035–1341.

Chronological List of Secondary Works on the New York Edition

The following is a selective list of reviews, critical articles, book chapters, dissertations, and bibliographical studies focused on the New York Edition. The list includes key studies of the prefaces, frontispieces, and revisions, but articles devoted to individual prefaces and to studies of James's revisions of individual works have been excluded. I have noted only a few of the most important contemporary reviews; for additional citations of early reviews of the Edition, see the entries under Foley (1944), Ricks (1975), and Taylor (1982).

1907

"The Novels and Tales of Henry James" [publisher's prospectus for the New York Edition]. *The Book Buyer* 32 (Dec.): 212.

1908

Conrad, Joseph. Editorial. *English Review* 1: 158–59.
Ford, Ford Madox. Editorial. *English Review* 1: 159–60.

1909

Lubbock, Percy. "The New York Edition of the Novels and Tales of Henry James." *Times Literary Supplement* 8 (July).
Marsh, Edward Clark. "Henry James: Auto-Critic." *Bookman* 30: 138.
"Why Mr. James Revised." *The Literary Digest* 29 (Aug. 21): 275–76.

1910

Fullerton, Morton. "The Art of Henry James." *Quarterly Review* (Apr.): 393–408; and *Living Age* (June): 643–52.

1912

Gretten, Sturge. "Mr. Henry James and His Prefaces." *Contemporary Review* (Jan.): 69–78; and *Living Age* (Feb.): 287–95.
McIntyre, Clara F. "The Later Manner of Mr. Henry James." *PMLA* 20: 354–71.

1918

Beach, Joseph Warren. *The Method of Henry James*. New Haven, Conn.: Yale University Press.

Bosanquet, Theodora. "The Revised Version." *The Little Review* 5 (Aug.): 56–62.

1920

Gosse, Edmund. "Henry James." *Scribners* 67 (Apr.): 422–30, and (May): 548–57.

1921

Lubbock, Percy. *The Craft of Fiction*. New York: Scribner's.

1923

Herrick, Robert. "A Visit to Henry James." *Yale Review* 12 (July): 724–41.

1924

Bosanquet, Theodora. *Henry James at Work*. The Hogarth Press: London.

1929

Roberts, Morris. *Henry James's Criticism*. Cambridge, Mass.: Harvard University Press.

1931

Edel, Leon. *The Prefaces of Henry James: Thèse Complémentaire pour le Doctorat ès Lettres* (L'Université de Paris). Paris: Jouve & C. [Reprint, n.p.: Folcroft Press, 1970].

1934

Blackmur, R. P. Introduction. In Henry James, *The Art of the Novel: Critical Prefaces by Henry James*, ed. Richard P. Blackmur, vii–xxxix. New York: Charles Scribner's Sons. [Reprinted from *Hound and Horn* 7: 444–47.]

1935

Aiken, Conrad. "Review of *The Art of the Novel: Critical Prefaces*." *Criterion* 14: 667–69.

1937

Leavis, F. R. "Henry James." *Scrutiny* 5: 398–417.

1944

Foley, Richard Nicholas. "Survey of the Criticism of James's Works: The New York Edition." In his *Criticism in American Periodicals of the Works of Henry James From 1866 to 1916*, 121–27. Washington, D.C.: Catholic University of America Press.

Matthiessen, F. O. "The Painter's Sponge and Varnish Bottle." In his *Henry James: The Major Phase*, 152–86. New York: Oxford University Press. [Reprint, New York: Oxford University Press, 1963.]

1948

Lucas, John S. "Henry James' Revisions for His Short Stories." Ph.D. diss., University of Chicago.

1951

Edel, Leon. "The Architecture of Henry James's 'New York Edition.'" *New England Quarterly* 24 (June): 169–78.

1955

Firebaugh, Joseph J. "Coburn: Henry James' Photographer." *American Quarterly* 7: 215–33.

Volpe, Edmond L. "The Prefaces of George Sand and Henry James." *Modern Language Notes* 70: 107–8.

1956

Traschen, Isadore. "Henry James and the Art of Revision." *Philological Quarterly* 35: 39–47.

1958

Wellek, René. "Henry James's Literary Theory and Criticism." *American Literature* 30: 293–321

1960

Hicks, Priscilla Gibson. "'The Story In It': The Design of the New York Edition." Ph.D. diss., Boston University.

Paterson, John. "The Language of 'Adventure' in Henry James." *American Literature* 32: 291–301.

1962

Shumsky, Allison. "James Again: The New York Edition." *Sewanee Review* 70: 522–25.

1963

Stafford, William T. "Literary Allusions in James's Prefaces." *American Literature*
35: 60–70.

1964

Gale, Robert. "Imagery in James's Prefaces." *Revue des Langues Vivantes* 30: 431–
45.
Holland, Laurence Bedwell. "The Prefaces." In his *The Expense of Vision: Essays
on the Craft of Henry James*, 155–82. Princeton, N.J.: Princeton University
Press.

1966

Coburn, Alvin Langdon. "Illustrating Henry James." In *Alvin Langdon Coburn:
Photographer; an Autobiography*, ed. Helmut and Alison Gernsheim, 52–60.
London: Faber & Faber.
Franklin, Rosemary F. *An Index to Henry James's Prefaces to the New York Edition*.
Charlottesville: Bibliographical Society of the University of Virginia.
Leonard, Vivien Rose. "An Introductory Study of Imagery in the Prefaces of the
New York Edition of the Novels and Tales of Henry James." Ph.D. diss., Co-
lumbia University.

1969

Bersani, Leo. "The Jamesian Lie." *Partisan Review* 36: 53–79.

1971

Poirier, Richard. *The Performing Self: Compositions and Decompositions in the Languages of Contemporary Life*, 86–111. New York: Oxford University Press.

1972

Bertolotti, David Santo, Jr. "A Concordance of Foreign Words and Phrases for
the New York Edition." Ph.D. diss., Michigan State University.
Edel, Leon. *Henry James: The Master, 1901–1916*, 321–39. Philadelphia: J. B.
Lippincott.
Raunheim, John P. "A Study of the Revisions of the Tales Included in the New
York Edition." Ph.D. diss., New York University.

1975

Frank, Ellen Eve. "Promises in Stone: The Architectural Analogy in Walter Pa-
ter, Gerard Manley Hopkins, Marcel Proust, Henry James." Ph.D. diss.,
Stanford University.

Ricks, Beatrice. *Henry James: A Bibliography of Secondary Works*, 224. Metuchen, N.J.: Scarecrow Press.

1976

Stone, Edward. "Edition Architecture and 'The Turn of the Screw.'" *Studies in Short Fiction* 13: 9–16.

1978

Cixous, Hélène. "L'Ecriture Comme Placement ou De l'Ambiguité de l'intérêt." In *L'Art de la Fiction: Henry James*, ed. Michel Zéraffa, 203–22. Paris: n.p.
Jablow, Betsy Lynn. "Illustrated Texts from Dickens to James." Ph.D. diss., Stanford University.
Zéraffa, Michel, ed. *L'Art de la Fiction: Henry James*. Paris: n.p.

1979

Auchincloss, Louis. "The Late Jamesing of Early James." In his *Life, Law, and Letters: Essays and Sketches*, 91–96. Boston: Houghton.
Blasing, Mutlu Konuk. "The Story of the Stories: James's Prefaces as Autobiography." In *Approaches to Victorian Autobiography*, ed. George P. Landow, 311–22. Athens, Ohio: University of Ohio Press.
Goetz, William R. "Criticism and Autobiography in James's Prefaces." *American Literature* 51: 333–48.

1980

Kappeler, Susanne. "Reader and Critic Writ Large." In her *Writing and Reading in Henry James*, 174–90. New York: Columbia University Press.

1981

Leitch, Thomas. "The Editor as Hero: Henry James and the New York Edition." *Henry James Review* 3: 24–32.

1982

Carroll, David. *The Subject in Question: The Language of Theory and the Strategies of Fiction*, 51–66. Chicago: University of Chicago Press.
Higgins, Charles. "Photographic Aperture: Coburn's Frontispieces to James' New York Edition." *American Literature* 53: 661–75.
Taylor, Linda J. *Henry James, 1866–1916: A Reference Guide*, 397–421, passim. Boston: G. K. Hall. Taylor lists more than 60 notices of the New York Edition which appeared in newspapers and magazines throughout the United States.

1984

Bogardus, Ralph F. *Pictures and Texts: Henry James, A. L. Coburn, and New Ways of Seeing in Literary Culture*. Ann Arbor, Mich.: UMI Research Press.

Caramello, Charles. "The Author's Taste, Or, Unturning the Screw." *Dalhousie Review* 64: 36–45.

Culver, Stuart. "Henry James's New York Edition: The Organic Text and the Mechanics of Publication." Ph.D. diss., University of California, Berkeley.

———. "Representing the Author: Henry James, Intellectual Property, and the Work of Writing." In *Henry James: Fiction as History*, ed. Ian F. A. Bell, 114–36. New York: Barnes and Noble.

Parker, Hershel. "The Authority of the Revised Text and the Disappearance of the Author: What Critics of Henry James Did with Textual Evidence in the Heyday of the New Criticism." In his *Flawed Texts and Verbal Icons: Literary Authority in American Fiction*, 85–114. Evanston, Ill.: Northwestern University Press.

———. "Henry James 'In the Wood': Sequences and Significances of His Literary Labors, 1905–1907." *Nineteenth-Century Fiction* 38: 492–513.

Rowe, John Carlos. "Forms of the Reader's Act: Author and Reader in the Prefaces to the New York Edition." In his *The Theoretical Dimensions of Henry James*, 219–52. Madison: University of Wisconsin Press.

1985

Jackson, Wendell P. "The Theory of the Creative Process in the 'Prefaces' of Henry James." In his *Amid Visions and Revisions: Poetry and Criticism on Literature and the Arts*. Baltimore: Morgan State University Press.

Jones, Vivien. "The Prefaces." In her *James the Critic*, 162–213. New York: St. Martin's Press, 1985.

Kimball, Jean. "A Classified Subject Index to Henry James's Critical Prefaces to the New York Edition (Collected in *The Art of the Novel*)." *Henry James Review* 6: 89–135.

Margolis, Anne T. "A Substitute Peformance." In her *Henry James and the Problem of Audience: An International Act*, 183–93. Ann Arbor, Mich.: UMI Research Press.

1986

Anesko, Michael. "The Eclectic Architecture of Henry James's New York Edition." In his *"Friction with the Market": Henry James and the Profession of Authorship*, 141–62. New York: Oxford University Press.

Goetz, William R. "The Prefaces: Criticism and Autobiography." In his *Henry*

James and the Darkest Abyss of Romance, 82–110. Baton Rouge: Louisiana State University Press.

1987

Brown, Margaret Ellen. "The 'Unabashed Memoranda' of the Prefaces: Henry James's Letter to the World." Ph.D. diss., University of Illinois, Urbana.

Miller, J. Hillis. "Re-Reading Re-Vision: James and Benjamin." In his *The Ethics of Reading: Kant, de Man, Eliot, Trollope, James, and Benjamin*, 101–27. New York: Columbia University Press.

Murphy, James G. "An Analysis of Henry James's Revisions of the First Four Novels of the New York Edition." Ph.D. diss., University of Delaware.

Shloss, Carol. "Henry James and Alvin Langdon Coburn, The Frame of Prevision." In her *In Visible Light: Photography and the American Writer, 1840–1940*, 55–89. New York: Oxford University Press.

1988

Mülder-Bach, Inka. "Genealogy und Stil: Henry James's *Prefaces*." *Poetica* 20: 104–30

1989

Cameron, Sharon. "The Prefaces, Revision, and Ideas of Consciousness." In her *Thinking in Henry James*, 32–82. Chicago: University of Chicago Press.

Horne, Philip. "Writing and Rewriting in Henry James." *Journal of American Studies* 23: 357–74.

Pearson, John. "Frames of Reference: The Prefaces of Henry James." Ph.D. diss., Boston University.

1990

Horne, Philip. *Henry James and Revision: The New York Edition*. Oxford: Clarendon Press.

Ringuette, Dana. "The Self-forming Subject: Henry James' Pragmatistic Revision." *Mosaic* 23: 115–30.

1991

McWhirter, David. "(Re)Presenting Henry James: Authority and Intertextuality in the New York Edition." *Henry James Review* 12: 137–41.

Weltzien, O. Alan. "The Seeds of James's Grand Monument, or When Growing Becomes Building." *Henry James Review* 12: 255–70.

1992

Millgate, Michael. "Henry James." In his *Testamentary Acts: Browning, Tennyson, James, Hardy*, 73–109. Oxford: Clarendon Press.

1993

Leitch, Thomas M. "The Prefaces." In *A Companion to Henry James Studies*, ed.
Daniel Mark Fogel, 55–71. Westport, Conn.: Greenwood Press.

1994

Parker, Hershel. "Deconstructing *The Art of the Novel* and Liberating James's
Prefaces." *Henry James Review* 14: 284–307.

Henry James, Alvin Langdon Coburn, and the New York Edition: A Chronology

Compiled by Ira B. Nadel

In the following chronology, references to James's letters are to *Henry James Letters*, ed. Leon Edel, 4 vols. (Cambridge, Mass.: Harvard University Press, 1974–84), unless otherwise noted. Citations of this source will use the abbreviation "*Lett.*" The abbreviation "NYE" refers to the New York Edition.

1905

January ?   Alvin Langdon Coburn writes to Henry James in New York requesting permission to photograph him.

April 26   Alvin Langdon Coburn, age 22, photographs Henry James, age 62, in New York for *Century Magazine*.

1906

February ?   James views Coburn's first one-man show at the Royal Photographic Society in London, held February 5–March 31, 1906. Preface to the show catalogue written by George Bernard Shaw.

May 9 ?   James and Coburn meet at the Reform Club, London. This is the probable time of James's first sitting for a portrait for later use as the frontispiece of Volume I of the NYE, for he wrote on May 9, 1906: "I was photographed the other day, by an American operator here, for a frontispiece (very well, artistically, and suitably, as I believe)" (*Lett.* 4: 404). Unsuccessful results.

June 8   James telegrams Coburn and invites him to Lamb House, Rye, for more photographing.

June 11   Coburn photographs James at Lamb House. James will write to Scribner's on June 12, 1906: "I spent yesterday afternoon in being again 'artistically' photographed here on my own premises by a young American expert, A. L. Coburn, who had already done me in London, but without satisfactory success, and who came down from town for an earnest second attack. He is quite the best person going, here, I think, and this time I hope for good results; which he promises me within ten days, when I will promptly send you the best" (*Lett.* 4: 407). James prefaces this section of his paragraph with a general comment on his worry over the question of illustrations for his Edition. Cf. his letter to his agent James B. Pinker, June 14, 1906 (*Lett.* 4: 409–10).

July 3   Coburn photographs James's House. The front door is selected as the frontispiece for Volume IX of the New York Edition, *The Awkward Age*, and labeled "Mr. Longdon's."

July 13   Pinker writes to Scribner's about Coburn's photographs: "Mr. James thinks these so highly successful that he is anxious that Mr. Coburn should do as much more of the work as is possible. There is . . . in Paris an old house which Mr. James suggests would make an appropriate frontispiece for 'The American,' and this Mr. Coburn could photograph under Mr. James' direction" (cited in Ralph F. Bogardus, *Pictures and Texts: Henry James, A. L. Coburn, and New Ways of Seeing in Literary Culture* [Ann Arbor, Mich.: UMI Research Press, 1984], 7). He encloses Coburn's portrait of James, a view of London for *Princess Casamassima*, plus four views of Lamb House. He adds that he will look after Coburn's interests.

July 26   James praises his portrait to Coburn in a letter but suggests cropping the photo in the middle; he then outlines the next image: "It is now important that you should do my (this) little house (for the same use)—and could you come down for the purpose some day early next week?" (Henry James to A. L. Coburn, [July] 26, 1906, James Collection, Alderman Library, University of Virginia).

September 3   James urges Coburn to go to Paris to photograph.

September 7   James writes to Pinker of his frustration with delays of Volume I and questions the illustrations: "the accursed picture business must still, for the start, be allowed more of a margin" (Yale University).

September 27   James to Pinker: "had on Tuesday a really successful couple of hours with Coburn in St. John's Wood" (Yale University). Coburn writes in his autobiography, "it was a lovely afternoon, I remember, and H.J. was in his most festive mood" (*Alvin Langdon Coburn: Photographer; an Autobiography* [London: Faber and Faber, 1966], 58). Plate made for one volume of *The Tragic Muse*.

October 2   Coburn travels to Paris to photograph with instructions from James. (See *Lett.* 4: 416–18.)

October 9   James writes to Coburn that he is anxious to see results but adds, "I have no doubt of my being able to make my pick, for each required plate" (James Collection, Alderman Library, University of Virginia).

November 2   James in London views and approves Coburn's Paris photos. Six images are selected.

November–December   Coburn takes photographs of London and English scenes, including "St. John's Wood," "The Curiosity Shop," and "Portland Place." James assists and travels about London searching for locations. "The Dome of St. Paul's" is the only image Coburn made without suggestion from James. It was suggested by Coburn for the frontispiece of Volume V of the NYE, *The Princess Casamassima*, Volume I. (See *Lett.* 4: 429–30 for details on London locales, especially for "In the Cage.")

December 6   James instructs Coburn regarding his Italian journey. (*Lett.* 4: 426–28.)

December 7   James writes to Coburn that he is unsure whether the Edition will be 23 or 24 volumes. (*Lett.* 4: 429–30.)

December 9   James writes to Coburn that permission to photograph Room 21 of the Wallace Collection has been granted. (*Lett.* 4: 431.)

December 10?   Coburn photographs Room 21 of the Wallace Collection at Hertford House, Manchester Square, London; the image is used for the frontispiece of Volume X, *The Spoils of Poynton*. (See *Lett.* 4: 431.)

mid-December   Coburn travels to Venice and Rome, taking with him James's written instructions for those photographs to be taken in Venice. (See *Lett.* 4: 426–29.) This Italian trip resulted in four photographs, two in Venice—"Juliana's Court" and "The Venetian Palace"—and two in Rome—"The Roman Bridge" and "By St. Peter's."

1907

January 2   Coburn returns from Italy; James approves the Italian photos in early January. Coburn and James travel about London seeking further locales to complete the remaining London plates. (Preface, *Golden Bowl*, NYE *23*: x–xiii.)

February 15   James writes to Scribner's that Coburn will go to New York "a week hence" with *all* the illustrations save one or two to be taken in the states. (Princeton University.)

February 22   Coburn journeys to America to photograph. Two plates are selected: "'On Sundays, now, you might be at Home?'" for "Lady Barbarina," in Volume XIV, and "The New England Street," for Volume XVI, which included "Europe."

March ?   Two more English photos are selected: "The English Home," for Volume III, the first volume of *The Portrait of a Lady*, and "The Doctor's Door," for Volume XIX, the first volume of *The Wings of the Dove*.

March 11–April 10   One-man show by Coburn at the Little Galleries of the Photo-Secession, 291 Fifth Avenue, New York.

December 2   Scribner's tells James "the volumes of tales reach proportions destructive of almost all expectation of profitable publication." Additional volume needed. (Princeton University.)

December 14   Scribner's publishes Volumes I and II of the NYE, *Roderick Hudson* and *The American.*

1908

December 14–15   James writes to Scribner's asking them to get Coburn to do a "Julia Bride" frontispiece for the extra volume of the NYE. (Princeton University.)

December 19   An additional frontispiece is needed for Volume XVII. Coburn is told by James to contact Scribner in America. Coburn is in America at the time.

1909

January 12   Scribner's writes to James that Coburn's photograph for "Julia Bride" has been made and will be sent to James for a caption. (Princeton University.)

January 18–February 1   Coburn has another one-man show at the Little Galleries of the Photo-Secession, 291 Fifth Avenue, New York.

January 22   James tactfully writes to Coburn that he is disappointed with Coburn's "The Halls of Julia," taken for the newly added Volume XVII, containing "Julia Bride": "it had all your technical merit, and it's not your fault if the subject, quite prescribed and imposed by our fatal conditions, isn't more entrancing" (James Collection, Alderman Library, University of Virginia).

June 21   James visits Coburn at his Hammersmith home, in London, at 5 P.M.

1913

April 29   James writes to Coburn regarding a possible frontispiece for an additional volume, suggesting two images: one from Paris, the other a New York skyscraper. (James Collection, Alderman Library, University of Virginia.)

May 2   James writes to Coburn to say he likes Coburn's suggestion of a view of Montmartre from a high point. Nothing came of the extra volume or photo. (James Collection, Alderman Library, University of Virginia.)

June 15   James visits Coburn at Hammersmith.

June 28   James visits Coburn at Hammersmith for tea at 5 P.M. This is apparently their last meeting.

Reference Matter

Notes

McWhirter: Introduction

1. Henry James to Edmund Gosse, Aug. 25, 1915, *Henry James Letters*, ed. Leon Edel, vol. 4 (Cambridge, Mass.: Harvard University Press, 1984), 776–77. James repeats the reference to Shelley's poem elsewhere in the letter, describing his "poor old rather truncated edition" as having "the grotesque likeness for me of a sort of miniature Ozymandias ('look on my *works*, ye mighty, and despair!')—round which the lone and level sands stretch further away than ever."

2. John Carlos Rowe, *The Theoretical Dimensions of Henry James* (Madison: University of Wisconsin Press, 1984), xi.

3. Recent reconsiderations of the Edition that I have found especially valuable include Michael Anesko's study "The Eclectic Architecture of Henry James's New York Edition," in his *"Friction with the Market": Henry James and the Profession of Authorship* (New York: Oxford University Press, 1986), 141–62; Hershel Parker's research on the "sequence and significances" of James's "literary labors" on the Edition, in his *Flawed Texts and Verbal Icons: Literary Authority in American Fiction* (Evanston, Ill.: Northwestern University Press, 1984), 85–114, as well as in "Henry James 'In the Wood': Sequences and Significances of His Literary Labors, 1905–1907," *Nineteenth-Century Fiction* 38 (1984): 492–513, and in "Deconstructing *The Art of the Novel* and Liberating James's Prefaces," *Henry James Review* 14 (1993): 284–307; Stuart Culver's essay "Representing the Author: Henry James, Intellectual Property, and the Work of Writing," in *Henry James: Fiction as History*, ed. Ian F. A. Bell (New York: Barnes and Noble, 1984), 114–36; Charles Caramello's discussion of the Edition in "The Author's Taste, Or, Unturning the Screw," *Dalhousie Review* 64 (1984): 36–45; Michael Millgate's chapter on the Edition in his *Testamentary Acts: Browning, Tennyson, James, Hardy* (Oxford: Clarendon Press, 1992); and Philip Horne's book-length study of James's theory and practice of revision, *Henry James and Revision: The New York Edition*

(Oxford: Clarendon Press, 1990). Certain discussions of James's prefaces for the Edition—a subject on which much has been written—also move towards a broader apprehension of the significance of the Edition as a whole: see Mutlu Konuk Blasing, "The Story of the Stories: James's Prefaces as Autobiography," in *Approaches to Victorian Autobiography*, ed. George P. Landow (Athens, Ohio: University of Ohio Press, 1979), 311–22; Thomas Leitch, "The Editor as Hero: Henry James and the New York Edition," *Henry James Review* 3 (1981): 24–32; and David Carroll, *The Subject in Question: The Language of Theory and the Strategies of Fiction* (Chicago: University of Chicago Press, 1982), 51–66. A checklist of these works and others—the most important reviews and criticism devoted to the Edition—appears in Appendix B at the end of this volume.

4. Rowe, *Theoretical Dimensions*, 28.

5. Henry James, quoted in Elsa Nettels, *James and Conrad* (Athens, Ga.: University of Georgia Press, 1977), 8–10.

6. Percy Lubbock, "The New York Edition of the Novels and Tales of Henry James," *Times Literary Supplement* 8 (July 1909). Lubbock recapitulated his argument in *The Craft of Fiction* (New York: Scribner's, 1921), a book that proved extremely influential in early New Critical circles.

7. Blackmur's isolation of the prefaces from the context of the Edition as a whole, while welcome insofar as it made the prefaces more widely available, has also served to obscure the full complexity of the Edition as a text. For a related critique of Blackmur, see Hershel Parker's essay "Deconstructing *The Art of the Novel*."

8. Leon Edel, "The Architecture of Henry James's 'New York Edition,'" *New England Quarterly* 24 (June 1951): 171. Edel repeats and elaborates his argument in *Henry James: The Master, 1901–1916* (Philadelphia: J. B. Lippincott, 1972), 321–39.

9. Richard Blackmur, Introduction to *The Art of the Novel: Critical Prefaces by Henry James*, ed. Richard P. Blackmur (New York: Charles Scribner's Sons, 1934; reprint, Boston: Northeastern University Press, 1984), xv.

10. Michel Foucault, "What Is an Author?," in *Textual Strategies: Perspectives in Post-Structuralist Criticism*, ed. Josué V. Harari (Ithaca, N.Y.: Cornell University Press, 1979), 159.

11. Anne T. Margolis, *Henry James and the Problem of Audience: An International Act* (Ann Arbor, Mich.: UMI Research Press, 1985), 186.

12. H. James to W. D. Howells, Aug. 17, 1908, *The Letters of Henry James*, ed. Percy Lubbock, vol. 2 (New York: Scribner's, 1920), 98–104.

13. Margolis, *Henry James and the Problem of Audience*, 191.

14. H. James, quoted in Horne, *Henry James and Revision*, 3.

15. See especially Anesko, *"Friction with the Market,"* and Marcia Jacobson,

Henry James and the Mass Market (University: University of Alabama Press, 1983).

16. See Anesko's and Stuart Culver's essays in this volume. Culver also discusses the deluxe edition format in his "Representing the Author," 115–17. Philip Horne suggests, however, that James may have had another sort of model in mind, exemplified by Browning's final collected edition of his works in sixteen volumes (1888–89) and the nine-volume Eversley edition of Tennyson (1907–8). See Horne, *Henry James and Revision*, 35.

17. Henry James to James B. Pinker, June 6, 1905, quoted in Horne, *Henry James and Revision*, 5.

18. Henry James to James B. Pinker, Sept. 29, 1905, quoted in Horne, *Henry James and Revision*, 7.

19. See, in addition to the essays by Anesko and Culver in this volume, Anesko's *"Friction with the Market"* and Culver's "Representing the Author."

20. Archibald Constable to Scribner's, Mar. 14, 1906, quoted in Horne, *Henry James and Revision*, 10.

21. See Anesko, *"Friction with the Market,"* 147–54. Scribner's prospectus for the Edition, "The Novels and Tales of Henry James," was published in *The Book Buyer* 32 (Dec. 1907): 212.

22. Culver, "Representing the Author," 134.

23. Anesko, *"Friction with the Market,"* 143–54.

24. James described the Edition in these terms in a letter of Aug. 7, 1905. The letter continues, "I exercise a control, a discrimination, I treat certain portions of my work as unhappy accidents—(many portions of many—of all—men's works are)." See *Henry James Letters* 4: 371.

25. *Selected Letters of Henry James to Edmund Gosse, 1882–1915: A Literary Friendship*, ed. Rayburn S. Moore (Baton Rouge: Louisiana State University Press, 1988), 313.

26. James wrote that the Edition designation "refers the whole enterprise to my native city—to which I have had no great opportunity of rendering that sort of homage." *Henry James Letters* 4: 368. For a darker reading of the significance of "New York," see Alfred Habegger's essay in this volume.

27. Edel, *Henry James: The Master*, 321.

28. H. James, quoted by Blackmur in James, *Art of the Novel*, xvi.

29. H. James, quoted in Edel, *Henry James: The Master*, 321.

30. See Parker, *Flawed Texts and Verbal Icons*, 96 and passim. F. O. Matthiessen's influential study of the revisions, "The Painter's Sponge and Varnish Bottle: Henry James' Revision of *The Portrait of a Lady*," appears in *Henry James: The Major Phase* (New York: Oxford University Press, 1944), 152–86.

31. See the readings of the revisions for *The Portrait of a Lady* by Nina Baym

("Revision and Thematic Change in *The Portrait of a Lady*," *Modern Fiction Studies* 22 [1976]: 183–200) and Anthony J. Mazzella ("The New Isabel," in the Norton Critical Edition of *Portrait* [New York: W. W. Norton, 1975], 597–619). Baym describes the revised text as "a different work"; Mazzella insists that in reading it "we are responding in a new way to new characters in a new work."

32. The captions accompanying the frontispieces for volumes 6 and 14 are the only instances in which James quotes directly from the illustrated text.

33. Roland Barthes, "From Work to Text," in *Textual Strategies: Perspectives in Post-Structuralist Criticism*, ed. Josué V. Harari (Ithaca, N.Y.: Cornell University Press, 1979), 73–81.

34. Foucault, "What Is an Author?," 159.

35. Balzac, quoted in V. S. Pritchett, *Balzac* (New York: Alfred Knopf, 1973), 161.

36. Henry James, *The American Scene*, ed. Leon Edel (Bloomington: Indiana University Press, 1968), 204.

37. Shoshana Felman, "Turning the Screw of Interpretation," in *Literature and Psychoanalysis. The Question of Reading: Otherwise*, ed. Shoshana Felman (Baltimore: The Johns Hopkins University Press, 1977), 205.

38. Rowe, *Theoretical Dimensions*, xiii.

39. Seán Burke, *The Death and Return of the Author: Criticism and Subjectivity in Barthes, Foucault and Derrida* (Edinburgh: Edinburgh University Press, 1992), 166.

40. Jacques Derrida, "Freud and the Scene of Writing," in his *Writing and Difference*, trans. Alan Bass (Chicago: University of Chicago Press, 1978), 226–27.

41. Jacques Derrida, "Signature Event Context," trans. Samuel Weber and Jeffrey Mehlman, in Derrida, *Limited Inc* (Evanston, Ill.: Northwestern University Press, 1988), 18.

42. See Nancy K. Miller, "Changing the Subject: Authorship, Writing, and the Reader," in her *Subject to Change: Reading Feminist Writing* (New York: Columbia University Press, 1988), 102–21.

43. Michel Foucault, "Afterword: The Subject and Power," in Hubert L. Dreyfus and Paul Rabinow, *Michel Foucault: Beyond Structuralism and Hermeneutics* (Brighton, Eng.: Harvester Press, 1982), 208.

44. Phillipe Lacoue-Labarthe, "Diderot: Paradox and Mimesis," trans. Jane Popp, in *Typography: Mimesis, Philosophy, Politics*, ed. Christopher Fynsk (Cambridge, Mass.: Harvard University Press, 1989), 258–60; emphasis in the original.

45. Millgate, "Henry James," in his *Testamentary Acts*, 100–101 and passim.

46. Ross Posnock, *The Trial of Curiosity: Henry James, William James, and the Challenge of Modernity* (New York: Oxford University Press, 1991), 16.

47. Paul Ricoeur, *Oneself as Another*, trans. Kathleen Blamey (Chicago: University of Chicago Press, 1992), 116, 2.

48. Ibid., 118.

49. Ibid., 123.

50. Ibid., 123–24.

51. Posnock, *Trial of Curiosity*, 285.

52. Dorothea Krook, *The Ordeal of Consciousness in Henry James* (Cambridge, Eng.: Cambridge University Press, 1967).

53. Barthes, "From Work to Text," 78.

54. James, *American Scene*, 77.

Posnock: Breaking the Aura of Henry James

1. Henry James, *Literary Criticism: Essays on Literature, American Writers, English Writers*, ed. Leon Edel and Mark Wilson (New York: Library of America, 1984), 651.

2. Jean-Paul Sartre, *Critique of Dialectical Reason*, trans. A Sheridan-Smith (London: NLB, 1976), 771–72.

3. Claude Lefort, *The Political Forms of Modern Society*, trans. John Thompson (Cambridge, Mass.: MIT Press, 1986), 304–5.

4. Henry James, *The American Scene* (Bloomington: Indiana University Press, 1968), 12.

5. James, *American Scene*, 126, 83, 177, 131.

6. Richard Blackmur, Introduction to *The Art of the Novel: Critical Prefaces by Henry James*, ed. Richard P. Blackmur (New York: Charles Scribner's Sons, 1934; reprint, Boston: Northeastern University Press, 1984), xlvi, xxiii.

7. Michael Jennings, *Dialectical Images* (Ithaca, N.Y.: Cornell University Press, 1987), 169. This sense of "aura" is only one of its meanings for Benjamin. As is well known, he was ambivalent about the "contemporary decay of the aura." For him, aura is also a "unique phenomenon of a distance, however close it may be," a phenomenon being eclipsed by mass culture with its bias toward homogeneity. Walter Benjamin, *Illuminations*, trans. Harry Zohn (New York: Schocken Books, 1969), 222–23. This meaning of aura as distance, rather than as cultural fetish, would clearly be supported by Henry James, who conceives the richest intimacy as premised on distance.

8. One of the remarkable aspects of this renewal is that it continued despite a period of two years (1909–11) when James virtually ceased writing, so afflicted was he by physical illness, depression over the financial failure of the New York Edition, and grief over William's death in 1910. That his memoirs were, in significant degree, a therapeutic working through of his assorted troubles is a warranted and often-made inference, especially since its logic repeats an earlier dynamic established with the *Guy Domville* humiliation of 1895. Then James

transformed his failure and depression into a stunning creative renewal. I concur in general, if not in particular, with Leon Edel's estimate that despite all the personal and professional tribulations of James's last two decades, in his last twenty years he "became looser, less formal, less distant; he writes [letters] with greater candor and with more emotional freedom . . . ; [he is] less rigid and more experimental in spite of his aging." Leon Edel, Introduction, *Henry James Letters*, ed. Leon Edel, vol. 4 (Cambridge, Mass.: Harvard University Press, 1984), xiii. Edel's belief that James underwent "considerable alteration in his personality" has been criticized as exaggeration. While Edel may be typically overdramatic in his sense of discontinuity, his theory at least alerts us to the remarkable efflorescence in James's late life and work.

9. Melville's novel and James's late works strikingly converge in the effort to unsettle the repressions of monadic individualism. Their shared strategy to disorient radically the experience of reading by estranging the reader's conventional expectations is part of a larger project of seeking a more relaxed mode of being that escapes the rigid control of the bourgeois self. This effort to unsettle social and ontological vigilance is the aim of the confidence man within Melville's novel and is embodied by the "restless analyst" in James, *American Scene*.

10. Ralph Waldo Emerson, *Essays and Lectures* (New York: Library of America, 1983), 413.

11. Wyndham Lewis, *Men Without Art* (Santa Rosa, Calif.: Black Sparrow, 1987), 115.

12. H. G. Dwight, quoted in Roger Gard, *Henry James: The Critical Heritage* (New York: Barnes and Noble, 1968), 439.

13. Dwight, quoted ibid., 444.

14. Frederick Taber Cooper, quoted ibid., 435.

15. W. C. Brownell, quoted ibid., 411, 418, 397.

16. William James, *A Pluralistic Universe* (Cambridge, Mass.: Harvard University Press, 1977), 43–50.

17. John Dewey, *Experience and Nature* (LaSalle, Ill.: The Open Court, 1929), 48.

18. Theodor Adorno, *Aesthetic Theory*, trans. C. Lenhardt (Boston: Routledge, 1985), 460. Adorno also salutes Dewey's "wholly humane" version of pragmatism at the start of *Negative Dialectics*, trans. E. B. Ashton (New York: Continuum, 1973), 14.

19. James, *American Scene*, 121–22, 124.

20. Walter Benjamin, *The Origin of German Tragic Drama*, trans. John Osborne (London: NLB, 1977), 33, 43, 29.

21. Dewey, *Experience and Nature*, 27.

22. Henry James, *Literary Criticism: French Writers, Other European Writers, the Prefaces to the New York Edition*, ed. Leon Edel (New York: Library of America, 1984), 41.

23. This Comtean image of Balzac is not James's only sense of the novelist; indeed the Frenchman also embodies an opposite impulse of indeterminacy (see *AN*, 343).

24. Henry James, *Autobiography*, ed. Frederick W. Dupee (New York: Criterion, 1956), 412.

25. H. James, *Literary Criticism: American*, 383.

26. Fredric Jameson, *The Political Unconscious* (Ithaca, N.Y.: Cornell University Press, 1981), 221.

27. Adorno, *Aesthetic Theory*, 327, 8, 446.

28. *The Golden Bowl* is an even more dramatic example of how James cultivates tension between central and centered consciousness: the fall into knowledge that dissolves Maggie's identity coincides with the novel's formal shift to her perspective.

29. J. Hillis Miller subjects this passage to close and illuminating scrutiny in his *The Ethics of Reading: Kant, de Man, Eliot, Trollope, James, and Benjamin* (New York: Columbia University Press, 1987), esp. 101–17. My reading of Henry James as pragmatist concurs with Miller's emphasis that in James praxis and ethics always take precedence over epistemology and aesthetics (102). But I would revise Miller by arguing that, for James, the aesthetic *is* praxis embedded in social experience.

30. Indeed prior to Lubbock's idealist reading of James's "craft of fiction," critics like Brownell faulted James for a lack of organic harmony.

31. Laurence Holland's seminal *The Expense of Vision: Essays on the Craft of Henry James* (1964; reprint, Baltimore: Johns Hopkins University Press, 1982) was the first to dissent from Blackmur's influential reading of the prefaces as magisterial and to stress their insistent eliciting of crisis, risk, and uncertainty. See also David Carroll's important discussion of the mobile, irresolvable tensions and displacements that circulate throughout the prefaces: *The Subject in Question: The Language of Theory and the Strategies of Fiction* (Chicago: University of Chicago Press, 1982), 51–66.

32. Adorno, *Aesthetic Theory*, 485.

33. Ibid., 161.

34. *Henry James Letters*, ed. Leon Edel, vol. 1 (Cambridge, Mass.: Harvard University Press, 1974), 181.

35. Adorno, *Aesthetic Theory*, 80.

36. James, *American Scene*, 121.

37. Ibid., 1.

38. H. James, quoted in F. O. Matthiessen, *The James Family* (New York: Knopf, 1961), 310.

39. H. James, quoted ibid.

40. H. James, *American Scene*, 407–8.

41. W. Benjamin, quoted in Jennings, *Dialectical Images*, 26.

42. Benjamin, *Origin*, 28.

43. Adorno, *Negative Dialectics*, 160.

44. H. James, *American Scene*, 273.

45. Ibid.

46. Ibid., 136. The fascination with the "mystic meaning of objects" shared by James, Benjamin, and Proust instances the positive meaning of "aura."

47. Matthiessen suggests something of my point when he describes James before his visit to America as needing to "break the web of his own enchantment." F. O. Matthiessen, *Henry James: The Major Phase* (1944; reprint, New York: Oxford University Press, 1963), 105.

Culver: Ozymandias and the Mastery of Ruins

1. The reference to "Ozymandias" appears in a letter to Edmund Gosse written in August 1915: *Henry James Letters*, ed. Leon Edel, vol. 4 (Cambridge, Mass.: Harvard University Press, 1984), 776–78. For Edel's discussion of the letter see Leon Edel, *Henry James: The Master, 1901–1916* (Philadelphia: J. B. Lippincott, 1972), 321–39.

2. Percy Bysshe Shelley, "Ozymandias," *Shelley's Poetry and Prose*, eds. Donald H. Reiman and Sharon Powers (New York: W. W. Norton, 1977), 103.

3. I have tried to describe the relations between this marketing strategy and the late style in general in my "Representing the Author: Henry James, Intellectual Property, and the Work of Writing," in *Henry James: Fiction as History*, ed. Ian F. A. Bell (New York: Barnes and Noble, 1984), 114–36. For a similar account of James's logic of delegation see Julie Rivkin, "The Logic of Delegation in *The Ambassadors*," *PMLA* 101 (Oct. 1986): 819–31.

4. For an account of the early years of American copyright law and the case made against international protection see James J. Barnes, *Authors, Publishers and Politicians: The Quest for an Anglo-American Copyright Agreement, 1815–1854* (London: Routledge, 1974).

5. Walter Hines Page, *A Publisher's Confession* (Garden City, N.J.: Doubleday and Page, 1905), 109.

6. James's letter was included in *What American Authors Think About International Copyright* (New York: American Copyright League, 1888), but it originally appeared in *The Critic* on Dec. 10, 1887.

7. Helmutt Lehmann-Haupt, *The Book in America* (New York: Bowker, 1952), and Charles A. Madison, *Book Publishing in America* (New York: McGraw-Hill, 1966), provide overviews of the deluxe boom of the 1890's.

8. Roger Burlingame, *Of Making Many Books* (New York: Scribner's, 1946), provides an in-house history of Charles Scribner's Sons, but see also Donald Sheehan, *This Was Publishing: The Book Trade in the Gilded Age* (Bloomington: Indiana University Press, 1952), 191–93.

9. Henry James to Rudyard Kipling, Sept. 16, 1899, *Henry James Letters* 4: 120.

10. *The Nation* 83 (Jan. 3, 1907): 2; and 84 (Feb. 14, 1907): 149.

11. Michel Foucault, "What Is an Author?," in *Textual Strategies: Perspectives in Post-Structuralist Criticism*, ed. Josué V. Harari (Ithaca, N.Y.: Cornell University Press, 1979), 159.

12. Joseph Conrad, "Henry James: An Appreciation," *North American Review* 180 (Jan. 1905): 102.

13. Ibid., 108.

14. For a sense of James's thinking at this time see his letter to Leroy Phillips, who was compiling a complete bibliography of the novelist: "Authors in general do not find themselves interested in a mercilessly complete resuscitation of their writings." *Henry James Letters* 4: 320.

15. See Michael Anesko, *"Friction with the Market": Henry James and the Profession of Authorship* (New York: Oxford University Press, 1986), chap. 7, for a detailed account of James's negotiations with the Scribners.

16. Henry James to Robert Herrick, Aug. 7, 1905, *Henry James Letters* 4: 371.

17. "Why Mr. James Revised," *The Literary Digest* 29 (Aug. 21, 1909): 275–76.

18. Anne Margolis has proposed that the later James was something of a divided artist who wanted to be both a vaudevillian playing to the public in general and an aesthete read by a discriminating and select audience. Thus, her argument goes, the New York Edition seemed to allow James to address both audiences at once. See her *Henry James and the Problem of Audience: An International Act* (Ann Arbor, Mich.: UMI Research Press, 1985). But I would argue that James explicitly rejects this "both/and" logic in "The Next Time": trapped by a more complicated paradox, Ralph Limbert has to try to please *le gros public* and fail in order to produce his works of genius and find his devotees in the first place (i.e., he fails to be the one in order to become the other).

19. William James, *The Principles of Psychology*, 2 vols. (New York: Holt, 1890) 1: 334. My attention was first drawn to this passage by Walter Benn Michaels. See his discussion of *The Principles of Psychology* in his *The Gold Standard and the Logic of Naturalism* (Berkeley: University of California Press, 1987).

20. W. James, *Principles of Psychology* 1: 340.

21. Ibid., 312.

22. In his persuasive account of the "psychic economies" of William and Henry James, Ross Posnock opposes the philosopher's fear of vastation and his tendency to regard the mind as "an engine of rationalistic control" to the novelist's willingness to be invaded by otherness and his readiness to see his passive gaze as in fact active and productive: where William is concerned to carefully cultivate

mental habits and avoid useless speculation, Henry is perfectly willing just to wonder. What I am arguing here may seem at first glance antithetical to Posnock's account, but I believe it merely takes it one step further: William cultivates habits to limit wonder, saving speculative energies for questions of pure philosophy, but Henry begins with wonder and then carefully cuts back, moving from the acceptance of otherness to an editorial disavowal. See Ross Posnock, "William and Henry James," *Raritan* 8 (Winter 1989): 1–26, and W. James, *Principles of Psychology* 2: 120–27.

23. Henry James to Charles Scribner's Sons, July 30, 1905, *Henry James Letters* 4: 367.

24. Brownell is cited in Anesko, *"Friction with the Market,"* 154, but cf. James's letter to the Scribners of Dec. 31, 1907, in which he accepts what he takes to be Brownell's decision to keep all the novels together. Anesko reads this as an example of James's readiness to compromise his design, but clearly Brownell's response indicates that he, at least, felt the novelist was too concerned with introducing into the collection rival forms of order that would compromise the chronological representation of his career. See *Henry James Letters* 4: 484–85.

25. Edel, in *Henry James Letters* 4: 366–68.

26. Henry James to Scribner's, July 30, 1905, *Henry James Letters* 4: 366.

27. Leon Edel, "The Architecture of Henry James's 'New York Edition,'" *New England Quarterly* 24 (June 1951): 176–77.

28. Henry James, "Honoré Balzac (1902)," in his *Notes on Novelists* (New York: Scribner's, 1914): 109–42, 121, 115, 117, 118.

29. Henry James to the Scribners, July 30, 1905, *Henry James Letters* 4: 368.

30. Anesko, *"Friction with the Market,"* 162.

Blair: In the House of Fiction

1. Recently influential readings of James that very differently privilege the moral or ethical dimensions of his art include Deborah Esch's "The Senses of the Past: The Rhetoric of Temporality in Henry James" (University Microfilms: Yale University Press, 1985); Martha Nussbaum's *Love's Knowledge: Essays on Philosophy and Literature* (New York: Oxford University Press, 1990); and John Carlos Rowe's *The Theoretical Dimensions of Henry James* (Madison: University of Wisconsin Press, 1984).

2. The terms of this critical debate are usefully rehearsed by Ross Posnock and Martha Banta; see their essays in this collection.

3. More recently, Carren Kaston's Introduction to her *Imagination and Desire in Henry James* (New Brunswick: Rutgers University Press, 1984), 1–17, usefully allows the notion of the house of fiction to stand for James's practice in order to generate a reading of the doubleness of his investments in renunciation.

4. In this gesture, the Preface exemplifies what Richard Brodhead, *The School of Hawthorne* (New York: Oxford University Press, 1986), has called James's "will to completion," a drive encoded in the late style to "give his writing the retroactive character of a completed *oeuvre*" (171, 138). Crucial to that aura of completion, however—as the figure in question makes clear—is its accommodation of infinite variety, excess, the "spreading field" of social and semantic possibilities.

5. An exception is Lynn Wardley's richly suggestive reading in "Woman's Voice, Democracy's Body, and *The Bostonians*," *English Literary History* 56 (Fall 1989) 3: 648–50.

6. Recent feminist readings of James that play out and against this ambivalence include Alfred Habegger's controversial *Henry James and the "Woman Business"* (New York: Cambridge University Press, 1989), which tends to replicate the imagination of mastery it critiques in its privileging of James's oedipal desires and designs; Beth Ash's "Frail Vessels and Vast Designs: A Psychoanalytic Portrait of Isabel Archer," in *New Essays on "The Portrait of a Lady*," ed. Joel Porte (New York: Cambridge University Press, 1990), 123–62; Donna Przybylowicz's *Desire and Repression: The Dialectic of Self and Other in the Late Works of Henry James* (University, Ala.: The University of Alabama Press, 1986); and Judith Fetterley's "Henry James's Eternal Triangle," in her *The Resisting Reader: A Feminist Approach to American Fiction* (Bloomington: Indiana University Press, 1978), 101–53. More recently, readers of James's fictions as texts of queerness have displayed a homologous ambivalence about the unstably homoerotic, homosocial, and homophobic resonances of his textuality; see particularly Eve Kosofsky Sedgwick, "The Beast in the Closet," in her *Epistemology of the Closet* (Berkeley: University of California Press, 1991), 182–212, whose unstably queered James contends with the more openly queer textual production asserted in Sedgwick's "Is the Rectum Straight? Identification and Identity in *The Wings of the Dove*," in her *Tendencies* (Durham: Duke University Press, 1993), 52–72, and Michael Moon's "Sexuality and Visual Terrorism in *The Wings of the Dove*," *Criticism* 28 (Fall 1986): 427–43.

7. Habegger, *Henry James and the "Woman Business*," 230; throughout, he is particularly interested in James's authority to "impose" "moral integrity" on women's fiction and to author master fictions of women's historical experiences and practices (122).

8. My reading draws on a number of influential studies of the uses made of the ideology of separate spheres for staking claims for literature as a cultural practice; they include: Cathy Davidson, *Revolution and the Word: The Rise of the Novel in America* (New York: Oxford University Press, 1986); Jane Tompkins, *Sensational Designs* (New York: Cornell University Press, 1978); Mary Kelley, *Private Woman, Public Stage: Literary Domesticity in Nineteenth-Century America* (New

York: Oxford University Press, 1984); and Nancy Armstrong, *Desire and Domestic Fiction: A Political History of the Novel* (New York: Oxford University Press, 1987).

9. I recapitulate the widely influential argument of Ann Douglas, *The Feminization of American Culture* (New York: Alfred A. Knopf, 1977), that discourses of domesticity develop in an (ultimately spurious) attempt within genteel culture to combat the ascendancy of the middle classes and to erase—as James's indictments of enterprising America intermittently do—the continuities between genteel or high culture and the culture of the marketplace it seeks to contain.

10. In "The Portrait of a Lack," in Porte, ed., *New Essays on "The Portrait of a Lady,"* 95–121, William Veeder argues that the distinction raised in the novel itself between downtown and uptown "does not square finally" with the difference of "man versus woman" but rather with a "thematic" distinction between "business" and "pleasure" (98). Clearly, James's acts of identification with female experience and values imply that "woman" is a gendered construct, a "fate available to individuals" (99), yet such fates are themselves gendered, as Veeder's linking in James of pleasure, failure of identity, and feminization or castration would suggest.

11. Amy Kaplan considers this analogy with close attention to the site of the home as a self-transcending locus for women writers' self-constructions in "Edith Wharton's Profession of Authorship," in her *The Social Construction of American Realism* (Chicago: University of Chicago Press, 1988), 65–87.

12. Henry James's remarks on America's capital city in *The American Scene* [1907] (Bloomington: Indiana University Press, 1968), 339–52, evince the same discomfort with a breached boundary, or "contract," of difference between the private sphere of femininity and the public sphere of male institutionality; he argues that the cost of America's uniquely "woman-made society" is the dehumanization of the American woman, who, having taken "upon herself a certain training for freedom," has been transformed into "a new human convenience"—but also hints that she no longer serves as the vehicle for the male novelist's representational desires. In James's lectures to and about American women, more straightforwardly regulatory motives prevail; his comments linking the problematic composition of America, for the returning master, with a feminization of its values were reproduced in *Harper's Bazaar* of Nov.–Dec. 1906 and Jan.–Feb. 1907.

13. Rowe, *Theoretical Dimensions*, 87. Freud's etymology in "The 'Uncanny,'" in his *On Creativity and the Unconscious: Papers on the Psychology of Art, Literature, Love, Religion* (New York: Harper and Row, 1958), 124–29, is apposite.

14. Habegger, *Henry James and the "Woman Business,"* 116–17 and chap. 7, "The Fatherless Heroine and the Filial Son: Deep Background for *The Portrait of a Lady,"* 150–81. Surprisingly, given his insistence on the oedipal exorcism per-

formed by the *Portrait*, Habegger doesn't stress the regulatory dimension of James's Preface except in regard to its treatment of Minny Temple; he remarks that James wrote it "three decades after first working on *The Portrait*, and he inevitably forgot a great deal. He also boasted" (115). Finally, Habegger dismisses James's misreadings in the Preface as "huffing and puffing three decades later" rather than regarding them as strategic revaluations.

15. As Habegger notes, James misrepresents even the formal achievement of the *Portrait* as a *bildungsroman*; the response of a contemporaneous critic, Charlotte Porter, in "The Serial Story," *Century Magazine* 30 (Sept. 1885): 812–13 (cited in Habegger, *Henry James and the "Woman Business,"* 115), makes the nature of this misrepresentation clear. She argues that most serial novels of the period employ the very narrative strategy James claims as original to the *Portrait*—that is, to "'[p]lace the centre of the subject in the young woman's own consciousness" (*3*: xv; *AN*, 51)—and thereby to "revea[l] the individuality of the heroine" in "an altogether new estimate of woman's moral value." Likewise, a thoroughly Jamesian F. R. Leavis, in *The Great Tradition* (New York: Penguin Books, 1948), 20 n. 1, remarks parenthetically that James "can't have failed to note with interest that *Emma* fulfills, by anticipation, a prescription of his own: everything is presented through Emma's dramatized consciousness, and the essential effects depend on that." Susan Fraiman, in *Unbecoming Women: British Women Writers and the Novel of Development* (New York: Columbia University Press, 1993), cogently theorizes the consequences for readings of the *bildungsroman* of reconsidering the location of narrative within women's experience and the female "center" of consciousness.

16. In *Thinking in Henry James* (Chicago: University of Chicago Press, 1989), 53–54, Sharon Cameron discusses James's "skewing" of Eliot's literary doctrine in his foreshortened version of this passage. Although her remarks are extremely suggestive with regard to James's gendered anxiety of influence, Cameron focuses on the ways in which James's censorship of Eliot analogizes the Preface's nostalgic representation of consciousness as autonomous, distinct, "free" of the tangle of circumstances and "unified," as against James's novelistic, and masterful, treatment of consciousness as "disseminated" (54, 76–77).

17. A *ficelle* is a string or thread; a dodge, a stage trick. To show (*montrer*) the *ficelle* is to betray a secret motive; to know (*connaître*) the *ficelle* is to know the tricks of the trade; to pull on (*tirer sur*) the *ficelle* is to go too far.

18. In her extraordinarily supple study of Jamesian epistemology, *Language and Knowledge in the Late Novels of Henry James* (Chicago: University of Chicago Press, 1976), Ruth Bernard Yeazell lucidly recovers the joint image-making engaged in by James's "central" consciousnesses and their associated *ficelles*, and in particular Maria Gostrey. Yeazell also identifies James's disclaimer for the *ficelle* as a "disingenuous" denial of her power and his own (52–53 and 67–76, from two apposite chapters: "The Imagination of Metaphor" and "Talking in James").

Anesko: Ambiguous Allegiances

NOTE: Funding to secure the photographs that accompany this essay was generously provided by the Hyder Rollins Fund of the Department of English and
American Literature and Language, Harvard University. Permission to quote
from unpublished sources has gratefully been received from Alexander R. James;
The British Library; William Heinemann Ltd.; Macmillan Publishers Ltd.;
John Murray (Publishers) Ltd.; the New York Public Library; Princeton University Library; and the Collection of American Literature, Beinecke Rare Book
and Manuscript Library, Yale University.

    1. See, for example, Herbert Croly, "Henry James and His Countrymen,"
The Lamp 28 (1904): 47–53.

    2. "The Novels and Tales of Henry James," *The Book Buyer* 32 (Dec. 1907):
212.

    3. "Uniform Editions," *Publishers' Weekly*, Aug. 5, 1882, p. 171.

    4. My earlier work on James, *"Friction with the Market": Henry James and the
Profession of Authorship* (New York: Oxford University Press, 1986), discusses the
Edition's complicated American publishing history (141–62). For Howells, see
my *Profession of Letters: The Correspondence of Henry James and William Dean
Howells* (New York: Oxford University Press, forthcoming 1996) and Edwin H.
Cady, *The Realist at War: The Mature Years 1885–1920 of William Dean Howells*
(Syracuse, N.Y.: Syracuse University Press, 1958), 253–54.

    5. Henry James to Charles Scribner's Sons, May 9, 1906, *Henry James Let-
ters*, 4 vols., ed. Leon Edel (Cambridge, Mass.: Harvard University Press,
1974–84) 4: 403, James's emphasis.

    6. Henry James to James B. Pinker, [Dec. 31, 1907] (Collection of Ameri-
can Literature, Yale).

    7. Edward Clark Marsh, "Henry James: Auto-Critic," *Bookman* 30 (1909):
138. Linda J. Taylor has compiled more than 60 notices of the New York Edition
which appeared in newspapers and magazines throughout the United States; see
Henry James, 1866–1916: A Reference Guide (Boston: G. K. Hall, 1982), 397–
421, passim.

    8. James's work was not always so handsomely treated. When the Macmillans
published the author's first collected edition in 1883, they dispensed with fair-
margined pages in favor of compact presentation and low price. While the idea of
issuing his works in a uniform edition appealed to James, he openly wondered
whether sufficient charm and physical attractiveness could be obtained at eighteen
pence a volume. Macmillan's sample page did not discourage him from pursuing
the enterprise, the material signal of James's true coming of age in the London
literary world. See Henry James to Frederick Macmillan, Apr. 19, 1883, *Henry
James Letters* 2: 410–11.

9. Henry James, "The Future of the Novel" [1899], in *Literary Criticism: Essays on Literature, American Writers, English Writers*, ed. Leon Edel and Mark Wilson (New York: Library of America, 1984), 103.

10. "Novels and Tales of Henry James," 212.

11. Henry James to Charles Scribner's Sons, Dec. 31, 1907, *Henry James Letters* 4. 484, Archibald Constable & Co. Ltd. to James B. Pinker, Jan. 16, 1908 (Collection of American Literature, Yale).

12. Archibald Constable & Co. Ltd. to Charles Scribner, Mar. 14, 1906 (Scribner Archive, Princeton).

13. Charles Scribner to William Meredith, Mar. 28, 1906, Charles Scribner Letterbooks 26: 42 (Scribner Archive, Princeton).

14. On June 6, 1905, James urged Pinker to remember, when he was first negotiating with Scribner's, that "my idea is a Handsome Book, distinctly, not less so than the definitive RLS or the ditto GM" (Collection of American Literature, Yale). The latter example may have been especially important to James, because Meredith had also used the occasion of collecting his works as an opportunity for extensively revising them. As the publisher's prospectus revealed, "for some time Mr. George Meredith has been carefully revising his works, and the text of Constable's Edition is the one which Mr. George Meredith wishes to be considered as final." The Scribner's prospectus for the New York Edition would boast a similar claim. See Michael Collie, *George Meredith: A Bibliography* (Toronto: University of Toronto Press, 1974), 259–60.

15. Archibald Constable & Co. Ltd. to Charles Scribner, Mar. 14, 1906 (Scribner Archive, Princeton University).

16. James B. Pinker to Charles Scribner's Sons, Feb. 28, 1908 (Scribner Archive, Princeton University).

17. Henry James to James B. Pinker, Feb. 29, 1908 (Collection of American Literature, Yale).

18. John Murray, Jr., to [Lemuel] Bangs, Feb. 27, 1908 (Scribner Archive, Princeton). Bangs was the Scribners' representative in London; his correspondence with the New York office frequently includes letters from English publishers forwarded on to the United States.

19. Charles Scribner's Sons to James B. Pinker, Mar. 24, 1908 (Berg Collection, New York Public Library).

20. Charles Scribner to Lemuel Bangs, Mar. 31 1908, Charles Scribner Letterbooks 7: 101 (Scribner Archive, Princeton).

21. "I simply couldn't live without him," James wrote Edith Wharton on July 2, 1906; see *Henry James and Edith Wharton Letters: 1900–1915*, ed. Lyall Powers (New York: Scribner's, 1990), 65.

22. Charles Scribner to Lemuel Bangs, June 23, 1908, Charles Scribner Letterbooks 7: 105 (Scribner Archive, Princeton).

23. Frederick Macmillan to William Heinemann, June 18, 1908, Add. MS 55491, p. 160 (Macmillan Archive, British Library).

24. William Heinemann to Frederick Macmillan, June 19, 1908, Add. MS 54887, f. 74; Macmillan to Heinemann, June 26, 1908, Add. MS 55491, p. 312; Heinemann to Macmillan, July 2, 1908, Add. MS 54887, f. 75; Macmillan to Heinemann, July 3, 1908, Add. MS 55491, p. 458 (Macmillan Archive, British Library).

25. Henry James to Frederick Macmillan, Sept. 6, 1908, *The Correspondence of Henry James and the House of Macmillan, 1877–1914*, ed. Rayburn S. Moore (Baton Rouge: Louisiana State University Press, 1993), 215.

26. See, for example, *Publishers' Circular* 89 (Oct. 3, 1908): 487.

27. See Leon Edel, Dan H. Laurence, and James Rambeau, *A Bibliography of Henry James*, 3rd ed. (Oxford: Clarendon Press, 1982), 138–39.

28. Evidence of continued demand is scattered through a long series of letters from Lemuel Bangs back to the New York office. It is more than likely that records of additional orders have not survived. Significantly, the numbers trace a wavelike motion in demand, rippling according to the sequence of publication, which suggests that purchasers of the early volumes stayed loyal and continued to buy the remainder as they appeared. Volumes 7 and 8 of the Edition (*The Tragic Muse*), as well as volume 14 (*Lady Barbarina, . . .*) are interesting exceptions, however; sales of these (225 copies) lagged behind all the rest by 10–25 percent. Predictably, the highest number tallied is for volume 1—*Roderick Hudson* (312 copies ordered as of Aug. 1916). The relevant Bangs letters are contained in folders 56–72, "To Charles Scribner from London" (Scribner Archive, Princeton).

29. Henry James to James B. Pinker, Oct. 13, 1908 (Collection of American Literature, Yale).

30. Henry James to James B. Pinker, Mar. 17, 1909 (Collection of American Literature, Yale).

31. Henry James to Frederick Macmillan, Mar. 17, 1909, *Correspondence of James and Macmillan*, 217.

32. Frederick Macmillan to Henry James, Mar. 18, 1909, *Correspondence of James and Macmillan*, 218.

33. For James's earnings beyond the advance, see his letters to James B. Pinker, Nov. 2, 1912, and May 4, 1915 (Collection of American Literature, Yale). For the publishers' proposals, see James to Pinker, Aug. 1, 1914, and Oct. 17, 1915 (Yale); Thomas Nelson & Sons to Pinker, Oct. 20, 1915, and J. M. Dent & Sons to Pinker, Oct. 25, 1915 (Houghton Library, Harvard).

34. Percy Lubbock to Frederick Macmillan, Sept. 21, 1919, Add. MS 55033, ff. 157–58; Macmillan to Lubbock, Sept. 23, 1919, Add. MS 55556, p. 977 (Macmillan Archive, British Library).

35. Henry James to James B. Pinker, June 6, 1905 (Collection of American Literature, Yale).

36. "Novels and Tales of Henry James," 212.

37. Levin L. Schücking, *The Sociology of Literary Taste* (1944; reprint, Chicago: University of Chicago Press, 1966), 54.

Nadel: Visual Culture

1. The following are my primary sources: Henry James, Preface to *The Golden Bowl*, vols. 23–24 of the New York Edition; idem, *The Art of the Novel: Critical Prefaces by Henry James*, ed. Richard P. Blackmur (New York: Charles Scribner's Sons, 1934), 331–35; Joseph J. Firebaugh, "Coburn: Henry James' Photographer," *American Quarterly* 7 (1955): 215–33; Charles Higgins, "Photographic Aperture: Coburn's Frontispieces to James' New York Edition," *American Literature* 53 (1982): 661–75; Ralph F. Bogardus, *Pictures and Texts: Henry James, A. L. Coburn, and New Ways of Seeing in Literary Culture* (Ann Arbor, Mich.: UMI Research Press, 1984); Carol Shloss, "Henry James and Alvin Langdon Coburn, The Frame of Prevision," in her *In Visible Light: Photography and the American Writer: 1840–1940* (New York: Oxford University Press, 1987), 55–89; Stuart Culver, "How Photographs Mean: Literature and the Camera in American Studies," *American Literary History* 1 (1989): 190–205.

2. See in particular Michael Anesko, *"Friction with the Market": Henry James and the Profession of Authorship* (New York: Oxford University Press, 1986), 11–24, 141–66. On page 21 Anesko refers to James's "burning desire for popular acclaim." See also Philip Horne, *Henry James and Revision: The New York Edition* (Oxford: Clarendon Press, 1990), 1–20.

3. In that year the critic Charles Caffin published *Photography as a Fine Art* (1901; Hastings on Hudson, N.Y.: Morgan and Morgan, 1971). In February 1902 Alfred Stieglitz formed the Photo-Secessionist group to counter the conservative, conventional, and traditional elements that dominated American photography. It coincided with the exhibition arranged by Stieglitz at the National Arts Club in New York which he titled "American Pictorial Photography Arranged by the 'Photo-Secession.'" See William Innes Homer, *Alfred Stieglitz and the American Avant-Garde* (Boston: New York Graphic Society, 1977), 28.

4. See Miles Orvell, *The Real Thing: Imitation and Authenticity in American Culture 1880–1940* (Chapel Hill: University of North Carolina Press, 1989), for a discussion of this transformation.

5. See James B. Colson, "Stieglitz, Strand and Straight Photography," in *Perspectives in Photography*, ed. David Oliphant and Thomas Zigal (Austin, Tex.: Ransom Humanities Research Center, 1982), 103–23.

6. Alvin Langdon Coburn, "Pythagoras," in Mike Weaver, *Alvin Langdon*

Coburn, Symbolist Photographer, 1882–1966 (New York: Aperture, 1986), 11.

7. Roland Barthes, *Camera Lucida*, trans. Richard Howard (London: Jonathan Cape, 1982), 76.

8. To the illustrator Joseph Pennell, who was to provide pictures for James's essay "London," James explained that the images "ought to be freely and fancifully drawn; *not* with neat, definite photographic 'views.'" *Henry James Letters*, ed. Leon Edel, 4 vols. (Cambridge: Mass., Harvard University Press, 1974–84) 3: 218.

9. Ibid. 3: 227.

10. Ibid. 4: 384; for a reproduction see 4: 385.

11. Ibid. 4: 394–95.

12. Ibid. 4: 406. For a photograph of James and Andersen in the sculptor's Rome studio see 4: 452.

13. Walter Benjamin provocatively remarks that captions turn "all the relations of life into literature, and without [them there] are signs that all photographic construction must remain bound in coincidences." "A Short History of Photography" (1931), in *Classic Essays on Photography*, ed. Alan Trachtenberg (New Haven, Conn.: Leete's Island Books, 1980), 215.

14. See *Henry James Letters* 4: 366.

15. Ibid. 4: 371.

16. Ibid. 4: 403, James's emphasis.

17. Ibid. 4: 368.

18. On Coburn and the Photo-Secessionists see Shloss, *In Visible Light*, 56, 61–62.

19. *Eclectic Magazine* (1854), quoted in Russel B. Nye, "Notes on Photography and American Culture, 1839–1890," in *Toward a New American Literary History*, ed. Louis J. Budd et al. (Durham, N.C.: Duke University Press, 1980), 254, emphasis in the original.

20. "Handsomely Illustrated," *Atlantic Monthly* 93 (1904): 137.

21. Leon Edel, *Henry James: The Master, 1901–1916* (Philadelphia: J. B. Lippincott, 1972), 333. See *Henry James Letters* 4: 368, 408. In "The Real Thing," the narrator is an illustrator preparing drawings for a definitive edition of an author's work.

22. *Henry James Letters* 4: 408.

23. See Appendix C for a chronology that documents the association between Coburn and James and chronicles the picture-taking process of the frontispieces.

24. *Henry James Letters* 4: 408.

25. See Horne, *Henry James and Revision*, 3–14, and Anesko, *"Friction with the Market."*

26. Horne, *Henry James and Revision*, 2, 349–51.

27. In Horne, *Henry James and Revision*, 351.

28. Henry James to James B. Pinker, May 20, 1914, in Anne T. Margolis, *Henry James and the Problem of Audience: An International Act* (Ann Arbor, Mich.: UMI Research Press, 1985), xiv. James's reaction to the poor reception and dismal "performance" of the New York Edition precipitated, of course, a crisis of confidence and his nervous breakdown of 1909–10. During this period, on a particularly bad day, James burned most of his letters and literary archive. See Edel, *Henry James: The Master*, 437.

29. Nathaniel Hawthorne, *The Scarlet Letter*, 3rd ed., ed. Seymour Gross et al. (New York: W. W. Norton, 1988), 9.

30. Ibid., 21.

31. Ibid., 22.

32. Henry James, *Hawthorne*, intro. Tony Tanner (New York: St. Martin's Press, 1967), 23.

33. Henry James, "Emerson," in his *Partial Portraits* (1887; Ann Arbor: University of Michigan Press, 1970), 15; cited by Tanner in H. James, *Hawthorne*, 7.

34. H. James, *Hawthorne*, 45.

35. Ibid., 46.

36. Henry Adams, *The Education of Henry Adams*, ed. Ernest Samuels (Boston: Houghton Mifflin Riverside, 1973), 297.

37. Ibid., 306, 328.

38. "Editor's Easy Chair," *Harper's New Monthly Magazine*, 34 (Jan. 1867): 261.

39. Hawthorne, *Scarlet Letter*, 34.

40. *Education of Henry Adams*, 243.

41. Henry James to Claude Phillips, Keeper of the Wallace Collection, in Leon Edel, *Henry James: The Master*, 337–38.

42. *Henry James Letters* 4: 430–31, James's emphasis. Another literary inspiration at the Wallace Collection is Poussin's seventeenth-century painting *A Dance to the Music of Time*, the title of which was used by Anthony Powell for his series of novels.

43. For a discussion of arches and bridges in the New York Edition see Higgins, "Photographic Aperture," 670–74. Higgins does not identify the Ponte Sant' Angelo, however. Bernini's work appears in another Coburn photograph: "By St. Peter's," the frontispiece to vol. 18, containing *Daisy Miller* and nine other stories. Visible in the picture is a portion of the 96 saints and martyrs by Bernini that embellish his magnificent colonnade composed of Doric columns four deep at Vatican square.

44. *Henry James Letters* 4: 429.

McGann: Revision, Rewriting, Rereading

1. Henry James, *The Ambassadors*, ed. S. P. Rosenbaum, Norton Critical Edition (New York: W. W. Norton, 1964).
2. Quoting Robert E. Young, "An Error in *The Ambassadors*," *American Literature* 22 (Nov. 1950): 245. Further page references to this article will be included in the text.
3. Another essay, by Susan M. Humphreys, discussed the chronological problems of the two chapters, but Humphreys did not reach Young's conclusion. Indeed, she seems to have written her piece without knowing of Young's essay, which had been published four years earlier. See Humphreys, "Henry James's Revisions for *The Ambassadors*," *Notes and Queries* 199 (Sept. 1954): 397–99.
4. Edel accepted it in the first of his responses to Young's essay; see Leon Edel, "A Further Note on 'An Error in *The Ambassadors*,'" *American Literature* 23 (Mar. 1951): 128–30; and see Young's reply, "A Final Note on *The Ambassadors*," *American Literature* 23 (Jan. 1952): 487–90.
5. For a convenient general narrative of the bibliographical events see S. P. Rosenbaum's discussion "Editions and Revisions," in his Norton Critical Edition, 353–67. But see Brian Birch's important essay on the process of the novel's revisions: "Henry James: Some Bibliographical and Textual Matters," *The Library* (1965): 108–23. Birch's essay corrects a number of crucial misrepresentations in Edel's work and Rosenbaum's.
6. See Yvor Winters, "Problems for the Modern Critic of Literature," *Hudson Review* 9 (Autumn 1956): esp. 348–50.
7. Leon Edel, "The Text of *The Ambassadors*," *Harvard Library Bulletin* 14 (1960): 460.
8. Leon Edel, Dan H. Laurence, and James Rambeau, *A Bibliography of Henry James*, 3rd ed. (Oxford: Clarendon Press, 1982), 125.
9. See Birch, "Henry James," esp. 114–23, where the deficiencies of the Methuen text are clearly exposed.
10. See Birch, "Henry James," 114.
11. "If you read The Ambassadors (it's long) kindly remember that it is an *old* book—I mean it was finished 2 years before the W. of the Dove was published; and I feel myself a kind of staleness and mistimedness in it." Henry James to Mrs. Humphry Ward, Oct. 27, 1903, C. Waller Barrett Collection, University of Virginia Library. The letter of December 16, discussed below, is also in the Barrett Collection. Both letters are printed here with permission.
12. In fact, Edel quotes salient parts of the December 16 letter in his *Harvard Library Bulletin* essay and wonders if James were writing to Ward about "the misplaced chapter." But he dismisses his thought because "Mrs. Ward would almost certainly have been reading the English edition, where the chapters are in

proper sequence" ("Text of *The Ambassadors*," 456). But of course Edel has missed the evident significance of the letter only because of his (misguided) faith in the accuracy of the Methuen text. (See also Rosenbaum's Norton Critical Edition, 408, where a brief passage from Edel's essay is quoted, including salient passages from James's letter to Ward.)

13. The Harper edition was not published until November and would not have been available to Mrs. Ward. We don't know—but have to presume—that James saw the Harper edition by the time of his second letter to Mrs. Ward.

14. As the rest of the conversation shows, Henry clearly believes that the problems of the text have been put to rest by his editorial revelation and analysis. That this may be a naive view is strongly suggested in Jerome McGann, "The Case of *The Ambassadors* and the Textual Condition," in *Palimpsest: Editorial Theory in the Humanities*, ed. George Bornstein and Ralph G. Williams (Ann Arbor: University of Michigan Press, 1993), 151–66.

15. James himself saw this set of circumstances as the climactic focus of the novel's emotional interest. See his "Project of Novel by Henry James," reprinted from F. O. Matthiessen and Kenneth Murdock's edition of *The Notebooks of Henry James*, in Rosenbaum's Norton Critical Edition, 375–404; see esp. 402–3.

16. See Winters, "Problems for the Modern Critic," 348–49.

17. Ibid., 351.

18. Because of the dialogue form of this work, an odd ambiguity appears in this final Tennyson allusion. Orally the statement might be taken to say exactly the opposite of what its printed form says; for we can *hear* the words as "Oh, that were possible." How is a reader to read it?—PRINTER'S DEVIL.

Armstrong: Reading James's Prefaces

1. J. Hillis Miller, *The Ethics of Reading: Kant, de Man, Eliot, Trollope, James, and Benjamin* (New York: Columbia University Press, 1987), 118. Miller would no doubt contest this definition of translation. As is well known, he is skeptical of the ability of any reading, including any translation, to render a text faithfully: "genuine reading is a kind of misreading. The value of a reading, against all reason, lies in its difference and deviation from the text it purports to read" (118). Differing slightly but significantly from Miller, I will argue that the deviation of the prefaces from the texts they present aims to educate readers to read in ways appropriate to James's novels, so that a notion of "right reading" is preserved by the prefaces through their very act of transgressing it.

2. See E. H. Gombrich, *Art and Illusion* (Princeton, N.J.: Princeton University Press, 1969), 4–5.

3. For more extensive analyses of this doubleness, see my book *The Challenge of Bewilderment: Understanding and Representation in James, Conrad, and Ford* (Ithaca, N.Y.: Cornell University Press, 1987), 45–62, 72–77.

4. See Leon Edel, *Henry James: The Master, 1901–1916* (Philadelphia: J. B. Lippincott, 1972), 322–23.

5. On the complexities of James's handling of point of view in *The Golden Bowl*, see my book *The Phenomenology of Henry James* (Chapel Hill: University of North Carolina Press, 1983), 146–48, 232.

6. See Martin Heidegger, *Being and Time*, trans. John Macquarrie and Edward Robinson (New York: Harper and Row, 1962), 188–95.

7. See my *Challenge of Bewilderment*, 94–95.

8. My argument here implies that Sharon Cameron errs in attributing to the prefaces an "idea of consciousness . . . as centered, subjective, internal, and unitary" which the fictions then call into question (*Thinking in James* [Chicago: University of Chicago Press, 1989], 77). Although the acts of doubling I find invoked by both the prefaces and the novels are "subjective," their temporal and spatial dislocations suggest that nowhere in James is subjectivity a unitary structure.

9. This is also one of the morals of "The Figure in the Carpet," a story that has been widely recognized as a parable about how to read. Hugh Vereker's double act of insisting on the existence of his undiscovered plan while refusing to disclose it asserts the defining authority of the artist's intention but asks that the reader take a responsibility of analysis and appreciation equal to the writer's responsibility of creation.

10. On the ambiguity of the evidence of James's intentions in writing *The Turn of the Screw*, see my book *Conflicting Readings: Variety and Validity in Interpretation* (Chapel Hill: University of North Carolina Press, 1990), 105–7.

11. This relation of reciprocal obligation and respect between writer and reader entails an "ethics of reading" different from the curiously impersonal, even transcendental relation Miller describes: "Reading is subject not to the text as its law, but to the law to which the text is subject. This law forces the reader to betray the text or deviate from it in the act of reading it, in the name of a higher demand that can yet be reached only by way of the text" (*Ethics*, 120). Ethics has to do with relations between people and their responsibilities toward one another. If reading has an ethical dimension (and I think it does), then that is because of the ways texts mediate between people and require them to behave in certain ways if the act of mediation is to succeed (and what will count as "success" implies the establishment of ethical norms that may be subject to dispute). The transtextual "law" that Miller has in mind would displace the reciprocal obligations binding reader and writer, and it thereby transcends the ethical realm. As "a higher demand" that suspends the ethical responsibilities of one person toward another, it belongs to the sphere of religion rather than to morality, as Miller himself suggests by referring to it as "an ontological law" or an "Absolute" (122). His theory advocates, I think, not an eth-

ics but a religion of reading. On the distinction between the ethical and the religious spheres, see Søren Kierkegaard, *Fear and Trembling* (1844).

12. The phrase "glory in a gap" is praise James gives to Conrad, but it applies equally well to himself. See James, "The New Novel" (1914), in *Literary Criticism: Essays on Literature, American Writers, English Writers*, ed. Leon Edel and Mark Wilson (New York: Library of America, 1984), 148. Also worth recalling is Ford Madox Ford's praise of James for his ability to "convey an impression, an atmosphere of what you will, with literally nothing" but indeterminacies (*Henry James: A Critical Study* [1913] [New York: Boni, 1915], 153).

Miller: The "Grafted" Image

1. Stéphane Mallarmé, "Sur le Livre Illustré," in his *Oeuvres Complètes*, ed. Henri Mondor (Paris: Editions Gallimard, Bibliotheque de la Pléiade, 1945), 878.

2. Ibid.

3. This passage is cited and discussed in Ezra Pound's Introduction to *Ezra Pound in Italy* and in the chapter "Illustrating Henry James" in *Alvin Langdon Coburn: Photographer; an Autobiography* (London: Faber and Faber, 1966), 52–60.

4. Henry James, *Autobiography*, ed. Frederick W. Dupee (New York: Criterion, 1956; reprint, Princeton, N.J.: Princeton University Press, 1983), 69.

Rivkin: Doctoring the Text

1. Hershel Parker, *Flawed Texts and Verbal Icons: Literary Authority in American Fiction* (Evanston, Ill.: Northwestern University Press, 1984), 41. Here is Parker's position at somewhat greater length: "There seems no reason to doubt the obvious assumption that the farther a writer gets away from the time the creative process on a book ended, the more difficult it is for him to remember the function of individual parts and the ways those parts worked together. No hard and fast limits can be drawn: some writers have better memories than others, some re-read their own works more often than others, some wait until one novel is published and reviewed before subjecting themselves to the physical and mental distraction of undertaking a new novel, and a great deal always depends on how prolonged and overwhelming the creative process has been and how thoroughly the author is compelled to put it behind him and go on with a new work" (40). This passage gives voice to some of Parker's most important assumptions: that there is a self-contained "creative process" and that the particular knowledge available to the author during that process is the relation of part to part and part to whole. I emphasize this second attribute because it shows such an affiliation with New Criticism, the critical position he nonetheless sets out to demolish.

2. Philip Horne, *Henry James and Revision: The New York Edition* (Oxford:

Clarendon Press, 1990), 20. I am quoting from a chapter entitled "The Rights and Wrongs of Revision," which begins with this startling statement: "Dogs are notorious for returning to their own vomit." One wonders where this analogy comes from in a book that defends James's "returns" with tenacious loyalty, except in those rare instances in which they lead to factual or grammatical error (as in pronoun reference). One oddity about this chapter is that although it initially takes its title in the largest sense and examines theories of literary composition from Keats's inspiration to Tennyson's incorporation of reader's reactions, it ultimately settles with the narrow question of whether James got more things right or wrong when he revised them for the New York Edition.

3. Horne, *Henry James and Revision*, 324.
4. Ibid., 152.
5. Ibid.

Holly: The Emotional Aftermath

1. All the material quoted in this paragraph is taken from Leon Edel, *Henry James: The Master, 1901–1916* (Philadelphia: J. B. Lippincott, 1972), 433–36.
2. *The Complete Notebooks of Henry James*, ed. Leon Edel and Lyall H. Powers (New York: Oxford University Press, 1987), 260.
3. Edel, *Henry James: The Master*, 440.
4. *Henry James Letters*, ed. Leon Edel, 4 vols. (Cambridge, Mass.: Harvard University Press, 1974–84) 4: 547; *The Letters of Henry James*, ed. Percy Lubbock, vol. 2 (New York: Scribner's, 1920), 155.
5. Edel, *Henry James: The Master*, 439, 434.
6. *A Dictionary of Psychological Medicine*, ed. D. Hake Tuke (London: J. and A. Churchill, 1892), 94.
7. Howard Feinstein, "Family Therapy for the Historian?—The Case of William James," *Family Process* 20 (1981): 97.
8. Harvey Green, *Fit for America* (New York: Pantheon, 1986), 294, 295.
9. For an overview of Fletcher's career, see James Whorton, *Crusaders for Fitness: The History of American Health Reformers* (Princeton, N.J.: Princeton University Press, 1982), 168–200.
10. Horace Fletcher, *The A. B.–Z. of Our Own Nutrition* (New York: Frederick Stokes, 1903), xxi.
11. Whorton, *Crusaders for Fitness*, 180; promotional brochure for Horace Fletcher filed with William James's letters to Fletcher, James Family Papers, Houghton Library, Harvard University.
12. See William James, *The Varieties of Religious Experience* (New York: Macmillan, 1961), 154, 93.
13. Quoted in Green, *Fit for America*, 297.
14. William James to Henry James, Jan. 1, 1904, Houghton Library. This

passage and all subsequent passages taken from letters in the James Family Papers at the Houghton Library are quoted by permission of Alexander R. James and the Houghton Library, Harvard University.

15. William James to Henry James, Mar. 7, 1904; Henry James to William James, Feb. 23, 1904, Houghton Library.

16. Henry James to William James, Mar. 21 and May 6, 1904, Houghton Library; *Henry James Letters* 4: 415; Henry James to Horace Fletcher, Aug. 4, 1905, and Jan. 5, 1906, Houghton Library.

17. H. Montgomery Hyde, *Henry James at Home* (New York: Farrar, Straus and Giroux, 1969), 138.

18. Henry James to Horace Fletcher, Sept. 21, 1905; Henry James to William James, Feb. 3, 1909, Houghton Library.

19. See, for example, James's letter to his sister Alice on Oct. 6, 1869, in which he characterizes his "digestive organs" as the "bane of my existence," or his letter to William on Oct. 26, 1869, in which he discusses the "intolerable nature" of his "chronically affected . . . constipated state" (*Henry James Letters* 1: 148, 158).

20. Leon Edel, *Henry James: The Untried Years, 1843–1870* (Philadelphia: J. B. Lippincott, 1953), 312.

21. For discussions of the relationship between James's anxieties about his personal integrity, his sense of his place in the family, and his psychosomatic illnesses, see Howard Feinstein, *Becoming William James* (Ithaca, N.Y.: Cornell University Press, 1984), chap. 12; and Owen King, *The Iron of Melancholy* (Middletown, Conn.: Wesleyan University Press, 1983), chap. 2.

22. In *Becoming William James*, Feinstein interprets James's costiveness in Eriksonian terms: "As Erikson has pointed out, psychological issues recur in later stages of the life cycle. Earlier crises are constantly reexperienced and earlier solutions perpetually reworked. In young adulthood, which Erickson has labeled a time of identity formation, following one's will becomes a paramount issue once more. In a family context [like the James's] that has made separation difficult, it may have to be fought out symbolically, once again through control of one's own stool" (229).

23. Joan Brumberg, *Fasting Girls: The History of Anorexia Nervosa* (New York: New American Library, 1989), 115.

24. In his *Anorexia Nervosa: A Guide for Sufferers and Their Families* (New York: Penguin, 1980), R. L. Palmer explains that the "exercise of rigid self-control" over one's intake of food "can be viewed as a way of coping with or avoiding emotional turmoil which might otherwise be or seem to be unmanageable" (31).

25. Quoted in Feinstein, *Becoming William James*, 47. Feinstein also quotes Henry, Sr., as saying that, after his graduation from Union College, he "rarely

went to bed sober" (57). Also see Feinstein on the incidence of "affective disorder, alcoholism, and other forms of psychopathology" in the first three generations of the James family (305).

26. See Feinstein, *Becoming William James*, 305, for information on Robert Temple, and *The Diary of Alice James*, ed. Leon Edel (New York: Penguin, 1934), 95, 149.

27. For discussions of the power of the secrets of Henry, Sr., on his children, see Feinstein, *Becoming William James*, 59–60, 64–66, and Alfred Habegger, "Lessons of the Father," *Henry James Review* 8 (1986): 1–36.

28. Saul Rosenzwieg, "The Ghost of Henry James: Study in Thematic Aperception," *Character and Personality* 12 (1943–44): 79–100; Michael Kerr, "Chronic Anxiety and Defining a Self," *Atlantic Monthly* (Sept. 1988): 35.

29. Kerr, "Chronic Anxiety," 35.

30. Feinstein, "Family Therapy," 98.

31. Ibid.

32. Henry James, *Autobiography*, ed. Frederick W. Dupee (New York: Criterion, 1956), 4 (my emphasis).

33. R. D. Laing, *Politics of the Family* (New York: Pantheon, 1971), 4, 6.

34. These letters are quoted in Leon Edel, *Henry James: The Conquest of London, 1870–1881* (Philadelphia: J. B. Lippincott, 1962), 343. In an unpublished essay, "The Jamesian Body: Two Oral Tales," Susan Griffin observes that these "letters display fat as a sign of health, proof to his parents that he is doing well physically and socially; it is the dinners out that shape him. Nurturing himself . . . he finally begins to break the James children's pattern of falling ill in order to get emotional and economic attention from their parents" (15). See also William Veeder, "The Feminine Orphan and the Emergent Master," *Henry James Review* 12 (1991): 21–22.

35. See in particular chaps. 5–8 in Feinstein, *Becoming William James*.

36. *Henry James Letters* 2: 156. The entire passage states, "It is time I should rend the veil from the ferocious ambition which has always *couvé* beneath a tranquil exterior; which enabled me to support unrecorded physical misery in my younger years."

37. *Complete Notebooks of Henry James*, 232–33.

38. *Henry James Letters* 4: 495, James's emphasis.

39. Ibid. 4: 372.

40. Leon Edel, *Henry James: The Treacherous Years, 1895–1901* (Philadelphia: J. B. Lippincott, 1969), 15–16.

41. Veeder, "Feminine Orphan," 48–49.

42. *Complete Notebooks of Henry James*, 109. I am grateful to Professor William Veeder for sharing with me his interpretation of this passage.

43. *Letters of Henry James* 2: 15; Hyde, *Henry James at Home*, 152, 154.

44. *Henry James Letters* 4: 167, 169. James discusses the fate of his father's writings in a letter to William concerning the publication of William's edition of his father's *Literary Remains*: "And we [Alice and Henry] talked of poor Father's fading away into silence and darkness, the waves of the world closing over this System which he tried to offer it, and of how we were touched by this act of yours which will (I am sure) do so much to rescue him from oblivion" (*Henry James Letters* 3: 62). *The Literary Remains of the Late Henry James* did not succeed in rescuing their father's reputation, and after the appearance of a hostile review in *The Nation*, James wrote to the editor, Godkin: "I have a tenderness for my poor Father's memory which is in direct proportion to the smallness of the recognition his work was destined to obtain here below and which . . . fill[s] me with a kind of pious melancholy in presence of the fact that so ardent an activity of thought, such a living, original, expressive spirit may have passed into darkness and silence forever, the waves of time closing straight over it, without one or two signs being made on its behalf" (*Henry James Letters* 3: 73).

45. *Henry James Letters* 4: 416.

46. Michael Anesko, *"Friction with the Market": Henry James and the Profession of Authorship* (New York: Oxford University Press, 1986), 144.

47. *Henry James Letters* 4: 366–67.

48. See *Henry James Letters* 4: 498.

49. Henry James to William James, Feb. 3 and July 18, 1909, Houghton Library. See also Henry James to William James, Feb. 26, 1909, in *Henry James Letters* 4: 516–17.

50. Quoted in Edel, *Henry James: The Master*, 433; *Henry James Letters* 4: 498.

51. Harvey Green notes that James "cabled his brother in February that he had 'stopped Fletcherizing. Perfectly well.' William relayed the message to Fletcher, who responded that 'a bugbear like your brother's message would set back my work tremendously'" (*Fit for America*, 298).

52. *Henry James Letters* 4: 516, James's emphasis.

53. Henry James to William James, July 18, 1909, Houghton Library.

54. *Henry James Letters* 4: 521.

55. Henry James to James B. Pinker, July 21 and Aug. 17, 1909, MS Collection of American Literature, Beinecke Library, Yale University; quoted by permission of Alexander R. James and the Beinecke Library. Focusing on the "vocational locus" of James's psychological "troubles," Cushing Strout believes that the revival of "his theatrical ambitions" in 1909 was responsible for "plunging him . . . into [the] disabling depression" of 1910 (*The Veracious Imagination* [Middletown, Conn.: Wesleyan University Press, 1981], 279).

56. Edel, *Henry James: The Master*, 436.

57. Henry James to William James, Oct. 31, 1909, Houghton Library.

58. Theodora Bosanquet to William James, Jan. 23, 1910, Houghton Library; quoted by permission of the Houghton Library. William writes to Henry on February 18, 1910: "I imagined nervous prostration as the chief name for it [Henry's illness]. Evidently it was that, but with *starvation* as a cause. It shows how complex is the human system! Starvation in you had evidently thrust the alimentary function quite out of gear. I find myself asking if you still had kept corpulent thru-out the ordeal. It is discouragingly mysterious, and shows, I think, that one's subjective feelings, appetite, etc. are not altogether trustworthy guides" (Houghton Library). Harvey Green notes: "Relations between Henry James and Fletcher deteriorated by 1911 when James evidently let it be known that he had 'starved' while holding to the regime. 'As for Henry James,' wrote Fletcher to Kellogg, 'If he has "starved" as a result of fletcherizing, he has done something else than fletcherize'" (*Fit for America*, 298).

59. Merle Fossum and Marilyn Mason explain that when "a person forms a primary relationship with a substance or an activity, we call the behavior addictive. . . . Clinically, it is often difficult to determine just when a habit becomes an addiction. Our criterion is: 'When you can't control when you start or stop the activity, when it begins to damage you and your close relationships, you're addicted'" (*Facing Shame* [New York: W. W. Norton, 1986], 123–24). James's inability to control his Fletcherizing once it had resulted in debilitating symptoms is apparent in his attempt to thwart his doctor's orders and to Fletcherize in secret; see Edel, *Henry James: The Master*, 439.

60. Quoted in Edel, *Henry James: The Master*, 441; William James to Alice Gibbens James, May 8, 1910, Houghton Library. William writes that "the symptoms" as "described" by Henry in a recent letter "are necessary parts of a case like his, & are doubtless what made Dr. Skinner describe it as a sort of hysteric imitation. Evidently he is best dealt with by not losing one's own steadiness of conviction, and at the same time by avoiding argumentation." For Henry's response to William's earlier statement that he had experienced a nervous breakdown, see Edel, *Henry James: The Master*, 441. William also referred to Henry's condition as "neuresthenic melancholia" (William James to Henry James, May 28, 1910, Houghton Library). The variety of terms used to describe Henry's affliction reveals that, as Elaine Showalter notes, neuresthenia "shared so many of hysteria's symptoms that even specialists could not always distinguish between the two" (*The Female Malady* [New York: Penguin, 1985], 134).

61. For a description of Doctor Skinner's treatment, see Edel, *Henry James: The Master*, 439.

62. For discussions of James's "feminine bent" or psychological identification with women, see Lisa Appignanesi, *Femininity and the Creative Imagination* (New York: Barnes and Noble, 1973), 21; Edel, *Henry James: Treacherous Years*, 209–10; Feinstein, *Becoming William James*, 233; Virginia Fowler, *Henry James's*

American Girl (Madison: University of Wisconsin Press, 1984), 4–5; and Veeder, "Feminine Orphan."

63. For a discussion of anorexia and hysteria in men, see Brumberg, *Fasting Girls*, 12, and *Dictionary of Psychological Medicine*, 619, 624–25.

64. Writing of his breakdown in *Society the Redeemed Form of Man*, Henry, Sr., claims that when "I sat down to dinner on that memorable chilly afternoon in Windsor, I held it [faith in selfhood] serene and unweakened by the faintest breath of doubt; before I rose from table, it had inwardly shrivelled to a cinder. One moment I devoutly thanked God for the inappreciable boon of selfhood; the next, that inappreciable boon seemed to me the one thing damnable on earth, seemed a literal nest of hell within my own entrails" (quoted in *The Literary Remains of Henry James*, ed. William James [Boston: Houghton Mifflin, 1884; reprint, Upper Saddle River, N.J.: Gregg Press, 1970], 71). John Owen King also notes a correlation between the desire of Henry, Sr., to "attain . . . detachment" from his much-hated worldly self and his decision to starve himself to death at the end of his life (*Iron of Melancholy*, 90; see also 138). For discussions of the relationship between James's anxieties about his personal integrity, his sense of his place in the family, and his psychosomatic illnesses, see Feinstein, *Becoming William James*, chap. 12; and King, *Iron of Melancholy*, chap. 2.

Habegger: New York Monumentalism

1. Henry James, *The Complete Tales* (Philadelphia: J. B. Lippincott, 1962), 283.

2. *Henry James Letters*, ed. Leon Edel, 4 vols. (Cambridge, Mass.: Harvard University Press, 1974–84) 4: 366–68.

3. Leon Edel, *Henry James: The Master, 1901–1916* (Philadelphia: J. B. Lippincott, 1972), 321.

4. *Henry James Letters* 4: 367.

5. Assessors Books, 15th Ward, 1843–46, New York City Municipal Archives; *Record of Will Libers/Surrogates Court/New York City*, Liber 95, pp. 235–42; *The Wyckoff Family in America: A Genealogy*, ed. Mr. and Mrs. M. B. Streeter (Rutland, Vt.: Tuttle, 1934).

6. Henry James, *Washington Square* (Harmondsworth, Eng.: Penguin, 1986), 39–40.

7. Assessors Books, 15th Ward, 1844 and 1854, New York City Municipal Archives.

8. Henry James, *The Bostonians* (Indianapolis: Bobbs-Merrill, 1976), 177–78.

9. Alfred Habegger, *Henry James and the "Woman Business"* (New York: Cambridge University Press, 1989), 126.

10. Katharine Hastings, "William James (1771–1832) of Albany, N.Y., and

His Descendants," *The New York Genealogical and Biographical Record* 55 (Apr., July, Oct., 1924): 101 19, 222–36, 301–13.

11. *The Letters of William James*, ed. Henry James III (Boston: Atlantic Monthly, 1920), 1: 7.

12. Henry James, *A Small Boy and Others* (New York: Scribner's, 1913), 182–84.

13. Henry James, Sr., to Edmund Tweedy, May 30, 1851, typescript, Houghton Library, Harvard University. All quotations from the James family papers at Harvard are by permission of Alexander R. James and the Houghton Library.

14. Henry James, Sr., to [Edmund Tweedy?], [Feb. or Mar. 1851?], Houghton Library.

15. "Lectures and Lecturing," *New York Tribune*, Nov. 24, 1852, p. 5.

16. [Henry James, Sr.], "Thackeray," *New York Tribune*, Nov. 13, 1852, p. 4. Attribution based on a clipping preserved among Senior's ephemera in the Houghton Library.

17. See Habegger, *Henry James and the "Woman Business,"* chap. 2.

18. William James, Introduction to *The Literary Remains of the Late Henry James*, ed. William James (Boston: Houghton Mifflin, 1884), 11.

19. H. James, Sr., *Literary Remains*, 146.

20. *Henry James Letters* 3: 62. Quotations from this letter have been corrected against the Jan. 2, 1885, holograph at Houghton Library.

21. Ibid.

22. Ibid.

23. *The Nation* 40 (Jan. 15, 1885): 60–61.

24. *Henry James Letters* 3: 74.

25. Fred Kaplan, *Henry James: The Imagination of Genius* (New York: Morrow, 1992), 281–85.

26. *Henry James Letters* 3: 102.

27. William James to J. R. Osgood, Dec. 3, 1883, Miller Library, Colby College; W. James, Introduction to *Literary Remains*, 117, W. James's emphasis.

28. *The Complete Notebooks of Henry James*, ed. Leon Edel and Lyall H. Powers (New York: Oxford University Press, 1987), 240.

29. H. James, *Small Boy*, 193. For another telling of John Barber James's story, see "Dupine Tracks J.J.," *Southern Review* 27 (Oct. 1991): 803–25.

30. Henry James, *Autobiography*, ed. Frederick W. Dupee (New York: Criterion, 1956).

31. Henry James, Sr., to [Edmund Tweedy?], [Feb. or Mar. 1851?], Houghton Library.

32. H. James, *Small Boy*, 180, 191–92.

33. Page of typescript headed "John B. James," Houghton Library, bMS Am 1092.9 (4600), folder 14.

34. Leon Edel, *Henry James: The Untried Years, 1843–1870* (Philadelphia: J. B. Lippincott, 1953), 137–38.

35. Teachers Insurance and Annuity Association of America, *The Twenty-Ninth Annual Report for the Year Ended December 31, 1947*, Schaffer Library, Union College.

36. Letters dated Oct. 6, 1838; Dec. 4, 1839; and May 12, 1840, file labeled "James Family—Albany, New York," New-York Historical Society.

37. "The Last Will & Testament of John B. James," dated July 25, 1855, and proved May 27, 1856, Albany County Surrogates Court.

38. "Cash Book. Estate of John B. James," pp. 4, 8, 24; "Ledger. Estate of John B. James," pp. 121, 122; New York State Library, accession number 16640. Quoted here and below by permission.

39. *Henry James Letters* 2: 371. I know of no sound basis for Edel's claim that "Johnny" was John James (1793–1866 [or 1865, the year he drew up his will]), a nephew of William of Albany. R. W. B. Lewis offers up the identical error without attribution in *The Jameses* (New York: Farrar, Straus and Giroux, 1991), 334–35. Edel's mistake probably rests on a hasty appropriation of Hastings, "William James," 308.

40. Wm. Q. in a Corner, "The Tribune and the Gamblers," *New York Tribune*, Feb. 6, 1858, p. 3.

41. *The Diary of George Templeton Strong* (New York: Macmillan, 1952) 2: 391.

42. "Cash Book. Estate of John B. James," pp. 59, 60, 54, 66, New York State Library.

43. "Vice and Its Prevention," *New York Tribune*, Feb. 1, 1855, pp. 5–6.

44. H.J., "An American in Europe . . . I. From New-York to Geneva—The Schools There. Special Correspondence of The N.Y. Tribune," *New York Tribune*, Sept. 3, 1855, p. 3.

45. Joel Munsell, *The Annals of Albany* (Albany, N.Y.: Munsell, 1854) 5: 335. The appointment was reported July 28, 1853.

46. H. James, *Small Boy*, 174.

47. I have discovered (too late to incorporate the fact in this essay) that John was served with a summons early in 1855, after losing at faro and writing a bad check to the tune of $2,975. For details, see Alfred Habegger, *The Father: A Life of Henry James, Sr.* (New York: Farrar, Straus & Giroux, 1994), chap. 21.

48. Henry James, Sr., to Edmund Tweedy, Sept. 14, 1856, Houghton Library.

49. "The Last Will and Testament of Catharine James," typescript at Houghton Library.

50. New York directories from 1852–53 to 1855–56; Recorded deeds, Liber 573, p. 440, New York Hall of Records.

51. H. James, *Small Boy*, 92–95.

52. "Our Best and Worst Society," *New York Tribune*, Mar. 12, 1855, p. 4. Attribution of this and the following editorial is based on two clippings preserved among Senior's ephemeral publications at the Houghton Library, bMS Am 1094.8 (77), boxes 10 and 11.

53. "Mayor Wood and the Gamblers," *New York Tribune*, Mar. 23, 1855, p. 4. A third editorial, "The Magistracy and Crime," *New York Tribune*, Mar. 29, 1855, p. 4, might be attributed to Senior on internal evidence.

54. Leonard Chalmers, "Fernando Wood and Tammany Hall: The First Phase," *New-York Historical Society Quarterly* 52 (Oct. 1968): 379–402.

55. New York State census for 1855, New York City, ward 8, election district 1, dwelling 213.

56. "The Lesson of the Sickles Tragedy," *New York Tribune*, Apr. 16, 1859, p. 9; "Marriage—Divorce," *New York Tribune*, Apr. 23, 1859, p. 5; "Marriage—Divorce—H.J.," *New York Tribune*, May 4, 1859, p. 6. A clipping of the first letter is among Senior's ephemera in the Houghton Library.

57. *Letters of William James* 1: 51.

58. See "American Observations in Europe. From Our Special Correspondent," *New York Tribune*, Aug. 26, 1856, p. 5; Henry James, Sr., to Eunice (Macdaniel) Dana, Mar. 26, [1857], Houghton Library.

59. Henry James, *Notes of a Son and Brother* (New York: Scribner's, 1914), 59.

60. "Cash Book. Estate of John B. James," p. 25, New York State Library.

61. Henry James, Sr., to Edmund Tweedy, May 23, 1856, Houghton Library; house number from *Sommier foncier* D.Q^{18}, Art. 2, folio 197, Archives de Paris.

62. Maurice Quentin-Bauchart, *Paris—les anciens quartiers* (Paris: n.d.), 26.

63. H. James, *Small Boy*, 327.

64. Henry James, Sr., to Edmund Tweedy, Sept. 14, 1856, Houghton Library.

65. H. James, *Small Boy*, 42.

66. Henry James, Sr., "The Order in American Disorder," *The Leader* 7 (Sept. 13, 1856): 879.

Sedgwick: Shame and Performativity

NOTE: This essay is taken from an ongoing project on queer performativity and shame. Sections of it have appeared previously in the sources credited at the front of the present volume. Timothy Gould, James Kincaid, Joseph Litvak, Michael Moon, Andrew Parker, and Judith Butler have been generously instrumental in my process of framing these still very tentative formulations.

1. Judith Butler, "Performative Acts and Gender Constitution: An Essay in Phenomenology and Feminist Theory," in *Performing Feminisms: Feminist Critical*

Theory and Theatre, ed. Sue-Ellen Case (Baltimore: Johns Hopkins University Press, 1990), 272–73.

2. Jean-François Lyotard, *The Postmodern Condition: A Report on Knowledge*, trans. Geoff Bennington and Brian Massumi (Minneapolis: University of Minnesota Press, 1984).

3. Paul de Man, *Allegories of Reading: Figural Language in Rousseau, Nietzsche, Rilke, and Proust* (New Haven, Conn.: Yale University Press, 1979), 298.

4. "Far from closing off the tropological system, irony enforces the repetition of its aberration" (de Man, *Allegories*, 301).

5. J. L. Austin, *How to Do Things with Words*, ed. J. O. Urmson (New York: Oxford University Press, 1970).

6. Shoshana Felman, *The Literary Speech Act: Don Juan with J. L. Austin, or Seduction in Two Languages*, trans. Catherine Porter (Ithaca, N.Y.: Cornell University Press, 1983).

7. Austin, *How to Do Things with Words*, 150.

8. Ibid., 6.

9. Ibid., 4.

10. Ibid., 16.

11. It's interesting that in Latin even to say "*I* am ashamed"—*pudet mihi*—doesn't permit of a first-person subject.

12. Erving Goffman, *Stigma: Notes on the Management of Spoiled Identity* (New York: Simon and Schuster, 1963).

13. Michael Franz Basch, "The Concept of Affect: A Re-Examination," *Journal of the American Psychoanalytic Association* 24 (1976): 765.

14. Francis J. Broucek, "Shame and Its Relationship to Early Narcissistic Developments," *International Journal of Psychoanalysis* 63 (1982): 369.

15. Basch, "Concept of Affect," 765–66.

16. See Joseph Litvak, *Caught in the Act: Theatricality in the Nineteenth Century English Novel* (Berkeley: University of California Press, 1992), 195–269, for the richest description of James's account of theatricality in the novels.

17. Silvan S. Tomkins, *Affect Imagery Consciousness*, vol. 2: *The Negative Affects* (New York: Springer, 1963), 123.

18. *The Notebooks of Henry James*, ed. F. O. Matthiessen and Kenneth B. Murdock (New York: Oxford University Press, 1947), 318, quoted in Eve Kosofsky Sedgwick, *Epistemology of the Closet* (Berkeley: University of California Press, 1991), 208.

19. *The Poems of Alexander Pope*, ed. John Butt (New Haven: Yale University Press, 1963), 787 (Book IV, ll. 387–94).

20. William James, *The Correspondence of William James*, vol. 1: *William and*

Henry: 1861–1884, eds. Ignas K. Skrupskelis and Elizabeth M. Berkeley (Charlottesville: University Press of Virginia, 1992), 73.

21. Ibid.

22. Another essay in which I have broached this material much more briefly is "Is the Rectum Straight?: Identification and Identity in *The Wings of the Dove*," in my collection *Tendencies* (Durham: Duke University Press, 1993).

23. *William and Henry*, 113. 24. Ibid., 84.

25. Ibid., 113. 26. Ibid., 63.

27. Ibid., 105. 28. Ibid., 108.

29. Kaja Silverman, "Too Early/Too Late: Subjectivity and the Primal Scene in Henry James," *Novel* 21: 2–3 (Winter/Spring 1988), 165.

30. Ibid., 149.

31. Or again, on going back to the magazine where an old story had been published: "I recently had the chance to 'look up' [and note *these* scare-quotes!], for old sake's sake, that momentary seat of the good-humoured satiric muse—the seats of the muses, even when the merest flutter of one of their robes has been involved, losing no scrap of sanctity for me, I profess, by the accident of my having myself had the honour to offer the visitant the chair" (*14*: xxi; *AN*, 214).

32. That it is thus also the smell of excitement can seem to involve grotesquely inappropriate affect—as the passage I've just quoted from continues: "No dreadful old pursuit of the hidden slave with bloodhounds and the rag of association can ever, for 'excitement,' I judge, have bettered it at its best" (*21*: ix; *AN*, 311). It is nauseatingly unclear in this sentence whether the "'excitement'" (note the scare-quotes) attaches to the subject position of the escaping slave or of the enslaving pursuer. The way I'm inclined to read this sentence—though I could be quite wrong—ties it back up with the matter of puppetry: James's ostensible reference, I think, with the flippant phrase "*dreadful old* pursuit of the hidden slave" is not to slavery itself but to the popular forms of theatrical melodrama and audience interpellation based on (for instance) *Uncle Tom's Cabin*. But condensed in the flippancy of this citation are two occasions of shame that were enduring ones for James: first, that he did not enlist to fight in the Civil War, what he describes in another preface as the "deluge of fire and blood and tears" needed to "correct" slavery (*14*: xxi; *AN*, 215); and second, the unattenuated but often fiercely disavowed dependence of his own, rarefied art on popular melodramatic forms and traditions.

Banta: The Excluded Seven

1. Michael Anesko, "The Eclectic Architecture of Henry James's New York Edition," in his *"Friction with the Market": Henry James and the Profession of Authorship* (New York: Oxford University Press, 1986), 153.

2. Ibid., 154, 160. Anesko's careful gleanings from the extensive three-way correspondence between James, Pinker, and Brownell put to rest Leon Edel's be-

lief that James maintained firm control over every step of the construction of the New York Edition. See Anesko's comments (149–50) on Edel's assertions in "The Architecture of Henry James's 'New York Edition,'" *New England Quarterly* 24 (June 1951), an argument Edel repeats in *Henry James: The Master, 1901–1916* (Philadelphia; J. B. Lippincott, 1972), 321–29.

3. Letter of Dec. 14, 1908, in Anesko, "Eclectic Architecture," 161. As Anesko puts it, Scribner's knew it would receive full value of its expenditures in any case. Even if the New York Edition did not sell, the publishing house would gain the coin of "an indefinable aura of quality" by having James on its list (143).

4. In another context, Toni Morrison has indicated how "the unspeakable" facts of the Afro-American experience exist as a powerful plane of narrative alongside mainstream literary texts precisely because of their exclusion. Such blanks are presences, existentially there, not to be overlooked, even though unspoken. See Toni Morrison, "Unspeakable Things Unspoken: The Afro-American Presence in American Literature," *Michigan Quarterly Review* 28, no. 1 (Winter 1989), 1–34. Note also the attempt by many feminist critics to analyze ellipses within women's writings, spaces where silence presses upon a domain of male words.

5. *Watch and Ward* appeared in serial form in the *Atlantic Monthly* in 1871 but was not published in book form until 1878—after the publication of *Roderick Hudson* (1876) and *The American* (1877). *Confidence*, serialized in *Scribner's Monthly* during 1879–80, was published as a book in 1880.

6. For James's dismissive characterizations of *Watch and Ward*, expressed both at the time of its serial appearance and at the time of its publication as a book, see Leon Edel, *Henry James. A Life* (New York: Harper and Row, 1985), 124.

7. James's statement concerning *The American* that he remained so "enamoured of my idea" that he continued to trust in it comes from the Preface to vol. 2 (*2*: vi; *AN*, 21).

8. On the final page of his final Preface appended to *The Golden Bowl*, James concludes his ruminations on the growth of taste to which the entire New York Edition gives testimony (*23*: xvii; *AN*, 340). As he looked back over all his fictions, he faced the question of whether what he found there was "a series of waiting satisfactions or an array of waiting misfits" (*23*: xix; *AN*, 341). The former are recognizable by the fact they still possess possibility, are alive; the latter reveal themselves as being "done," as being dead (*23*: xxv; *AN*, 348).

9. Leon Edel's Preface to the 1959 Grove Press edition of *Watch and Ward* notes that Nora Lambert is a dry run for Isabel Archer, Nanda Brookenham, and Milly Theale (14); but so is Angela Vivian of *Confidence*. Citations of *Watch and Ward* below are from this edition.

10. H. James, *Watch and Ward*, 213.

11. H. James, *Watch and Ward*, 109; *The Europeans* (Oxford: Oxford University Press, 1985), 76; *The Bostonians* (New York: Macmillan, 1886), 318.

12. For one example, see Edel's Preface to *Watch and Ward*, 6–8.

13. II. James, *The Europeans*, 35, 38, 58.

14. Ibid., 70.

15. The one "American" capable of letting herself go is Gertrude Wentworth. She is up to breaking vows to be "good"; she can risk excitement; she will become the "folded flower" that Felix (a nice version of Gilbert Osmond) will knock out of the pure empyrean in order to rescue her from the living death of Wentworthian tranquillity and rectitude. An example of the sort of hidden text that readers gain pleasure from detecting, Felix's remark, "She's a folded flower. Let me pluck her from the parent tree and you will see her expand" (*The Europeans*, 139) is "L'Allegro" to "Il Penseroso" of the situation James sets up in *The Portrait of a Lady*. There Ralph Touchett wishes to provide Isabel with wings so that she may soar above the limitations of existence, but the result is that she is knocked from the heavens by a man named Gilbert—a name that means "bright promise."

16. Henry James, *The Other House* (New York: Macmillan, 1896), provides an interesting conflation of these two tendencies: a charming male who succeeds too well in pleasing everyone and by shifting hard decisions onto women. Unlike Chad Newsome, however, Tony Bream finally finds himself burdened with the terrible fate of being "liked" so well—"too much"—that no one will ever confront him with his guilts (388).

17. Henry James, *Washington Square* (New York: Harper, 1894), 21–22.

18. Ibid., 20.

19. The disclosure that James might have actually undergone the torments of Scrooge during his night of self-revelation may well be the purpose of other essays in this collection. At issue here, however, is the nature of *the observed presence* that centers the New York Edition.

20. James's constant use in the prefaces of references to the magician figure is also suggestive of the strategies he employs. Like any successful illusionist, this figure displaces the attention of the audience from what is *not there* (a white rabbit) so that it will be beguiled by what appears to be present (a rabbit pulled from nowhere) precisely because the atmosphere he manipulates appears *to envelop everything*. Manipulated by the expert magician, readers of the prefaces are made to forget what is not so (not present) in order to focus upon what he wishes us to think constitutes the whole scene.

21. The act of working through *Roderick Hudson* provided James with the trope, used in the Preface to that novel, of the spice islands and the dangers and pleasures it promised (*1*: vi; *AN*, 4).

22. The exceptions are *Watch and Ward* and *The Other House*, which arguably contain too much seriousness of the adolescent and postadolescent variety.

23. The relation of the Jamesian satiric mode to James's notions of vulgarity, and the role this issue may have had in the effacements James made from the rec-

ord, is an entirely different matter from the view that James felt he had to censor lapses that exposed him to the charge of introducing emotional crudities. Let us revise the notion that James might have found it necessary to distance himself from the "vulgarity" of *The Bostonians, The Other House*, and *The Sacred Fount* because of the violent angers, the aberrant behavior, the loaded sexuality they contain. If these three and the other four excluded novels now seem less "normal" and more "marginal," it is largely because of their exclusion. That is, those texts were not left out simply because they were less easy to authorize. After all, the rest of James's fictions only appear "normal" as the result of their inclusion. When it came time for James to censor his own productions, "the aberrant" and "the normal" would have seemed a trivial basis for determining how he was best to advance his self-installation as the master of the forms of high art.

24. *Watch and Ward* contains James's notation that plain women, who have no hope of being desired, may settle on being thought clever (45). Mrs. Tom Tristram of *The American* will also go in that direction, in contrast to Catherine Sloper, who (because not clever enough to be other than good) is assigned the fate of being dull, without the capacity to elicit desire. Fanny Assingham, on the other hand, is plain, clever, desirous of being "desired," yet she also craves to be "good," or at least "right." These issues are played out, I suggest, within James's own formulation of the type of the artist he placed before his public in the New York Edition.

25. The following two quotations are from Henry James, *Confidence* (Boston: Houghton, Osgood, 1880), 257, 301–2.

26. Elizabeth Hardwick's comments about *Washington Square* in regard to its perfect balance, its narrow focus, its "rather claustrophobic" nature bear out the rightness of the artistic container James provided this novel of 1881; but James already realized that *The Portrait of a Lady* of the same year would show him off as a "major" talent. Elizabeth Hardwick, "On Washington Square," *New York Review of Books* (Nov. 22, 1990), 28.

27. H. James, *The Bostonians*, 308. The next quotations are from pp. 8, 72, 248, 270.

28. James wrote to William Dean Howells that *The Bostonians* had never "received any sort of justice"; but he also admitted that it would take "a great deal of artful redoing" to bring it into line with his later views on the novelistic craft, an effort he believed he could not give to its revision. In Edel, *Henry James. A Life*, 625.

29. Henry James, *The Sacred Fount* (New York: Scribner's, 1901), 168, 295.

30. H. James, *The Bostonians*, 86. Olive remarks that Goethe's words come by way of Bayard Taylor's translation. James's dismissal of Taylor's aesthetic as carried out in the "genteel tradition" of James's Boston was one of the reasons he transplanted his professional career abroad.

31. See Munro Beattie, "Henry James: 'The Voice of Stoicism,'" in *The Stoic*

Strain in American Literature, ed. Duane J. Macmillan (Toronto: University of Toronto Press, 1979), 63–75, C. B. Cox, "Henry James and Stoicism," in *Essays and Studies Collected for the English Association*, vol. 8, ed. D. M. Low (London: John Murray, 1955), 76–88; Steven H. Jobe, "The Discrimination of Stoicism in *The American*," *Studies in American Fiction* 16, no. 2 (Autumn 1988): 181–94. I wish to thank Andrew Soven for calling my attention to this continuing strain of reference to the qualities of classical Stoicism in James's writings.

32. The following citations are from Geoffrey Galt Harpham's *The Ascetic Imperative in Culture and Criticism* (Chicago: University of Chicago Press, 1987), 31, 36. Harpham's argument refers to T. S. Eliot—who, like the later James, valorizes the self-effacement of the artist into the anonymity of art—as a practitioner of cenobitic art, acting to make the link between the self-effacement of the artist and the anonymity of art upheld by both Eliot and the later James. Even more telling are the quotations Harpham takes from *The Varieties of Religious Experience*, by William James, published in 1902. One comes hauntingly close to his brother's urgencies of the same period with the following description of the need to keep oneself secure and clean within the world by adopting "the law which impels the artist to achieve harmony in his composition by simply dropping out whatever jars, or suggests a discord. . . . To omit, says Stevenson, is the one art in literature." William James goes on to say, "the holy-minded person finds that inner smoothness and cleanness which it is torture to him to feel violated at every turn by the discordancy and brutality of secular existence" (quoted in Harpham, *Ascetic Imperative*, 24–25).

33. Comment by Harpham in paraphrase of both Nietzsche and Foucault (*Ascetic Imperative*, 235). The quotations from Chanel and Vreeland appeared in Holly Brubach's essay for *The New Yorker* of Feb. 27, 1989, pp. 71–76. The full setting for Chanel's remarks regarding her decision to be the "revolutionary" was this: "It was not to create what I liked, but rather, first and foremost, to do away with all the things I didn't like." "I invented my life by taking for granted that everything I did not like would have an opposite, what I would like." In her article for *The New Yorker* of Dec. 31, 1990, Brubach brings the international *couture* scene up to date, citing the fashion editor who predicts that "'the new vulgarity' . . . would be the style of the nineties." Brubach goes on to declare: "The new vulgarity is abstract and purely aesthetic, a kind of postmodern rococo, which might take as its slogan 'When too much is not enough.' . . . Not coincidentally, elegance is almost completely lacking in the clothes this season—it's not a virtue that fashion aspires to anymore."

34. These terms are used to describe the outer dress (and to imply the inner lives) of the fashionable women at Newmarch, the country house that forms the scene of *The Sacred Fount*, a most de Wolfian novel (200).

35. Poiret's view as paraphrased in an article of 1922 by Pierre de Lanux,

titled "A Tyrant Artist Who Sways the Taste of the Parisians. The Place of Paul
Poiret in the Modern Scheme of Dress, House and Stage Decoration," *Arts and
Decoration* (Sept. 1922), 332. Lanux goes on to comment that fashion "lends itself
continuously to protests, since it continuously upsets habits and proposes to abandon existing standards and adopt new ones. It is revolutionary by essence. That is
perhaps why (see Freud) it is carried on with greatest passion by those society people who are the most conservative in their political opinions" (383).

36. Baudelaire, "In Praise of Make-Up," quoted by Joan Juliet Buck in
Vogue, Oct. 1989. The original passage reads as follows: "La mode doit donc être
considérée comme un symptôme du goût de l'idéal surnageant dans le cerveau hu-
main au-dessus de tout ce que la vie naturelle y accumule de grossier, de terrestre
et d'immonde, comme une déformation sublime de la nature, ou plutôt comme un
essai permanent et successif de réformation de la nature." Note that Buck does not
include the final clause: "or rather like a continuous, successive testing of nature's
reformation." The Preface to *The Golden Bowl* (the vessel in which James poured
his thoughts concerning the art of re-vision) provides striking imagery in support
of James's notion of the artist as the "dresser" of his texts. Since he here speaks of
his "first-born" novels, he uses the language of the nurse who goes to the nursery
intent upon the "tidying-up of the uncanny brood" prior to bringing them down-
stairs to show them off before company. But since these early texts have also aged
over *the natural course of time*, he also refers to the "removal of accumulated dust,"
the "washing of wizened faces," and the "straightening of grizzled locks." In any
case, the dresser accepts the need to arrange—"to a better effect"—the "superannuated garments," however "expensive" the task. In turn, the texts undergoing the
artist/dresser's re-reading, re-seeing, re-visioning are "touchingly responsive to
new care of any sort whatever," since all involved in the process agree upon the
need for "the finer air of a better form" (*23*: xiv, xvi, xviii, xxii; *AN*, 336–45).

37. Ezra Pound incorporated reference to the complex nature of Paquin's
prewar style, reflecting ambivalence to a period of "marvellous reign, no violence
and no passports," but also a time when artifice contended against nature's elegance. See Walter Baumann, "Carleton, Paquin and Salzburg," *Paideuma: A Journal Devoted to Ezra Pound Scholarship* 11 (1982): 445.

38. See Valerie Steel, *Paris Fashion: A Cultural History* (New York: Oxford
University Press, 1988); Martin Battersby, *Art Deco Fashion: French Designers
1908–1925* (New York: St. Martin's Press, 1974); James Laver, *Taste and Fashion, from the French Revolution to the Present Day* (London: Harrap, 1946); and
Georgina O'Hara, *The Encyclopedia of Fashion* (New York: Abrams, 1986).
Scholars of fashion design differ over the dates marking the watershed moments
in design revolution. Laver believes that 1909–14 forms a single, and significant,
moment. Battersby views 1900–1908 as a low tide, with its timid return to "in-
sipid banality." Most place importance upon the Secessionist movement backed by

the furniture design exhibitions in Munich and Vienna of 1911; all point out the stunning impact of the Ballets Russes and the costume designs of Bakst in introducing an Orientalism that was pared back in shape but fantastic in mood.

39. Nicole Thornton, Introduction to her *Poiret* (New York: Rizzoli, 1979), n.p.

40. Also note both the extravagant costume Madame de Vionnet wears (Book Sixth, chap. 3), which marvelously manipulates nature into an ideal vision, and the look she assumes (Book Twelfth, chap. 2) as of a maidservant weeping over the loss of her lover which draws her into "the gross, the mundane and the despicable" of the world James also incorporates with care into *The Ambassadors*.

41. Valuable information concerning Elsie de Wolfe's career as an entrepreneur of "refusal" largely comes from Jane S. Smith's *Elsie de Wolfe. A Life in the High Style* (New York: Atheneum, 1982).

42. Ibid., 128.

43. Ibid., 63.

44. As we know, James's personal taste in furnishings, paintings, music, and the theater was distinctly conservative and anything but avant-garde. Therefore no literal connections between those tastes and the ways in which his literary aesthetics was developing between 1897 and 1907 can be made.

45. Smith, *Elsie de Wolfe*, 112.

46. From de Lanux, "A Tyrant Artist," 383.

47. Buck, *Vogue*, Oct. 1989.

Index

In this index an "f" after a number indicates a separate reference on the next page, and an "ff" indicates separate references on the next two pages. A continuous discussion over two or more pages is indicated by a span of page numbers, e.g., "57–59." *Passim* is used for a cluster of references in close but not consecutive sequence.

literary authority, 9–10, 58–65 *passim*, 290–91nn3–4, 291n7; misrepresentations performed on, 69–73 *passim*, 293nn15–18; regulation of, 65–69, 292nn9–10, 292n12, 292–93n14
Gender Trouble (Butler), 206
Gestures of refusal, *see* Aesthetics of refusal
"The Ghost of Henry James" (Rosenzweig), 173
Glove/gage signifier, 234–35, 314n32. *See also* Homoeroticism
Godkin, E. L., 194, 307n44
Goethe, Johann, 255, 317n30
Goffman, Erving, 211
The Golden Bowl, 16, 23f, 47, 52, 177, 245–46, 287n28
Green, Harvey, 169, 307n51, 308n58
Griffin, Susan, 306n34
Guy Domville, 176, 214, 285–86n8

Habegger, Alfred, 18, 66, 291n7, 292–93nn14–15
"Halls of Julia" (frontispiece to "Julia Bride"), 277
Harbinger, 190
Hardwick, Elizabeth, 317n26
Harper's (publisher), 78, 114ff, 117, 301n13
Harper's Magazine, 97, 100
Harpham, Geoffrey Galt, 255, 318n32
Hastings, Katharine, 197
Hawthorne, Nathaniel, 31, 45, 98–99, 100–101
Hearne, P. L., 198–99, 200f
Hegel, Georg Wilhelm Friedrich, 28f
Heidegger, Martin, 130
Heinemann, William, 83–84, 87
Henry James and Revision (Horne), 142
Henry James Sesquicentennial Conferences (1993, New York), xxiii
Henry James: The Imagination of Genius (Kaplan), xxiv
Henty, G. A., 94

Herrick, Robert, 94
Higgins, Charles, 299n43
Hileman, Charles H., 198f
Holland, Laurence, 287n31
Holly, Carol, 18
Homoeroticism, xxiv, 215, 314n32; clumsy style and, 245–46; constipation and, 224–25; digestion and, 233–34; in prefaces, 229–36, 314n32; and queer identity, 236–39; spatial metaphors of, 226–28; wealth and, 223–24. *See also* Shame
Horne, Philip, 142, 147, 283n16, 303–4n2
Houghton Mifflin, 45
Hound and Horn, 25
House of fiction trope, 8, 59–60, 61, 290–91nn3–4, 291n4. *See also* Domestic sphere; Monument
Howells, William Dean, 78, 317n28
How to Do Things with Words (Austin), 208f
Humphreys, Susan M., 300n3

Ibsen, Henrik, 94
Identity: cenobitic and eremitic representations of, 255–56, 318n32; and central vs. centered consciousness, 15, 31–32, 287n28; dissolution of, 26, 28–29, 286n9; and nonidentity thinking, 29–35, 286n9, 287n29; selfhood concept of, 15–17; and shame's recirculation, 172–73, 212–13, 237–38, 239; between thinking subject and past selves, 50–51, 289–90n22. *See also* Author; Literary authority
Illustrated London News, 42
Illustrations, 55–56, 96f, 138–40, 298n21. *See also* Frontispieces; Photography
Individualism, 31, 286n9. *See also* Identity
Inner child metaphor, 213, 215–16
"In Praise of Make-up" (Baudelaire), 257, 319n36

Index   333

Library of Congress Cataloging-in-Publication Data

Henry James's New York edition : the construction of authorship /
edited by David McWhirter.
 p.   cm.
 Includes bibliographical references and index.
 ISBN 0-8047-2564-0 (alk. paper)
 1. James, Henry, 1843–1916—Authorship.   2. Authors and
publishers—New York (N.Y.)—History—20th century.   3. Fiction—
Publishing—New York (N.Y.)—History—20th century.   4. Authors and
readers—United States—History—20th century.   5. James, Henry,
1843–1916—Publishers.   6. James, Henry, 1843–1916—Editors.
7. Authorship—History—20th century.   I. McWhirter, David Bruce.
PS2127.A9H46   1995
813'.4—dc20   95-1325
                                                                 CIP